JAMES BOND
WILL RETURN

JAMES BOND WILL RETURN

*Critical Perspectives
on the 007 Film Franchise*

EDITED BY
CLAIRE HINES,
TERENCE McSWEENEY,
AND STUART JOY

Wallflower Press
New York

Wallflower Press is an imprint of Columbia University Press
Columbia University Press
Publishers Since 1893
New York   Chichester, West Sussex
cup.columbia.edu

Library of Congress Cataloging-in-Publication Data

Names: Hines, Claire, editor. | McSweeney, Terence, 1974– editor. | Joy, Stuart,
    editor.
Title: James Bond will return : critical perspectives on the 007 film franchise /
    edited by Claire Hines, Terence McSweeney, and Stuart Joy.
Description: New York : Columbia University Press, [2023] | Includes
    bibliographical references and index.
Identifiers: LCCN 2023024026 (print) | LCCN 2023024027 (ebook) |
    ISBN 9780231207409 (hardback) | ISBN 9780231207416 (trade paperback) |
    ISBN 9780231556965 (ebook)
Subjects: LCSH: James Bond films—History and criticism.
Classification: LCC PN1995.9.J3 J38 2023 (print) | LCC PN1995.9.J3 (ebook) |
    DDC 791.43/651—dc23/eng/20230727
LC record available at https://lccn.loc.gov/2023024026
LCebookrecordavailableathttps://   lccn.loc.gov/2023024027

Printed and bound by CPI Group (UK) Ltd, Croydon, CR0 4YY
Cover design: Elliott S. Cairns
Cover images: PictureLux / The Hollywood Archive / Alamy Stock Photo (*top*);
MGM / Columbia Pictures / Photofest (*bottom*)

CONTENTS

ACKNOWLEDGMENTS

M y first encounters with James Bond were in the 1980s. My grandparents took me to the cinema to watch the latest Bond films on the big screen, my mum bought me some of the Ian Fleming novels from her book club magazine, and at one point I also remember eating a lot of Shredded Wheat in order to get *Octopussy* (1983) stickers and send off for the badge and Secret Agent code card. This book is in part the product of that earlier fascination, which later combined with an academic interest in the larger-than-life character who is highly problematic yet somehow endlessly watchable. Thanks go to my brilliant coeditors on this shared Bond project for selecting me to be part of this particular mission, and to the wonderful contributors who joined us out in the field. I am also grateful to family, friends, and colleagues at UEA for enduring my ongoing Bond obsession. Most of all, thanks to Jaqueline Furby, who still lets me watch Roger Moore as Bond at (almost) any opportunity.

—Claire Hines

* * *

Like many of us, I would imagine, the character of James Bond has been a part of my life for longer than I can remember. Some of my earliest film memories are Bond-related, both at the cinema and the then-perennial but now long-gone "James Bond film at Christmas" tradition. It is for these reasons and many others that this project has been a real pleasure to work on from its opening gun barrel to its closing credits. I would like to sincerely thank my delightful coeditors, Claire Hines and Stuart Joy, for going on this journey with me. While it has not been quite as adventure-packed as a Bond film, it has certainly been an eventful project with its very own memorable twists and turns. I would also like to thank my young son Wyatt for watching the films with me, especially those from the Moore era, which I watched for the first time when I was just about his age so long ago. His questions about the films were no doubt very different to my reactions to them back in the 1970s and 1980s ("Daddy, why is James Bond so mean to those ladies?"), but at the same time the delight he found in them even now perhaps explains in part why the character still resonates for audiences and has endured for so long.

—Terence McSweeney

* * *

I was first introduced to James Bond by my older brother. As a child, I vividly recall watching the opening scene of *GoldenEye* (1995), in which the fictional British spy (at the time played by Pierce Brosnan) performs a daring bungee jump off the Verzasca Dam. It was then that I became instantly captivated by the figure, a feeling that persisted throughout my formative years and adolescence. Like many other Bond fans, 007 has remained a perennial feature of my adulthood, thanks in no small part to the character's ability to transcend time periods and trends, but also through his capacity to connect us through shared memories to the people we care about. Therefore, I consider myself fortunate to have been a part of a project that holds a special place in my heart and to have been privileged to work with such amazing coeditors and contributors, whose dedication and work made this collection a delight from pitch to page. I am also extremely grateful to the staff and students at Solent University for their support and enthusiasm for the project. Finally, thank you to my wife for always being my guiding light and for politely enduring a lockdown-induced Bond movie marathon.

—Stuart Joy

JAMES BOND
WILL RETURN

INTRODUCTION

James Bond—Agent of Continuity and Change

CLAIRE HINES, TERENCE MCSWEENEY, AND STUART JOY

I n a joint statement published prior to the release of *No Time to Die* (2021), Barbara Broccoli and Michael G. Wilson, veteran producers of the official James Bond franchise, acknowledged that the world's longest-running film series was at a "critical juncture" due to the impending departure of its longest-serving lead actor, Daniel Craig.[1] The periodic recasting of a new actor in the iconic role of the fictional British spy has been a regular feature of the franchise ever since Sean Connery was replaced by George Lazenby in *On Her Majesty's Secret Service* (1969). Yet there was something different about the issues faced after the release of *No Time to Die*, the twenty-fifth Bond film made by Eon Productions. Bond's seemingly definitive onscreen death in the film, a first for the franchise, and the departure of Craig at a time when some people were (again) speculating that the character was no longer relevant for the modern era, led to something of an existential crisis for the future of Bond. However, the critical and commercial success of *No Time to Die* might seem to suggest otherwise; its $774 million take at the global box office was not quite as much as the two previous films, *Skyfall* (2012) and *Spectre* (2015), but still a considerable achievement considering that it was released into international markets suffering from the effects of the Coronavirus (COVID-19) pandemic, which, for a time, had shut down film industries and theaters all around the globe.

For these reasons and more, the editors of *James Bond Will Return: Critical Perspectives on the 007 Film Franchise* contend that it is the perfect time for this volume's wide-ranging retrospective of the enduring cinematic icon and the more than sixty-year-old series. Although the character's status as a perennial and even integral part of British cultural identity and worldwide phenomenon has been explored on numerous occasions in the decades since *Dr. No* in 1962, this collection proposes to do something different in the field of Bond scholarship. It adopts a chronological anthological structure that moves through the film series in chapters written by established Bond scholars and new voices in order to bring a diverse range of perspectives to the subject. Interrogating the film franchise in such a way calls attention to elements of continuity and change, especially in relationship to the Bond formula that many of our authors return to in their respective chapters. In doing so, the collection is able to take us from the opening of *Dr. No*, after the introduction of the iconic gun barrel, to the final moments of *No Time to Die*, when Daniel Craig's tenure as Bond comes to a dramatic climax.

Aside from being notable for the breadth of its engagements with the long-running series, this collection hopes to be engaging for readers, both those with a casual interest in the franchise and more serious Bondophiles, because of the variety and originality of its critical approaches, among them analyses of color in *Goldfinger* (1964), the costume design and characterization of May Day (Grace Jones) in *A View to a Kill* (1985), the UK press reception of *The Living Daylights* (1987), Cold War nostalgia in *GoldenEye* (1995), and the impact of contemporary progressive politics on *No Time to Die*. In some ways, the Bond canon has become a tapestry of iconic moments playing on repeat in the cultural imaginary: the first time Connery says "The name's Bond, James Bond"

Figure 0.1 "Bond, James Bond." 007 (Sean Connery) delivers the iconic line for the first time. *Dr. No* (1962).

in *Dr. No* (figure o.1), Tracy's shocking death in *On Her Majesty's Secret Service*, Roger Moore's Union Jack parachute in *The Spy Who Loved Me* (1977), and the exhilarating parkour scene that opens *Casino Royale* (2006), which did so much to establish the viscerality that would define Craig's time as the character. The contributors to this volume call upon many such moments to collectively argue for the enduring importance of James Bond in ways reserved for those rare fictional creations that come to last so long and mean so much, not just to the cultures in which they are created, but to audiences all around the globe. This results in a collection spanning what we might call the "Bond experience," which readers may dip into film by film or actor by actor according to the era. More ambitious Bond devotees can read the whole of the volume cover to cover, but the editors certainly suggest a few breaks and perhaps a Vesper Martini (shaken, not stirred, of course) along the way.

Present and Past Bond, James Bond

It is well documented that Ian Fleming's Bond debuted during a period in British postwar history when Britain's influence as a global superpower was waning.[2] Correspondingly, Bond has been widely read as functioning as a "nationalist fantasy," self-consciously designed to mask the failures and inadequacies of a crumbling Empire.[3] In Fleming's novels, the character operated in an imagined alternative reality that ran counter to the prevailing real-world geopolitical narrative that saw Britain's influence and status undoubtedly declining on the international stage in the decades after the end of World War Two. In these stories, Bond was an artificial projection of British imperial strength in a postimperial age; his intellect, physical prowess, virility, and cross-cultural consumerism catered to a nostalgic longing for Britain's former glory, while the character's ideological rhetoric sustained a neo-imperial ethos that implicitly endorsed prejudices and attitudes that became more outdated as the decades passed, but are still embraced by many. All of this helps to explain why some critics, scholars, and even fans have often criticized what they have seen as the sexist, racist, elitist, and xenophobic attitudes of the Bond novels and the films they inspired.

Despite such criticisms, the enduring appeal of the Bond film franchise has been rooted in the character's ability to successfully navigate more than sixty years of political, social, and cultural change, at once adapting with the times but just as importantly never deviating too far from the formula on which it was built. Tony Bennett and Janet Woollacott, for example, state, "If Bond has functioned as a 'sign of the times,' it has been as a *moving sign of the times*." In this way, the series is defined by the continually shifting balance of continuity and change, which some other franchises have found hard to reconcile and which can be seen very clearly in the chronological structure adopted by this edited collection. What we see, and what this volume will attest to, is how Bond "has functioned as a shifting focal point for the articulation of historically specific ideological concerns."[4] Notably, James Bond, as played by Connery (1962–1967, 1971), Lazenby (1969), Moore (1973–1985), and Timothy Dalton (1985–1987), found himself embroiled in, and indeed contributed to, the ideological and geopolitical rivalry between the United States and the USSR known as the Cold War. Even though they came after that conflict had ended, the seven years and four films during which Pierce Brosnan (1995–2002) played the role were also defined by its looming shadow and the complicated political realities that were left in the aftermath of the dissolution of the Soviet Union.[5] Brosnan's last Bond film, *Die Another Day* (2002), was released more than a year after the events of September 11th, 2001, but it was not until Craig's tenure as the character (2006–2021) that Bond could really be said to exist in what has been described by many as the post-9/11 and "War on Terror" years.

The Craig films recalibrated the Bond formula in a variety of ways never attempted before by the producers of the franchise, characterized, as Christoph Lindner suggests, by their status as "a re-evaluation, a reinvention and a renewal."[6] They did this by introducing a continuing overarching narrative across Craig's five films and a characterization of Bond that evolved as previous Bonds had never done before (figure 0.2). Craig's Bond is demonstrably more vulnerable, more fallible, and more human than he was ever allowed to be in the past, in ways that audiences seemed to demand from action heroes in the first two decades of the twenty-first century. Craig's Bond is certainly an example of those whom Fran Pheasant-Kelly referred to as the "wounded hero" and Vincent M. Gaine as "damaged," the likes of whom became so prominent in post-9/11 action cinema.[7] Just as important were the Craig era's attempts to update certain areas of representation in light of progressively growing discourse concerning gender and ethnicity, which can be seen as culminating in the emergence of the Black Lives Matter, #MeToo, and Time's Up movements and the broader debates they engendered. How far these developments were integrated into the Craig films has been widely and vigorously debated. Some insiders, such as producer Michael G. Wilson, stress that the series "has been embracing Me Too for many Bond films. I don't think that any of our films would not be acceptable—certainly since Daniel [Craig] started."[8] However, other observers saw the Craig era very differently, like Jonathan Murray, who considered it an "unthinking continuation of regressive stereotypes long associated with the 007 franchise," or Patrick Anderson, who wrote that *Skyfall*, the most commercially successful film in the history of the franchise with earnings of $1 billion worldwide, sought to "salvage heteronormativity, patriarchy, white supremacy, and imperial power."[9]

Figure 0.2 "The name's Bond, James Bond." Unlike his predecessors, this Bond (Daniel Craig) must earn his "00" status and in doing so takes on many of the hallmarks of the post-9/11 wounded hero. *Casino Royale* (2006).

These very different interpretations of the franchise have been a hallmark of how producers, commentators, fans, and academics have understood the character and the films, perhaps one of the reasons Bond has continued to resonate well beyond the diegetic frame. What will be clear to readers of *James Bond Will Return* is that the series and the films within in it are able to function as remarkable historical and cultural artifacts, immersed in the sociocultural, geopolitical, and industry trends of their respective moments, time capsules of their eras in ways the most resonant of culture products have always been. The anthological structure of this volume brings into stark view, as Barbara Broccoli has argued, that "Over the years, attitudes have changed, and so have the Bond films. The films are representative of the times they're in."[10] Yet given the popularity of Bond in both popular and academic arenas, it is not just the films that have evolved, but also the body of work that has been written about them.

Bond Studies: Then and Now

With the present moment and the longevity of the franchise in mind, *James Bond Will Return* contributes to over sixty years of Bond scholarship, much of which interrogates the meanings of Bond as a fictional character. Popular attention on James Bond predated the cinematic franchise, beginning with responses to Ian Fleming's novels, but academic study developed in recognition of the huge success and cultural impact of the films. In the spirit of this volume, the milestones and "phases" of Bond studies may be mapped broadly across the eras defined by different actors who have portrayed Bond in the official series to also give a sense of the emergent approaches and scholarship variously drawn on in some chapters, and the contributions made by our authors to further evolve the range of topics and perspectives brought to the films.[11]

The height of the Connery era and Bondmania in the mid-1960s saw the first formative phase of Bond scholarship appear in the form of articles and essays, but most significantly Kingsley Amis's *The James Bond Dossier* (1965), on the literary Bond.[12] The next year, another collection, *The Bond Affair* (1966), extended attention to the film series and recognized that Bond had become the "popular phenomenon" we know today.[13] Some twenty years on, at the end of the Moore era, a major contribution to the wider field of cultural studies was produced, which remains a landmark of Bond scholarship. Published in 1987, Tony Bennett and Janet Woollacott's *Bond and Beyond* extensively analyzed the "political career of a popular hero" to date, identifying the different periods and ideological concerns that are important in relation to the contributions in this collection, no matter what approach is taken.[14]

The next significant milestone was around the turn of the century, during Brosnan's tenure as Bond. While the film franchise tackled the new millennium, in scholarship the works of James Chapman and Jeremy Black called further attention to Bond's relationship to cultural and political history. Notably, Chapman's first edition of *Licence to Thrill* (1999) gave a strong rationale for taking the Bond franchise seriously and observed the negotiations of past and present, continuity and change, in connection with film culture, popular culture, and society.[15] After these studies came a number of scholarly collections, including interdisciplinary approaches to Bond in different media and from different critical angles. For instance, Christoph Lindner's *The James Bond Phenomenon* (2003) collected foundational writings on the figure of Bond, the films, and the novels plus newer scholarship (broadened further and updated in the second edition of the collection).[16] Even when the film series was in a period of uncertainty in the early 2000s, these academic works reflected the continuing popularity and great critical value of studying Bond.

When the Bond films took a new direction in the mid-2000s with the beginning of the Craig era, this encouraged a growth in scholarship, bringing forward other voices and diverse critical perspectives about the franchise. These include books and edited collections that focus on gender, geopolitics, and fashion and analyses of Bond's relationship with popular culture.[17] This latest phase of Bond scholarship builds upon the legacy of past works but also makes other connections, engaging with Bond in different ways across media, from adaptation to fandom, chronicling evolutions of the character, and some specifically examining the Bond of the post-millennial "reboot" films.[18] Another milestone happened in 2017 when the online open-access *International Journal of James Bond Studies* was launched, "dedicated to critical readings of all aspects of the Bond franchise. Bringing together a variety of new voices and leading scholars in the field, the journal seeks to expand on existing criticism—and to develop new critical and theoretical paradigms by which to view the Bond universe—and through which to view wider cultural, social, and political issues."[19] The importance of this mission statement is recognized by this collection, although, in this case, with specific focus on the official Eon films that remain central to the franchise. Our authors employ a range of approaches to (re)situate the meanings of the cinematic Bond in relationship to contemporary society and British and American film cultures and engage with debates that (re)frame the film series. As this introduction and our short academic overview attest, James Bond matters to the entertainment industry, audiences, society, and culture and to scholarship, negotiating issues of wider importance throughout more than sixty years on film in ways that we argue surpass any other film series.

Critical Perspectives on the 007 Film Franchise

As previously stated, this volume adopts a chronological approach to the Bond film franchise, with an original chapter on every installment in the series from *Dr. No* until *No Time to Die*. Each of the twenty-five chapters has been written as a stand-alone interaction with the film in question. But, as will quickly become apparent, these individual engagements navigate the shifting coordinates of the series, demonstrating the elements of continuity and change that have shaped and defined this long-lived franchise. Each contributor to the anthology was empowered to approach the film from a new or different critical perspective, with the directive from us as editors being that the chapter should provide an original take on some aspect of the film, either by developing a particular approach or introducing ideas and arguments that have not been covered extensively in literature on the franchise.

Starting at the beginning of Connery's tenure and the first big-screen Bond adventure, Laura Crossley's chapter argues that *Dr. No* is not just an escapist fantasy, but rather captures its political, historical, and social moment nearly a decade into the New Elizabethan age. This is a recurring theme evident throughout the edited collection, and it is certainly one of the reasons that Bond has endured since the Sixties. Bond himself is, of course, another reason why the films are so popular. In Lucy Bolton's chapter focusing on *From Russia with Love* (1963), she suggests that the film consolidated many of the defining features of the character, notably establishing sex and sexual appeal as crucial aspects of Bond's identity. By Connery's third appearance as Bond, both star and character had become international icons, but *Goldfinger* is also important to the franchise for many other reasons. In his analysis, Keith M. Johnston considers how color technology and aesthetics play an essential role in creating the film's memorable set pieces, promotional material, and iconic imagery, which continues to shape the franchise today. The fourth entry, *Thunderball* (1965) had a budget that exceeded those of the previous three Bond films combined, and the creative ambition of the production was even larger. In his chapter, Klaus Dodds examines how the people, places, and prevailing geopolitical climate of the film help to legitimize 007's claims to authority, effectively blending and blurring the real-life realities of the Cold War. Robert Shail's discussion of *You Only Live Twice* (1967) also explores Bond's place in the world in the mid-1960s, but approaches the film from within the framework of Orientalism as defined by noted cultural critic Edward Said. His analysis is one of several in this collection that acknowledges how the franchise can, at times, make for uncomfortable viewing, especially for modern audiences. In the popular historiography of Bond, the sixth film, *On Her Majesty's Secret Service*, which starred Lazenby, has provoked perhaps the most divisive responses of almost any entrant in the series: some viewers consider it a critical and commercial misfire and some regard it as one of the most original films in the canon, even the closest adaptation of Fleming's writing. James Chapman's chapter intervenes in this debate and examines the development and production history of *On Her Majesty's Secret Service*, drawing on archival research to challenge some of the perceptions around the film.

The first Bond film of the 1970s was also the last official film to feature Connery. Ian Scott's chapter examines the franchise's movement into its second decade. Scott convincingly argues that the plot, setting, characters, and framings of *Diamonds Are Forever* (1971), while very much influenced by the early '70s, seem to anticipate aspects of Bond and British and American culture and politics that would later come to pass. Yet, the 1970s were to be Moore's decade as Bond and he continued in the role into the mid-1980s. The chapters on the Moore era begin with Fran Pheasant-Kelly's reading of how the spatial dichotomies, locations, and spaces of *Live and Let Die* (1973) are reflective of its complex and sometimes paradoxical cultural histories. This and the following chapter examine the role of the criminal antagonist. Julie Lobalzo Wright focuses on Christopher Lee's distinctive Bond villain Francesco Scaramanga in *The Man with the Golden Gun* (1974), arguing that, while the film is undoubtedly a testament to the decade that "taste forgot" through its safari suits, animatronics, and energy crisis storyline, the presence of Lee provides it with much more than just a kitsch quality. The next two chapters engage with aspects of Bond as operating within the realms of fantasies of both a personal and a national nature. Terence McSweeney explores *The Spy Who Loved Me* as a wish-fulfilment fantasy on the national scale at a very specific moment in British history, when the country was pulled between the poles of the Queen's Silver

Jubilee celebrations and the realities of political and economic turmoil. In this chapter, McSweeney reads Moore's Bond in a way similar to how scholars have engaged with iconic American superheroes, seeing the British icon as a vivid synechdochal figure of national identity. This idea of the Moore era of Bond embracing escapism continues in Steven Gerrard's writing on *Moonraker* (1979) which uses theories of escapism to argue for a reexamination of, to put it diplomatically, one of the least well-regarded films in the franchise.

The 1980s saw the final three films of the Moore era: *For Your Eyes Only* (1981), *Octopussy* (1983), and *A View to a Kill* (1985). Stuart Joy argues that vengeance is the central motif of *For Your Eyes Only*, but, in a rare move for the series, not only James Bond's but also the female love interest's, Melina Havelock (Carole Bouquet). The centralization of her experience of loss drives the narrative forward in ways that make her one of the most interesting and active female characters in the history of the franchise. Not surprisingly, such a focus on gender remains critical to this collection, but costume is also a common theme in the chapters on the last of the Moore-era Bond films. Claire Hines examines the emphasis on Bond's use of disguise in *Octopussy* in relationship to the iconic image of the stylishly suited male hero. By contrast, Randall Stevens spotlights another criminal antagonist, arguing that Grace Jones's henchwoman May Day in *A View to a Kill* is unique in the film series by considering her position as a woman of Bond and the range of striking designs created in collaboration with couture designer Azzedine Alaïa.

Timothy Dalton's two-film tenure as the character was brief but impactful, and both of his films are connected in different ways by our authors to the changing social, political, and cultural moments of their release. Stephanie Jones uses a reception study to examine references to AIDS and safe sex, which reviews of *The Living Daylights* (1987) mention again and again. Jones explains and interprets those references in response to an installment of the series where Bond took markedly fewer sexual partners than usual. Stacey Peebles explores *Licence to Kill* (1989), a film considered by many to be a critical moment in the evolution of the franchise, as to how far it is influenced by the shifting power dynamics occurring in the world at large during the time of its production: both geopolitical ones, in the form of the end of the Cold War, and cultural, in the emergence of third-wave feminism.

If the 1980s was divided between two very different interpretations of the Bond character, the next decade was defined only by Brosnan. His final film, *Die Another Day* (2002), was released in the 2000s but had yet to embrace the tumultuous era as Craig's films would later do so wholeheartedly. Even so, his films navigated the end of one world order, the Cold War, and speculated as to what might replace it. This is the central focus of Tatiana Konrad's chapter on *GoldenEye*, which examines the transition, or lack thereof, to the post–Cold War world, focusing on the film's thematic and aesthetic ambiguity as it attempts to chart the changing geopolitical dynamics of a world order that had fueled the entire history of Bond since *Dr. No.* The great promise of *GoldenEye* was followed by *Tomorrow Never Dies* (1997), discussed by Llewella Chapman in a close examination of how the "Bondian" formula and tropes and former Bond films, as well as the social, political, and cultural contexts, influenced scriptwriter Bruce Feirstein. The Bond formula is also the subject of Tobias Hochscherf's chapter that considers *The World Is Not Enough* (1999) as a transitional Bond film. Hochscherf argues that, while Brosnan's third film comprises many of the elements of the Bond formula that have historically made the franchise so successful, the producers carefully tried to update the series by challenging some of its characteristics, including gender politics, the use of technology, and the representation of contemporary geopolitics. Brosnan's last outing as Bond in *Die Another Day* marked the franchise's fortieth anniversary, but the film is widely regarded as another low point in the series. In the decades since its original theatrical release, its less-than-favorable reputation has often been associated with its embrace of Computer Generated Imagery (CGI), which diverged from the series' longstanding tradition of practical effects. Yet Christopher Holliday argues that Brosnan's final appearance as Bond served as a crucial template for exploring the innovative potential of CGI, especially during a period when digital technologies were creating new aesthetic possibilities for filmmakers working in Hollywood.

The 9/11 attacks and the ongoing War on Terror seemed to signal for the producers of the Bond franchise that something had to change after *Die Another Day.* The Brosnan films had perhaps become too disconnected from their political and cultural moments, and audiences seemed to be demanding more complicated characters and narratives from the action genre that Bond had shaped and contributed to for so many years. This led to a new Bond in the form of Daniel Craig. The parameters of what was new about the Craig-era Bond are delineated in Christine Muller's chapter on *Casino Royale*, in which she tackles the film's origin story, which resets James Bond as a plausible operative under the torturous and merciless conditions of contemporary international espionage. Estella Tincknell argues for a reappraisal of *Quantum of Solace* (2008), asserting that the film distils multiple elements from the Bond universe into a hyperintensified, visually spectacular speed tour of the canon. The next two chapters of the collection take a decidedly gothic turn in approaching Bond. Monica Germanà's reading of Craig's third film, *Skyfall*, examines uncanny technology and Bond's traumatic past to further shed light on the complicated relationship with modernity that has defined Bond, whereas James Smith's chapter on *Spectre* (2015) analyzes the images of haunting that proliferate the twenty-fourth entry in the Bond franchise. Bringing Craig's tenure and this volume to a conclusion, Terence McSweeney and Stuart Joy explore the impact of contemporary sociocultural discourse on the portrayal of women in *No Time to Die*. As mentioned earlier, by the time this entry was made there were more vocal calls for substantive changes to the franchise. Such claims had been made for decades about the character and aspects of the Bond formula. However, the directness and frequency of similar critiques prior to the release of *No Time to Die* was notable, as several commentators and journalists asked whether the cultural institution of James Bond was still relevant for audiences as we began the third decade of the twenty-first century.

Together, the twenty-five chapters in this collection engage with the wide range of ways that the Bond franchise has achieved historical and cultural impact, charting the repetitions and innovations navigated by this famous agent of continuity and change over the years throughout the late twentieth and early twenty-first centuries. At the time of writing, how and when exactly Bond will next return to our screens remains to be seen, but for an understanding of the future we might look back to the past that this anthology richly documents.

Notes

1. Erin Clarey, "They Resurrected MGM. Amazon Bought the Studio. Now What?," *New York Times*, July 6, 2021, www.nytimes.com/2021/07/06/business/media/mgm-amazon-michael-deluca-pamela-abdy.html.

2. Timo Müller, "The Bonds of Empire: (Post-) Imperial Negotiations in the 007 Film Series," in *Post-Empire Imaginaries?*, ed. Barbara Buchenau and Virginia Richter (Leiden: Brill, 2015), 305–26.

3. James Chapman, *Licence to Thrill: A Cultural History of the James Bond Films* (New York: Columbia University Press, 2000), 4.

4. Tony Bennett and Janet Woollacott, *Bond and Beyond: The Political Career of a Popular Hero* (London: Macmillan, 1987), 19.

5. Tobias Hochscherf, "Bond for the Age of Global Crises: 007 in the Daniel Craig Era," *Journal of British Cinema and Television* 10, no. 2 (2013): 298–320.

6. Christoph Lindner, "Introduction," in *Revisioning 007: James Bond and Casino Royale*, ed. Christoph Lindner (London: Wallflower, 2009), 1–7.

7. Fran Pheasant-Kelly, *Fantasy Film Post 9/11* (New York: Palgrave Macmillan, 2013), 144; Vincent Gaine, "Remember Everything, Absolve Nothing: Working Through Trauma in the Bourne Trilogy," *Cinema Journal* 51 (2011): 160.

8. Baz Bamigboye, "We'll Never Have Jane Bond But We Will Still Rise to the Occasion in the #MeToo Era, Says Barbara Broccoli," *Daily Mail*, April 26, 2021, www.dailymail.co.uk/tvshowbiz/article-6961695/BAZ-BAMIGBOYE-never-Jane-Bond-says-Barbara-Broccoli.html.

9. Jonathan Murray, "Containing the Spectre of the Past: The Evolution of the James Bond Franchise During the Daniel Craig Era," *Visual Culture in Britain* 18, no. 2 (2017): 247–73; Patrick Anderson, "Neocon Bond: The Cultural Politics of *Skyfall*," *Quarterly Review of Film and Video* 34, no. 1 (2016): 20.

10. See Bamigboye, "We'll Never Have Jane Bond."

11. For a fuller outline of scholarship, we refer our readers to Ian Kinane's account of evolutions in critical studies of James Bond, the novels and films, and wider media,

"James Bond Studies: Evolutions of a Critical Field," *International Journal of James Bond Studies* 1, no. 1 (2017): 1–11.

12. Kingsley Amis, *The James Bond Dossier* (London: Jonathan Cape, 1965).

13. Lietta Tornabuoni, "A Popular Phenomenon," in *The Bond Affair*, ed. Umberto Eco and Oreste del Buono (London: Macdonald, 1966), 13–34.

14. Bennett and Woollacott, *Bond and Beyond*, 22–43.

15. Chapman, *Licence to Thrill*. Chapman updated a second edition of *Licence to Thrill* in 2007. A third edition is in process at the time we are writing this introduction.

16. Christoph Lindner, ed., *The James Bond Phenomenon: A Critical Reader* (Manchester: Manchester University Press, 2003). The second edition was published in 2009. Also see the collection from Edward P. Comentale, Stephen Watt, and Skip Willman, eds. *Ian Fleming and James Bond: The Cultural Politics of 007* (Bloomington: Indiana University Press, 2005).

17. On gender and James Bond, see Lisa Funnell, ed., *For His Eyes Only: The Women of Bond* (New York: Wallflower, 2015); Steven Gerrard, ed., *From Blofeld to Moneypenny: Gender in James Bond* (Bingley, UK: Emerald, 2020). On fashion, see Monica Germanà, *Bond Girls: Body, Fashion and Gender* (London: Bloomsbury, 2019); Llewella Chapman, *Fashioning James Bond: Costume, Gender, and Identity in the World of 007* (London: Bloomsbury, 2022). On geopolitics, see Lisa Funnell and Klaus Dodds, *Geographies, Genders, and Geopolitics of James Bond* (London: Palgrave Macmillan, 2017) and journal articles such as Klaus Dodds, "Screening Geopolitics: James Bond and the Early Cold War Films (1962–1967)," *Geopolitics* 10, no. 2 (2005): 266–89. On Bond's relationship with popular culture, see Robert G. Weiner, B. Lynn Whitfield, and Jack Becker, eds., *James Bond in World and Popular Culture: The Films Are Not Enough* (Newcastle upon Tyne, UK: Cambridge Scholars, 2010) and Claire Hines, *The Playboy and James Bond: 007, Ian Fleming and* Playboy *Magazine* (Manchester: Manchester University Press, 2018).

18. On adaptation, see Jeremy Strong, ed., *James Bond Uncovered* (London: Palgrave Macmillan, 2018). On fandom, see Claire Hines, ed., *Fan Phenomena: James Bond* (Bristol: Intellect, 2015). On James Bond in the film series and beyond, see Jaap Verheul, ed., *The Cultural Life of James Bond: Specters of 007* (Amsterdam: Amsterdam University Press, 2020). On Craig-era Bond, see, for example, Lindner, *Revisioning 007*; Klaus Dodds and Lisa Funnell, eds., "James Bond in the Daniel Craig Era," special issue, *Journal of Popular Film and Television* 46, no. 1 (2018), and other journal articles such as Katherine Cox, "Becoming James Bond: Daniel Craig, Rebirth, and Refashioning Masculinity in *Casino Royale* (2006)," *Journal of Gender Studies* 23, no. 2 (2014): 184–96; Hochscherf, "Bond for the Age of Global Crises."

19. Kinane, "James Bond Studies," 8.

CHAPTER 1

BOND AND THE NEW ELIZABETHANS

Tradition and Modernity in *Dr. No* (1962)

LAURA CROSSLEY

In 2012 the BBC commissioned a series on Radio 4 to mark the Queen's Diamond Jubilee and, from suggestions from the general public, selected a list of sixty people whose "actions during the reign of Elizabeth II have had a significant impact on lives in these islands and given the age its character, for better or worse."[1] It is a disparate list that crosses racial, gender, and class lines and takes in virtually every facet of contemporary British life, including as it does the Conservative politician Enoch Powell, cultural theorist Stuart Hall, ballet dancer Margot Fonteyn, and musician/producer Goldie. Spy fiction is admirably represented by Graham Greene, a literary novelist who termed his espionage books "entertainments," as he deemed them to carry no message; yet even those works—*Stamboul Train* (1932) and *Our Man in Havana* (1958), for example—center on themes of treachery and moral guilt.[2] Greene's reputation as a serious novelist established him as a writer in tune with the moral and social concerns of the era—not the sort of conversation that is usually associated with the creator of James Bond, novelist Ian Fleming. Yet if the list of influential New Elizabethans were to run to fictional characters, it would, I think, be fair to wager that Bond would figure prominently. As "the most successful adventure hero in history" and the protagonist in the world's longest-running film franchise, Bond holds a unique place in cinema history and in the British and global cultural imagination.[3]

While Bond is clearly descended from the clubland heroes and sons of empire who defined British heroism through the nineteenth century and into the twentieth, he is also a modern figure. The blatant sexuality and violence of the first

Bond film, *Dr. No* (1962), were far removed from the more restrained cinema of the 1950s and was already looking toward the more permissive society that would emerge throughout the 1960s. *Dr. No* embodies the Cold War pre-occupations with sex and spies that would erupt spectacularly with the Pro-fumo Affair in 1963. It navigates the traditional and the progressive, and its upbeat tone prefigures the ethos of the "Swinging Sixties," that era in British cultural history popularly characterized through fashion, music, commerce, and an ostensibly more open attitude toward sex.[4] Its optimism is lacking in Fleming's novels. It is often stated that the loss of empire translated into Brit-ain's being a reduced figure on the world stage, yet the transition from the empire to the Commonwealth was part of that sense of renewal and optimism in the 1960s. It seems fitting that the film that kick-started one of the most suc-cessful franchises in cinema history should share its inception with Jamai-can independence.

Many scholars have pointed to the situating of the Bond novels and films in relation to the decline of empire and the specific "diminishing state of national sovereign power" that constitutes the Bondian world as providing a form of escape: a fantasy that situates Britain as being far more important on the world stage than it is, with the most recent films overtly acknowledging the postim-perial geopolitical landscape.[5] This is most clearly evident in *Skyfall* (2012), in the film's narrative but also with the formal linking of Bond, in the person of Daniel Craig, with the Queen during the "Happy and Glorious" section of the London 2012 Olympic Games opening ceremony. It is, perhaps, a natural asso-ciation: Bond made his first appearance in print in *Casino Royale* in 1953, the Queen's Coronation year. At the climax of this opening sequence, Queen Eliz-abeth II ostensibly jumps from a helicopter into the Olympic stadium, deploy-ing a Union Flag parachute on the way down, while Monty Norman's James Bond theme echoes around the arena. The symbolism linking Bond, the royal family, and British cultural identity is made manifest: in one scholar's words, "British communities may have lost their empire, and over the years they may have had to witness the declining status of a nation that was once a massive superpower, but the 2012 ceremonies showed that they could nevertheless cel-ebrate their continued relevancy."[6]

But why is this idea of empire—or the lack of it—so important to discus-sions around the figure of James Bond? As James Chapman has pointed out, the Britain of Bond, as established in the novels, "may be characterised as a Brit-ain at the twilight of empire."[7] Much of it is to do with the character's origins: the template for the patriotic, upper-class, gentlemanly protagonist laid down by John Buchan in his creation of Richard Hannay.[8] Hannay himself has all the traits of the "Heroes of Empire"—duty, stoicism, courage, perseverance—associated with characters such as Gordon of Khartoum, Clive of India, or the fictitious *Sanders of the River* (1911). Clive and Sanders both had their stories committed to film in 1935, with Gordon's being told in *Khartoum* in 1966. These traits were, for much of the nineteenth and early twentieth centuries, folded into constructions of national identity and national character. This national character is, therefore, the justification for empire. As film historian Jeffrey Richards states, it stems from the "moral superiority of the British to everyone else by virtue of their commitment to a code of behaviour which involves the preservation of law, order and justice for love of those qualities."[9] Bond and his fellow adventurers, such as *The Avengers'* (ITV, 1961–1969) John Steed (Patrick Macnee), act as signifiers of continuity and "stability."[10] This tension between tradition and modernity has been at the heart of much evolution of cultural life from the mid-twentieth century onward and could, arguably, be seen to be a defining characteristic of the New Elizabethans.

The 1950s occupies a curious space in the British cultural imagination; with its coming before the Swinging Sixties but after the upheaval of the Second World War, the decade can be somewhat overlooked and is more often the setting for cozy crime dramas such as *Marple* (ITV, 2004–2013) or *Grantchester* (ITV, 2014–). It is a decade that still had rationing, high unemployment, housing shortages, and a rising crime rate. As Heather Wiebe states:

> The anxiety about a changing British society perceived to be in a state of decline, especially in London, was evident in the coverage of the second big news story of 1953, the grisly Christie murders in Notting Hill. Here was inner city decay, a morally decadent world peopled by prostitutes and drug addicts, tensions between English poor and Jamaican immigrants living side by side in Notting Hill, all wrapped up in a narrative of shocking violence.[11]

As the decade progressed, fear around the increase of "shocking violence" was laid at the door of youth subcultures, in particular the dreaded and much-vilified Teddy boys, who became the byword for delinquency.[12] But even in the 1950s, there were calls to retract the label, not least from Labour MP George Isaacs, who, in a speech in 1955, stated: "Teddy boys are youngsters with youthful spirits who like to have their own kind of clothes. There are bad ones among them here and there, but you will find darn fine lads in Edwardian clothes going to the Boys' Brigade and the Sea Cadets. The name Teddy boy is beginning to stink; I would rather call them 'the New Elizabethans.'"[13] His plea failed, but what is interesting here is the merging of the modern figure of the Teddy boy with the very traditional and solid Brigade and Cadet movements. Implicit in Isaacs' words is the idea that the combination of modern individualism and traditional institutional service is inherent to how we might define the New Elizabethan.

Against the somewhat tumultuous backdrop of the early 1950s, we also have the figure who gives the New Elizabethans their name. The Coronation of

Elizabeth II in 1953 was both a statement of continuity and stability and assertion of youth and modernity: she was, after all, only twenty-five when she came to the throne and would become a figurehead not of empire but of the rapidly expanding Commonwealth. The coronation itself "articulated an optimistic British modernity in self-consciously different terms, emphasizing social hierarchy and individual achievement rather than egalitarianism, and reinvoking Empire (in the new form of the Commonwealth) rather than focusing more exclusively on Britain as an island nation."[14]

The 1950s had myriad social problems but the decade also had a focus on technological change, economic stimulus, and, crucially, the switch from empire to the much more equitable Commonwealth of Nations. The end of rationing in 1955 and the eventual economic boom that led Prime Minister Harold Macmillan to declare that Britons had "never had it so good" paved the way for what Diana Vreeland would later term the "Youthquake."[15] The traces of the focus on youth and modernity can be seen much earlier in the emergence of rock 'n' roll in the late 1950s and by 1962, the year of *Dr. No*'s release, it is very evident. The Beatles made their first recording at Abbey Road in June 1962, while the Rolling Stones played their debut gig at the Marquee Club the following month. On August 6, 1962, after months of buildup and preparation, Jamaica became the first Caribbean island to gain independence. While the transition to Commonwealth did cause consternation and wariness in some quarters, this seemed to stem less from concerns over the end of imperial rule and more from the impact that Jamaican independence would have on the Federation of the West Indies.[16] Such concerns proved valid when the Federation faced dissolution as a result of its being "deserted" by Jamaica and Trinidad, which followed Jamaica to independence a few weeks later on August 31.[17] For many communities, however, it was seen as the ongoing and very welcome process of modernization; a photograph donated to the National Museums Liverpool shows a multiethnic and multigenerational ball held in the city to celebrate Jamaican Independence Day.[18]

It was in October 1962 that *Dr. No* opened in Britain. In many ways the film was visually exciting, vibrant, and fresh. The posters, with their bright red-and-yellow color scheme, depict a suave Sean Connery casually wielding both a cigarette and a gun; beside him are the sketches of four women, all in various states of undress. Sex and violence are implicit before we even get to the film itself. There had not really been a film quite like it before, certainly not in Britain. While British cinema of the 1950s is not quite as staid as its reputation might allow—the introduction of the X Certificate by the British Board of Film Classification in 1951 resulted in a steady rise of films with increased violent and sexual content—*Dr. No* feels almost un-British in its sheer lack of inhibition and unashamed glamour. There had been successful franchises centered on British gentleman adventurers prior to Bond, notably RKO's B-movie series of

The Saint (1938–1941) and The Falcon (1941–1946). While both characters were at ease with gunplay and had a weakness for beautiful women, the films were very much characterized by traditional notions of British upper-class mores and reticence.

On screen, despite its tight budget of $1.1 million, *Dr. No* brings a sophisticated sheen to its proceedings by leaning into the opportunities afforded by filming on location in Jamaica, and the soon-to-be independent Jamaica at that. The film avoids any ruminations on the imminent postimperial nature of the island's identity and still positions the incumbents of Government House as the ruling body (an untruth, even at the time of filming).[19] Despite this, some of that end of empire can be felt in the film: as a character, Bond seems modern and brash against the colonial administrators at Government House. This may also have something to do with the casting: Bond has all the trappings of a privileged upbringing, but Sean Connery brings an edginess to the role that would not have been given by a performer such as David Niven, who was once considered for the part. Similarly, MI6 chief M's (Bernard Lee) relationship with Bond is that of the stolid Establishment figure trying to rein in and control the much more dynamic, youthful, and modern agent.

Today, it easy to spot the elements that would go on to be so recognizable in every Bond film that followed: beautiful locations, an assortment of glamorous women (some allied with Bond, some not), advanced technology, nefarious villains, and a hypercompetent secret agent whose loyalty to Queen and country is never in doubt. However, watching *Dr. No*, it is also evident how unlike the rest of the franchise it is. The superficial differences are easy to spot from the start: the lack of a pre-credits cold open, no prancing nudes while a popular singer of the day belts out the theme tune. The Maurice Binder–designed credits sequence is a proto-psychedelia of flashing multicolored dots accompanied by Monty Norman's theme; both dots and music segue into dancing silhouettes and then eventually silhouettes of the three blind assassins who open the action, with Byron Lee and the Dragonnaires' version of *Three Blind Mice* playing over the images. From this opening, inconsequential though it may be, elements of Jamaican culture are already embedded into the film. James Robertson's exemplary examination of the Jamaican links in the production argues that the film's "engagement with some Jamaican concerns" provides one of the distinct elements in *Dr. No* that is never quite replicated in subsequent installments.[20]

The Jamaica of *Dr. No* is captured in glossy, beautifully lit and composed shots that show off the island's natural beauty, but there is also an element of authenticity. As we follow the three assassins through the streets of Kingston, there is no attempt to disguise or prettify the surroundings: cars and buses pass by, locals go about their business. As the assassins tap their way through the streets, they pass women carrying oversized bundles balanced on their heads and a man having a smoke by the harbor wall (figure 1.1), until they reach the road taking them out of the city and to the colonial Queen's Club, where the only black faces are the staff. For an outsider unfamiliar with Jamaica, it is establishing local color; for an islander, these would be known locations that fix *Dr. No* into a very specific geography. Similarly, later in the film, when Bond receives directions from the duplicitous Miss Taro (Anglo-French actor Zena Marshall playing a Chinese character), the instructions are so precise that they would be easily recognized by the local population: "Take the Port Royal Road out of Kingston. Drive on the Windward Road 'til you pass the cement factory . . ." It is one of the least glamorous locations for Bond to be lured to in this or any other film in the franchise, but these spots make very visible the burgeoning infrastructure, the investment in the island's future as it headed toward independence.

To a domestic British audience at a time before low-budget mass travel, the view of Jamaica provided not just a form of escapism but also an insight into a world that they would have little hope of experiencing. The use of authentic Jamaican locations—recognizable to both the local island populace and the Jamaican diaspora—alongside a number of Jamaican actors and a background of calypso and ska music (the latter also provided largely by the popular local group Byron Lee and the Dragonnaires) grounds the film in its locale. It is a very different experience of the Caribbean to that offered eleven years later in *Live and Let Die* (1973), where the island locations merely act as a backdrop to the action and (at best) questionable representations of race and a wholly distorted version of voodoo practices. For this first film, the presence of Fleming,

Figure 1.1 The three assassins on the harbor road. *Dr. No* (1962).

working on further Bond novels at his home, Goldeneye, and his involvement in the life of the island gave *Dr. No* "remarkable local entrée."[21] Even by the second film, *From Russia with Love* (1963), this sort of embedding in the setting is signally absent. Given the involvement of Jamaican locals in the production, it is disappointing that the only Jamaican character of note, Quarrel (John Kitzmiller) is downgraded to a more "stereotypical eye-rolling" and servile role as opposed to the relative agency he has in the novel.[22] Despite this, Marguerite LeWars, who featured as the photographer Annabel Chung in the film and was crowned Miss Jamaica in 1961, speaks of the excitement and pride in *Dr. No* among local audiences and the "magic" of seeing footage of different locations around Jamaica spliced together.[23]

London as a location is not as showcased as Jamaica in the film and is limited to the casino where we first encounter Bond, his apartment, and M's office; taken together, they signify a London of some glamour, power, and tradition. There is, however, a knowingness in the presentation of an idea of traditional, privileged Britishness, with the filmmakers clearly inviting the audience to recognize and enjoy the absurdity of the story and its characters. While the film is neither comedy nor satire, it is playful and this sense of playfulness and knowingness at the expense of received ideas of upper-class Britishness contribute to the feeling of freshness and modernity. In a DVD commentary, director Terence Young explains how the slow reveal of Connery in Bond's introductory scene at the casino, Le Cercle, was intended to be funny.[24] This includes the lighting of his cigarette to break up the line "Bond . . . James Bond," with the timing designed to elicit a laugh from the viewers. Bond's flirtation across the gaming table with Sylvia Trench (Eunice Gayson) introduces another aspect of the character—that he is not, perhaps, the best spy around, given that he cheerfully uses his real name in all situations, that he hands over his telephone number to a woman he has just met, and that his address is so easy to find that she locates his flat and is able to let herself into it with no apparent difficulty. The playful banter between Bond and Sylvia hints that they may have been previously acquainted but, because this is never made explicit in the film, there is always the possibility that they are not. Sandwiched in between his encounters with Sylvia is Bond's briefing by M. It is in these scenes that the more traditional elements of Bond's and *Dr. No*'s world are most evident.

The opulence of the casino gives way to the drab corridor and Moneypenny's plain office, hidden behind the door of "Universal Exports." Beyond that is M's office, which, as production designer Ken Adam explains, is intended to invoke tradition and stability—even if the wood panelling was actually grained paper and the padded red leather door was fake.[25] As Bond first enters M's inner sanctum, he checks himself, with a glance across at his boss, who has not as yet acknowledged his presence, and for an instant he has the guilty look of a child caught sneaking back into the house after curfew. That is exacerbated when M, still reading his notes, responds to Bond's "Good evening, sir," with the deflating statement "It happens to be three a.m." The briefing proceeds and, while M clearly considers Bond a trusted and valued agent, as an embodiment of the more Victorian values of discipline and self-denial he also clearly disapproves of his lifestyle. Bond's hedonistic tendencies are much more aligned with the individualism of the 1960s. Individualism is one of the elements that form the backbone of historian Arthur Marwick's characterization of the 1960s.[26] It is a discernible trait in myriad heroes and antiheroes across the decade that, according to Jeffrey Richards, encapsulates everyone from the Dracula of the Hammer horror cycle (1958–1974) to Arthur Seaton of *Saturday Night and Sunday Morning* (1960): "Initially symbols of a ruthless and exploitative upper class, they soon became transformed into the heroes of an era of sex, style and 'anything goes.' Like other heroes of the 1960s, their concern was with the self— 'What I want is a good time. All the rest is propaganda.' "[27]

Individualism and tradition are also in evidence when Bond returns to his flat, which has a similar décor to M's office: forest green walls, prints of vintage cars, walnut hall tables, and bronze fixtures (figure 1.2). It has a distinctly old-fashioned feel, especially when contrasted with the bright colors and clean lines of the fashionable 1950s aesthetic in the wake of the forward-looking Festival of Britain in 1951. The festival was focused on promoting British industry, technology, and design and the overall style was "Contemporary," characterized as "clean, bright and new . . . In an island hitherto largely given up to gravy browns and dull greens, 'Contemporary' boldly espoused strong primary

Figure 1.2 Bond (Sean Connery) at home. *Dr. No* (1962).

colours."[30] The dull greens identified here are clearly visible in Bond's apartment, visually placing him in the tradition of the British gentleman. The contrasting individualism becomes apparent when Bond, aware of an intruder, enters his bedroom and discovers Sylvia clad only in his pajama top and her gold evening court shoes. His instruction that he has to leave "immediately" for Jamaica soon becomes "almost immediately"—Bond's devotion to duty always has the potential to be sidelined, temporarily at least, for more personal pleasures.

Once Bond is in Jamaica, the aesthetic of traditional Britain exemplified in the décor of his flat and M's office is associated almost exclusively with the colonial environs of Government House and the Queen's Club. But these are places in which Bond spends little time and he appears both bored with and dismissive of the officials involved in the administration and governance of Jamaica. There are some traces of tradition evident in the lair of Dr. No himself (Joseph Wiseman), whose brass lamps, bearskin rugs, and artworks would not look out of place in a gentleman's club in London. The trappings of power for a Bond supervillain reflect the privileged power of imperial Britain: the most prominent painting on display is Goya's portrait of the Duke of Wellington, which had been stolen from the National Gallery in 1961. Bond's hotel in Kingston, on the other hand, is light, airy, and (again) modern, reflecting the vibrancy of the soon-to-be independent nation. His allies during his mission are not the British stationed on the island, but the local fisherman-cum-fixer, Quarrel, and C.I.A agent Felix Leiter (Jack Lord)—an acknowledgment of the United States as the popular embodiment of modernity, as well as the growing sphere of American influence, especially as Britain continued to withdraw from its former colonies in the Caribbean. The American presence points to the wider importance of U.S. culture on the global stage but it is also worth remembering that the image of "Swinging Britain" was itself influenced and, to some extent, shaped by American culture.[29] While this is not central to the film's narrative, the placing of Leiter as one of Bond's key associates is another example of how Bond and Dr. No in particular engage with negotiating the end of empire and all of its traditional trappings and the embracing of Britain's new role on the global stage and in the Commonwealth.

Much like Isaacs' identification of the Teddy boys as "darn fine lads" with "youthful spirits," Bond holds a dialogue between tradition and modernity that runs through Dr. No and beyond: into the franchise and more widely across the 1960s. This dialogue, which, as previously discussed, affords potential for humor, also highlights a more complex issue: retaining traditional elements that are still situated as sites of stability and power in the face of a changing world inevitably gives rise to nostalgia and a sense that something of value has been lost in the process of change and renewal. Heather Wiebe's examination of the 1953 Coronation identifies the problematic tension that arose when the quest for renewal was undertaken with an eye on the past: "Loss lurks in the rhetoric of New Elizabethanism, in the obsessive talk of war and hardship that the Elizabethans and the New Elizabethans had in common. The quest for renewal is intermingled with an awareness of loss, which is expressed through the preoccupation with the past itself; the past, after all, can be many things, but it is always lost by definition."[30] This loss in the 1950s and 1960s is almost always associated with the move away from the imperial structures of prewar Britain. The decline of empire, the end of empire, the loss of empire—all these phrases have been used in relation to the postimperial era and specifically in relation to James Bond: the son of empire when the empire was gone. Yet this sense of loss is seemingly absent from *Dr. No*: even now, the film has a freshness and a vibrancy. Today we can certainly identify problematic areas around race, gender, and class, and these are areas that should be and are discussed, debated, and analyzed in this collection and elsewhere. But the film is also fun and funny. It sets out to entertain and it does. In the background of the scenes is a Jamaica that is diverse, that is full of national pride and on the cusp of its independence. The empire has gone but the ever-burgeoning Commonwealth links diverse communities across the globe and the emphasis is on equality rather than subservience to an imperial center. Bond inhabits Jamaica with as much self-possession and confidence as he does Le Cercle and his own home and with the acceleration of British technological advances, design, creativity, and sexual expression that would only increase as the 1960s advanced. These characteristics do not make him anachronistic but rather a man of his times.

The 2012 list of New Elizabethans encompasses so-called high and low culture and crosses class, gender, and racial lines—you have to appreciate any list that includes playwright Harold Pinter and actor Barbara Windsor as figures of equal cultural importance. It feels fitting to be writing this more than sixty years after *Dr. No* came to our screens and seventy years after Elizabeth II came to the throne. In the years before her death there was much reflection on the years of her reign and the changes that occurred. Attitudes around class, sex, gender, and race have been central to much of these discussions and the change from empire to Commonwealth is spoken of, on all sides, with apparent optimism—but there is noticeably much more clear-eyed anger and justifiable criticism about the abuses and exploitation that were endured by nations and individuals under British imperial rule. In the coverage in Britain, overall, there is no sense of decline but rather of evolution, but evolution that acknowledges and incorporates elements of tradition and continuity, very much the way that Bond has done and probably will do for some time to come. *Dr. No* does not offer any definitive resolutions to the social and cultural concerns of 1962: increased American-Soviet tensions, the U.S. sphere of influence spreading into the Caribbean, for example. But it does show a Jamaica that will be just fine in its independence and a Britain that will be just fine without an empire—better, perhaps, with willing allies rather than coopted subjects. If a New Elizabethan is someone who can recognize both the good and ill of the past, can retain what is worth keeping—even if it is as superficial as a taste in interior decoration that runs to wood panelling and leather Chesterfields—while engaging with the modern world on their own terms, then shake yourself a vodka martini and reflect on the fact that a New Elizabethan is a pretty good thing for James Bond to be.

Notes

1. BBC, *The New Elizabethans*, www.bbc.co.uk/programmes/articles/5P7MYJ7Z2JlX-gYDXLWJq6jd/about.
2. Cedric Watts, *A Preface to Greene* (London: Routledge, 2014 [1997]), 149.
3. Jeremy Black, "The Geopolitics of James Bond," *Intelligence & National Security* 19, no. 2 (2004): 292.
4. Danny Powell, *Studying British Cinema: The 1960s* (New York: Columbia University Press, 2009), 5.
5. Davide Cannadine, "James Bond and the Decline of England," *Encounter* 53, no. 3 (1979): 46; Samuel Goodman, "England's Green, Unpleasant Land: Memory, Myth and National Identity in the Novels of Ian Fleming," *Bristol Journal of English Studies* 3 (2013): 2.
6. Marouf Hasian, "*Skyfall*, James Bond's Resurrection, and 21st-Century Anglo-American Imperial Nostalgia," *Communication Quarterly* 62, no. 5, (2014): 569–70.
7. James Chapman, "James Bond and the End of Empire," in *James Bond Uncovered*, ed. Jeremy Strong (Basingstoke, UK: Palgrave Macmillan, 2018), 209.
8. Barry Forshaw, *British Crime Film: Subverting the Social Order* (Basingstoke, UK: Palgrave Macmillan, 2012), 216.
9. Jeffrey Richards, *Films and British National Identity: From Dickens to Dad's Army* (Manchester: Manchester University Press, 1997), 40.
10. David Stafford, "Spies and Gentlemen: The Birth of the British Spy Novel, 1893–1914," *Victorian Studies* 24, no. 4 (1981): 503.
11. Heather Wiebe, "'Now and England': Britten's 'Gloriana' and the 'New Elizabethans,'" *Cambridge Opera Journal* 17, no. 2 (2005): 146.
12. Nick Bentley, "New Elizabethans: The Representation of Youth Subcultures in 1950s British Fiction," *Literature & History* 19, no. 1 (2010): 18. "Teddy boy" was a name given to members of a youth subculture that arose in the early 1950s. These largely young working-class boys dressed in Edwardian-style jackets and waistcoats and became associated with a rise in knife crime and gang violence. While there were documented incidents of Teddy boys involved in violence—notably the 1958 Notting Hill race riots—the majority had no involvement in criminal delinquency.
13. Bentley, "New Elizabethans," 18.
14. Wiebe, "'Now and England,'" 147.
15. Harry McPhail, "#ThrowbackThursday: Harold MacMillan's 'never had it so good' Speech," *Bedford Independent*, September 5, 2015, www.bedfordindependent.co.uk/throwbackthursday-harold-macmillans-never-had-is-so-good-speech/; Jennifer Coates, "Introduction: Representing Youth and Gender in Japanese Popular Culture," *U.S.-Japan Women's Journal* 54 (2018): 3.

16. "Jamaica Gives Cooperation Pledge," *Times*, February 10, 1962.
17. "Impassioned Plea to Britain by Sir Grantley Adams," *Times*, March 6, 1962.
18. "An Archive Can Be Your Story," National Museums Liverpool, www.liverpoolmu seums.org.uk/stories/archive-can-be-your-story.
19. James Robertson, "Rewriting *Dr. No* in 1962: James Bond in Jamaica," *Small Axe* 47 (July 2015): 64.
20. Robertson, "Rewriting *Dr. No*," 75.
21. Robertson, "Rewriting *Dr. No*," 63.
22. James Chapman, *Licence to Thrill: A Cultural History of the James Bond Films* (London: I. B. Tauris, 1999), 78.
23. Marguerite LeWars, "Commentary," *Dr. No* (Los Angeles: MGM, 2012), DVD, directed by Terence Young.
24. Terence Young, "Commentary," *Dr. No* DVD.
25. Ken Adam, "Commentary," *Dr. No* DVD.
26. Arthur Marwick, *The Sixties* (Oxford: Oxford University Press, 1998), 17–18.
27. Richards, *Films and British National Identity*, 166.
28. Harry Hopkins, *The New Look: A Social History of the Forties and Fifties in Britain* (London: Secker and Warburg, 1963), 271–72.
29. Powell, *Studying British Cinema*, 5.
30. Wiebe, "'Now and England,'" 172.

CHAPTER 2

"A REAL LABOUR OF LOVE, AS THEY SAY"

James Bond as a Sexual Plaything in
From Russia with Love (1963)

LUCY BOLTON

The language of barter, competition, and sport runs alongside the brutal reality of impending death throughout *From Russia with Love* (1963). Whether it is the villainous organization SPECTRE using live targets for shooting practice, the faceless Number One and his Persian cat being entertained by Siamese fighting fish locked in deadly combat, gypsy girls prepared to fight to the death over a man, or James Bond's (Sean Connery) willing participation in a high-stakes trap set by the Russians (or so he believes), the film's narrative proceeds through a variety of contests, battles, and games.[1] Central to this, and frequently the object in play, is the body of Bond, which, as film historian Toby Miller observes, is often, across the franchise, "both shaken *and* stirred, by people, technologies, and events beyond his ken."[2] Certainly, Bond's body is the focus of many of the characters in this second installment of the series: some want him dead, and others simply want him. The succession of games and contests in *From Russia with Love* (hereafter *FRWL*) draws attention to Bond's sexual experience and ability, thereby developing the character from *Dr. No* (1962) in terms of his desirability to women and also setting some limits on Bond's autonomy and inviolability. These limits are carried forward into the following films in the franchise and became integral to the Bond screen persona.

The Set-Up

The pre-credit action sequence of *FRWL* plays a trick on us. The James Bond we think we recognize is actually a live target wearing a Bond mask: his anxious expression, overly-powdered face, and irregular suit indicate, upon closer viewing, that this is not the real Bond, but initially we are duped by our prior knowledge of Sean Connery.[3] We witness Bond's apparent garroting by Donald "Red" Grant (Robert Shaw), but when the rubber mask is pulled off the dead body, we see an auburn-haired man with a moustache. This is a training exercise for Grant, whom we will meet again when he is tasked with the assassination of the real 007. Grant's use of a "live target," as Morzeny (Walter Gotell) explains to Rosa Klebb (Lotte Lenya), is common practice at the SPECTRE training facility: games in this film are lethal and not to be taken lightly.

The film opens with Kronsteen (Vladek Sheybal) swiftly winning his chess tournament when summoned by Number One. The character is established as a masterful brain, a champion at chess and gamesmanship, and the SPECTRE agent who has come up with a plot to destroy Bond. His plan is meant both to trick the British Secret Service into obtaining the Lektor, the Russian decoding machine, and to exact revenge for Dr. No's death by killing Bond, the agent he predicts will be sent on the mission. Bond is to be lured not only by the prospect of the decoding machine, which SPECTRE can then take from him and sell back to the Russians, but also by the beautiful bait, the unwitting Tatiana Romanova (Daniela Bianchi), who believes she is working for her Soviet comrades. The premise of the film, then, is a trap to catch and kill Bond.

At the British Secret Service headquarters in London, M (Bernard Lee) explains the mission to Bond. A Russian cypher clerk has fallen in love with Bond's file photograph and wants to defect to the West, bringing the Lektor, on the condition that Bond comes to meet her and brings her across. M and Bond are both well aware that the plan is most likely a trap, but they cannot pass up the opportunity of getting their hands on a code-breaking machine. As Kronsteen predicted, the British mentality has read the trap as a challenge. The photograph of Tatiana appeals to Bond, but he worries that, when they meet in the flesh, he won't live up to her expectations. M says, with a knowing intonation, "Just see that you do." From the outset of the mission, Bond is a pawn in intermingling games played by various characters, and the subject of the film's main ploy as well. In Ian Fleming's novel, Bond wonders what his younger self would "think of the dashing secret agent who was off across the world in a new and most romantic role—to pimp for England?"[4]

The Women

In the first film, *Dr. No*, Bond has a frustrated encounter with Sylvia Trench (Eunice Gayson) and a ruthless tryst with Miss Taro (Zena Marshall), before ending up in a clinch with Honey Ryder (Ursula Andress). In *FRWL*, women feature more significantly in the story and the plot, displaying "the prominent roles that women play in his romantic life." The character's "preparedness to hit Tatiana when he thinks she's lying to him demonstrates his capacity for brutality towards women as well."[5] It is often argued that the women in this film, and indeed the Bond franchise generally, are simply objectified, disposable sketches of women rather than meaningful characters. Moya Luckett argues, "So forgettable are some that they can even reappear as another character: *From Russia with Love*'s . . . Zora (Martine Beswick) resurfaces in 1965's *Thunderball* . . . as the no more memorable Paula Caplan. Even those who linger across films, like Bond's (would-be) girlfriend Sylvia Trench (Eunice Gayson) in the first two installments, link seriality to failure or even death. Trench never secures Bond, and her role is quickly dropped."[6] In particular, Tatiana is often seen as having no agency in *FRWL*: In Helena Bassil-Morozow's words, "Tasked with seducing Bond, Tatiana Romanova . . . is objectified from the very start, by men and women on both sides of the iron curtain." She suggests that the black velvet ribbon tied around Tatiana's neck is "like a domestic cat wearing a bow," while Lisa Funnell and Klaus Dodds see it as making her look like a gift for Bond to unwrap.[7] James Chapman assesses the film's gypsy fight as being "entirely for the erotic gratification of the spectators (both the characters in the film who are watching and the spectator in the cinema)."[8]

Much has been written about the objectification of these women, and although I would argue that they are more than "pretty props," in what follows I want to shift the focus onto Bond's sexual standing and consider how, in Britni Dutz's words, "Bond himself (Sean Connery) is highly eroticized."[9] Before progressing, however, a word about Connery. The way in which Connery as Bond is presented in the film is undoubtedly tailored to the actor's particular features. That Connery was "a beautiful specimen of well-honed manhood: six foot two inches tall, with the biceps of a road driller and eyes like chipped anthracite" meant that his face and body could be presented convincingly as an erotic spectacle.[10] Producer Albert "Cubby" Broccoli's assessment of Connery as a Greek god who needed some grooming and refining goes a long way to explaining the appeal of the actor's confident and edgy incarnation of 007. This analysis of *FRWL* is firmly grounded in Connery's particular sexual appeal, and indeed it is a challenge to conceive of any of the other Bond actors being so convincing in this particular role.

Bond the Sex Object

Following the trick played by the pre-credit sequence, we meet the "real" Bond, moored in a punt with Sylvia Trench, the woman he had met in his first-ever film scene in the casino in *Dr. No*. A young man punting past exclaims what great sport it is, and Bond says that he couldn't agree more, but of course he is not referring to the punting. Bond is reclining in an embrace with Trench, with his right leg stretched out toward the side of the punt. A bottle of champagne, on a rope that passes down his thigh and through his toes, is cooling in the river (figure 2.1). Bond's body is in an overtly exhibitionist position, clad in shorts that come only just below his groin, which is central in the frame. His stomach and chest are on show in an open short-sleeved shirt draped around his shoulders, and his posture, stretched across into the embrace with Sylvia, who is lying on his left, displays his physique for audience appreciation. This shows us Bond off duty, a very different look from the initial sight of the tuxedo-clad Bond in *Dr. No.*

Sylvia caresses Bond's back and sees the scar on his side when he tests the temperature of the champagne. She wonders if it is "a souvenir from another jealous woman," conveying her competitiveness with Bond's other lovers. (In due course, this scar will also be felt and commented upon by Tatiana as an identifying mark.) Bond's beeper announces that there is a call for him and he goes to his car to take it, wearing only the small shorts, carrying his jacket and shirt. Sylvia grasps at his clothes as he is trying to dress to prevent him from leaving. Although Moneypenny (Lois Maxwell) has stressed he is needed, Sylvia's persistence persuades Bond to extend his journey time back to the office from an hour to an hour and a half, which prompts Sylvia to clap her hands with realization of a battle won. Already, in Bond's first scenes, his body is the object of a contest between women: the lustful and determined "old case" Sylvia and the knowing and tolerant Moneypenny. As Bond lifts his car roof to

Figure 2.1 Bond (Sean Connery) reclines while keeping the champagne cool and offering himself as an erotic spectacle. *From Russia with Love* (1963).

create a den for his tryst with Sylvia, it is plainly sex that Sylvia wants and sex that Moneypenny knows Bond is having. When he eventually arrives at the office, Moneypenny's comment that "it will be a miracle if he can explain where he's been all day" refers directly to his sexual interlude. This sets up Bond's sexual performance as a topic of conversation and bartering, a theme that will become central to the film's story.

Several parties await Bond's arrival at the Istanbul airport for his mission as he immerses himself in a well-established web of espionage. When Bond meets the head of the Turkish station, Kerim Bey (Pedro Armendáriz), and his son, they explain that the Bulgarians, who work for the Russians, are following them, and that they all know who is following whom and when—the whole set-up is like a game, with players acting according to rules known by all parties. Kerim tells Bond he's wasting his time on this suspicious trip to obtain the Lektor. Bond is notably impotent to effect any of the plot and must wait for the next move to be played. We don't have to wait long, however, as Kronsteen's machinations to disrupt the rules of the game soon get underway.

At his hotel, Bond rejects his bugged room and requests a change of accommodation, saying it is because the bed is too small. The receptionist is told to offer him the bridal suite as an alternative, which he accepts. The reason for this room switch will soon become apparent, but a limpet mine explodes at Kerim's quarters, so they consider it safer not to stay at the hotel but to go to visit Kerim's friends at the gypsy camp. Bond is made welcome by Kerim's friend Vavra (Francis De Wolff) and shown to a table, where the dancer (Lisa Guiraut) makes Bond the object of her provocative performance. Then there is to be a fight between Vida (Aliza Gur) and Zora (Martine Beswick), who are in love with the same man. The contest is a fight to the death, and the scantily clad women struggle and claw at each other in a dramatic and vicious duel. Before either emerges as the victor, however, the camp is attacked by Krilencu (Fred Haggerty) and his men, and a battle ensues among the gypsies, the Bulgarians, and the Russians, during which Grant covertly saves Bond. When the raid is over and Vavra thanks Bond for saving his life, Bond asks for the gypsy fight to be called off. Vavra says that Bond is too soft to be a real gypsy and gives him the task of settling the contest between the women: "Decide," Kerim says. "They're both yours." As the seemingly reconciled women pose seductively in front of him, Bond observes, "this might take some time." The two are next seen in the morning, tending to him—sewing on a button, giving him food (figure 2.2). We do not know his decision, but we know that he has been involved in a sexual contest, and that his sexual experience is being called upon to decide who is the winner. This explicit evocation of the threesome again puts sex central to Bond's off-screen experience. The outcome of his sexual activity is less important than the fact that he is having it, and that everybody knows.

Figure 2.2 Bond (Sean Connery) receives the ministrations of the women he is charged with deciding between. *From Russia with Love* (1963).

Toby Miller has considered Bond's penis at length, including the possible psychoanalytic perspectives on this brandishing of the penis in the context of cultural imperialism and masculinity.[11] The main thrust of my argument about Bond's sex organ, however, accords more with that of Funnell and Dodds, who simply point out that the character is called upon to "use his physical and sexual prowess to his and Britain's advantage." They continue, "His body and demeanour, while not without their limits when it comes to sheer endurance, are renewable resources to be exploited time and again for the sake of his mission."[12]

As Bond is undressing for a bath back at his hotel, he hears someone in the bedroom. Bond, wearing only a hand towel wrapped around his hips, sees through a transparent curtain that a woman is getting into his bed. It is Tatiana, called Tania by her friends. She is naked except for her black choker—she is there to make love and to test him "in the flesh." She says he looks just like his photograph, consistent with the idea that he's been assessed and chosen, even if, in fact, it was not done by her. Bond tells her she's one of the most beautiful girls he's ever seen, to which she replies, "thank you—but I think my mouth is too big." A close-up on her parting lips, as Bond assesses them, is followed by his judgment, "It's just the right size—for me, that is." Although Bond moves in for a kiss on the lips, the innuendo clearly suggests the contemplation of oral sex. Tania checks the scar on his back and says she knows all about him from his file. Knowledge about Bond's body, it seems, is as available as knowledge about the other object of desire, the Lektor. When Bond asks if she is disappointed now that she has seen him, she says she will tell him in the morning. As Bond and Romanova begin to make love, the camera moves up from the bed to the mirror at the head of the bed, then to the other side of the mirror, and we can see that they are being filmed by Klebb and her henchman through a two-way glass. Both Tania and Bond are victims in this voyeuristic plot, which once more throws focus onto characters and audience thinking about Bond having sex, coupled with an assessment of his ability to please Tania. Bond's sexual prowess is integral to Romanova's conversion to Bond's side. On the boat on the Bosphorus, she asks, "Will you make love to me all the time when we are in England?" and he promises that he will, "day and night."

On the Orient Express train, after the Lektor has been taken from the Russian Consulate and the couple are making their getaway, Bond and Tania pretend to be Mr. and Mrs. Somerset. For her cover identity, Bond gives Tania a wedding ring and a wardrobe of clothing that is clearly intended for the bedroom. Tania dresses up in the nightdresses and negligees, playfully inhabiting her unwitting role in the plot. However, Bond becomes suspicious of her when Kerim is killed, supposedly by Benz (Peter Bayliss). In fact, both Kerim and Benz were killed by Grant as part of the SPECTRE plan. Bond's conversation with Grant, who is posing as British agent Nash, tests both their professional acumen. They are plainly getting the measure of each other, with Bond at a distinct disadvantage. Bond observes that Nash "looks very fit," to which Grant replies that he "tries to keep in shape." He also notices that Nash orders red wine at dinner to accompany his fish, a cardinal sin in the eyes of the gourmet Bond. And Bond sees Nash slip a drug into Tania's drink, but fails to react or do anything about it. Back in the cabin, the uneasy conversation continues. Bond makes the mistake of turning his back on Grant, enabling Grant to cosh him over the head.

When Bond comes around, the penny finally drops: "You've been playing us off against each other." Grant admits, in response, "I get a kick out of watching the great James Bond find out what a bloody fool he's been making of himself." Grant explains the plan, including that he had saved Bond's life at the gypsy camp, and scoffs that Tania "thinks she's doing it all for Mother Russia." He tells Bond about the film secretly taken in the bridal suite, and how the planned headlines would be "British Agent murders beautiful Russian spy, then commits suicide." Grant's sadism is evident from the plans he has for Bond's death: he tells the agent that the first, second, and third bullets won't kill him, and that he won't put Bond out of his painful misery "until you crawl over here and you kiss my foot." Humiliation is integral to the killing of Bond, as is the infliction of physical agony. Bond's body is the basis of a different type of fantasy for Grant than it is supposed to be for Tania. Bond tricks Grant by tempting him with the gold sovereigns and the tear gas canister from Q's (Desmond Llewelyn) briefcase of tricks. Then a brutal fight ensues, and Bond eventually garrotes Grant in much the same way that Grant strangled the live target in the pre-credit sequence.

The games appear to be over once Bond and Tania arrive in Venice, and, as Bond believes, it should be "routine from here on in." However, Klebb enters their hotel suite, dressed as a chambermaid, and, once exposed, cries "Romanova!" demanding her loyalty and cooperation. As Klebb fights with Bond, trying to kick him with the poisoned blade in the toe of her shoe, Tania, who has been knocked to the floor, holds Klebb's gun, apparently wavering between whom to shoot: even at this final stage there is a contest, between Klebb, her mentor and boss, and Bond, her lover, who may be finished with her once the job is over. Tania chooses Bond, having been won over to his side through her love for him. Shooting Klebb, she saves Bond's life and secures the Lektor for the British. Although she has been, as Funnell and Dodds describe, "more ingénue than femme fatale," ultimately Tania has chosen to side with her lover, "a man who is a loyal servant of his country, rather than a fellow Soviet woman who is a traitor."[13]

Bond's Body

This second installment of the film franchise had a budget of $1.9 million, twice the cost of *Dr. No*, and consolidated Bond's popularity in Europe.[14] The popular novel on which the film is closely based, which Broccoli considered to be "one of Fleming's best stories," sees Bond having a strong central relationship with Tania, and also led to the film's being, as Chapman describes, "an excursion into a more traditional sort of spy story which was not to be repeated."[15] The visual style of the opulent train journey has featured in several Bond films since, notably *The Spy Who Loved Me* (1977), *Casino Royale* (2006), and *Spectre* (2015), but the considerable time spent on the train in *FRWL*, allowing the various strands of the plots and subplots to unravel, remains a unique episode in the franchise's history.

Thomas Barrett argues that Tatiana Romanova "holds a crucial position in the western re-visioning of Soviet and Russian woman" and plays a significant role in the process of making "Soviet women ripe for Western consumption."[16] The contrast between the lithe, beautiful, and stylishly dressed Romanova and the stocky, uniform-clad Klebb, with its insinuations of lesbianism, certainly offers two archetypes of Soviet women for the Bond films to develop in the future.[17] As noted above, Sylvia Trench reappears from *Dr. No* and has her lust for Bond sated, but we do not meet her again. And the fate of the gypsy girls remains unknown—was Bond able to choose who should win the man they both love? Or did a night with him ruin them for any other man so that now neither of them wants anyone else? As with the majority of Bond's romantic encounters, these questions remain unresolved, including the relationship with Tania. However, what has become clear through the development of this film is that women want to have sex with Bond and that, as Toby Miller notes, "the series opened a world for some women where sex was about pleasure, not commitment; fun, not family; action, not inertia; taking, not waiting."[18]

Alongside the development of the collection of characters who became known collectively as "the Bond girls" and a substantial contribution to the panoply of villains, with arguably the best of any of the films, *FRWL* emphasizes that James Bond is a sex object. He will become renowned for his cavalier attitude toward women, happy to seduce and have sex with them despite this leading to their deaths.[19] However, in this film, his sexual adventures are largely planned and orchestrated by others—Sylvia, SPECTRE, M, and Vavra. This narrative trope leads to Bond being somewhat disempowered without being totally powerless. Sylvia is persuasive and relentless, and Bond concedes; Vida and Zora are placed before him with an instruction to decide the fight, and he acquiesces to the task; and he is instructed to meet Tania's demand to be her lover, which he accomplishes, albeit the whole encounter has been contrived, staged, and filmed by SPECTRE. Perhaps unsurprisingly, Bond does not appear to find these demands unpleasant or objectionable, but his acquiescence is not the element of interest. What is significant is that his sexual experiences, attractiveness, ability, and encounters are consolidated in this film as an intrinsic part of his work.

Claire Hines argues about Connery, "[I]t is generally agreed that he defined the screen character, and his model of masculinity, sexuality, and Britishness, set a standard against which subsequent Bonds are measure and judged."[20] It is certainly the case that the Bond of *FRWL* develops the Bond of *Dr. No* in terms of a romantic and emotional life and in relation to his attitude toward women. He is an enthusiastic embracer of his role as sexual plaything. This does not, however, mean that he has a consistently loving or sympathetic attitude. Even this early in the franchise, we have seen him have sex with Miss Taro when he knows she is working for Dr. No and has just called for the police to arrest her, and in *FRWL*, we see that he is willing to slap Tania across the face and to witness her being drugged without intervening.

Bond's sexual confidence also exposes an area of vulnerability. As well as his body being used in the course of government and SPECTRE business, he is made vulnerable in the act of lovemaking when he is filmed by Klebb. Further, he does not appear to look beyond his conquering of Tania in the plan to steal the Lektor, such that Grant's revelations about the plot astound him and he is unprepared for Klebb's final appearance at the hotel. Bond says of Tania, "She'll do anything I say," prompting Kerim to observe that he has been caught by the old adage, "Give a wolf a taste, then keep him hungry. My friend, she's got you dangling." Bond shows awareness of his role in the trap but presses ahead regardless and largely in ignorance. Another element that is consolidated in this film, then, is that Bond often fails and needs others to save him. Miller refers to Bond's "repeated, hapless failure," and we see this in evidence throughout *FRWL* as he fails to understand the complexity of the trap in which he finds himself, the players behind it, or the reality of his surroundings.[21] Without Tania's intervention to knock the gun out of Klebb's hands and her choice to shoot Klebb instead of Bond, it looked like his number was up.

We might recall the sight of Number One's Siamese fighting fish battling to the death, observed by his patient cat, who waits until the fight is over so that both fish can be easily eaten. Perhaps the perspectives of Number One and his cat invite us to see the characters, plots, and subterfuges within *FRWL* as a series of similarly staged contests, at the end of which Bond manages, through a combination of allure, resourcefulness, and quick thinking, to be the last man standing. As Jeremy Black concludes, "survival of the fittest is the theme."[22] But although it is popular to stress the simplicity and the old-fashioned nature of *FRWL*, it can be seen that the film's villains, sharply edited fights, and set pieces and the range of women in Bond's personal and working life developed the character and his lifestyle and established the vital role that sex and sexual attractiveness would play in the Bond films to come. The character has triumphed, bringing home the Lektor and the girl: has trounced his foes and emerged victorious. What we have witnessed, however, is the instrumentalization of Bond's penis as a pawn in a series of games. His sexual appetites having been taunted, his sexual prowess assessed, and his sexual experience employed as a means of settling a feud, in *FRWL* James Bond has to utilize sexual talents that are on display far more than in the preceding film. These encounters serve to establish the sexual appetites of the Connery Bond as voracious and renowned and his sexual appeal as mesmeric and irresistible, both of which would be consolidated in the next installment of the film franchise.

Notes

1. Umberto Eco describes each Bond novel as a "sequence of 'moves'" and sets out a scheme of nine basic recurring ones. He notes that *From Russia with Love* is a "highly complicated" scheme. Umberto Eco, "The Narrative Structure in Fleming," in *The Bond Affair,* ed. Oreste Del Buono and Umberto Eco, trans. R. A. Downie (London: Macdonald, 1966), 35–75.
2. Toby Miller, "Paradoxical Masculinity: James Bond, Icon of Failure," in *The Cultural Life of James Bond: Specters of 007,* ed. Jaap Verheul (Amsterdam: Amsterdam University Press, 2020), 135.
3. Llewella Chapman, *Fashioning James Bond: Costume, Gender, and Identity in the World of 007* (London: Bloomsbury Academic, 2022), 34.
4. Ian Fleming, *From Russia with Love* (Chatham, UK: Hodder and Stoughton, [1957] 1988), 93.

5. Lucy Bolton, "The Phenomenology of James Bond," in *Fan Phenomena: James Bond*, ed. Claire Hines (Bristol, UK: Intellect Books, 2015), 68.
6. Moya Luckett, "Femininity, Seriality and Collectivity: Rethinking the Bond Girl," in Verheul, *Cultural Life of James Bond*, 153.
7. Helena Bassil-Morozow, "The Soviet Woman in Bond Films," in *From Blofeld to Moneypenny: Gender in James Bond*, ed. Steven Gerrard (Bingley, UK: Emerald, 2020), 94, 95; Lisa Funnell and Klaus Dodds, *Geographies, Genders, and Geopolitics of James Bond* (London: Palgrave Macmillan, 2017), 82.
8. James Chapman, *Licence to Thrill: A Cultural History of the James Bond Films* (London: I. B.Tauris, 1999), 97.
9. Bassil-Morozow, "Soviet Woman in Bond Films," 96; Britni Dutz, "James Bond and the Evolution of the Gaze through Female Spectatorship," in *James Bond in World and Popular Culture: The Films Are Not Enough*, ed. Robert G. Weiner, B. Lynn Whitfield, and Jack Becker (Newcastle upon Tyne, UK: Cambridge Scholars, 2011), 184.
10. Cubby Broccoli, with Donald Zec, *When the Snow Melts: The Autobiography of Cubby Broccoli* (London: Boxtree, 1998), 167.
11. Toby Miller, "Cultural Imperialism and James Bond's Penis," in *The James Bond Phenomenon: A Critical Reader*, 2nd ed., ed. Christoph Lindner (Manchester: Manchester University Press, 2009), 122–53.
12. Funnell and Dodds, *Geographies, Genders*, 8.
13. Funnell and Dodds, *Geographies, Genders*, 84, 86.
14. James Chapman, *Licence to Thrill*, 93.
15. Broccoli, *When the Snow Melts*, 183; Chapman, *Licence to Thrill*, 93.
16. Thomas M. Barrett, "Desiring the Soviet Woman: Tatiana Romanova and *From Russia with Love*," in *For His Eyes Only: The Women of James Bond*, ed. Lisa Funnell (New York: Wallflower, 2015), 41.
17. Lisa Funnell and Klaus Dodds consider and develop how geopolitics, gender, and sexual orientation convey powerful messages about these women in *Geographies, Genders, and Geopolitics of James Bond*, 87.
18. Miller, "Paradoxical Masculinity," 130.
19. In *License to Thrill*, James Chapman considers the sexism in the films and the treatment of women as commodities "to be consumed by Bond, and then discarded, often meeting grisly ends" (117).
20. Claire Hines, *The Playboy and James Bond: 007, Ian Fleming, and* Playboy Magazine (Manchester: Manchester University Press, 2018), 63. Hines explores the significance of the Connery Bond for *Playboy*, and how determined the magazine was to interview him. Hines also goes on to examine Connery's interview comments about hitting women, which haunted him for the rest of his life and that also contributed to the conflation of Connery with the character of Bond in the 1960s.
21. Miller, "Paradoxical Masculinity," 135.
22. Jeremy Black, *The Politics of James Bond: From Fleming's Novels to the Big Screen* (Westport, CT: Praeger, 2001), 115.

CHAPTER 3

THE MIDAS TOUCH

Eastmancolor, the Bond Franchise, and *Goldfinger* (1964)

KEITH M. JOHNSTON

Sixty years on, it is almost impossible to imagine *Goldfinger* (1964) in black and white. Eon's Bond universe had been in color since the opening images of *Dr. No* (1962), a calculated use of Eastmancolor that differentiated the film from previous adaptations, including the American early color television version of *Casino Royale* (CBS 1954), or the black-and-white *Daily Express* comic strips that began in the UK in the 1950s.[1] The Bond novels had used color covers, and several 1962 *Sunday Times* color supplements used colorful illustrations for stories and articles by Ian Fleming, but the world of James Bond was not especially colorful until it was adapted for cinema.[2] Since then, the Eon series' use of color across cinematography, production design, set design, and costume has fueled key sequences and moments in the franchise and deepened many of the key claims made for the films' links to modernity, fashion, ideology, nationality, and gender politics.

Despite that potent link between the Bond films and color, there has been little in-depth focus on color within studies of the franchise. Where color is discussed, it is most closely associated with the title sequences, particular aspects of production design, or brief mentions of the series' use of exotic locations.[3] In part, this matches a similar lacuna in film scholarship around studies of color, albeit one that scholars over the last fifteen years have been working to rectify.[4] A recent assessment of British Eastmancolor films has referenced some key chromatic moments in the Bond series: Christopher Lee's titular golden gun–equipped assassin, *The Spy Who Loved Me*'s (1977) resplendent red-white-and-blue parachute, and the "vibrant red blood dripping down the screen" in the gun barrel sequence, "a portal through which the audience enters the world of James Bond."[5] Outside of such limited examples, however, the broader role of color within the franchise remains an elision that this chapter hopes to address through a focus on perhaps the most famous Bond film of them all.

What does it mean, though, to study *Goldfinger* through the lens of color? The third Bond film had the franchise's largest budget to date, sending 007 (Sean Connery) on a mission across Europe and North America to foil a plot by Auric Goldfinger (Gert Fröbe) that would irradiate the gold reserves at Fort Knox. The film looms large in franchise history, described as "the peak of the series, the most perfectly realized of all the films" and "the archetypal Bond film."[6] Can color say anything new about a film that remains so intrinsic to understandings of the Bond films, and which set so many of the narrative and thematic standards that would follow? It is worth starting by acknowledging that color in the Bond universe can be read from different perspectives. Color is rarely ideologically neutral: Bond's assertion of Britishness is done "as a white man who exercises regional superiority over non-white women. . . . to reaffirm and entrench his privilege"; while the colorful location work of the Bond series was "used as both advertising and as a way of exploring ideas about empire . . . beautiful and exotic locations formed the backdrop to the adventures."[7] Even though it lacks authentic location filming, *Goldfinger*'s pre-credit sequence relies heavily on ethnic stereotypes (here, Mexican) that are enhanced via color in makeup and costume. Similar issues link color and ideology in the depiction of the blue-and-yellow-costumed Chinese and Korean henchmen Goldfinger and his "Red Chinese" partners employ. Color, then, has immediate connotations within the Bond films, and can usefully highlight those existing scholarly analyses of the franchise, its narratives, and its characters. Before moving on to a closer study of how color is used in *Goldfinger*, it is important to consider the place of the Bond film productions in the context of other color filmmaking of the early-to-mid 1960s and what that can reveal about Eon's approach to color in the series.

Color and *Goldfinger*

In retrospect, it may seem obvious that a British-American production like *Goldfinger* would opt to film using the recently introduced Eastmancolor stock. Adopted in British film production from 1953 on, although in use in Hollywood since 1951, "Eastmancolor's cheaper single-strip stock . . . revolutionized the ways in which colour films were made," not least breaking up Technicolor's previous monopoly on color film production and processing, expanding the number of color films made.[8] Improvements to the original Eastman-Kodak color negative film were made through the 1950s and early 1960s, with *Gold-finger* shooting on Eastmancolor Color Negative Film 5251: a stock that improved speed but was largely "developed to reduce grain . . . primarily instigated by the higher magnification employed by widescreen images."[9] The recurring credit "Color by Technicolor" on publicity materials and prints of the film helps identify the laboratory that processed the rushes, color-graded the final prints, and produced the lucrative release prints. Technicolor's involvement here may have included the creation of the more expensive three-strip imbibition processing, but this was not always the case, particularly later in the Bond franchise when Technicolor phased out that process and laboratory work shifted between Technicolor and Rank Laboratories.

In the first half of the 1960s a decision to film in color was not without its problems, coming at a time when color film was by no means a dominant force in the cinema marketplace. Color film production, particularly in Britain, was at a low ebb. In "the first four years [of the 1960s] three out of four feature films" were in black and white; while that statistic would be reversed by 1966, Eon's decision to opt for color on *Dr. No* was more of a gamble than it first appears.[10] Two years later, in 1964, *Goldfinger* was still competing against a mixture of black-and-white and color releases during its release. In the UK, *Sight and Sound* featured *Goldfinger* alongside thirty-five other films on release (only fourteen in color), while US trade press publications listed six November 1964 releases (two in color, four in black and white) and six Christmas 1964 films (six in color, two in black and white).[11] It seems likely that the success of blockbuster films such as *Goldfinger* and its competitors *Mary Poppins* (1964) and *My Fair Lady* (1964) were part of that slow conversion to full color film production through the 1960s.

By adopting color as a central aesthetic pillar of its emerging Bond franchise, Eon was faced with a recurring industry issue around the combination of Eastmancolor and existing production techniques such as back projection. With the budget for *Goldfinger* not allowing the largely UK-based cast and crew to film in the United States, cinematographer Ted Moore was forced to rely heavily on back projection to combine material he had shot on location with filmed moving images (taken on the same location shoot) projected behind the actors on the set at Pinewood Studios. While this was common practice within black-and-white and color filmmaking, the color matching in the finished film reveals an unintended yellow hue to the studio-shot elements when cut in with the stronger white balance of the location shots. *Goldfinger* director Guy Hamilton has stated his dislike of using rear-projected plates and the problems of combining the two elements; color film added extra complexity to the process.[12]

In the early 1960s, the two techniques of combining studio and location shots in one image were either rear (or back) projection and travelling mattes. Both allowed the placement of actors in different locations or added realistic back-grounds to studio set-ups: most commonly, as seen throughout *Goldfinger*, in reverse shots not possible on location or shots showing actors driving or trav-elling in a car. Back projection had the advantage of speed and immediacy: "[T]he background scene is projected on to a translucent screen placed behind the foreground action . . . the director can see the background scene in relation to the foreground action while it is taking place, and the composite scene is ready with the rushes the next day."[13] Rank had introduced a new rear-projection system at Pinewood during the time *Goldfinger* was shooting at the studios, claiming this "triple-head rear projection unit with VistaVision Gates" was set-ting "new standards in picture definition and has the additional advantage of better exposure times."[14] Although introduced to keep Pinewood competitive with UK and US studios, such new technologies could still cause color match-ing issues for both the cinematographer and laboratory color grader. The alter-native to rear projection was to use a "travelling matte" system, an optical technique where actors were filmed in front of a blue or green screen and back-ground sequences added later in the film laboratory. The latter can also be seen in *Goldfinger* during the Aston Martin chase around the Auric Enterprises factory. Travelling matte sequences through the film also appear to have made use of a special camera developed by Rank for use at Pinewood: the BS 3 Beam Splitter. This camera used "a beam-splitting mechanism" that split the filmed image onto two separate pieces of film, "one to record the foreground action, the other to record the matte."[15] Either technique required precise control in both the lighting and shooting of the separate elements for a convincing color match to be completed.

Such production issues were common in the first decade of Eastmancolor, although elsewhere in *Goldfinger* the color process clearly strengthens the com-bination of special effects techniques. In a room dominated by dark wood paneling, golden sculptures, and banks of blue-grey computer equipment, Gold-finger leaves Bond to die on a gleaming metal table as a laser beam inches up between his legs. In terms of practical effects, special effects technician Bert Luxford was underneath the table with an acetylene torch, causing the orange flame and sparks to lick up into the air.[16] To create the full illusion, the final red-orange laser beam was an optical effect added in the laboratory. Here, rather than create problems with effects, the use of Eastmancolor could add empha-sis and danger to a well-worn sequence of the hero in peril.

Color in *Goldfinger*

The work of production designer Ken Adam across the series has been cele-brated for its style and scale but the focus on his contribution does tend to overshadow the other members of the crew responsible for color composition and design. Ted Moore, for example, had a steady record of color filming behind him, yet his work tends to suffer in comparison with discussions of Adam's visual artistry. Duncan Petrie has described how Moore's "assured cinematography set the style for the Bond movies" but sees Moore as a solid and dependable cinematographer rather than a visually exciting one.[17] For Petrie, Moore belongs to an older group of cinematographers, with his work on *Dr. No* favoring a "traditional and rather garish use of high-contrast, hard-edged lighting combined with unobtrusive camera movement, leaving the leading players, exotic locations, and Ken Adam's sets to provide the necessary aura of cosmopolitan glamour and modernity."[18] Guy Hamilton's comment that "Ted had huge sets to light and he lit them well" offers similar slim praise for Moore's chromatic contribution.[19] Indeed, a 1964 reviewer had already raised a similar point, claiming "Ted Moore's lensing does justice to Adam's astute sets."[20]

Moore's work was perhaps not as visually innovative as Adam's sets have become; the implied lack of a precise cinematographic vision may speak in part to why the Bond series has not yet been analyzed deeply in terms of its use of color. Looking more closely at Moore's chromatic approach across *Goldfinger* does reveal some moments that push beyond the traditional into what could be described as a more expressionistic mode. In the pre-credits sequence, red lighting is used in three distinct places: the first illuminates the sides of the metal silos of the heroin plant; the second casts some of that tone in the background of the café after the explosion has gone off. These are more traditional uses, adding light to emphasize the scale of the silos and then suggesting the off-screen effect of the flames and explosion. The third occurs when Bond knocks the electric heater into the bath, electrocuting his assailant. This is unmotivated by anything diegetic. There is no sense that the heater is what causes the red flare of light. It appears more fueled by a desire to heighten the immediate emotional impact of this moment, offering a link back to Bond's actual mission (destroying the factory) and the blood in the initial gun barrel sequence.

Electrocution is also a chromatic feature on two other occasions: one where light is used without an apparent narrative motivation and one where it matches narrative action. The first occurs when Goldfinger uses a nerve gas to kill the gangsters he has trapped in his rumpus room. As the gas is invisible, the flashes of blue light that occur as the gangsters fight to escape seem unmotivated by the specific action on screen and more to create a similar expressionistic effect as in the pre-credits, a heightening of the emotional stakes. When a similar blue lighting effect occurs later in the film it accompanies the electrocution of Oddjob (Harold Sakata) in Fort Knox and is linked more to that diegetic action than the less narratively motivated emotional jolt in the rumpus room.

Elsewhere, the film's nuanced treatment of color includes discrete chromatic shifts for different sections. In the opening Fontainebleau hotel sequence, for example, the dominant chromatic element is blue. This is seen in location images in Miami and matching studio-based set design and decoration: the deep blue of the pool from above and through the glass wall; the blue/red striped awnings and blue-topped tables on the patio; the blue walls of the hotel corridor outside Goldfinger's room; and the blue towels on which Jill Masterson (Shirley Eaton) lies on her hotel room balcony. Blue dominates the costuming here as well, from Bond's blue terry cloth poolside outfit through the patterned blue swimsuit worn by Dink (Margaret Nolan) to Bond and Jill sharing a pair of light blue pajamas. It is only in the moments leading up to Jill's death that other colors start to intrude, using a combination of set design and lighting to herald Goldfinger's revenge. There are pale yellow in the pillows, a yellow-ochre tone on the bedroom walls, bronze lampshades, and gold fixings on the bedframe: a set of chromatic elements that offer a link to the film's villain. After he is knocked out by Oddjob, Bond's entry back into the bedroom is lit with bronze-orange tones. While retaining a practical narrative link (the sequence takes place at sunrise), these tones build up to the reveal of Jill's golden body (figure 3.1) and the chromatic influence that Goldfinger will have across the rest of the film.

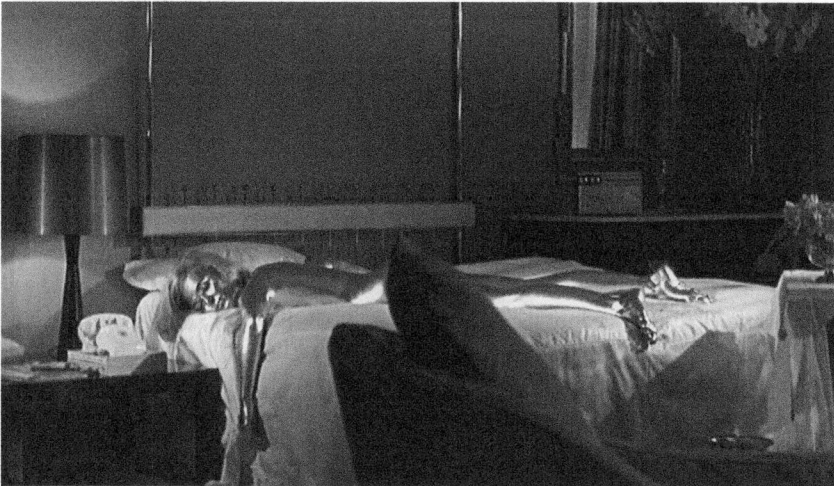

Figure 3.1 The iconic image of Jill Masterson (Shirley Eaton) covered in gold. *Goldfinger* (1964).

This use of a range of colors that are related to or can stand in for gold is continued across the film. It is more obvious in some places than others and can lack nuance in its repeated usage. Elizabeth Ladenson has commented on the presentation of Auric Goldfinger in both book and film, where "everything about the character has to do with that metal. . . . [He] wears yellow and orange clothing; drives a yellow car (which turns out in fact to be made entirely of gold)."[21] Certainly, Gert Fröbe's villain is never far from yellow or gold elements in his costume: a yellow terry cloth top and shorts at the Fontainebleau hotel, yellow cardigan and waistcoat, a golden sheen on the lapels of his brown coat, and gold buttons. Equally, he is given a range of golden props: snapping a yellow pencil in Miami, playing with a golden putter at the golf course, displaying a gold-bronze bomb in the rumpus room, or brandishing a golden gun in the Fort Knox sequence. There are also links to supporting characters involved in his plans: the yellow belts on his minions, the golden sunbursts on the uniforms of the Pussy Galore Flying Circus, and the golden cropped top Mei-Lei (Mai Ling) wears on board Goldfinger's Lockheed JetStar (which itself features gold accessories and highlights).

Despite this emphasis on yellow and gold, those colors rarely dominate the film after Jill's murder and, apart from the brief moments outlined above, are rarely central hues until the Fort Knox sequence. This is, of course, regularly linked to color through Ken Adam's production design, helped in part by Adam's own recollections of the set and his approach to creating its imagined interior. Adam recalls producer Albert R. "Cubby" Broccoli's desire for a "cathedral of gold" and notes that regular bank vaults were "not interesting visually to an audience" because gold is too heavy to be stacked high.[22] Adam's solution was to create "a huge glittering vault piled high with stacks of gold that reach almost to the ceiling," which he called "the perfect space to stage the last fight . . . a gold arena and Bond was able to use gold bars as weapons."[23] This has remained the dominant understanding of color and its relationship with the Fort Knox ending. Yet the filming and editing of the set highlights far stronger metal and steel-grey tones than the golden palace suggested by Adam and other commentators. The huge set is built around the central brown-black pillar that supports the lift, with concrete pillars, cream marble walls, and an array of steel shutters, doors, and barred cages (figure 3.2). Those high stacks of gold, regularly visible in long and medium shots, are impressive but remain secondary to the action on display. Indeed, Bond's frantic attempts to defuse the atomic bomb emphasize the importance of stainless steel and aluminum to the production and prop design of the Fort Knox interior. The bomb, with its colorful switches, lights, and rotating discs, also offers the film's final chromatic touch: the gold-tinged numbers of the countdown clock, which freeze on "007."

Figure 3.2 Ken Adam's Fort Knox set was designed as a gold arena where Bond (Sean Connery) would battle Oddjob (Harold Sakata). *Goldfinger* (1964).

Golden Girls: Promoting *Goldfinger*

The most detailed academic look at the chromatic elements of *Goldfinger* focuses on Robert Brownjohn's infamous title sequence, where scenes from the film are projected "across the human canvas of a bikini-clad, gold-painted woman . . . [and] that turns her into a literal trophy."[24] As argued above, despite that central sequence and its iconic status within the franchise, gold is not aesthetically dominant within the color scheme of the film. The cultural association of that color with this film, and the entire series, is crucially linked as much to the film's official publicity and promotional campaign and the actions of individual cinema exhibitors as to the title sequence. Eon and United Artists set a golden tone before the film's release, encouraging a publicity focus on Shirley Eaton in press visits and pieces that centered on the importance of her gold-painted body. While the film was in production at Pinewood Studios, the UK *Daily Mirror* newspaper ran a photo-feature with two separate behind-the-scenes photographs of Eaton and two unnamed makeup artists.[25] Although they only hint at the soon-to-be-iconic image of Eaton, these black-and-white shots capture something of the metallic reflective tones captured on film. The emphasis put on Eaton's body continued in other press and promotional materials, including its inclusion on almost all the film's posters, in pressbooks, and in the November 1964 edition of *Life* magazine, where Eaton featured on the cover and feature article.

This promotional theme reached its apex at the *Goldfinger* premiere, "one of the most golden, glittering premieres ever seen in London's West End." Five thousand fans outside the Odeon Leicester Square watched "a body of four golden girls" in an armored car delivering the film print, before star Honor Blackman arrived "dazzling in white and gold and wearing a fabulous diamond and gold finger."[26] The *Daily Mirror,* clearly a fan of both the Bond franchise and printing photographs of attractive young women, had followed the production with great interest, publishing photo-articles on Shirley Eaton, Margaret Nolan, Gilda Sherman, June Cooper, and others. The newspaper detailed preparations for the premiere for several days, including a report on Kathy Austin, "one of twelve lovelies who will keep a date . . . at the premiere of the new James Bond film, 'Goldfinger.' . . . They will sell programmes."[27] There was no shortage of gold-tinged "lovelies" in the run-up to the premiere. As well as Austin, who was photographed wrapped in gold lamé, and the young women in the armored car, four additional "golden girls" were photographed wearing special golden shoes for the premiere.[28]

The prominence given to Eaton's female body as the "key art" from the film, and the producer's identification of it through press briefings, newspaper articles, and film-specific promotion, has made this brief screen appearance the chromatic image most associated with the film. The film's press kit and campaign book highlighted different "Golden Stunts" a theatre could adopt, including the use of a "Golden Girl." Encouraged by this, many UK and US cinema exhibitors created their own golden and female-body-oriented promotional ballyhoo. Toronto's press premiere featured "two models splashing gold colors" while "another group of gold costumed models gave out gold lettered programs."[29] A Lima, Ohio theater cashier "dusted her hair with gold and . . . dressed in a gold brocade evening gown with elbow-length gloves" and "prominently displayed her right index finger, which was painted gold."[30] In Cambridge, UK, "a 'gold girl' took part in the University rag . . . this brave young lady wore only a bikini— and gold paint—and carried a machine gun."[31] While "a pretty model painted from head to foot with gold paint and wearing a gold bathing suit and gold shoes" promoted the film at the Kimo Theatre, Albuquerque, the ABC Falkirk, UK cinema had a more budget-conscious option, creating a "gold-painted 'lady' . . . [from] an old female dummy which was spray painted with gold paint."[32]

Given that Eaton's golden appearance remains "one of the most fetishized spectacles in British cinema," its appropriation by the film's publicity campaign strengthens the argument that "the covering of the female form in gold serves to . . . signify the body as commodity."[33] Gold was prominent in other showmanship ideas, including a giant golden hand hanging over the lobby entrance of a Lexington, Kentucky cinema; or selling gold bricks, adding golden decoration to "lady finger" cakes and handing out gold nail polish in Bellefontaine,

Ohio.[34] The fact that the commodified golden female body remains the dominant chromatic image speaks to the power *Goldfinger* had in its initial moment of release, and also its impact in the decades since. It shows the power that color film had to create key imagery but reiterates that color cannot be understood as separate from contemporary debates on gender and representation.

＊＊＊

When focusing on color in a film like *Goldfinger* it can be difficult to separate extraneous elements of color from those that recur and gain chromatic importance. After the Miami sequence there is the now-traditional London briefing from M (Bernard Lee), a brief flirtation with Moneypenny (Lois Maxwell), a scene at the Bank of England, and then a visit to equipment officer Q (Desmond Llewelyn). This expository five-minute section contains color elements that speak to the wider Bond franchise as well as the specifics of this film. M's office is a contrast to the bright and modern pastel colors of Miami: a dark brown wood–paneled location with hints of a gentleman's club in the red leather-backed chairs and the faded green tones of its lampshades and Bakelite phone. Moneypenny's office is simpler, muted, although dominated by a colorful map of the world on one wall. The Bank of England scene is gloomier, the long dark wooden table surrounded by grey walls, white cornices, and a black-and-white checkered floor. Q branch is more utilitarian, a concrete bunker in which white-coated scientists and engineers bustle around doing tasks; and which serves as the site to reveal the film's other potent chromatic body, the silver Aston Martin.

All four rooms contain potentially important color elements. There is a gold telescope in the back of M's office, pointing up at the ceiling; Moneypenny wears a blue dress and has a colorful scarf draped over her bag; the dining room has yellow/gold curtains, gold rims to the coffee cups, and gold picture frames, candlesticks, and light fittings; the background of Q branch features a red van, two red fire extinguishers, and a "No Smoking" sign. The recurring hints of gold in M's office and the Bank of England might briefly reclaim that metallic hue for these bastions of the English establishment who wrap gold bars in green velvet rather than melt them down. Moneypenny's dress might recall the more carefree and sexually active world of Miami, while her world map speaks to broader cartographic issues around MI6's perceptions of colonial ownership and stewardship. The placement of the red images in the back of Q branch offers a reminder of who manufactured the murderous equipment recently used by Bond in Mexico, while also being suggestive of a sight gag that never made the final cut, another precursor for the more comedic tone that Bond–Q exchanges would gain as the franchise progressed.

None of these appear as essential to a chromatic understanding of *Goldfinger* as the recurring usage of blue and red expressionist lighting techniques, the blue tones of Miami, the insistent foregrounding of gold around the villain Goldfinger or, indeed, the engraving of Eaton and Nolan's golden bodies on the wider public consciousness via Eon's publicity and marketing techniques. Yet what they point to is the complexity of understanding color as an aesthetic element, as part of the largely unseen technological apparatus of the film industry, and as a shared chromatic collaboration on the part of cinematographers, production designers, costume designers, effects teams, and laboratory workers.

Notes

1. Tony Bennett and Janet Woollacott, *Bond and Beyond: The Political Career of a Popular Hero* (Basingstoke, UK: Macmillan, 1987); Robert Shail, "Adapting the Male Hero: The Comic Strip Adaptations of James Bond," in *From Blofeld to Moneypenny: Gender in James Bond*, ed. Steven Gerrard (Bingley, UK: Emerald, 2020), 11–24.
2. Ian Fleming, "Berlin Escape," *Sunday Times Colour Supplement*, February 4, 1962; Ian Fleming, "James Bond's Hardware," *Sunday Times Colour Supplement*, November 18, 1962.
3. Shelley O'Brien, "Babes and Bullets: The Representation of Gender in Bond Themes and Title Sequences," in Gerrard, *From Blofeld to Moneypenny*, 103–15; Catherine Howarth, "Pussy Galore: Women and Music in *Goldfinger*," in *For His Eyes Only: The Women of James Bond*, ed. Lisa Funnell (New York: Wallflower, 2015), 159; Bennett and Woollacott, *Bond and Beyond*.
4. See, for example, Paul Coates, *Cinema and Colour: The Saturated Image* (London: British Film Institute/Palgrave Macmillan, 2020); Sarah Street, *Colour Films in Britain 1900–1950* (London: BFI Palgrave, 2012); Joshua Yumibe, *Moving Color: Early Film, Mass Culture, Modernism* (New Brunswick, NJ: Rutgers University Press, 2012); Barbara Flückiger, Eva Hielscher, and Nadine Wietlisbach, eds., *Color Mania: The Material of Color in Photography and Film* (Zurich: Fotomuseum Winterthur/Lars Müller, 2020).
5. Sarah Street, Keith M. Johnston, Paul Frith, and Carolyn Rickards, *Colour Films in Britain: The Eastmancolor Revolution* (London: Bloomsbury, 2021), 121.
6. John Brosnan, *James Bond in the Cinema* (New York: Tantivy Press, 1972), 55; James Chapman, *Licence to Kill: A Cultural History of the James Bond Films* (London: I. B. Tauris, 1999), 111.
7. Travis L. Wagner, "'The Old Way Are Best': The Colonisation of Women of Color in James Bond," in Funnell, *For His Eyes Only*, 52; Jennie Lewis-Vidler, "The Patriotic Spy: For Queen, Empire, and Dry Martinis," in Gerrard, *From Blofeld to Moneypenny*, 35.
8. Street et al., *Colour Films in Britain*, 1.
9. Street et al., *Colour Films in Britain*, 322.
10. Richard Farmer, Laura Mayne, Duncan Petrie, and Melanie Williams, *Transformation and Tradition in 1960s British Cinema* (Edinburgh: Edinburgh University Press, 2019), 18.

11. "A Guide to Current Films," *Sight and Sound* 33, no. 4 (1964): 212; Vincent Canby, "Film Code's Crepe-Hung Xmas," *Variety*, December 16, 1964; "Goldfinger," *Boxoffice*, November 16, 1964.

12. "Audio Commentary Featuring Guy Hamilton," *Goldfinger* (Beverly Hills, CA: MGM Home Entertainment, 2000), DVD.

13. Victor L. A. Margutti, "Some Practical Travelling Matte Processes," *British Kinematography* 36, no. 5 (1960): 131.

14. The Rank Organisation Limited, "Annual Report and Accounts 1965," accessed January 24, 2022, memoriesofrxmp.info/wp-content/uploads/2017/10/Rank-Organisation-ARA-1965.pdf.

15. "BS 3 Beam Splitter for Travelling Matte Cinematography," accessed January 24, 2022, collection.sciencemuseumgroup.org.uk/objects/co8339361/bs-3-beam-splitter-for -travelling-matte-cinematography-35-mm-camera.

16. Albert J. Luxford and Gareth Owen, *Albert J. Luxford the Gimmicks Man: Memoirs of a Special Effects Maestro* (Jefferson, NC: McFarland, 2002), 46.

17. Duncan Petrie, *The British Cinematographer* (London: BFI, 1996), 123.

18. Duncan Petrie, "A Changing Visual Landscape: British Cinematography in the 1960s," *Journal of British Cinema and Television* 15, no. 2 (2018): 213.

19. Adrian Turner, *Goldfinger* (London: Bloomsbury, 2000), 123.

20. "*Goldfinger*," review, *Variety*, September 23, 1964: 6.

21. Elizabeth Ladenson, "Pussy Galore," in *The James Bond Phenomenon: A Critical Reader*, ed. Christoph Lindner (Manchester: Manchester University Press, 2003), 186–87.

22. Turner, *Goldfinger*, 16.

23. Brosnan, *James Bond in the Cinema*, 68; Ken Adam, quoted in Bennett and Woollacott, *Bond and Beyond*, 165.

24. Howarth, "Pussy Galore," 159.

25. "Shirley—She's Gold All Over. Almost," *Daily Mirror* (London), April 21, 1964, 3.

26. "Goldfinger," *Kinematograph Weekly*, September 24, 1964, 6.

27. "Golden Girl Kathy," *Daily Mirror* (London), September 3, 1964, 11.

28. "Girls with a Touch of Gold," *Daily Mirror* (London), September 18, 1964, 3.

29. "Obsession with Gold Marks Toronto Preview," *Variety*, November 25, 1964, 13.

30. "'Goldfinger' Stunt Pays in Lima, Ohio," *Boxoffice*, August 30, 1965, 3.

31. Frank Ratcliffe, "Showmanship," *Kinematograph Weekly*, November 26, 1964, 23.

32. "Gold Girl," *Boxoffice*, February 15, 1965, 22; Frank Ratcliffe, "Showmanship," *Kinematograph Weekly*, June 17, 1965, 124.

33. O'Brien, "Babes and Bullets," 107.

34. "Gold Brick Sale Leads 'Goldfinger,'" *Boxoffice*, March 8, 1965, 35.

CHAPTER 4

THE POPULAR GEOPOLITICS OF *THUNDERBALL* (1965)

Look Up, Look Down, and Look Everywhere!

KLAUS DODDS

The fourth James Bond film in the Eon Productions franchise, *Thunderball* (1965), was a commercial success on its release. World-wide, with appropriate adjustments, *Thunderball* has been described as a "billion-dollar film."[1] Even without adjustments, a $9 million budget generated some $63 million in box-office receipts in the U.S. domestic market and $141 million worldwide.[2] As James Chapman notes, the film represents a "new vitality of British popular culture, the prominence of science and technology, and the increasing permissiveness in sexual attitudes and behaviour."[3] Trade press reviewers such as *Variety* were fulsome in their praise for the film's panache:

> "Thunderball" packs a wallop in its tongue-in-cheek treatment of agent-at-work . . . There's visible evidence that the reported $5,500,000 budget was no mere publicity figure; it's posh all the way, crammed with pop values, as company moves from France to England to the Bahamas. . . . The result is a tight, exciting, melodrama in which novelty of action figures importantly . . . Terence Young [the film's director] takes advantage of every situation in his direction to maintain action at fever-pitch.[4]

The *Motion Picture Herald* adopted a more critical edge and connected the film's appeal to the "same formula": "Remember 'Goldfinger?' And what exhibitor doesn't! Well, take another great big handsome hunk of that same formula, wrap it up in the same kind of production values, with all the trimmings, plus a whole flock of new and intriguing gimmicks, and you have 'Thunderball.'"[5] Despite the popularity and acclaim, at the time, Bond actor Sean Connery called for more attention to be given to "dialogue" and expressed some misgivings about the use of "gimmicks" in the Bond film.[6]

As this chapter will discuss, hydrofoils, miniature underwater breathing apparatuses, rocket packs, a Geiger counter, underwater propulsion systems, an aerial skyhook system, and other items play a crucial role in enabling both the projection of power and James Bond's eventual mission success in *Thunderball*.[7] For the early Bond films, Eon Productions drew creatively on prevailing Cold War geopolitical atmospherics that were able to sustain and empower outlandish plots. Stealing nuclear bombs, hiding in plain sight, and fighting underwater fitted in well with a world where there was suspicion aplenty about what the other side might be planning. But who were the other side? Part of the creative genius of the Bond franchise was to introduce a transnational criminal network into the popular geopolitical calculus—an organization that thrived on exploiting the bifurcated world of Cold War geopolitics.

The introduction of SPECTRE, while first noted in Ian Fleming's novel *Thunderball*, published in March 1961, became embroiled in an artistic/creative dispute between the novelist and the screenplay writers, Kevin McClory and Jack Whittingham.[8] At the heart of the matter was accreditation, with accusations traded that Fleming appropriated collective creative endeavor without due acknowledgment. The result of the legal action brought by McClory against Fleming in 1963 was that the literary and film rights for the screenplay were granted to McClory. Fleming retained the rights to the novel but with the caveat that it was "based on a screen treatment by Kevin McClory, Jack Whittingham and the Author."[9]

This chapter offers a reading of James Bond and *Thunderball* as illustrative of popular geopolitics.[10] It is different from earlier work on the geopolitics of James Bond, which tended to focus on how the Bond franchise engaged with the realities of Cold War geopolitics.[11] My interest in James Bond, by way of contrast, is focused more on how these cultural and geopolitical worlds co-constitute one another.[12] A fictional British super-spy, working with US allies, tackling outrageous threats posed by transnational terror/criminal networks and sponsoring states, became popular precisely because Bond engaged with a prevailing zeitgeist. Building on my collaborative work with fellow Bond scholar Lisa Funnell, this chapter's approach to the popular geopolitics of James Bond is to consider how people, places, and the wider geopolitical order are made and remade each time 007 is called upon to save the UK, close allies, or even the globe. Bond, in each film, must be both resourceful and literally "in touch" with the elemental and intimate side of his missions.[13]

As popular geopolitical scholarship on Bond and film more generally also emphasizes, the locations are integral to the narrative arc of the film.[14] They are not mere backdrops; in *Thunderball*, Bond's mission is defined by his inter-action with places, from the darkly light interiors of Whitehall in central Lon-don to underwater fights in the tropical waters off the Bahamas. Using the skill of production designer Ken Adam and the technical adroitness of those respon-sible for filming the underwater elements, *Thunderball* remains the most sub-merged Bond film of them all. Adam immersed himself in this film, literally. He and others went on a scuba-diving course in the Bahamas prior to filming.[15] *Thunderball*, of all the Bond films, is the underwater film par excellence, with a nine-minute underwater fight scene involving forty-five divers as part of the finale. No other Bond film, including *The Spy Who Loved Me* (1977) and *For Your Eyes Only* (1981), which have strong subsurface plots involving, respec-tively, the mysterious disappearance of nuclear-powered submarines and the quest for a sunken spy ship, has quite as much screen time devoted to activities below the waterline. A movie poster for *Thunderball* captioned "Look Up! Look Down! and Look Out!" captures not only the marketing brio but also "elemen-tal geopolitics"; Bond is forced throughout the film to battle with heat, height, pressure, and depth.[16] Critics and fans remain divided by the overall balance between above and below water, but the net result is to emphasize the degree to which Bond's quest for a lost NATO bomber is dependent on frantic under-water searches and spectacular confrontation with SPECTRE's diving force.

James Bond, SPECTRE, and "Geopolitical Atmospherics"

Spy films were hugely popular in the 1960s. There was a gap of four years between the publication of the novel *Thunderball* and the release of the film in 1965. It was one of Fleming's last novels (with all the controversy noted earlier about its genesis and artistic creation) and centered on a plot by SPECTRE to steal nuclear weapons. The first Bond film, *Dr. No* (1962), had defined SPEC-TRE to viewers for the first time. Over a dinner conversation with James Bond and his companion Honey Ryder (Ursula Andress), the eponymous Dr. No (Joseph Wiseman) explains the organization's genesis and is dismissive of the conventional geopolitical coordinates of the Cold War. East and West for Dr. No are mere "points on the compass." The schism between the United States and the Soviet Union is, as successive films suggest, enabling of SPECTRE's crimi-nal planning.

In *Thunderball*, we learn early in the film that SPECTRE is behind a daring heist involving the theft of two nuclear bombs. A recorded message warns the United Kingdom and other NATO powers that they have a very limited time to pay a $280 million ransom. Failure to do so will result in nuclear detona-tion. In popular cultural terms, the idea of nuclear weapons being stolen and held for ransom was still quite novel, with early television examples such as

Alas, Babylon (CBS 1950) featuring a plotline involving a nuclear war between the United States and the Soviet Union. Later dramas, such as *Forbidden Area* (CBS 1956), starring Charlton Heston, explore in more detail the proposition that ownership of nuclear weapons could become a source of national insecurity. In *Thunderball*, the theft is made possible because a NATO pilot is replaced by an imposter who is then able to steal the plane and make off with the accompanying nuclear bombs. A "routine NATO training flight" proves to be anything but routine. The UK's loss of an Avro Vulcan bomber served as a reminder that military alliances, however robust in appearance, were not immune to security breaches. The rogue agent was integral to the narrative arc, as in other spy and thriller films such as *The Manchurian Candidate* (1964).

  Thunderball's genesis and critical reception serve as a reminder that the Bond films were not guaranteed box office success. It had to be worked at. What the Bond production team wanted to ensure was that, whatever James Bond was up against, it could work in a real-life world punctuated by spectacular threats and dangers such as the 1962 Cuban Missile Crisis. The Cold War strategies of the United States and the Soviet Union were audacious, and a well-funded fictional SPECTRE and its villainous individuals had to be shown to be up to the task of pursuing their outlandish plans. Dr. No, Ernst Blofeld (played in *Thunderball* by Anthony Dawson and voiced by Eric Pohlmann), and later evil geniuses such as Stromberg (Curd Jürgens) and Drax (Michael Lonsdale) recognized only too well that money and access can secure organizational sophistication, group loyalty, and infrastructural prowess.

Set-Designing, Filming Underwater, and Operating Above and Below

In an interview with Christopher Frayling, Ken Adam did not understate the challenges facing *Thunderball*. As Adam recalled, "*Thunderball* was definitely a new dimension because it took place above and below water, which was exciting."[17] On the plus side, Adam and the production team enjoyed a far larger operating budget than they had on *Goldfinger*. The fourth Bond film was technically the most challenging of the Connery era.[18] For the underwater elements, Albert "Cubby" Broccoli and Harry Saltzman hired Florida's Ivan Tors diving company (which had been responsible for the popular 1964–1967 NBC television series *Flipper*) to organize underwater filming, which eventually involved eighty-three separate scenes and eighteen sequences. The production team worked with another Miami-based engineering outfit, which built mini-submarines. Later, Adam travelled to Florida to share his proposed designs for the film, including the hydrofoil for the villain Emilio Largo's (Adolfo Celi) super-yacht, the *Disco Volante*.[19] The production team also experimented with avant-garde technology, such as the portable jetpack used by Bond to effect his escape from the French château early in the film. *Thunderball* saw the use of other novel elements such as underwater submersibles, diving equipment, and specialist equipment that helped to cultivate a sense of the spectacular.

A good example of this was the use of a special hook attached to a B-17 aircraft, which permitted the rescue of Bond and Dominique Derval (Claudine Auger) from the aftermath of the loss of Largo's yacht. Originally the film screenplay suggested that Bond would pursue Largo via a hovercraft and then seek to board the ship to stop him from exploding the bombs. However, it was decided to change the ending of the film because a retired U.S. Air Force colonel advising on set managed to secure the services of a modified B-17 operated by Inter-Mountain Aviation, based in Arizona. Their plane had a skyhook and Bond could effect a spectacular rescue as the plane gathered the inflatable raft and winched him and his companion into the aircraft. Reportedly, the B-17 pick-up did not actually retrieve the dummies standing in for Bond and Dominique.[20]

The Avro Vulcan bomber is another strikingly important element in the film. Adam recalled in an interview that the model plane was built in the Bahamas, and that he was given special permission to inspect real-life Vulcan bombers.[21] A genuine Avro Vulcan fighter bomber was around 97 feet in length (29.5m) and a similar size wingspan of 100 feet (30m). For the purposes of the film, a 12-to-13-foot model was constructed out of fiberglass by the special effects team, led by Johnny Stears. This was suspended by a wire system and slowly propelled toward the water as part of the filming of the crash-landing sequence. Sunk in sixty feet of water, the plane's presence is integral to the quest aspect of the film—the theft and disappearance of nuclear weapons from a British bomber conducting a routine NATO training mission.[22]

Lamar Boren, a veteran cinematographer, was responsible for the underwater sequences of the film, having pioneered watertight filming equipment in earlier TV shows such as *Sea Hunt* (1958–1961). By the time of *Thunderball*, Boren and the team were using Panavision cameras designed to showcase the dramatic sequences of underwater fighting and intrigue. The division's budget was large, including $45,000 for gear for the divers involved in the complex underwater fight scenes. To help the audience distinguish sides, the SPECTRE operatives wear black gear and the U.S. naval forces and Bond are dressed in highly visible orange outfits. Multiple ships were involved in the filming process, including an opportunistic inclusion of a British cruiser which just happened to be on a Caribbean tour at the time.[23] The larger filming budget gave license to those closely involved in the making of *Thunderball* to use equipment and gadgets to achieve two fundamental things: to cement Bond's reputation for spectacular escapes and miraculous survival, and to dramatize the infrastructural and financial power of SPECTRE.

Film Locations and the Place-Making of *Thunderball*

Overseas filming started in France in February 1965 and moved to the Bahamas in March of the same year. The French-based filming occurred in the heart of Paris and Château d'Anet, located some eighty kilometers west of the capital. The château played host to the opening scene of the film, involving Bond confronting the "widow" (Rose Alba) of a former French agent. Interspersed between Paris and the Bahamas are a series of locations in southern England, ranging from the Shrublands health farm where Bond meets SPECTRE operative Count Lippe (Guy Doleman) and a pub located close to an RAF base (although NATO is referred to in the film itself), where the pilot is ambushed violently and replaced by a SPECTRE pilot.

There are three particularly key locations to consider. The first is No. 35 Avenue d'Eylau in Paris. In the novel, SPECTRE is said to be located along Avenue Haussmann. It is an important scene-setter for the introduction of SPECTRE and its global network of criminal operations. Following the progress of its second-in-command, Largo, we learn that the Centre International d'Assistance aux Personnes Déplacées is a front organization for SPECTRE. Largo is clearly known to a passing police officer, who apologizes for troubling him about parking restrictions. As Largo walks through the front office, it would appear at first sight to be dedicated to the well-being of stateless peoples. However, an anteroom reveals the secret location for SPECTRE, an operations room carefully designed by Adam to convey the secretive and sinister nature of the organization. While No. 1 (the head of SPECTRE, Blofeld) is partially hidden behind a venetian blind, the remaining senior operatives sit on an elevated platform ready to update him about the global state of play. As Adam recalled, "I was getting pretty fed up with boardrooms and long tables. It was getting more and more difficult to come up with new concepts for conference rooms. So, I decided they would just be sitting on armchairs with a little shelf attached to all the buttons and lamps: the control console."[24] This interpretation helps to establish the highly hierarchical nature of SPECTRE and the resources that it can call upon to generate mayhem, extract money, and, when necessary, exact revenge (figure 4.1).

SPECTRE's centers of operations have several things in common in the Bond films. They are hidden in plain sight behind front organizations and/or located underground or underwater, often close by to other activities that are managed by the criminal parties concerned (e.g., *Dr. No* and a neighboring bauxite mine). A world map (or globe, in the case of Stromberg's ship-based HQ in *The Spy Who Loved Me*) often features notably. In *Thunderball*, the large black-and-white map in the SPECTRE headquarters provides a visual entrée into what follows. No. 1's review of their transnational operations offers the audience an insight into scale and scope, with activities including blackmailing a Japanese agent, the assassination of a French scientist in Russia, and drug importation from China to the United States. We understand that SPECTRE is ruthless in eliminating those who are thought to be anything less than loyal and obedient. Even Largo bows to No. 1 as he enters the secret room. The scene affords an introduction to Largo and his plans for the "most audacious" SPECTRE project. This theme of audaciousness is both tongue-in-cheek and yet also reinforced by evidence of SPECTRE's infrastructural capabilities: they have access to people in high office, enjoy the use of sophisticated technologies, and operate a global network of agents, informants, and influential victims.

Thunderball's second key location type is a thoroughly British meeting space. In complete contrast to the SPECTRE HQ in Paris, the interior of the Whitehall conference room is baroque, including tapestries and high-backed Vatican-style chairs, decidedly not modern minimalist in style. Civil servants are shown drawing the large curtains and the nine 00s are seated in a circular pattern listening to M (Bernard Lee) give his briefing. Bond is last to enter the room, cementing his reputation as a maverick figure in the organization. The briefing from M and the Home Secretary is delivered after SPECTRE has carried out its devilish operation. Two atomic bombs are now in its possession and a city in either England or the United States faces the prospect of a nuclear attack if the ransom is not paid within a week. Another oversized map is unveiled, and a senior RAF officer explains how far the Vulcan bomber could have flown. Despite the NATO references, it is evident that it is the United States and the United Kingdom that are the most exposed to a SPECTRE attack and that the Prime Minister and President are in conversation with one another. The briefing is short, but the geopolitical qualities of the film are developed markedly. SPECTRE's audacity has confused the UK and the United States, and NATO faces an extraordinary crisis—one that if more widely known may have deleterious consequences for the security organization and public support.

Figure 4.1 The SPECTRE command and control room. *Thunderball* (1965).

In M's private office, we learn that Bond's destination is originally Canada, but the agent has an alternative in mind. Having opened the intelligence file, his eye is captured by a photograph of the missing pilot (thought to be François Derval) and his sister Dominique. The photograph was taken by a shop in downtown Nassau. Perhaps, as he tells M, the sister will be able to shed light on what has happened. As Bond has demonstrated in earlier missions, charming, manipulating, and seducing women of interest is a preferred modus operandi. In this film, Bond works effectively with one Bahamian woman (Paula), seduces a British woman (Patricia), becomes embroiled with a SPECTRE operative (Fiona), and manipulates a French woman (Dominique). Bond's first encounter with Dominique proves to be highly significant in creating not only a personal (later, intimate) connection, but also a way of negotiating a mission that is shaped as much by elemental encounters underwater as it is by interaction with Largo and his henchmen. Pre-departure, the audience learns that Bond's relationship with M is not without its tense elements. Through their conversations, we gather how he intends to interpret the mission and negotiate the up-and-coming fieldwork. His way of operating is the antithesis of SPECTRE's: it is nonhierarchical, instinctive, and at times indifferent to authority figures. Part of Bond's mass screen appeal is that his way of operating is highly individualistic and idiosyncratic. He bends rules, breaks rules, and ignores rules to achieve mission success.

The final location of note is the Bahamas, specifically the capital, Nassau, and its immediate environs. As soon as we get to the Bahamian element of the film, there is a noticeable shift in brightness, with accompanying sandy beaches and crystal-clear waters. As with Jamaica in *Dr. No*, the location filming accentuates the chic elements of this island in the Caribbean. Bond's experiences are shaped by social privilege and access to vehicles such as motorboats and helicopters. While many scholars have been drawn to the role of exotic places in the Bond canon and how an international network of locations has been used to locate, promote and market 007, the Bahamas (and Jamaica, in the case of *Dr. No*) provided an opportunity to showcase a part of the world where Britain's historic and imperial power could mingle with the Cold War superpower, the United States.[25]

The underwater environment off the coastline of Nassau is integral not only to the narrative arc of *Thunderball* but also the idealization of the special U.S.–UK relationship. The sea enables three types of activity that are crucial to the development of the plot and, later, the personal relationship between Bond and Felix Leiter (Rik Van Nutter). We learn, early on, that the audacious plot to steal a bomber and the nuclear bombs will involve a deliberate crash landing into the sea. Once on the surface of the sea, the plane is sunk by the pilot in shallow water. A reception team composed of SPECTRE divers not only recovers the bombs from the plane, but then hides the plane. The sea becomes, in effect, a natural storage space for the duration of the operation. Preventing Bond and others from discovering its location is crucial to avoiding detection more generally. The sea (and even Largo's swimming pool) is also an arena for noticeable gadgets, including underwater jetpacks and submersibles. It is also a place of intense conflict and cooperation. Bond, working with Leiter alongside US naval forces, becomes embroiled in a set-piece confrontation where the combatants attack each other with knives and harpoon guns. While Leiter pilots the helicopter that helped to locate the stricken bomber, it is Bond who battles SPECTRE forces below the water. There is an obvious and notable division of labor here—Bond engages, and Leiter supports him (figure 4.2).

The release of the film in 1965 coincided with an "oceanic" turn more generally in both filmography and science.[26] Scientific exploration of the underwater worlds had been popularized by high-profile explorers such as Jacques Cousteau and films such as *The Silent World* (1956) to science fiction television programs and films such as *Voyage to the Bottom of the Sea* (1961) and *The Underwater City* (1962), respectively. The popularization of the aqualung offered unprecedented opportunity for recreational diving and underwater photography gave viewers vivid portrayals of clear, warm-water tropical environments. The coral reef was framed as a site for spectacular image-hunting—exotic fish, shark attacks, and beguiling changes in light and darkness. In *Thunderball*, Bond must repeatedly negotiate sharks in a range of underwater environments from the swimming pool to the waters where the stolen bomber was hidden. The manipulative use of the former becomes yet another definer of Largo's ruthlessness as a SPECTRE agent is thrown into one of his shark pools.

At the time, there was considerable interest in the ocean as a resource and geopolitical frontier. International legal developments were enabling coastal

Figure 4.2 James Bond (Sean Connery) prepares to dive in search of the Avro Vulcan Bomber while Felix Leiter (Rik Van Nutter) flies the helicopter. *Thunderball* (1965).

states to expand their interests beyond territorial seas toward the continental shelf. Cold War adversaries were investing more in submarine technologies and ocean mapping and surveillance.[27] NATO, in the late 1950s, established a sub-committee on oceanographic research and started to track and trace, where it could, the advancements made by the Soviet Union in underwater technolo-gies such as sonar, ocean mapping, and surveying. Monitoring the activities of third parties took on added importance in the 1960s when coastal states began to develop commercial fishing and offshore drilling. In the case of the Baha-mas in *Thunderball*, SPECTRE is portrayed as an organization that thinks it can act with impunity onshore and in coastal waters. As Bond and Leiter come to appreciate, however, this level of power carries with it strategic implications. The Bahamas is less than 160 nautical miles from the U.S. city of Miami. As with Crab Key in *Dr. No*, in the Bond franchise remoter islands and the sur-rounding sea are commonly coded as enablers of malfeasance far removed from the sovereign control of recently decolonized states such as Jamaica. In 1965, the Bahamas was still under British colonial rule.

The crystal waters off the islands offer opportunities to showcase Bond's movements through the water in pursuit of others and hidden objects such as the lost bomber. SPECTRE's use of the sea to hide, move, and strategize is an equally notable element in the film. It also highlights a persistent feature of *Thunderball*: that the underwater domain is not represented as an environment for local Bahamian communities. There are no shots of local divers, fishers, and sailors. Instead, the underwater and coastal environment is shown to be a place for visitors such as Dominique (the only woman shown in the sea), or a site for the professional SPECTRE divers (all men) and spies such as Bond to work through. The final confrontation is one where the U.S. Navy launches a deci-sive attack on the SPECTRE underwater force and foils the plot to detonate a bomb in Miami.

A Popular Geopolitical Conclusion

James Bond continues to entertain audiences around the world, and consider-able opportunities remain to investigate further how popular cultural figures such as spies and superheroes help to shape our collective geopolitical imagi-nations.[28] Popular media such as film and television are integral to the produc-tion and circulation of representation, knowledge claims, and the propagation of power and authority. James Bond's claims to authority, heroism, and power are not only embodied in diverse ways, but also enacted in sites and spaces that prove crucial to who, what, and where is considered justified and legitimized. The fourth Bond film embodies all of that as Bond confronts SPECTRE oper-atives above and below the waterline. Bond has, of course, been the subject of

multiple interpretations ranging from his being a misogynistic and racist imperial agent to a fantasy figure who contributed to popular cultural engagements
of postwar Britain.[29] In Bond's world, Britain is the senior partner in the Anglo-
American special relationship and Bond and Britain are significant global
geopolitical players, especially in the Caribbean.

As an example of popular geopolitics, the Bond films provide rich opportunities to blend and blur the real-life geopolitical circumstances of the Cold War.
The creative mindset of the franchise found scope for a transnational organization to traverse borders and spread its malign influence through corruption,
extortion, and terror. Notably, after the September 11, 2001 attacks on the United
States, some commentators reached to the Bond movies of the 1960s and compared Al-Qaeda to SPECTRE, and continue to reference SPECTRE when contemplating future enemies Bond might yet confront.[30] Fact and fiction are perfectly capable of working alongside one another, and Eon Productions worked
creatively with that interface in *Thunderball*.

Notes

1. See "POP Diving: 007 Thunderball," *Alert Diver*, March 8, 2017, alertdiver.eu/en_US
   /articles/pop-diving-007-thunderball.
2. "Thunderball," *Box Office Mojo*, www.boxofficemojo.com/title/tt0059800/ (accessed
   March 30, 2022).
3. James Chapman, "A Licence to Thrill," in *The James Bond Phenomenon*, ed. Christoph Lindner (Manchester: Manchester University Press 2003), 93.
4. "Thunderball," *Variety*, December 22, 1965.
5. "Thunderball, Great Britain, 1965," *Motion Picture Herald*, January 5, 1966, 433.
6. Matthew Field and Ajay Chowdhury, *Some Kind of Hero: The Remarkable Story of the
   James Bond Films* (Stroud, UK: The History Press, 2015), 147.
7. "James Bond's Weird World of Inventions," *Popular Science*, January 1966, 62, 178.
8. On the dispute over the rights to the screenplay, see Robert Sellers, *The Battle for Bond:
   The Genesis of Cinema's Greatest Hero* (Sheffield, UK: Tomahawk Press, 2007).
9. Bond biographers and scholars continue to disagree about who should be credited with
   the invention of SPECTRE. See, for example, the discussion in Andrew Lycett, *Ian
   Fleming* (London: Weidenfeld & Nicolson, 1995).
10. On popular geopolitics, see Klaus Dodds, *Geopolitics: A Very Short Introduction*
    (Oxford: Oxford University Press, 2019).
11. For example, Jeremy Black, *The Politics of James Bond: From Fleming's Novels to the
    Big Screen* (Lincoln: University of Nebraska Press, 2005).
12. Klaus Dodds, "Licensed to Stereotype: Geopolitics, James Bond and the Spectre of Bal-
    kanism," *Geopolitics* 8 (2003): 125–56; see also Adam Svenden, "Painting Rather Than
    Photography: Exploring Spy Fiction as a Legitimate Source Concerning UK–US Intel-
    ligence Co-Operation," *Journal of Transatlantic Studies* 7 (2009): 1–22.
13. Lisa Funnell and Klaus Dodds, *Geographies, Genders, and Geopolitics of James Bond*
    (London: Palgrave, 2017).

14. Klaus Dodds and Lisa Funnell, "Popular Culture," in *International Encyclopedia of Human Geography*, ed. Audrey Kobayahsi (Amsterdam: Elsevier, 2020), 223–28.

15. The diving course undertaken by Ken Adam in preparation for the set design and filming of *Thunderball* was discussed with me when I interviewed him at his London home in October 2004.

16. Klaus Dodds and Lisa Funnell, "Going Atmospheric and Elemental: Roger Moore's and Timothy Dalton's James Bond and Cold War Geo-Politics," in *Media and the Cold War in the 1980s: Between Star Wars and Glasnost*, ed. Henrik G. Bastiansen, Martin Klimke, and Rolf Werenskjold (London: Palgrave, 2019), 63–85.

17. Laurent Bouzereau, *The Art of Bond* (Basingstoke, UK: Boxtree, 2006), 67.

18. Barry Parker, *Death Rays, Jet Packs, Stunts and Supercars* (Baltimore, MD: Johns Hopkins University Press, 2005), 27–54.

19. Christopher Frayling, *Ken Adam: The Art of Production Design* (London: Faber and Faber, 2005), 151.

20. The details regarding the screenplay development are available to consult via the Richard Maibaum Papers held at the University of Iowa, Box 31 *Thunderball*, Correspondence, notes, and treatment, 1965. My thanks to Lindsay Moen, Public Services Librarian, Special Collections and Archives, University of Iowa Libraries.

21. Frayling, *Ken Adam*, 151.

22. See David Leigh, "The Avro Vulcan Bomber from Thunderball," *The James Bond Dossier*, April 3, 2013, www.thejamesbonddossier.com/content/the-avro-vulcan-bomber -from-thunderball.htm.

23. "James Bond's Weird World," 178.

24. Cited in Frayling, *Ken Adam*, 153.

25. Stijn Reijnders, "On the Trail of 007: Media Pilgrimages into the World of James Bond," *Area* 42, no. 3 (2010): 369–77; James Chapman, "James Bond and the End of Empire," in *James Bond Uncovered*, ed. Jeremy Strong (Chelmsford, UK: Palgrave Macmillan, 2018), 203–22.

26. Margaret Cohen, "The Underwater Imagination: From Environment to Film Set, 1954–1956," *English Language* 57 (2019): 51–70.

27. Antony Adler, *Neptune's Laboratory: Fantasy, Fear, and Science at Sea* (Cambridge, MA: Harvard University Press, 2019), 101–34.

28. Klaus Dodds, "Screening Geopolitics: James Bond and the Early Cold War Films (1962–1967)," *Geopolitics* 10 (2005): 266–89.

29. See Simon Winder, *The Man Who Saved Britain: A Personal Journey into the Disturbing World of James Bond* (New York: Picador, 2006).

30. Al Horner, "What the Future of Bond Movies Could Look Like," *BBC Culture*, September 14, 2021, www.bbc.com/culture/article/20210913-what-the-future-of-bond -movies-could-look-like.

CHAPTER 5

BOND IN THE EAST

Orientalism and the Exotic in *You Only Live Twice* (1967)

ROBERT SHAIL

J ust as the producers structured the narrative of *Thunderball* (1965) and built its marketing campaign around the concept of an underwater James Bond adventure, *You Only Live Twice* (1967) was devised and promoted as the film that would take Bond to the Far East, with all the latent potential that held for exotic locations, unfamiliar customs, and an East-against-West culture clash. Bond had always been a dilettante traveler, sampling the delights of foreign climes on behalf of an audience presumed to identify as Anglo-American, but this film would take him to new tourist levels of exoticism. Colonial discourses underpin the representations of the exotic in the film and thereby condition the pleasures it offers. These pleasures also give expression to specific anxieties of the 1960s about the growing influence of Japan on the world stage and its potential industrial superiority, while continuing to recycle the implicit ideology of Orientalism.

Ian Fleming had made his first trip to Japan in 1959, a three-day visit undertaken as part of his ongoing day job as a journalist; despite the enormous success of his Bond novels, he continued this sideline to the end of his life, seemingly for the additional financial security it provided him. He was compiling a series of colorful travel pieces called "Thrilling Cities" for publication in the *Sunday Times*. In 1962 he made a return trip with two journalist friends, Richard Hughes and Tiger Saito, who were eventually to become incorporated as key characters in the narrative of his next Bond novel, to be called *You Only Live Twice* after a Japanese proverb. The second visit became a scouting trip for what was already firming up to be his twelfth and last Bond installment, the

eleventh novel in the series alongside a collection of short stories.[1] It also formed
the third part of a loose trilogy of stories featuring master criminal Ernst Stavro
Blofeld. It was subsequently published by Jonathan Cape early in 1964; Fleming died in August the same year. According to the account of the trip given by
Graham Thomas, Fleming was very much the white, Western male tourist on
these trips, sampling the delights of the East with currency in his pocket ready
to spend. What particularly struck Fleming was the seeming contrast between
traditional Japanese culture and the emerging youthful embrace of technology,
qualities that are reflected both in his book and the film adaptation. He was
also concerned more generally with what he saw as a decline in Britain's international standing and influence in the world.[2] A firm colonialist by inclina-
tion, he had been convinced by an earlier visit to Hong Kong (alongside the
impressions he took from his long-term residence in Jamaica) of the benefits
of Western imperialism and he lamented its decline, even in terms of the ben-
eficial influence that he might have expected to find in Japan but could not.

Screenwriters Sydney Boehm and Harold Jack Bloom worked on early drafts
of an adaptation before Fleming's friend Roald Dahl was brought in to write
his first film script. Dahl was fairly open with the press about the challenge of
adapting Fleming's novel, dismissing it as his worst and little more than a superficial tourist travelogue of the Far East, requiring him to come up with an
entirely new plot.[3] He was advised by the film's producer, Albert "Cubby" Broccoli, to watch previous entries in the series and essentially assemble a characteristic Bond storyline of his own based on them that incorporated the visually
exciting Japanese locales and unfamiliar cultural motifs. As James Chapman
confirms, in relation to the challenges posed by the novel "the solution was simply to discard Fleming's story entirely, keeping just the location and the character names."[4] Director Lewis Gilbert, along with the producer, contributed further ideas in preproduction and, accompanying a location scout over Japan by
helicopter, Broccoli devised the concept of the film's finale, which takes place
inside a dormant volcano.[5] Key personnel from previous Bond films were
retained, such as production designer Ken Adam and titles designer Maurice
Binder, who could build on the theme. This group also included composer John
Barry, who provided the score, with the main theme sung by Nancy Sinatra.
Sean Connery remained in the title role, although he made clear to the press
his intention to make this his last film as Bond, a decision he later reversed.[6]

Shooting began on July 4, 1966 at various locations in Hong Kong and Japan,
with studio work at Pinewood Studios near London. During the shoot at Pinewood, Dahl attended and continued to undertake rewrites to underline the
film's exoticism.[7] The premiere took place in June 1967 in London's West End.
Its budget was $10.3 million at 1967 rates, and it drew in a box-office return of
$111.6 million.[8] Although still high, this was a fall from *Thunderball* and the
first revenue drop in the series, which Ronald Milione suggests was due to an

oversaturation of spy thrillers at the box office.⁹ The critical reception was also muted, with many reviewers finding the formula tired and one critic suggesting that it was "disappointing, lacking the wit and zip, the pacing and punch of its predecessors." Roger Ebert went further: "[W]hat we're left with is a million-dollar playpen in which everything works but nothing does anything." Retrospective critical opinion hasn't shifted greatly, with James Chapman thirty years later complaining that "*You Only Live Twice* is a poorly constructed, episodic, meandering film in which one incident follows on from another without much sense of narrative development."¹⁰ The exotic Eastern locales, which aroused little of the anticipated excitement, hadn't succeeded in reenergizing the series but, nonetheless, have remained its defining characteristic within the franchise.

The film opens with a characteristically flamboyant pre-credits sequence, this time finding Bond making another romantic conquest while on foreign duty in Hong Kong. Assassins apparently succeed in machine-gunning him to death, but after the main titles we, of course, discover this has been a ruse to allow him to work undercover. After the usual briefing with M (Bernard Lee), he is assigned to investigate the hijacking of American and Soviet space rockets that are in orbit above the Earth. The storyline plays on the contemporary space race to the moon and on Cold War tensions, with Britain adopting a neutral stance, refusing to take sides but instead dispatching Bond to unravel the truth. The plot is revealed to be SPECTRE's attempt to provoke devastating nuclear conflict, leaving it free to dominate what remains of the globe. The hijackings are the work of another space probe that is being launched from Japan. Bond is sent to investigate at various striking locations, with the inevitable car chases, fist fights, and seductions building to a typically spectacular clash between Bond and SPECTRE, led by Blofeld (Donald Pleasance), marking the villain's first full appearance in a Bond film. There are many typical features, including gadgets and appearances by Q (Desmond Llewelyn) and Miss Moneypenny (Lois Maxwell). Dahl's script provides Bond with his usual array of dry one-liners, albeit leaning more toward sexual innuendo than in the past. Throughout, the attractions of the film's Eastern locations and the exotic qualities of Japanese culture are central to the intended appeal.

In retrospect, the film has been particularly celebrated for the production design of Ken Adam, who frequently incorporates a sense of Eastern "otherness" into his sets. He had initially joined the Bond team with *Dr. No* (1962), going on to work on three of the first four films.¹¹ He established a reputation for large, elaborate set constructions that were suited to the franchise, particularly when depicting the headquarters of Bond's enemies. James Chapman suggests that: "the distinctive 'look' of the films owes a great deal to the work of designer Ken Adam. The Bond films are noted for their lavish modernist sets: Adam's designs emphasise large, airy interiors, smooth surfaces of polished metal and glass, gleaming colours, and a dazzling array of technological gad-getry."[12] *You Only Live Twice* may well qualify as the apogee of Adam's work on the series, culminating with his designs for Blofeld's headquarters inside the dormant volcano. The main set of the rocket launch site and its control room are characteristic in their grandeur, providing a perfect setting for the finale; the set was 126 feet high and used 700 tons of structural steel, with a total build cost of £350,000.[13] Its complex design incorporated a movable heli-copter platform, working monorail system, and full-scale rocket mock-up that could simulate liftoff. All of these elements chime with the film's depiction of the superior ambition of postwar Japanese technology and innovation. How-ever, equally memorable is the set for Blofeld's private quarters, where he waits in his sleek white revolving chair, caressing his cat, before dispatching victims to a miserable end in the ornamental pond, which he keeps well-stocked with piranha fish. The overall cost was reputed to have been $1 million.[14] The sets incorporate distinctively Oriental motifs such as sliding doors and clean lines alongside their gadgetry. The opulence of these designs mirrors the film's fas-cination with Japanese traditions, technology, and modernity.

Viewed today, the most striking feature of the film remains its use of Japa-nese cultural iconography to add a distinctive quality to its generic elements. As Cynthia Baron has noted, the first Bond film, *Dr. No*, had already established a "discourse of Orientalism" as an exotic ingredient in the Bond formula, in this case specifically in the form of its sinister villain and his array of threat-ening technology.[15] This theme is established from the beginning of *You Only Live Twice* in the pre-credits sequence. Here, we find Bond in Hong Kong and, typically, in the bedroom of a beautiful Chinese woman. The dialogue estab-lishes the film's position, as Bond muses to himself: "Why do Chinese girls taste different?" When his female companion is rather mystified by his comment, he explains national differences in women by using a convoluted food meta-phor, comparing the differing pleasures offered by Chinese food, such as Peking Duck, as opposed to Russian caviar. Bond's position as an international tourist and conspicuous consumer is made clear (and mirrors Fleming's own position in his original travel articles), as is the role of women as commodities to be enjoyed, their national characteristics providing diverse flavors. This approach was confirmed in an episode of the popular British television program *Whick-er's World* (BBC, ITV 1958–1994), which visited the film on location during pro-duction. Host Alan Whicker's public image was a kind of sophisticated dilet-tante somewhat in the mold of Bond: he traveled to various exotic spots as the archetypal white man abroad and allowed the viewers at home to join in vicariously.[16] The theme was continued in the promotional campaign for the film, with the leading trailer telling us that "Bond rises in the East," as well as Maurice Binder's credits sequence, with its images of seductive Japanese women in traditional costume alongside silhouetted parasols. Even John Barry's theme music contains a stereotypically Eastern melodic phrase to emphasize the otherness at work. At the film's conclusion, the final credits play out over further images of Japanese women and silhouetted parasols, with the closing image of a seductive female Japanese face staring directly through the camera lens toward us. Some of these aspects didn't go unnoticed on the film's release in Japan, where, despite box-office success and media excitement, some local critics felt that the film "humiliated the country with its stereotypical depiction of the country and people."[17]

It's useful to frame the film's representations of the East within the critical perspective provided by the work of social theorist Edward Said. Said describes the development of Orientalism as a concept within Western culture, particularly in the eighteenth and nineteenth centuries, when it was centered on a particular geographic location in the Middle East: "The Orient is an integral part of European *material* civilization and culture. Orientalism expresses and represents that part culturally and even ideologically as a mode of discourse with supporting institutions, vocabulary, scholarship, imagery, doctrines, even colonial bureaucracies and colonial styles."[18] He qualifies this by adding a further development to Orientalism's geography with an American-based definition that developed later, and which draws in the Far East. As a result, the principles of Said's approach can be applied to geographical regions beyond the Middle East, where his studies originated. For Said, Orientalism as a phenomenon is remarkable in the manner in which it has adapted, and been adapted, to meet such historical variations: "Orientalists must learn to accept enormous, indiscriminate size plus an almost infinite capacity for subdivision . . . evidenced in its confusing amalgam of imperial vagueness and precise detail."[19] Nonetheless, Said argues that these discourses are definable through a direct response to Western colonialism, as nations in the Middle East and Far East were governed by a number of Western powers, with consequent development of commercial exploitation, trade, and travel. A dialogue developed between the two cultural worlds, rooted in an unequal power division that shaped that dialogue and framed its outcomes. Consequently, the history of Orientalism also inevitably encompasses resistance to that colonial discourse and to Western empire-building.

Said argues that Orientalism is "a system of representations framed by a whole set of forces that brought the Orient into Western learning;" forces that are fundamentally political in their implications.[20] He details the cultural manifestations of the Oriental discourse in the arts, particularly literature, in his landmark study *Orientalism* (originally published in 1978). Here, he demonstrates how its effects are manifest in ideas of exoticism, whose underlying mechanisms are designed to emphasize the "otherness" of the East, positioning it as not just different but fundamentally inferior to Western culture and therefore legitimizing colonialism. Referring to the culture of the Middle East, and specifically the Arab-Islamic world, Said shows how these Western cul- tural representations demonize the region as primitive, violent, crude, untrustworthy, and amoral. For Said, these are a "latent" expression of the underlying historical forces at work but no less potent for that. At the same time, as they act to represent otherness, the images also express a sense of the threat that the Orient embodied via a seductive, exotic appeal that acts to mask its underlying dangers. Said's analysis produces an analytical tool that regards both latent cultural representations and underlying ideological discourses as intrin- sically linked. Such qualities invite colonization as a justified response to this perceived threat.

Although Said's focus is largely on the Middle East and the Arab world, he implies the possibility of widening his critique to U.S. discourses regarding the Far East, and particularly China and Japan. Koichi Iwabuchi, among others, has shown how Said's approach can be applied to cultural discourses that under- pin international tourism to Japan by the construction of representations that focus on the culture of Japan as distinctively other, embodied in a seductive exoticism masking a national identity that is fundamentally ruthless, violent, and untrustworthy, as indicated by Japanese historical militarism.[21] For Said, the specific position of Japan in relation to Orientalism is directly linked to Western Christian traditions and the positioning of Japanese culture as a fundamental threat to them through its "primitive" religious discourses. At its heart, he perceives this as a form of colonial essentialism.[22] Tony Bennett and Janet Woollacott have linked these discourses directly to the Bond phe- nomenon, suggesting that Bond himself is an embodiment of "the imaginary possibility that England might once again be placed at the center of world affairs during a period when its world-power status was visibly and rapidly declining."[23]

Images of Japanese otherness abound in *You Only Live Twice*, especially in the form of tourist stereotypes. These images also confirm Iwabuchi's argument that colonial discourses of exoticism become embedded or normalized in a national sense of self. When Bond arrives in Tokyo, he is taken on a veritable coach tour of characteristic Japanese experiences. First, he makes contact with a local secret undercover agent during a visit to a sumo wrestling contest. Through Connery's reaction shots, we observe the bout as fundamentally strange and even unintentionally comic. The audience's enjoyment of the spectacle appears oddly childish, with Bond positioned as too sophisticated for such bizarre entertainments. Later, he visits what appears to be a geisha house, where young Japanese women remove his clothes and bathe him (fig- ure 5.1), followed by a massage. What occurs next remains off-screen but the implication is clearly that sexual services will also be provided. Bond adopts the position of the appreciative tourist, enjoying the pleasures that Japanese culture offers. The Japanese themselves, and particularly women, are essentially

Figure 5.1 The pleasures of the exotic East. *You Only Live Twice* (1967).

service-industry workers who are willingly complicit in a financial exchange, reducing themselves to little more than commodities. Bond is the knowledgeable tourist, speaking the Japanese that he apparently learned when he took a First in Oriental languages at Cambridge University. This sense of the otherness of Japanese culture sits alongside Bond's own remarkably wide knowledge of its complexities, as demonstrated by his familiarity with sake, of which he appears to be a connoisseur. This apparent contradiction serves both to elevate Western superior understanding while belittling the culture that is being addressed. Michael Denning acknowledges this in his critical essay on Bond when he refers to how "the loss of British world economic and political hegemony was accompanied by the loss of a cultural centrality; the obverse of imaginary centrality to the world of the British agent Bond is the marginality of Britain as a place of adventure."[24]

Japanese culture is identified as a mixture of tradition and modernity. Bond's first experience of Tokyo is a drive through its gleaming nighttime streets, where he sees contemporary high-rise buildings, sleek cars, and neon lights juxtaposed with kimono-clad women riding in rickshaws. Tradition is depicted as relentlessly other and is frequently mocked. Along with the sumo and geishas, he encounters Charles Gray's character in a hotel whose interior is decked out in traditional designs, with sliding doors and paper dividing walls. He drinks sake with his Japanese counterpart, Tiger Tanaka (Tetsurō Tamba). (Japanese actors were cast on the basis that they could speak English and wouldn't need to be dubbed or subtitled.[25]) Tanaka keeps his own troupe of ninja operatives whom Bond joins for training, setting up a montage of combat scenes that display their martial arts skills. The location used for these sequences was Himeji Castle, the largest and most-visited historical site in Japan and later to become one of the nation's first UNESCO World Heritage Sites.[26] The geisha house is also in traditional Japanese style and Bond approaches it through a characteristic garden with trees in blossom. Later, Bond joins a group of Japanese fishermen to begin the attack on Blofeld's hideout; all of the Japanese are clothed in stereotypical dress. This beautifully shot sequence is accompanied by music that uses Japanese motifs and instruments. During this section of the film, as part of his cover story Bond is married to a local girl in a traditional Japanese ceremony, which is shown at some length. Throughout these scenes, Japan is presented as if for a tourist brochure, with no attempt to complicate or enrich the clichés.

Modernity is also represented in many sequences. SPECTRE masks its presence within a Japanese technology company, Osato Chemicals and Engineering, whose headquarters is a massive high-rise structure packed with new technology; the filmmakers made use of the iconic New Otani Hotel, which at the time was the tallest building in Tokyo and boasted a revolving restaurant on its top floor. Tanaka and his secret agents are similarly depicted as part of this modernity. His underground office leads onto a private train system that runs under Tokyo, enabling him to move around without being spotted. The chief executive at Osato, Mr. Osato himself (Teru Shimada), combines the old world and the new, heading up his technology empire and employing contemporary gadgetry while adopting the appearance of a venerable, fatherly figure. Bond matches SPECTRE's arsenal of weapons with his own mini-helicopter, which proves more effective than the latest Japanese inventions. The height of Japanese technological progress is, of course, militaristic in nature: a space rocket that can outmaneuver both US and Soviet spacecraft, even managing to swallow them and transport them back, crew and all, to Blofeld's secret base. The base itself is a masterpiece of Japanese engineering, with mysterious computers and communication devices everywhere. It's clear that, for Blofeld to pursue his megalomaniac schemes, he is reliant on Japanese know-how, although this eventually proves inferior to British endeavor and bravery, in the form of Bond. Japanese modernity is depicted as a clear threat; even if its efficiency is admired, it is a threat that can be nullified (figure 5.2).

The use of Orientalism reaches its peak with the bizarre sequence in which Bond is disguised as a Japanese person himself. He submits willingly to his transformation, although we actually see very little of the details other than some female agents who are tasked with altering his hair and using makeup to change his facial appearance and his chest hair. He then dresses in traditional Japanese costume to blend in with the fishermen. The change largely takes the form of altering Connery's eyebrows and the corners of his eyes to give him an assumed stereotypical Asiatic appearance. The transformation is, apart from anything else, completely unconvincing; he is carefully lit in the following sequences so that he is frequently in shadow or has a hat pulled down to partly cover his face. These scenes display the film's appropriation of Japanese

Figure 5.2 East meets West: the perceived threat of modernity. *You Only Live Twice* (1967).

culture as if it were a mask that could be adopted and are now acutely uncomfortable to watch. The effect is to trivialize Japanese identity. Happily, once the action scenes on the volcano start, Connery's makeup seems to be abandoned.

Another discomforting element of the film is the way in which colonial discourses of Orientalism are combined with chauvinism. As we have seen, an early sequence sees Bond comparing the nationalities of his female companions as if they were items on a restaurant menu. Later, in the bathhouse, Tanaka tells him that there is a clear hierarchy of power between the sexes in Japan. Unapologetically, he refers to an old Japanese proverb that says that "men come first, women come second." Bond appears highly gratified to hear this. Later, Tanaka enjoys teasing Bond by telling him that his new wife will be a woman "with a face like a pig." Of course, this proves to be untrue and Tanaka has actually picked out a very beautiful mate for him. Nonetheless, in these scenes, even if handled in a somewhat tongue-in-cheek manner, women are overtly identified as commodities, little more than decorative and pleasure-giving servants. Bond has found a perfect home for himself. The only woman given any agency within the plot is Helga Brandt (Karin Dor), who, of course, is a sadistic and perverse villainess who threatens to torture Bond and who proves to be entirely treacherous. She is quickly dispatched by our hero but not before he has had sex with her. For Bennett and Woollacott, these discourses are symptomatic of Bond's position as "an ideological shorthand for the appropriate image of masculinity in relation to which feminine sexual identities were to be constructed."[27] For Denning, this is part of a commercial commodification of patriarchy whereby "sexuality becomes the master code into which all discourses—commercial, political, philosophical, even religious—are translated."[28] Commodification is confirmed as the dominant ideology.

Taken at face value, *You Only Live Twice* seems to have developed a reputation as a slightly formulaic and even rather tired entry in the Bond series. In plot terms, its narrative offers little that is new, settling for a combination of Cold War tensions and a characteristically fantastical scheme by Blofeld and SPECTRE to achieve world domination. Its pleasures are equally characteristic of the Bond formula: exotic locales, beautiful women, a dashing hero, and elaborately staged action sequences and stunts. There are even the typical gadgets provided by Q Branch and humorous encounters with M and Miss Moneypenny. The only new ingredients lie in its Japanese dimension. For critics who find virtues to extol, these seem to be largely due to its striking visuals, courtesy of cinematographer Freddie Young, and Ken Adam's sets. The element of tiredness resulted in disappointing reviews and poorer than expected box office. A change was due, perhaps also accelerated by the release of the Bond spoof *Casino Royale* (1967). The next Eon film, *On Her Majesty's Secret Service* (1969), would take the franchise in a new direction involving deeper characterization and even full-blown tragedy, as well as the arrival of a new Bond.

More than sixty years later, it is obvious that *You Only Live Twice* contains a number of disquieting elements that were to become prominent in future debates about the more reactionary content of the films and that would lead, eventually, to the reboot offered in the Daniel Craig films. However, Orientalist tendencies remained even then, as can be seen in *Skyfall* (2012). *You Only Live Twice* is built on a familiar bedrock of exotic imperialist attitudes and consumer materialism. The latter produces an overtly chauvinistic outlook where the female characters are permitted virtually no agency at all, instead providing a consumerist fantasy of conspicuous male consumption. The former underpins representations of Japan that conform to Said's concept of Orientalism, where Japanese culture is reduced to stereotypes of the exotic and archaic that conceal an underlying threat, often militaristic. If this was intended to reassure Western audiences of their superiority at the time, today it rather tends to make for difficult viewing.

Notes

1. For a full account of the writing of the novel and Fleming's interest in Japan, see Graham Thomas, *The Definitive Story of* You Only Live Twice: *Fleming, Bond, and Connery in Japan* (London: Sagus, 2020).
2. Thomas, *Definitive Story*, 94.
3. John Cork and Bruce Scivally, *James Bond: The Legacy* (New York: Harry N. Abrams, 2002), 100.
4. James Chapman, *Licence to Thrill: A Cultural History of the James Bond Films* (London: I. B. Tauris, 1999), 131.

5. See the documentary *Inside "You Only Live Twice"* on the Ultimate Edition *You Only Live Twice* DVD, MGM Home Entertainment, 2002.

6. Ronald Milione, *Behind the Scenes of* You Only Live Twice: *From a Director's View* (Amazon Prime, 2021) gives a detailed dossier of the film's production.

7. Thomas, *Definitive Story*, 132.

8. Cork and Scivally, *James Bond: The Legacy*, 301.

9. Milione, *Behind the Scenes*, 23.

10. Terry Clifford, "Review of *You Only Live Twice*," *Chicago Tribune*, June 18, 1967: 22; Roger Ebert, "Review of *You Only Live Twice*," June 19, 1967, www.rogerebert.com /reviews/you-only-live-twice-1967; Chapman, *Licence to Thrill*, 135.

11. For a detailed appreciation of Ken Adam's work, see Christopher Frayling, *Ken Adam and the Art of Production Design* (London: Faber and Faber, 2005) and Christopher Frayling and Ken Adam, *Ken Adam Designs the Movies: James Bond and Beyond* (London: Thames and Hudson, 2008).

12. Chapman, *Licence to Thrill*, 60.

13. Thomas, *Definitive Story*, 150.

14. Milione, *Behind the Scenes*, 19.

15. Cynthia Baron, "*Doctor No*: Bonding Britishness to Racial Sovereignty," in *The James Bond Phenomenon: A Critical Reader*, ed. Christoph Lindner (Manchester: Manchester University Press, 2003), 146.

16. "*You Only Live Twice*," episode of *Whicker's World*, BBC, first broadcast March 25, 1967.

17. Thomas, *Definitive Story*, 162.

18. Edward W. Said, *Orientalism* (London: Penguin, 2019), 2. Emphasis in original.

19. Said, *Orientalism*, 50.

20. Said, *Orientalism*, 202.

21. Koichi Iwabuchi, "Complicit Exoticism: Japan and Its Other," *Continuum* 8, no. 2 (1994): 49–82.

22. Said, *Orientalism*, 120.

23. Tony Bennett and Janet Woollacott, "The Moments of Bond," in *The James Bond Phenomenon: A Critical Reader*, ed. Christoph Lindner (Manchester: Manchester University Press, 2003), 19.

24. Michael Denning, "Licensed to Look: James Bond and the Heroism of Consumption," in Lindner, *James Bond Phenomenon*, 65.

25. Thomas, *Definitive Story*, 55.

26. Milione, *Behind the Scenes*, 160.

27. Bennett and Woollacott, "Moments of Bond," 24.

28. Denning, "Licensed to Look," 73.

CHAPTER 6

THE OTHER FELLOW

On Her Majesty's Secret Service (1969)

JAMES CHAPMAN

O*n Her Majesty's Secret Service* (1969) is the odd-one-out of the
Bond films, the joker in the pack, the embarrassing family member whom everyone would rather forget. In *The James Bond
Bedside Companion*, for example, Raymond Benson avers that "it has been forgotten by the general public" despite being "a fond favorite among Bond fans."[1]
Danny Peary, in the third of his books on cult movies, notes that in the United
States it is "rarely screened in repertory houses and rarely written about in Bond
overviews . . . And if it plays on television, it's usually a ridiculous, jumbled version with Bond serving as narrator."[2] A feature of much of the popular historiography on the Bond films, furthermore, is that authors often feel the need to
defend the film against its critics. In the Eon-endorsed *The Official James Bond
007 Movie Book*, for instance, Sally Hibbin contends that "this movie is a firm
favourite among Fleming fans—even without the appearance of [Sean]
Connery."[3]

There are two main reasons why *On Her Majesty's Secret Service* (hereafter
OHMSS) stands apart from the rest of the Bond series. Most obviously, it featured a one-time Bond: the Australian George Lazenby, a former car salesman
and male model, who was chosen to fill Sean Connery's shoes when the latter
announced that *You Only Live Twice* (1967) would be his last Bond picture.
While there are conflicting accounts whether Lazenby was dropped by Bond
producers Harry Saltzman and Albert R. "Cubby" Broccoli or he quit the role
of his own accord, Connery was lured back to the series for *Diamonds Are*

Forever (1971).[4] *OHMSS* therefore represents an interregnum in a run of six Connery Bond pictures. Lazenby became the "forgotten" Bond and the lesser box-office performance of *OHMSS* relative to the other films was laid at his door. As studio historian Ronald Bergan puts it: "The inexperienced Lazenby carried the can for the picture's comparative failure, but in fact the handsome ex-model was perfectly competent in carrying out the usual manoeuvres concocted by Richard Maibaum from Ian Fleming's novel, although the real stars were the skiing and sledding stuntmen."[5]

The other reason why *OHMSS* is something of an outlier is that it does not fit into the overall trajectory of the Bond film series. From *Dr. No* (1962) to *You Only Live Twice*, the trend had been toward ever greater degrees of visual spectacle and sumptuous production design at the expense of psychological realism. *You Only Live Twice* had been the first Bond picture to dispense entirely with Fleming's plot: it borrowed only the title and some character names from its nominal source text. By contrast, *OHMSS* was the closest of all the films to Fleming's book. As screenwriter Richard Maibaum remarked: "As a novel I think it's the best of them and the one we had to do the least with to make a good motion picture script. It was a solid novel, more of a serious effort than most of his books, which are really one hundred pages of brilliant exposition and then some good, swift action."[6] *OHMSS* was followed by *Diamonds Are Forever*, which maintained only marginally more of Fleming's book than *You Only Live Twice*. It therefore represents the last authentic Fleming adaptation in the Bond series until the much-vaunted "reboot" of the franchise in *Casino Royale* (2006).

This chapter seeks to place *OHMSS* in its historical contexts of production and reception based on archival and other primary sources. It demonstrates that the film did not start out as the close Fleming adaptation that it became. And in the process it challenges some of the myths and half-truths that have accumulated around the film. One of these is the idea—particularly common within the Bond fan culture—that *OHMSS* would have been close to the perfect Bond movie if only it had starred Connery rather than Lazenby. John Brosnan, for example, contends that *OHMSS* "could have been the best of the series had it not been fatally flawed by Connery's absence."[7] Other received wisdoms are that *OHMSS* was poorly received by critics (in fact it divided contemporary reviewers, with some considering it the best Bond picture of all) and that it was a box-office flop. The latter claim is simply untrue.

OHMSS was Ian Fleming's eleventh Bond book, written, as was his custom, in Jamaica, in the early months of 1962 (during the shooting of *Dr. No*) and published a year later in April 1963 by Jonathan Cape in the United Kingdom and the New American Library in the United States.[8] It was serialized in three parts in *Playboy* and was adapted for the *James Bond* comic strip in the *Daily Express*, drawn by John McLusky, between June 29, 1964 and May 17, 1965. It was welcomed by most reviewers as a return to form for Fleming and the Bond adventures, following the poorly received *The Spy Who Loved Me*. As Fleming himself wrote in a letter to Robert Kennedy after completing *OHMSS*: "My last book, *The Spy Who Loved Me*, has had an extremely mixed reception, due largely to the late appearance of James Bond. But I can now tell you that my next and longest to date, has James Bond in from the first page to the last, and all Kennedys will be receiving a copy around next Easter."[9]

A frequent complaint within Bond fandom is that *OHMSS* was filmed out of sequence with *You Only Live Twice*: this meant that the emotional and psychological context of *You Only Live Twice*, wherein Bond exacts revenge for the death of his wife Tracy at the end of *OHMSS*, was absent from the film version. However, the strategy of the Bond producers in the 1960s was oriented toward filming the most recent titles rather than internal continuity. It has been well documented that in 1961 Saltzman and Broccoli had intended that *Thunderball* (at the time the most recent book) should be the first Bond film. The first three Bond pictures—*Dr. No*, *From Russia with Love* (1963), and *Goldfinger* (1964)—were based on novels published between four to six years earlier. *For Your Eyes Only*, published in 1960, was a collection of five short stories that did not lend itself so easily to adaptation for film. Nor did *The Spy Who Loved Me*, published in 1962, with its atypical narrative.

It had been intended until shortly before the release of *Goldfinger* that *OHMSS* would follow as the fourth Bond picture: indeed, early prints of *Goldfinger* declared that "James Bond will return in *On Her Majesty's Secret Service*." United Artists' records reveal that by the end of August 1964, holding company Danjaq had spent $55,430 on the development of *OHMSS* compared to $21,339 on the development of *Thunderball*.[10] The decision to go with *Thunderball* instead of *OHMSS* was made in September 1964—the month that *Goldfinger* was released in London—when Saltzman and Broccoli reached an agreement with Kevin McClory to produce the film jointly.[11] Once the agreement with McClory had been made, *Thunderball* was brought forward, with *OHMSS* planned to follow for 1966–1967, "again starring Sean Connery."[12]

In August 1965, following the completion of principal photography on *Thunderball*, *Variety* reported that the producers "haven't determined which will be next, although they have a script near complete by Richard Maibaum on *Her Majesty's Secret Service*."[13] The same month, *Kine Weekly* reported that Saltzman had been scouting locations in Switzerland with the intention of shooting the following winter.[14] *OHMSS* remained slated as the next Bond until late in 1965: as in *Goldfinger*, the end credits of *Thunderball* originally announced, "James Bond will return in *On Her Majesty's Secret Service*." Charles Helfenstein's authoritative study of the making of *OHMSS* suggests that the decision to go with *You Only Live Twice* instead was due to the producers looking to capital-ize on Bond's popularity in Japan.[15] This is consistent with the oft-quoted *Time* magazine article in 1965 attesting to Bond's global popularity, including that in Tokyo "the queue for *Goldfinger* stretched for half a mile."[16] In December 1965, coinciding with the release of *Thunderball*, *Variety* reported that *You Only Live Twice* would begin production in Japan in March 1966.[17]

Richard Maibaum, the principal screenwriter for the first four Bond pictures, who had not been involved in scripting *You Only Live Twice*, was assigned to *OHMSS*. Maibaum's papers, held by the University of Iowa, include extensive script materials and drafts for *OHMSS*. The earliest is a full screenplay dated March 29, 1966 which includes some significant differences from both Flem-ing's novel and the finished film.[18] It opens with Bond rescuing Tracy from kid-nappers on a Mediterranean beach, during which his Aston Martin trans-forms into an amphibious vehicle complete with periscope and torpedoes. The submersible car was dropped from later scripts but would remain in the locker of unused Bond ideas until it was resurrected for *The Spy Who Loved Me* (1977). Blofeld's mountaintop lair at Piz Gloria includes a vast cave containing lifts, staircases, gantries, and a menagerie of wild animals (a note in the script remarks: "K. ADAM please dream up"). Eventually, of course, Adam did not work on *OHMSS*, for which Syd Cain was the production designer. Perhaps the most unexpected departure, however, is the revelation that Blofeld—who, when he first meets Bond, is wearing a mask that conceals his face—"looks amaz-ingly like Gert Frobe":

BLOFELD
I believe you knew my half-brother—Auric Goldfinger
(*sighing*)
Our mother often cautioned him about his reckless fetishism. Actually she
considered him somewhat retarded. Don't you agree?

It is part of Bond folklore that it was originally intended to bring back Gert Fröbe as Goldfinger's twin brother in *Diamonds Are Forever*, but it turns out that the idea had first been considered for *OHMSS*. This screenplay was probably written before it had been determined that Bond would meet Blofeld face to face in *You Only Live Twice*.

At this point, it does not seem that *OHMSS* was intended as a more serious and less gimmicky Bond picture. Indeed, the inclusion of a scene where Tracy is bound on a conveyor belt heading for a furnace—a device that became a cli-ché of the cliffhanger adventure serials of the silent era and that in the mid-1960s was already the subject of parody in the television series *Batman* (ABC 1966–1968)—indicates a semiparodic approach that sits uncomfortably with the tragic ending. The inclusion of various gadgets in this script, among them a wristwatch/bug detector and a 3-D television in Blofeld's lair, suggests the influence of *Goldfinger* and *Thunderball*. However, a number of circumstances would orient *OHMSS* toward a more serious treatment. One was Charles K. Feldman's Bond spoof *Casino Royale* (1967), which preceded *You Only Live Twice* in cinemas by several months.[19] Indeed, there had been such a glut of gimmicky Bond imitations and spoofs in the mid-1960s—including Dario Sabatelli's cash-in *O. K. Connery* (a.k.a. *Operation Kid Brother*, 1967)—that a shift back toward genuine Fleming material became a form of product differentiation. Another factor was the selection of Peter Hunt to direct *OHMSS*. Hunt, editor of the first four Bonds and second unit director of *You Only Live Twice*, was keen to put his own stamp on the film. In particular, he wanted to downplay the gadgetry that had featured so prominently in the previous three films: "We could have stuck to exactly the same formula, but we preferred to progress. Besides, *On Her Majesty's Secret Service* is better without the gadgetry and paraphernalia. It is a marvellous adventure story, with Bond surviving by his own physical skill and ingenuity, and at the same time it is a genuine love story, with 007 falling in love and marrying for the very first time."[20]

However, the most important factor in shaping the development of *OHMSS* was Connery's decision to quit Bond following *You Only Live Twice*. *OHMSS* therefore had to be reworked as the introductory vehicle for a new James Bond. A treatment of April 27, 1967 sketches out a new pre-title sequence where Bond is lured to a villa where he believes he has tracked down Blofeld. It turns out to be a trap and Bond is captured by SPECTRE agents who intend to shoot him and dump his body in a river. As they drive to the bridge in Bond's Aston Martin, he uses the ejector seat to effect his escape. The surprised SPECTRE agents lose control of the Aston Martin, which collides with a petrol tanker: the tanker explodes and plunges into the river, where it traps Bond. Following the main titles, the treatment picks up nine months later as Bond is discharged from hospital following plastic surgery and reports to headquarters. M "welcomes him back to active service, explains when Bond asks why his face was changed so drastically that it was thought a new face would prolong his life and be especially useful in pursuit of Blofeld who obviously by now is familiar with his old appearance." Otherwise the treatment still included a heavy dose of gadgetry, including a ski pole containing a blowpipe, boots with built-in skis, and a new car for Bond in the form of a Ford Grand Turismo Mark III equipped with a laser ("This is the new Double O Section standard issue").[21]

All the script materials have Bond tendering his resignation from the Secret Service: this is forestalled by Miss Moneypenny, who switches his resignation letter for a request for leave. However, Maibaum was evidently uncertain about the reason for Bond's resignation. This varies from one draft to another. Some versions follow the book insofar as Bond has become frustrated with what he regards as routine police work:

BOND

Sir, I never regarded myself as an Investigator of Missing Persons. I wasted two
years trying to run Blofeld down.

M

Obviously he knew what you looked like.

BOND

When he's found, I'll be delighted to kill him. Until then I respectfully request a
more congenial assignment.[22]

However, other versions have Bond resenting being taken off "Operation
Bedlam":

BOND

I'm keen to go back to Operation Bedlam, sir. Killing Blofeld's something of a
must with me.

M (*frowning*)

You spent two years trying to run him down. Without distinguishing yourself, I
must say.

BOND

He knew what I looked like. You've taken care of that difficulty very nicely.[23]

The finished film has Bond's resignation prompted by being relieved from
"Operation Bedlam." Another difference is that the 1967 scripts have Bond killing Blofeld and Irma Bunt at the end ("I returned their wedding present!")
before realizing that Tracy is also dead.

Following a complete script dated June 21, 1967, Maibaum seems to have put
OHMSS aside for a full year. In the second half of 1967 he wrote "additional dia-
logue" for Broccoli's production of *Chitty Chitty Bang Bang* (1968) and early in
1968 wrote three script drafts for George Pal's unrealized film of *Logan's Run*.
In October 1967 *Variety* reported that *OHMSS* would begin production in
August 1968 but that no replacement for Connery had been signed.[24] In Feb-
ruary 1968, in response to a report that Connery had relented and agreed to do
OHMSS, Saltzman told *Variety*: "I don't know where they got that one from.
Connery wants to do it, but I think it's time for a change. Frankly, I don't have
any idea yet who we'll cast for the part."[25] Maibaum returned to *OHMSS* in
June 1968 and wrote several drafts and revisions over the next three months.
The plastic surgery idea was dropped, but there were still references to acknowledge the as-yet-uncast "new" Bond. Script materials from this period all have
the pre-title sequence of Bond rescuing Tracy on the beach as per the finished
film, with Bond commenting ruefully as Tracy runs out on him: "This never
happened to Sean Connery." (Maibaum adds: "I know, we'll have to find another
line").[26] This was subsequently changed to: "This never happened before, 007."

Figure 6.1 "This never happened to the other fellow!" comments James Bond (George Lazenby) in *On Her Majesty's Secret Service* (1969).

Script revisions dated August 20, 1968 have changed it again to: "This never happened to the other fellow" (figure 6.1).[27]

The "Shooting Script" (September 5, 1968) is very close to the finished film in structure and dialogue (though reverting to "This never happened before, 007"). However, the one major difference from the film is that it is Tracy who proposes to Bond rather than vice versa:

TRACY

Did you miss me at all? Up there on the mountain?

BOND

I had . . . a lot to occupy me. Body and mind.

TRACY

I understand.

BOND

Not quite, you don't. I was using people, Tracy. Using women, for my job. And I
   enjoyed it.

TRACY *(level)*

If you didn't, you wouldn't do it well.

BOND

You don't mind?

TRACY

You forget, James. I've used people too. And without even the excuse of a job.
   Do *you* mind?

BOND *(after a pause)*

No. I can't afford to.

TRACY

So we understand each other at last. Very few people would. Marry me, James.
   That's what marriages are for . . . not for interference but for understanding . . .
   for a fellowship.[28]

Helfenstein avers that it was Peter Hunt who decided that Bond "should do the asking."[29] The rewritten proposal scene was probably one of those for which British playwright and novelist Simon Raven received an "additional dialogue" credit. Some sources suggest that Raven contributed the poem quoted by Tracy as she attempts to distract Blofeld prior to the helicopter attack on Piz Gloria ("Thy dawn, O Master of the World, thy dawn . . .").[30] However, the poem, a misquotation from James Elroy Flecker's play *Hassan*, is in the shooting script. Lazenby's casting was announced shortly before principal photography began in October 1968.[31]

United Artists undertook the usual high-profile release strategy for *OHMSS*. In August 1969 it was announced that the film would open at 1,700 sites worldwide on December 18, "highlighted by special premieres in New York, London, Paris and other world capitals."[32] The trade reviews predicted another smash hit. *Variety* forecast that the "latest Bond issue should prove to be the same bonanza at the box office that the previous masculine fantasies have been, boosted by favourable word of mouth and curiosity at seeing Lazenby in the role."[33] *Boxoffice* felt that Lazenby "manages to humanize Bond more than his predecessor did" and that "This film should prove to be exceptionally popular at the box office."[34] *The Hollywood Reporter* noted the changing nature of cinemagoing insofar as it thought the film would draw "many who make their only movie date of the year with Bond and those millions more who should continue to make Bond the screen's most profitable series."[35] *Kine Weekly* found it well up to par: "Most of the well-tried ingredients of the 007 success are included in this film and it should make a mint of money. Sure-fire attraction."[36] And *Today's Cinema* felt that the action sequences compensated for the absence of gadgets: "Bond without crazy gimmicks or off-beat humour, and with sex appeal at a minimum. However, the action of the last hour or so is superlatively exciting and as a result the film should do excellent business."[37]

It has become something of a received wisdom that *OHMSS* was not as well received as the previous Bond films and that Lazenby was universally panned for his performance. Even a brief survey of the contemporary reviews demonstrates this was not the case. For example, the *Independent Film Journal* proclaimed that "George Lazenby is a worthy successor to Sean Connery in the James Bond role . . . He doesn't possess Connery's good looks, but he gives Bond a human side, with his vulnerable quality and the sense of fun in his performance."[38] The *Motion Picture Herald* found that "Lazenby gradually dispels a viewer's reluctance to accept him as Connery's successor" and became more "easy and confident" as the film went on.[39] A. H. Weiler (*New York Times*) was more equivocal: "He's tall, dark, handsome, and has a dimpled chin. But Mr Lazenby, if not a spurious Bond, is merely a casual, pleasant, satisfactory replacement."[40] Pauline Kael (*New Yorker*) thought the new Bond "quite a dull fellow" but added that Peter Hunt "is a wizard at action sequences, particularly an ethereal ski chase that you know is a classic while you're watching it, and a mean, fast bobsled chase that is shot and edited like nothing I've ever seen before."[41] Charles Champlin (*Los Angeles Times*) pronounced it "by a long shot the very best of the James Bond epics" and suggested that it was "the first of the films in which Bond is allowed any genuine claim to humanity, real feeling and sentiment."[42] A dissenting note was sounded by Molly Haskell (*Village Voice*), who felt that the downbeat ending would deter some: "If you like your Bonds with happy endings, don't go" (figure 6.2).[43]

British critics were generally less favorably disposed toward Lazenby than were their American counterparts. There was also a sense in some of the reviews that the Bond series had run out of steam. Margaret Hinxman (*Sunday Telegraph*) declared that watching Lazenby "makes you appreciate how much style and subtlety Sean Connery, even at his worst, brought to the role . . . Peter Hunt handles the adventure as surely as anyone could. But I doubt if it will make any new converts."[44] Dilys Powell (*Sunday Times*) averred that "a new James Bond should stir regrets for the previous one. I can't help missing Sean Connery . . . His successor, George Lazenby, I find too amiable: one doesn't get the rasping indifference to danger which used to combine so happily with the sybarite's taste in drinks."[45] Penelope Houston (*Spectator*) felt that the last pretense of Bond being a real person had gone: "The new Bond, George Lazenby, is a slow reader, but in any case there is precious little left of the just human hero of the earlier films, or their style of nonchalance in the midst of conspicuous mayhem and extravagance."[46] Derek Malcolm (*The Guardian*) had the best putdown of Lazenby, whom he thought "looks like a Willoughby Brothers clothes

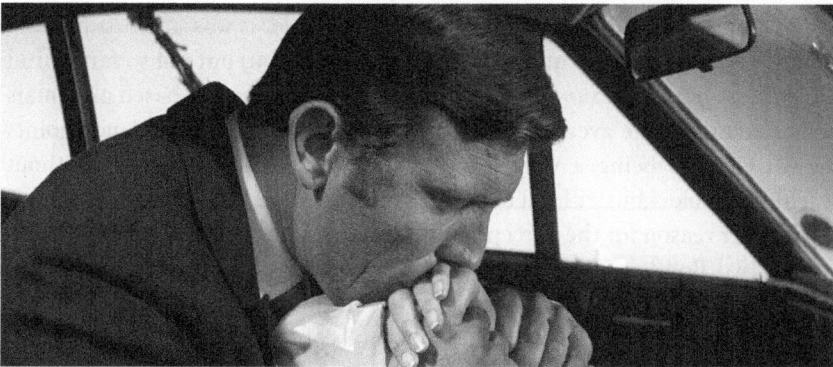

Figure 6.2 "If you like your Bonds with happy endings, don't go," Molly Haskell advised readers of the *Village Voice* in her review of *On Her Majesty's Secret Service* (1969).

peg and acts as if he's come out of Burtons short on credit."[47] Tom Milne (*Observer*) was another who felt that the Bond formula had run its course: "*On Her Majesty's Secret Service*, I equally fervently trust, will be the last of the James Bond films. All the pleasing additions and eccentricities and gadgets of the earlier films have somehow been lost, leaving a routine trail through which the new James Bond strides without noticeable signs of animation."[48]

The suggestion that *OHMSS* was a box-office flop is very wide of the mark. By 1975 it had returned total worldwide theatrical rentals of $24.4 million. This was significantly less than the three previous Bond pictures: *Goldfinger* ($49.6 million), *Thunderball* ($56.4 million) and *You Only Live Twice* ($44 million).[49] However, this reflects as much the exceptionality of those films, especially *Goldfinger* and *Thunderball*, which marked the height of "Bondmania" in the mid-1960s, as any real failure of *OHMSS*. The declining box office of the Bond films following *Thunderball*—*OHMSS* returned 45 percent less than *You Only Live Twice*, which in turn was 22 percent down on *Thunderball*—should be seen as a recalibration of the commercial expectations of the series as it moved, in Tony Bennett and Janet Woollacott's terms, from cultural phenomenon to "institutionalised ritual."[50]

The perception that *OHMSS* was a commercial failure rests largely on its performance in the U.S. (and Canadian) market. After its first year on release *OHMSS* had returned domestic rentals of $9 million, which placed it ninth at the annual box office. It was a long way behind the year's blockbuster, *Airport* ($37.6 million) and the runners up, *M*A*S*H* ($22 million) and *Patton* ($21 million). but was on a par with the antiwar satire *Catch-22* ($9.2 million) and ahead of the Steve McQueen vehicle *The Reivers* ($8 million).[51] Compared to other Bond films, *OHMSS* returned 50 percent less than *You Only Live Twice* ($18 million) in America and 67 percent less than *Thunderball* ($27 million).[52] However, *Boxoffice*, which tabulated the popularity of individual films based on their box-office gross in first-run situations in major cities against the average for those locations, reported that *OHMSS* grossed 322 percent of the average of films released in 1969 and 1970. In this table, it was again some way behind *Airport* (491 percent) and *M*A*S*H* (425 percent) but not so far behind *Butch Cassidy and the Sundance Kid* (340 percent).[53] Whether based on rentals or percentage of the average box-office gross, therefore, the evidence points toward *OHMSS* being a very solid box-office success in America without reaching the blockbuster level of previous Bonds.

Another reason for the perception that *OHMSS* was a failure is that the following two Bonds—Connery's return in *Diamonds Are Forever* and Roger Moore's debut in *Live and Let Die* (1973)—both did significantly better at the box office than *OHMSS*, with worldwide rentals of $45.7 million and $48.7 million respectively. Even allowing for inflation, the Bond pictures of the early 1970s proved more successful than *OHMSS*. However, the reputation of *OHMSS* within the Bond fan culture has grown in hindsight, to the extent that it now regularly features in polls of the best Bond films. Andrew Pilkington of the James Bond 007 Fan Club states: "To most informed Bond fans it is considered possibly the best film in the entire series . . . *On Her Majesty's Secret Service* rightly deserves its place at the top of the Bond chart, and serves as a reminder that at their best, the Bond films can be exceptional entertainment."[54] Perhaps the best way of situating *OHMSS* within the Bond series is to see it not so much as an outlier as one of those films—others include *Licence to Kill* (1989), *Skyfall* (2012), and *No Time to Die* (2021)—that demonstrate the bounds of difference within the Bond formula. And to realize that the "other fellow" more than merits his place in Bond's cinematic legacy.

Notes

Grateful thanks to Eon Productions and to Lindsay Moen of the University of Iowa Special Collections for allowing access to the digitized Richard Maibaum papers.

1. Raymond Benson, *The James Bond Bedside Companion* (London: Boxtree, 1998), 194.
2. Danny Peary, *Cult Movies 3: 50 More of the Classics, the Sleepers, the Weird, and the Wonderful* (New York: Simon & Schuster, 1988), 176.
3. Sally Hibbin, *The Official James Bond 007 Movie Book* (London: Hamlyn, 1987), 49.
4. Lazenby's account of his short tenure as 007 informs the documentary-drama *Becoming Bond* (Delirio Films, dir. Josh Greenbaum, 2017).
5. Ronald Bergan, *The United Artists Story* (London: Octopus Books, 1986), 247.
6. "Richard Maibaum: 007's Puppet Master," *Starlog* 68 (March 1983), 27.
7. John Brosnan, *James Bond in the Cinema* (London: Tantivy Press, 1972), 114.
8. Fleming was evidently quite smitten with Ursula Andress, whom he met during the location shooting of *Dr. No*. He gave her a "cameo" appearance in *OHMSS*, when Irma Bunt points her out in the public restaurant at Piz Gloria: "And that beautiful girl with the long fair hair at the big table, that is Ursula Andress, the film star. What a wonderful tan she has!" Ian Fleming, *On Her Majesty's Secret Service* (London: Penguin Classics, 2004 [1963]), 118.
9. Quoted in Fergus Fleming, *The Man with the Golden Typewriter: Ian Fleming's James Bond Letters* (London: Bloomsbury, 2015), 330.
10. Schedule of applications of Danjaq profits to August 28, 1964, United Artists Collection MCHC82–046 Box 3 Folder 5, Center for Film and Theater Research, Wisconsin Historical Society, University of Wisconsin–Madison.
11. "McClory and Partners Readying Next Fleming; Sean Connery Still 007," *Variety*, September 23, 1964, 4.
12. "UA Hits New Earnings Peak; Set Production Far Ahead," *Boxoffice*, June 1, 1964, 4.
13. "Broccoli and Saltzman Un-Bonded for 4 New Pix; Eight 007's to Go," *Variety*, August 18, 1965, 4.
14. *Kinematograph Weekly*, August 5, 1965, 14.
15. Charles Helfenstein, *The Making of "On Her Majesty's Secret Service"* (USA: Spies LLC, 2009), 26.
16. "Bondomania," *Time*, June 11, 1965, 59.
17. "'Thunderball': Global Explosion," *Variety*, December 29, 1965, 14.

18. *On Her Majesty's Secret Service*: Screenplay by Richard Maibaum, March 29, 1966, Richard Maibaum Papers, Box 28, University of Iowa Special Collections (hereafter Maibaum/Iowa).

19. "United Artists: 'We Got True Bond,'" *Variety*, March 15, 1967, 5.

20. Quoted in Herbert A. Lightman, "The 'Cinemagic' of 007," *American Cinematographer* 51, no. 3 (March 1970): 204–5.

21. *On Her Majesty's Secret Service*: Short outline by Richard Maibaum, April 27, 1967, Maibaum/Iowa Box 28.

22. *On Her Majesty's Secret Service*: Incomplete draft with holograph revisions, no date, Maibaum/Iowa Box 28.

23. *On Her Majesty's Secret Service*: Screenplay ("Second Draft"), no date, Maibaum/Iowa Box 28.

24. "Peter Hunt to Direct New James Bond Film, without Sean Connery," *Variety*, October 4, 1967, 24.

25. "Saltzman (Bond) & Kirsher (Disks) Plot With-It Pics for 18–24 Crowd," *Variety*, February 14, 1968, 4.

26. *On Her Majesty's Secret Service*: Screenplay, June–August 1968, Maibaum/Iowa Box 28.

27. *On Her Majesty's Secret Service*: Screenplay, August 1968 (Revised 20.08.1968), Maibaum/Iowa Box 28.

28. *On Her Majesty's Secret Service*: Shooting Script, September 5, 1968, Maibaum/Iowa Box 28.

29. Helfenstein, *Making of,* 33.

30. Matthew Field and Ajay Chowdhury, *Some Kind of Hero: The Remarkable Story of the James Bond Films* (Stroud, UK: The History Press, 2015), 184.

31. "TV Yields UA New James Bond & Wife," *Variety*, October 9, 1968, 3.

32. "New James Bond Feature Set for Global Openings," *Boxoffice*, August 4, 1969, 5.

33. *Variety*, December 17, 1969, 16.

34. *Boxoffice*, December 22, 1969, 4253.

35. *Hollywood Reporter*, December 17, 1969, xx.

36. *Kinematograph Weekly*, December 20, 1969, 8.

37. *Today's Cinema*, December 19, 1969, 5.

38. *The Independent Film Journal*, December 21, 1969, 1162.

39. *Motion Picture Herald*, January 7, 1970, 260.

40. *New York Times*, December 19, 1969, 68.

41. *New Yorker*, December 27, 1969.

42. *Los Angeles Times*, December 18, 1969, 68.

43. *Village Voice*, December 24, 1969.

44. *Sunday Telegraph*, December 21, 1969.

45. *Sunday Times*, December 21, 1969, 36.

46. *Spectator*, December 27, 1969.

47. *The Guardian*, December 16, 1969.

48. *Observer*, December 21, 1969, 3A.

49. "James Bond's 25th Anniversary," *Hollywood Reporter*, July 14, 1987, S-26.

50. Tony Bennett and Janet Woollacott, *Bond and Beyond: The Political Career of a Popular Hero* (London: Macmillan, 1987), 38.

51. "Big Rental Films of 1970," *Variety*, January 6, 1971, 11.

52. "All-Time Box-Office Champs," *Variety*, January 6, 1971, 12.

53. "The Hits of '69–'70," *Boxoffice*, June 7, 1971, D1.

54. "The James Bond 007 Fan Club at the BFT: 30 Years of James Bond in the Cinema 1962–1992," program notes in the BFI Reuben Library digitized clippings file for *OHMSS*.

CHAPTER 7

DIAMONDS ARE FOREVER (1971)

007 and Transatlantic States of Emergency

IAN SCOTT

On the 30th of December, 1971, *Diamonds Are Forever*, the seventh cinematic outing for Eon's James Bond, was premiered in the UK at the Odeon Leicester Square in London. Though designated as a 1971 release, much of the film's impressive box-office take ($116 million worldwide) was accumulated through the first months of 1972. Its theatrical run therefore occurred some way into a decade that was turning out to be a world away from the heady swinging sixties era into which the Bond film franchise had been born. By the early 1970s Britain was firmly in the grip of economic and social decline, a decline that in the country, if not the wider world, had not just become a watchword but a state of mind.

In January 1972 a coal miners' strike began that prompted Edward Heath's Conservative government to declare a state of emergency. Although resolved temporarily, further ruptures of discontent led to another strike almost exactly two years later that resulted in a three-day working week being imposed, power cuts, and, eventually, the fall of the Heath government in the first of two general elections in 1974. The Bogside Massacre in Derry on "Bloody Sunday," also in January 1972, saw British troops stationed in Northern Ireland kill fourteen civilians, while an IRA bomb a month later, at the end of February, killed six people at the Aldershot army barracks.

To say that industrial strife, political crises, and social disorder were becoming prominent issues in the life of the nation is to considerably undersell the unravelling of Britain's national fabric at the start of the 1970s. As James Chapman characterizes it, the Bond novels and films have often been perceived as working in tandem with Britain's "end of empire" decline and its descent into what Bond's arch enemy Ernst Stavro Blofeld (Charles Gray) calls in *Diamonds Are Forever* a "pitiful little island."[1] It wasn't as if, taking Bond as their cue, the movies were otherwise a means of escape either. On both sides of the Atlantic, 1971–1972 saw film delve ever more deeply into the gritty landscape and uncertain future the times were producing. This was perhaps best reflected in 1971 American releases such as the police thrillers *Klute* and *Dirty Harry* and the postapocalyptic science fiction films *The Andromeda Strain* and *The Omega Man*.

The British spy thriller had taken on a somber, cynical tone over the course of the previous few years. Although nothing like as popular across the Atlantic, as Simon Willmetts proposes, the move toward a more "realist" spy genre in the 1960s, epitomized by *The Spy Who Came in from the Cold* and *The Ipcress File* (both 1965), meant that Bond wasn't the only vision of British intelligence on offer to American audiences. The downbeat-ness of the John Le Carré adaptation in the first example was complemented by Len Deighton's establishment-averse hero Harry Palmer (Michael Caine) in the second film. Ironically enough, *The Ipcress File* included a number of the same production team responsible for Bond. But it was also clear to see from a domestic perspective how these movies made sense in terms of the collapse of empire theory and the revelations behind the Cambridge spy scandal that was ongoing in the 1950s and '60s and into the '70s, which "shattered the Bond image of the British intelligence establishment."[2] In the United Kingdom, just as with the U.S. films above, further cinematic exploration of contemporary and futuristic dislocation was well underway by the turn of the 1970s. *Get Carter* (1971), the directorial film debut for Mike Hodges starring Michael Caine, and most especially *A Clockwork Orange* (1971), Stanley Kubrick's adaptation of Anthony Burgess's dystopian novel with Malcolm McDowell, represented both the down-at-heel grime of the coming postindustrial north on the one hand and the casual violence usurping norms for a youthful generation cast as social renegades and now estranged from convention and consensus on the other.

Into this maelstrom came the latest adventure from Bond, and a film that proved to be one of the most commercially popular releases in the series up to that point. A need for escapism might be the natural conclusion to reach in accounting for the movie's box-office take when strife at home and bleak economic futures globally were the order of the day. Taking the audience into 007's alternative cosmopolitan universe, in *Diamonds Are Forever* Bond gets to stroll around Amsterdam and cavort in Las Vegas most particularly, as if the bright neon lights of the gambler's paradise would carry on boundlessly. And yet even in Vegas by the turn of the '70s, those lights were starting to flicker intermittently, with the "Rat Pack" heyday long past and a wholesome reinvention of the city as a family theme park a full twenty years in the future. It's symptomatic that one of the stalwarts of the Rat Pack collective, Sammy Davis, Jr., should be engaged for a cameo in *Diamonds Are Forever*—where he's playing at a rou- lette table—only for the scene to be eventually left on the cutting room floor.[3] As if symbolically casting aside the resort's faded 1950s and '60s chic by snip- ping Davis out of the action, the Bond film caught a moment in which the post- modern reinvention of Las Vegas had not yet begun to take shape, even while the old cloak was slowly starting to be shed.

In some ways, then, *Diamonds Are Forever* was a fantasy that diverted audi- ences from what the 1970s was becoming, but that was also a last hurrah for a lot of things. It was Sean Connery's last "official" performance as 007 (before he reaccepted the role in the one-off, outside-the-franchise film *Never Say Never Again* in 1983), a last nod toward '60s pizzazz and glamor, and a recoloring of Las Vegas one more time before the old-style Strip gave way to its brasher and bigger sibling. From the end of the 1980s, starting with the Mirage, a series of monolithic hotel complexes were built on a new strip in the neighborhoods of Paradise and Winchester, outside the city's formal limits. The Vegas Strip of old went into decline before reopening as the Fremont Street Experience in 1995, a reinvention that started to reinvigorate that older quarter of the city that fea- tures so heavily in this Bond film.

As well as these cultural and urban motifs, and notwithstanding the other fictional espionage already mentioned, *Diamonds Are Forever* continued to assert the Bond ideal that British intelligence, know-how, and diplomatic gain- saying were all still a ready part of the armor of the West in a Cold War envi- ronment battling totalitarian forces and megalomaniacal villains out for con- trol of the world. All these elements take their place in the film's fast-paced and action-fueled storyline. The latter contains an amalgam of threats, including the theft and sale of nuclear armaments and rogue warheads and a parade of gang members and lone/team assassins out for their own interests via diamond smuggling. There's even a reference to the reclusive billionaire Howard Hughes thrown in for good measure, in the guise of Willard Whyte (Jimmy Dean). Each of these constituent elements is collectively woven into a plot that pivots from the traditional European customs of the Netherlands to the glitzy and garish New World neon of the Nevada desert. Whyte, in particular, a not-so-subtle rendition of the still occasionally resident magnate of Las Vegas at the time, plays upon the past and future colliding at a moment when Hughes himself was in the process of buying several of the casinos, an act that later kick-started the reimagining of the city's wholesome, all-star future.

There was more to *Diamonds Are Forever* than the Cold War present, more to it than the impending retirement of Connery, and considerably more than a head-turn away from the realities of a recession-fueled world descending into drabness, though. Indeed, while *Diamonds Are Forever* is nothing if not a reaf- firmation of the franchise's considerable obsession with cars, girls, and gadgets, these familiar conceits disguise social and cultural shifts in the contours of transatlantic society at the time of production that were eventually to come into full force at decade's end. Postindustrialization became a reality as the 1970s progressed. The image of a great British past now lost to progress and instantaneousness would take hold in the minds of many creative people, and what was still vibrant at the time—music, films, culture generally—would be steadily wrapped up in an elegiac nostalgia for past glories. It didn't matter that those signifiers were partly contradictory—the Beatles set against the Sex Pistols, James Bond pitted against Harry Palmer—for they amounted to one thing nationally: influence on the world stage.

When Margaret Thatcher came to power at the 1979 General Election, she put much of her political energies into a plan for recovering influence so as to convey, in her eyes at least, success. By then, Bond's ability to spot social trends and reflect on current political and cultural tastes had long since waned. But before all that *Diamonds Are Forever* implied more than decline and hinted at realignments to come that the Thatcher years in Britain and the Reagan revolution in America would enthusiastically incorporate.

Bond Britannia

As Dominic Sandbrook has it, the Bond films after *Diamonds Are Forever* when Roger Moore took over the role were implausible pastiches of a bygone era. They were being made when there was no longer a "place for uncomplicated heroism," and in a franchise that gradually became antiquated and old-fashioned in a comparatively short space of time.[4] Sandbrook's is a tale that has become commonplace in the recollections of British society and culture during the 1970s. Decline and stagnation, grime and decay, the roots of a murky torpor are all around, and the waning of the Bond franchise, after *Live and Let Die* (1973) at least—Moore's first appearance in the 007 role, which dips, however regressively, into Louisiana's Southern bayou milieu with voodoo culture and tarot mysticism all in the mix—reflects on this wider deterioration for all to see.

Alwyn Turner's book *Crisis? What Crisis* (2008) develops the themes of cinematic social compulsion and cultural conditioning still further in contemplating the reaction of the authorities in charge of cinema as well as the government to *A Clockwork Orange* in 1971, released within a few weeks of *Diamonds Are Forever*. Here was the ultimate fracturing of society on screen: disaffected youths losing their moral and ethical compass amid the crumbling hinterland of suburban Britain as McDowell's Alex leads his gang of "droogs" on an ultra-violent rampage across an unspecified future landscape. This was a generation without Bond's sense of duty: least of all did they display any patriotic sentiment toward their nation and its past. The decade's culmination for Turner, as for Sandbrook, was the emergence of punk rock and most especially the rise of the Sex Pistols five years later. In "ironically" utilizing frayed and cut-up images of the Union flag and the Queen, the band seemingly broke the back of a new generation's devotion to the establishment routines of old.[5]

The real irony, however, was that, in their own ways, Bond and the Sex Pistols shared antiestablishment credentials, but these would in time be absorbed into the mainstream commodification of a British culture that likes its brash upstarts, using them ultimately as lightning rods for a particular unifying sensibility. It was hard to tell whether another musical icon of the time, David Bowie, was being sarcastic in his repeated calls through the mid-1970s for a right-wing takeover of the country. Sarcastic or not, such calls neither fell on deaf ears nor absently deferred responsibility from the cultural touchstones of British life who needed to recognize that change was coming.[6] The past was going to be reinvented as a marketing tool for what would eventually become "Cool Britannia" by the 1990s. Bowie's own dystopian contribution at the time even had connotations with the title of the Bond film. But *Diamond Dogs*, his 1974 concept album, envisaged a Britain in the throes of a postapocalyptic nightmare straight from the pages of George Orwell and William Burroughs, whose works were name-checked inspirations on the title track of the album and the song "1984."

Bowie was always good at reinvention, as countless critics observed throughout his career. He also saw how branding was starting to work and where it would most likely be appropriated to signify style or substance, whether that was a whole new invention or a reclaiming of previous attributes designed to fascinate and placate the masses. On screen, Bond had begun as a classic brand associated with luxury names such as Aston Martin and Martini, and was forever consolidating a timeless British type. In *Diamonds Are Forever*, however, Bond commandeers a Triumph Stag. It's meant to signal a contemporary relevance for splendid British engineering as the nation entered the unlimited prospects of the 1970s. He picks up the car at Dover after beginning his tracking of South African diamonds being offloaded on the Dutch market with a trail of dead bodies in their wake. He then travels to Calais on the British-invented, state-of-the-art Hovercraft, run by Seaspeed at the time (figure 7.1) before presumably driving the 225 miles in Triumph's Italian-styled convertible to Amsterdam.

Once arrived, Bond swings the Stag through the narrow streets and over the waterways of Amsterdam. Both the car and hovercraft therefore offer a keen sense of the early 1970s drive for innovation without any of the class of Bond's Aston Martin heritage. And so, while both capture what is meant to be a spirited new age, their subsequent reliability problems and failure to turn profits simply stopped the British economy in its tracks.[7] Indeed, their example served

Figure 7.1 Bond (Sean Connery) directs his Triumph Stag toward the Seaspeed hovercraft at Dover. *Diamonds Are Forever* (1971).

to reinforce the Thatcherite shift to leanness, efficiency, and a postindustrial service marketplace a decade later. These brands were, in other words, of their time but also pointing toward a sociocultural realignment by the end of the decade that began rejecting clunky British-made machinery in favor of European and Japanese reliability and practicality.

Illusory America

If the era's music scene at home was alive to rampaging social critique from glam rock to punk that hinted at Bond's increasingly anachronistic tone, and British production and engineering was about to be plagued by a capriciousness that questioned Bond's travel plans, then Las Vegas as a playground for the rich and famous was heading for a similar reckoning. The city's future is glimpsed in *Diamonds Are Forever* through Willard Whyte's brand new "Whyte House" hotel complex, with its towering façade looking over an imposing concourse entrance. Welcoming, spacious, and as manicured as the well-to-do suburbs of Los Angeles and Palm Springs from whence the new patrons of the city would spring, those locations are also the jumping-off spots that Bond passes through on his way to Nevada early in the film. By inserting a magnate character into the story, the producers were also taking liberties with the real billionaire rivalry going on at the time. The Las Vegas Hilton is the stand-in for the Whyte House—although a backdrop soaring façade that wasn't there is added in Ken Adam's design—and was at the time of its opening, only two years before filming, the tallest structure in Las Vegas. But the hotel's enviable modernism was the brainchild of Kirk Kerkorian, a rival to Howard Hughes. Hughes attempted to hinder and then halt Kerkorian's plans for the complex. Failing in that plot, Hughes ended up, in a fit of pique, buying the unfinished Landmark Hotel across the street and opening it before the Hilton, or International as it was then commonly known, had a chance to unlock its doors.[8] Having a Hughes impersonator inhabit his rival's casino in the film was at the very least, then, a tongue-in-cheek maneuver by the producers and writers Richard Maibaum and Tom Mankiewicz that hinted at the past and future colliding.

In any case, this skeleton blueprint of impending alteration is heavily contrasted against the gaudy chaos of the indoor circus scene in the middle of the movie, where Tiffany Case (Jill St. John) is followed by government agents as she attempts to retrieve the real diamonds that Bond—impersonating businessman Peter Franks—has secreted as insurance to find out who is siphoning off the precious stones for their own profit. Las Vegas in these scenes is a threatening place, as angular and hideously distorted as the hall of mirrors where Tiffany stops to check who is following her. Trapeze artists fly above patrons who are eating chicken-in-a-basket. Showgirls dance and parade with little modesty. Even the young kids at the shooting gallery where Tiffany picks up the diamonds are really in it only for the prizes rather than the fun.

This backdrop might contrast Bond (class) with Vegas (crass), but a relationship with the United States more generally had already been steadily cultivated in several films leading up to *Diamonds Are Forever*, notably *Goldfinger* (1964). Scholars such as Willmetts believe this is because Bond was just "so much more American; consumerist, individual and emblematic of a frontier spirit."[9] He's "almost a surrogate American hero," James Chapman reminds us when he refers to the next film, *Live and Let Die*.[10] Lisa Funnell and Klaus Dodds are at pains to stress, however, that while Fleming's novels as well as the films admire the United States, "there are also traces of disgust and displeasure at consumer culture, criminality, and currency." They argue for Bond's being "uncomfortable in urban America," which is often apparent, though it's noticeable that Las Vegas's illusory urbanism in *Diamonds Are Forever* is something he embraces, even if it is a somewhat British, white dinner-jacketed manner of wry appreciation and awareness.[11]

Connery is helped in his cultivation of the U.S. landscape and appeal to the country's cinemagoers by Jill St. John, an actor who was no stranger to espionage thrillers, having previously starred in the made-for-TV dramas *The Spy Killer* (ABC, 1969) and its sequel, *Foreign Exchange* (ABC, 1970). Both were made with director Roy Ward Baker and the latter, about Russian spies in London, nurtured St. John's transatlantic appeal (figure 7.2). Becoming the first American "Bond girl," Tiffany is far more street-savvy and brash than previous occupants of the role, her emerging independence meant to be cognizant of the times. She neglects to wear much in the way of clothes at times, for sure, but her hairstyle and fashion sense when it does appear has her at odds with the more overtly

Figure 7.2 Tiffany Case (Jill St. John) with Bond (Sean Connery). *Diamonds Are Forever* (1971).

sexualized Plenty O'Toole (Lana Wood), whom Bond meets at a craps table. Plenty is all long flowing hair, cocktail dress with plunging neckline, and obvious pick-up lines that nearly land her in bed with Bond within an hour of meeting him. In the famous scene that has her thrown out of Bond's hotel window into the swimming pool below her disposability is made clear. Tiffany's ability to play both sides against the middle in her fight to survive forces bigger than she is thus remains a different take on a Bond accomplice to that point.

But it wasn't just St. John's crossover appeal that meant Bond maintained a healthy fan base in the States, with his cultivated Englishness and inverted snobbery. American cinema was already recalibrating its appeal, having flirted with the countercultural milieu in movies such as *Easy Rider* (1969) and *Two-Lane Blacktop* (1971). The New Hollywood scene had plenty of mileage left in it, but Steven Spielberg, George Lucas, and other emerging talents were looking toward a commercial renaissance (which the 1980s would see come to fruition) rather than the socially challenging hippie cinema of Dennis Hopper and Monte Hellman.[12] *Diamonds Are Forever* fit into a cinematic conservatism for wholesome fun, battling countercultural influence and bleaker social critique alongside popular box-office hits in 1971 such as *Fiddler on the Roof* and *Bedknobs and Broomsticks*.

Cold War imagery and histrionics are not as prominent in *Diamonds Are Forever* as in other Bond films to that point, but the character's American persona is still heightened in this regard, helped by the return of Connery to the role. Indeed, as David Talbot outlines in his biography of Canadian spy William Stephenson, "Britain's point man in the underground war against Nazis in America" during World War II was just the sort of polished operator in the shadows who nevertheless managed to maintain a healthy appetite for the cocktail party circuit. It was there that he met Ian Fleming, who was based in Naval Intelligence. Stephenson's larger-than-life character was such that he influenced Fleming to give his developing fictional spy something of his own suave persona.[13] George Lazenby had captured Stephenson's brooding presence in the previous film, *On Her Majesty's Secret Service* (1969), and *Diamonds Are Forever* picks up on Lazenby's sole appearance as Bond by giving Connery's portrayal a slightly more mature transatlantic edge than on earlier occasions. The preceding film's storyline is pursued, too, but only insofar as Bond reengages in his personal mission to hunt down and kill Blofeld as head of SPECTRE, seeking revenge for the assassination of his new wife, Tracy (Diana Rigg), at the conclusion of *On Her Majesty's Secret Service*

Certainly the Cold War would resurface—though increasingly incongruously during Roger Moore's stint as Bond—but the Connery Bond movies, even allowing for Lazenby's intervention in the more serious-minded *On Her Majesty's Secret Service*, seemed to epitomize the way the world worked as the immediate postwar era gave way to the later years of the century. How else could it possibly function? Money bought power and villains had unimaginable wealth. Some hazy rejection of what by the end of the 1960s seemed the unending certainties of a bipolar Cold War future is often brought to the fore as a reason for altering the balance of world authority in favor of a Blofeld, a Goldfinger (Gert Fröbe), or an Emilio Largo (Adolfo Celi). Bond thinks he has disposed of Blofeld in *Diamonds Are Forever*, only to discover that he has slain a double. But in any case, the film seems to suggest, the world was already learning that there were plenty of other tyrants to go round, some masquerading as statesman in a world order that we only later discovered helped end the Cold War and then, in typical Bond fashion, made the planet a much more dangerous place.

Pleasant Little Country

Some critics see Bond going so far as to be in the business of single-handedly saving Britain's reputation globally as decolonization and deindustrialization became realities for the country's postwar worldview.[14] Historian David Kynaston even anticipates the rise of Britain as tea-towel souvenir state by referring to Ian Fleming's own cynicism about the condition of the nation at large. An American character in one of the early 1960s novels, *For Your Eyes Only* (a Roger Moore–era adaptation in 1981) referenced England as a "pleasant little country . . . a place to see old buildings and the Queen," ripe for the tourist markets opening up in the decade that wanted to see London in all its finery but broken as a world power.[15]

Diamonds Are Forever, then, through its personalities, settings, plot, and cinematically cultural framing, is a film that seems to be living in the past, but that is in fact prophesizing the future. The politics of the approaching Thatcher/Reagan years, the sociocultural moves for Las Vegas away from seedy associations with racketeering and organized crime toward more family-oriented entertainment, and gender dynamics that see female antagonists tackle Bond in a somewhat more progressive manner than had hitherto been seen, are all hints of what is to come. Mostly, though, *Diamonds Are Forever* anticipates the franchise's move toward offering Bond and British culture as commercial and corporate entities ripe for exploitation. Product names were not new to Bond, but a different sort of branding begins its inexorable rise not just in this film, but in the wider marketplace, where status and possession became equally as important as integrity and reputation in the "greed-is-good" 1980s. This branding is less in service to the economic welfare of the state than it is barter: material culture objects bought and sold signaling the commodification of British life that would take hold in the conservative New Right economic landscape of the later 1970s and across the succeeding decades.

Transatlantically, James Bond was passing through a cultural as well as cinematic screen test of sorts at the start of the 1970s. His persona suddenly looked pale in comparison to the edgy estuary English of Caine, McDowell, and John Hurt in *Get Carter*, *A Clockwork Orange*, or even *10 Rillington Place* (1971). But in reality, *Diamonds Are Forever* was bypassing the conflagrations at the heart of British and American life in the 1970s and already signaling a sociocultural intent about to reach its full political maturity in the elections of Thatcher and Reagan, only eighteen months apart at the turn of the 1980s.

Bond might have felt equally alienated from the seedier detritus of U.S. inner cities and the concreted council estates on the edge of urban spaces that later 1960s and '70s "progress" was throwing up in Britain. But there were already signs Bond would find his way in the next era: the Moore, Timothy Dalton, and even Pierce Brosnan incarnations of Bond that would sell the spy's patriotic and classical soul for brands as accessible as Seiko (rather than Rolex), Minolta, Pepsi, 7-Up, and eventually BMW. Even the British car market gave way to its European sophisticates in the 1990s and early 2000s, and Bond swanning about in BMW's Z3 convertible only served to signal attainment for the multitudes and social position for the upwardly mobile. It was in its own way Bond's more reliable, German-engineered equivalent of the Triumph Stag from two decades earlier. Late-era Brosnan and most certainly the Bond reboot with Daniel Craig and director Sam Mendes reclaimed the classical styling, and the Aston Martin DB5, but only as symbols of the bulldog spirit, like the Royal Doulton figure Judi Dench's M gives Bond in *Skyfall* (2012). The porcelain bulldog serves as a figurative posting of British popular culture's shift over the course of forty years from mercantile to marketing.

Scholars such as Steven Thomas see this branding process's apotheosis in Bond's immersion into globalization in the 1990s and 2000s. No other movie character has given us such a singular mirror reflection on the state of the world across more than sixty years, thinks Thomas. And while this "floating signifier" contributed to all manner of contradictory ideologies and social anxieties that were considerably more complex than the films suggested, he argues, they nevertheless served to displace potential social antagonisms that might otherwise have surfaced more pronounceably in the Reagan and Thatcher years.[16]

Diamonds Are Forever might have been a last hurrah for Connery's "classic" Bond and old-time Las Vegas, but it was also a chimera distracting from the times and prophesying a brighter, if transparent, future for Bond Britannia Ltd. It was therefore the beginning of trademark Bond, the sellable commodity that could divert attention from all other things and on which the country, and the franchise, began trading for fifty years after this film.

Notes

1. James Chapman, *Licence to Thrill: A Cultural History of the James Bond Films*, 2nd ed. (London: I. B. Tauris, 2008), 217.
2. Simon Willmetts, *In Secrecy's Shadow: The OSS and the CIA in Hollywood Cinema, 1941–1979* (Edinburgh: Edinburgh University Press, 2017), 11–12.
3. See "*Diamonds are Forever*: Deleted Scenes," Universal Exports, www.universalexports .net/Movies/diamonds-deleted.shtml#slideshow2, accessed July 5, 2022.
4. Dominic Sandbrook, *Seasons in the Sun: The Battle for Britain, 1974–1979* (London: Penguin, 2013), 86.
5. Alwyn W. Turner, *Crisis? What Crisis? Britain in the 1970s* (London: Aurum, 2008), 162–63.
6. Andy Beckett, *When the Lights Went Out: What Really Happened to Britain in the Seventies* (London: Faber and Faber, 2010), 178.
7. Dominic Sandbrook, *State of Emergency: Britain, 1970–1974* (London: Penguin, 2020), 97–98.
8. Jonathan Kandell, "Kirk Kerkorian, Billionaire Investor in Film Studios and Casinos, Dies at 98," *New York Times*, June 16, 2015, www.nytimes.com/2015/06/17/business/kirk -kerkorian-billionaire-investor-in-film-studios-and-casinos-dies-at-98.html.
9. Willmetts, *In Secrecy's Shadow*, 194.
10. James Chapman, "James Bond and the End of Empire," in *James Bond Uncovered: Palgrave Studies in Adaptation and Visual Culture*, ed. Jeremy Strong (London: Palgrave, 2018), 217.
11. Lisa Funnell and Klaus Dodds, *Geographies, Genders, and Geopolitics of James Bond* (London: Palgrave, 2017), 6–7.
12. David Hepworth, *1971: Never a Dull Moment* (London: Black Swan, 2017), 366–67.
13. David Talbot, *The Devil's Chessboard: Allen Dulles, the CIA, and the Rise of America's Secret Government* (New York: HarperCollins, 2015), 21–22.

14. "One man [Bond] silently maintained the country's reputation," says Simon Winder in his study of the spy, quoted in David Kynaston, *Modernity Britain, 1957–1962* (London: Bloomsbury, 2015), 123.

15. Kynaston, *Modernity Britain*, 405.

16. Steven W. Thomas, "The New James Bond and Globalization Theory, Inside and Out," *CineAction*, Winter 2009, 32–39.

CHAPTER 8

FROM HARLEM TO SAN MONIQUE

Spatial Dichotomies, Voodoo, and Cultural Identity in
Live and Let Die (1973)

FRAN PHEASANT-KELLY

U mberto Eco (2009) contends that a series of oppositions structure Ian Fleming's Bond novels. These binaries are principally
relevant to the characterization of James Bond, either in relation
to other characters or the qualities with which they are respectively associated.
In this regard, Eco recounts, Fleming's villains often have some physical anomaly, which is generally replicated in film adaptations of the novels. Eco further
states that "there is also a racial quality common to all Villains, along with other
characteristics . . . Usually, he is of mixed blood and his origins are complex and
obscure. He is asexual or homosexual or at any rate is not sexually normal."[1]
Mr. Big, alias Dr. Kananga (Yaphet Kotto), the villainous antagonist of Guy
Hamilton's film version of *Live and Let Die* (1973), varies somewhat from Eco's
account, other than the fact that he is Black, since he does not have any obvious anomaly. Indeed, all the villainous characters of the film are African Americans, partly reflecting the popularity of blaxploitation films at that time,
while there are allusions to Black cultural identity through scenarios involving voodoo rituals and jazz funerals. This aspect is a central point for previous
scholarship on the film, which frequently highlights potentially racist issues
regarding the stereotyping of Black characters, although, as James Chapman
concludes, "In hindsight, *Live and Let Die* seems less offensively racist than it
does merely dated . . . [T]he stupidity of the black villains. . . . is perfectly in line
with the characterisation of villains in other Bond movies, and indeed in popular action cinema generally. In other words, they are stupid because they are
villains, not because they are black."[2]

The film revolves around Bond's investigation of the deaths of three MI6 agents in New York, New Orleans, and a fictional Caribbean island, San Monique. It transpires that the agents have been assassinated by associates of Kananga, San Monique's president and its representative at a United Nations summit. However, Kananga is also a drug dealer who operates in New York City's Harlem as Mr. Big, the plot of the film revolving around his heroin operation. We learn that the operation is protected by the voodoo threat of Baron Samedi (Geoffrey Holder), one of Kananga's henchmen, and that Kananga plans to distribute the heroin through a chain of Fillet of Soul restaurants. Notably, the key locations of Harlem, New Orleans, and a fictionalized version of Jamaica are associated with Black cultural history and identity and are distinctive in the ways that they are represented, namely as sites of criminal activity.

This chapter therefore broadens Eco's influential binaristic model to argue that in *Live and Let Die* otherness extends beyond characterization and intriguingly manifests in settings and spaces, as well as in certain of the film's tropes (such as the tension between voodoo supernaturalism and technology). The claim accords with David Sibley's contention that "[f]eelings about others, people marked as different, may also be associated with places." Sibley develops this premise to suggest that such a connection "applies also to stereotypes of the other which assume negative or positive qualities according to whether the stereotyped individual or group is 'in place' or 'out of place.'"[3] On initial inquiry, *Live and Let Die* seems to correspond to such a juxtaposition in its alignment of abject, disorderly spaces with Black characters and criminality, and conversely, opulent spaces and orderliness with white male characters (specifically Bond). Employing Eco's model of binary structures, as well as Sibley's concept of spatial exclusion, the chapter textually analyzes the film's various dichotomies of space as they relate to class, gender, race, and cultural identity. While the primary suggestion is that the binary oppositions that structure characterization are spatially echoed, a concurrent complexity in this juxtaposition sees certain locations reflecting cultural histories and identities, which, like the criminal antagonists that tend to inhabit them, are more nuanced than straightforward oppositions might suggest. Overall, therefore, a spatial analysis that reflects on characterization tends to challenge claims of racism.

The Spaces of *Live and Let Die*

This analysis contributes to limited literature on spaces related to the Bond series, one exception being Lisa Funnell and Klaus Dodds' 2017 study of the films' various geographies. However, the authors do not consider these topographies in terms of Fleming's oppositions more broadly, nor as they manifest in *Live and Let Die*. Rather, in relation to the latter, they briefly mention Jamaica as a frequent location in Fleming's novels and observe that "not only are portions of the film set in New York and New Orleans, but the film taps into some of the conventions and aesthetics featured in American Blaxploitation films." Funnell and Dodds go on to comment that "Bond is shown to be out of place in urban America in a manner that is quite different to his experiences of being a white British man in the Caribbean."[4] So, too, does James Chapman refer to Bond as being "out of place" in *Live and Let Die* and identifies "an uneasy tension within the film between the use of [blaxploitation] themes and motifs on the one hand and the stereotyped representation of black characters as villains on the other."[5]

By contrast, Daniel McClure engages more definitively with place and space and argues that "the reverberation from British colonialism and white supremacist thought continued haunting English-speaking popular culture at the dawn of the 1970s. . . . *Live and Let Die* . . . set the infamous secret agent against the criminal activity of the Jamaican-Harlem villain, Dr. Kananga (Yaphet Kotto). The film revolved around the notion of black urban criminality combined with the Caribbean island imagery of voodoo. Both notions combined precisely at the same moment, in the early 1970s, when white British anxiety toward black migrants to Great Britain gained momentum."[6] McClure therefore focuses on the clearly relevant sociocultural and political zeitgeist of the film's production. However, *Live and Let Die* also achieves its spatial dynamic by both building on and then consciously disrupting the binary tropes established in Fleming's novels. The film accomplishes this through two avenues: the association of certain spaces with otherness and cultural identity and thematic oppositions related to characterization.

Other People, Other Spaces: Theorizing Otherness

Eco's survey of Fleming's novels details fourteen such binary oppositions, principally in relation to characterization but also concerning certain sets of values. These dichotomies, four of which relate to characters and the rest to values "personified by the four basic characters," include: Bond–M; Bond–Villain; Villain–Woman; Woman–Bond; Free World–Soviet Union; Great Britain–Non-Anglo-Saxon Countries; Duty–Sacrifice; Cupidity–Ideals; Love–Death; Chance–Planning; Luxury–Discomfort; Excess–Moderation; Perversion–Innocence; and Loyalty–Disloyalty.[7] As is evident, space and place are included in this taxonomy, although these are broad conceptualizations associated with nations and ideology rather than exact settings and, while they do relate to characterization and otherness, Eco does not elaborate upon them in terms of specific narratives.

In the case of *Live and Let Die*, the spaces occupied by Bond's adversaries generally display qualities that conform to Sibley's application of abjection, whereby "The sense of border between the self and other is echoed in both social and spatial boundaries." Ostensibly, Sibley correlates identity to space, noting that "both space and society are implicated in the construction of the boundaries of the self but . . . the self is also projected onto society and onto space." He subsequently refers to "border crossings" as those points where "crossing boundaries, from a familiar space to an alien one which is under the control of someone else, can provide anxious moments; in some circumstances it could be fatal, or it might be an exhilarating experience—the thrill of transgression." It is at the point of crossover that such threat is most potent. Sibley identifies such zones as liminal zones or zones of abjection. He notes that "images of 'other' people and 'other' places . . . are combined in the construction of belonging and exclusion, from the global to the local. . . . The imagery of defilement, which locates people on the margins or in residual spaces and social categories, is now more likely to be applied to 'imperfect people' . . . a list of 'others' including the mentally disabled, the homeless, prostitutes and some racialized minorities."[8] In a related vein, the organization of various social spaces in *Live and Let Die* correlates with certain groups and appears to follow a number of earlier films concerned with white domination in society, which, as Richard Dyer puts it, "associate whiteness with order, rationality, rigidity, qualities brought about by contrast with black disorder, irrationality and looseness."[9] However, at times, the film's spatial binaries also subvert such notions and, in this sense, disrupt Black stereotypes and challenge racist claims.

Spatial Dichotomies, Characterization, and Cultural Difference in *Live and Let Die*

The centrality of space, place, and associated cultural identity is signalled from the outset, with the murders of agents at a United Nations meeting taking place in New York, a funeral procession occurring in New Orleans, and in San Monique within the opening five minutes. These sequences quickly establish the aforementioned oppositions identified by Dyer in respect to characterization and in relation to liminal spaces as described by Sibley. Indeed, locations are important signifiers in the film, with New Orleans in particular having specific connotations; Owen Robinson describes the city as "the head-quarters of death" in view of its "rich and often discussed tradition of zombie imagery and mythology, tied in with its voodoo heritage."[10]

In the opening United Nations sequence, the camera zooms in from an establishing exterior panoramic shot of the skyline before cutting to the UN building's interior. Here, the delegates (all male) are seated uniformly around a semicircular plinth, each delegate labelled with the country that they are representing and linked to headphones through which translation takes place. (The UK representative, Dawes, is assassinated via the headphones, although the mechanism for this is not explained.) In short, the setting has an orderly arrangement. The second assassination occurs in New Orleans. Even though in reality the city center has a skyline similar to New York's, the scene unfolds at street level and instead exploits the city's associations with African American culture through a Black funeral procession headed by a jazz band. The procession is watched by Hamilton, the second MI6 agent soon to be assassinated, as he surveys a local restaurant named Fillet of Soul (the chain run by Kananga, the name of which signals a reference to Black music). As the coffin-bearers pass Hamilton, another bystander stabs him, the procession then suddenly transforming into an animated, lively affair with colorful feather umbrellas and upbeat music in a modified interpretation of the jazz funeral (figure 8.1). Tashel Bordere explains that typically, the jazz funeral comprises "a small band, family members and friends of the deceased, and a 'second-line' or people passing in the street, who desire to participate. The band plays upbeat music, moving the crowd to a dance-like strut."[11] Here, however, the implication is that the entire (Black) group participates in the murder.

A long shot of the dancing crowd cuts immediately to a parallel scene of wildly cavorting bodies in a voodoo ritual on San Monique in which a third agent, Baines, is tied up between two stakes and fatally attacked with a venomous snake. The sequence opens with an extreme long shot, framing the ritualistic activities of the group, all of whom are again Black, and several of whom are dressed in exotic costume. As McClure points out, "Alongside black urban

Figure 8.1 The New Orleans jazz funeral. *Live and Let Die* (1973).

criminality, *Live and Let Die* resuscitates the nineteenth-century imperialist binary of civilization and savagery, as well as the role gender plays in coding white supremacy. The first part of this system is the use of the occult . . . [which] helps reinforce the audiences' identification of the black characters with images of a 'savage' Africa and its inverse relation to white civilization."[12] This is to some extent because of the way that popular culture mediates voodoo, which Adam McGee describes as an "imagined religion" that moves away from its Haitian Voudou origins to serve "as a venue for the expression of more-or-less undiluted racial anxieties, manifested in lurid fantasies about black peoples."[13] These latter two events therefore appear to manipulate various aspects of Black cultural traditions and tie them to criminality/savagery.

Thereafter, the film begins to adopt the more typical features of a Bond adventure, opening with a close-up of a young, semiclad female agent in bed with James Bond (Roger Moore), who is awakened by M (Bernard Lee), head of MI6, to investigate the three murders. Antithetical to the voodoo and New Orleans scenes, Bond's apartment is perhaps the most opulent setting of the entire film, with wood-panelled walls throughout, arched doorways, leather armchairs, oil paintings, brass fittings, and generally formal geometric lines. Here again, place and space reflect characterization. The film then moves to a New York airport, Bond smartly dressed in shirt, tie, and overcoat and carrying a briefcase when his taxi is ambushed en route to the CIA headquarters. The setting at this point typifies New York, with long shots of the skyline and Brooklyn Bridge, the city's grid layout and highly geometric architecture constituting an organized mise-en-scène consistent with Bond's appearance and the earlier apartment scene. These introductory sequences establish a dichotomy of orderly spaces connected with whiteness versus frenzied scenes associated with Black culture and thus seem to conform to both Dyer's and Sibley's claims. However, while the representation of voodoo and the funeral appear to subscribe to a racist agenda, certain characters, including CIA agent Harry Strutter (Lon Satton), MI6 colleague Quarrel (Roy Stewart), Kananga and his fortune teller, Solitaire (Jane Seymour), and the spaces that they occupy do not fall into such clear-cut categories.

Meanwhile, at an MI6 surveillance site in the city, another of Bond's CIA colleagues, Felix Leiter (David Hedison), observes Kananga, together with Solitaire and one of his henchmen, enter the San Monique Embassy. Kananga is as smartly dressed as Bond and the Embassy that he occupies likewise parallels the sophistication of Bond's apartment in its gold-striped wallpaper, mahogany bookcases, and paintings. Inside the embassy, Kananga starts to make a speech before switching seamlessly to a prerecorded message (as a cover and suggesting that he is aware the building is under surveillance) and changing his costume. Two of his henchmen, along with Solitaire, then exit the building through a secret passageway concealed behind a wardrobe, this doubling of spaces reflecting both his dual identity and the polarized spheres in which he and his gang operate. For, unlike Bond, who later (as noted by Chapman), appears highly conspicuous in Harlem, Kananga easily slips between the roles of UN diplomat and drug baron. This fluidity matches the spaces that he inhabits, corresponding to the transgressive qualities described by Sibley as they relate to liminal zones.[14] Such ambiguity of character correlates with the various other spaces of the film that Kananga's gang occupy, which on the one hand appear shady and abject, but on the other house sophisticated technological mechanisms and have an underlying orderliness inconsistent with their outward appearance. Such a pattern begins to emerge when the car that ambushed Bond is traced to a voodoo shop, providing the first site where the smartly dressed spy appears completely out of place. Bond follows a suspicious-looking character (the same one involved in the car ambush) behind a curtain within the shop. Here, a series of passageways leads into an underground carport housing the vehicle associated with Bond's ambush. Bond witnesses Kananga's three colleagues get into another limousine, indicating that the passageway through the back of the wardrobe in the embassy connects to the voodoo shop.

As Bond hails a taxi to follow the limousine, the voodoo shopkeeper reports on his movements by telephone while the camera highlights the driver of a second car also clearly watching Bond: as this is another Black character, one might assume that he too belongs to Kananga's gang. Bond's taxi heads away from the city center, which falls away to the rear of the frame, toward Harlem, where street-level close-ups and medium close-ups of market stalls now foreground the visuals. These scenes, which are distinct in their framing from those of central New York, are also more vibrant and tend to be more disorderly than the city center, again reverberating with the spatial dichotomies previously described. "Can't miss him—it's like following a cue ball," comments the Black character seen tailing Bond, emphasizing how conspicuous the agent appears. This is particularly evident when Bond enters a Fillet of Soul restaurant (narratively connecting the Harlem setting to New Orleans), its flamboyantly dressed Black clientele providing a contrast to his markedly formal "English" disposition. In fact, while Kananga easily evades CIA surveillance, Bond's exact location is known by Kananga's henchmen at every stage, enabled in part by Solitaire, who is able to track his movements precisely via the tarot cards.

In the restaurant, a waiter assigns Bond to a specific booth that suddenly swivels around, revealing another concealed space, eclectic in its combination of white net curtains, white rug, and red-painted brick walls. Here, he encounters Solitaire and Mr. Big, although at this point, the spectator is unaware that Mr. Big and Kananga are the same, both because Mr. Big wears a prosthetic mask and because he adopts the patois of stereotyped blaxploitation characters rather than the formal enunciation typified by Kananga's earlier speech.

For instance, Mr. Big instructs his men to "take this honky out and waste him . . . now." The exterior of the building where Bond is to be "wasted" proves even more abject than its interior, with urban detritus and graffiti-covered ruins littering the mise-en-scène. The setting reflects the associations with otherness in white society indicated by Sibley. For example, Sibley states that "the association between black and dirt, between dirt and disease, emphasizes the threatening quality of blackness."[15] Several extreme long shots dominate the sequence, thereby accentuating the extent of the decrepitude. Bond, wearing leather gloves, looks even more inappropriately located but nonetheless overcomes the two Black characters supposed to "waste" him. He is then stopped by the Black character who has been tailing him. This turns out to be Strutter of the CIA, thereby confounding any association between criminality and race and disrupting the space/character connection implied by the exterior setting.

The film subsequently moves to San Monique, opening with a close-up of grinning voodooist Baron Samedi, who sports a painted face and white top hat, loincloth, and long coat, and performs a wild musical extravaganza alongside other performers, recalling the frenzied scenario of the opening sequence (figure 8.2). Samedi is introduced to the hotel audience as "chief of the legion of the dead, the man who cannot die," reinforcing a supernatural trope, while the performers contort their semiclad bodies into extreme and unusual positions, again providing a marked contrast to Bond's upright stature. In particular, one sequence cuts between a long shot of a besuited Bond carrying a briefcase to one of a seminaked contortionist walking along on his hands, with his legs unnaturally hooked over his shoulders. The entire performance is illuminated

Figure 8.2 Baron Samedi (Geoffrey Holder). *Live and Let Die* (1973).

with flaming torches and projects a tribal, ritualistic tone in keeping with popular cultural representations of voodoo.

While Bond's San Monique hotel room has modest concessions to luxury, it is somewhat lacking the decadence normally associated with the franchise and thus begins to undermine prior connections between whiteness and space. From here, Bond (now looking less conspicuous in denims and open-necked shirt) and Rosie Carver (Gloria Hendry), a CIA agent sent to support him, take a boat to Kananga's mansion. The Black skipper, Quarrel, however, arouses Rosie's suspicions when she discovers a concealed electronic communications system below deck and then, from Rosie's point of view, we see him coiling up a rope behind Bond, as if he is about to strangle him, an implication that is soon disrupted when Rosie aims a gun at Quarrel (although she forgets the safety catch). It transpires that Quarrel is working for MI6, the film thus continually destabilizing racist assumptions concerning links between race and criminality. Gender also plays a part, for Rosie is not only depicted as hysterical through repeated screaming episodes and her inability to handle a gun appropriately, but it emerges that she is working for Kananga.

Like Bond's apartment, Kananga's mansion provides one of the film's most luxurious settings, with exterior golden minarets and conservatory, while inside, it features tasseled curtains, leather-back chairs, and lavish décor. Paradoxically, the mise-en-scène of brightly colored feathers that frames the white character Solitaire (who reads tarot cards for Kananga) and her exotic red costume as the camera cuts from an extreme long shot of the building to its interior, is akin to that linked with Black culture witnessed previously, confounding the tropes suggested above by Sibley and Dyer. This supernatural element crops up further when Rosie and Bond approach Kananga's mansion—first, in Solitaire's reading of the cards and foretelling of Bond's imminent arrival. It also emerges in that the prediction associated with the "lovers" tarot card (which foretells that Bond and Solitaire will be lovers) actually comes to pass, again consolidating the supernatural veracity of the film and notably, that linked to a white English woman. In short, whiteness is linked to irrationality.

Other instances of supernaturalism are, conversely, often underlain by technology. For example, when Bond and Rosie land on San Monique, Rosie appears terrified of a scarecrow, its threat suggested by a rapid zoom to close-up. When Bond shows her a tarot card (delivered anonymously), which he indicates is that of a "deceitful perverse woman"—suggesting that he too seems to believe in the cards—she flees but is shot, the gunfire coming from one of a series of scarecrows strategically placed en route to the mansion. In a similar scenario, Bond and Solitaire, while investigating Kananga's heroin operation, later come across Samedi seated on a gravestone, playing a flute, recalling the myth of Pan. Once Bond and Solitaire are out of sight, Samedi then speaks into the "flute," which transpires to be a radio transmitter, again suggesting a juxtaposition of superstition and technology. Later, Bond and Solitaire commandeer an old double-decker bus and are chased by the island police across San Monique. The scene contrasts with the usual Bond car chase scenarios, which mostly feature high-profile cars equipped with elaborate gadgets, and thus once more deviates from prior correlations between whiteness and luxury. The bus also appears entirely incongruous in the Caribbean setting, emphasizing Bond's "out-of-placeness." When they finally rendezvous with Quarrel and escape by boat, Bond reassures an anxious Solitaire that "voodoo land was just poppy fields, a simple matter of heroin smuggling," his comments emptying voodoo still further of its religious origins.

Shortly thereafter, Bond meets Leiter in New Orleans. Just as they discuss locating the local Fillet of Soul restaurant, the scene cuts to a second New Orleans jazz funeral replicating the scenario that opened the film. This time, however, it is Strutter who is watching the restaurant, standing in the same place as Hamilton, his predecessor. The sequence duplicates the camera angles and close-ups of the same characters as previously, thus inviting the spectator to expect a similar outcome. Indeed, this is precisely the case, as the jazz band makes an identical switch in tone, although this time, we do not witness Strutter's demise. Arriving just as the funeral procession livens up, Leiter and Bond enter the restaurant, unaware of Strutter's death. They are invited to sit in a certain booth, but Bond politely requests a table closer to the stage, though this too turns out to be a mistake: the table suddenly descends below ground, Bond again finding himself in oddly furnished underground space. It is here that Mr. Big removes his prosthetic mask to reveal his alter ego, Kananga.

Bond eventually escapes in a speedboat via the Louisiana bayous. To evade Kananga's pursuing henchmen as well as the local police force, he launches the boat over various intervening strips of land. In one case, this involves a neatly mown estate that borders the bayou, where an affluent, middle-class white family are relaxing outside in their garden. His pursuers end up stranded in the family's swimming pool, further suggesting a dichotomy of spaces according to class and race. Here, being "out of place" corresponds not only to the fact that Black criminals find themselves in a speedboat in a private domestic swimming pool, but also because it belongs to a white middle-class family. In another parallel situation, the speedboats plough overland across the rolling lawns of the Treadway estate through an outdoor wedding ceremony. This constant intersection of discordant scenarios translates into the spatial liminality described by Sibley as a source of anxiety and abjection.[16] Such liminal zones, emphasized through the use of long shot, provide opportunities for narrative disorder, while culturally, they signal distinctions between class and race through spatial circumstances.

Elsewhere, for her betrayal of Kananga, Solitaire is subjected to the same voodoo ritual as Hamilton and is likewise strung between two poles with the threat of being poisoned by snake venom. A long shot opens the scene, with frenzied cavorting and ritualistic action as she is carried out and tied up. The tribal leader who attacked Hamilton, dressed in a loincloth and again adorned with a goat's head, picks up a snake and taunts Solitaire. Bond watches from behind a gravestone before the ritual suddenly stops and a figure of what appears to be Baron Samedi begins to rise from a grave. When Bond shoots the figure, it merely shatters despite appearing fully embodied moments earlier. Even though Bond subsequently throws him into a coffin full of venomous snakes, Samedi reappears once more at the end of the film, his return from the dead suggesting that his voodoo origins are authentic rather than merely a cover for criminal activity. When Bond and Solitaire thereafter stand on the spot from where Samedi emerged, they descend into an underground complex by mechanical means and find themselves in an architecturally labyrinthine system of caverns with highly organized sections, illuminated by chandeliers and complete with a monorail system. The two escape by killing Kananga. The film ends with Samedi sitting on the front of the train on which Bond and Solitaire are travelling, reinforcing the film's supernatural aspects.

✳ ✳ ✳

Several scholars have suggested that *Live and Let Die*, which features mostly Black actors as criminals, is racist, although others, such as Chapman, conclude otherwise. However, the narrative is more complex than it initially appears, and extends Eco's binaristic model that he uses to analyze Fleming's original novel. While Eco outlines certain binary oppositions based on characterization and tropes associated with key protagonists, such juxtapositions are reflected in the film's spatial topographies. Especially noticeable is the relationship of rundown places with Black communities and the way that these are filmed, while Bond is conspicuous in almost all the Black cultural settings in which he appears. However, Kananga subverts this opposition in the way that he switches easily between two personae, one a UN delegate and the other a drug baron. This dichotomy is reflected in the way that certain spaces he inhabits also have a dual nature: for example, the opulent embassy connecting through a secret passage to the cult voodoo shop. Each disordered or chaotic space therefore has a concealed technological, more sophisticated aspect. While one might argue that concealed spaces are common across the franchise, here they arise specifically in connection with Black cultural histories and identities. Meanwhile, Dyer's observations are also confounded by the fact that Solitaire, a white English woman, has a heritage of supernatural powers, and that Strutter and Quarrel operate on the side of the law whereas Black female CIA operative Rosie Carver is a go-between for Kananga. At the same time, voodooist Samedi's mystical abilities remain unexplained. The film does not, therefore, serve a racist agenda.

Even though it extends Eco's binaristic model from characters to the spaces that they occupy and the motifs attached to certain characters, there is a fluidity in this interpretation. Kananga in particular exhibits a credible dual nature, resonant with the instabilities of cultural identity. As postcolonial theorist Stuart Hall contends, this is unstable and unfixed because the past "is always constructed through memory, fantasy, narrative, and myth. Cultural identities are the points of identification, the unstable points of identification or suture, which are made, within the discourses of history and culture. Not an essence but a *positioning*. Hence, there is always a politics of identity, a politics of position, which has no absolute guarantee in an unproblematic, transcendental 'law of origin.'"[17] In other words, cultural identity is dynamic and reflects changes in time and space. As McClure notes, this instability corresponds to the contemporaneous zeitgeist of *Live and Let Die*, a period when Black culture became prominent and reflected 1970s radical political shifts and equal rights efforts. A spatial study of the film thus exposes racist assumptions and offers a nuanced reconsideration of Eco's binary analysis of characterization.

Notes

1. Umberto Eco, "Narrative Structures in Fleming," in *The James Bond Phenomenon*, ed. Christoph Lindner (Manchester: Manchester University Press, 2009), 40. Capitals in original.
2. Lisa Funnell and Klaus Dodds, *Geographies, Genders, and Geopolitics of James Bond* (London: Palgrave, 2017); Daniel McClure, "Defining, Re-Defining Colonial Legacies in Film: *Live and Let Die, The Harder They Come*, and the Cultural Geographies of Early 1970s Jamaica," in *James Bond in World and Popular Culture: The Films Are Not Enough*, ed. Robert G. Weiner, B. Lynn Whitfield, and Jack Becker (Newcastle upon Tyne, UK: Cambridge Scholars, 2011), 290–302; Walter Metz, "Breaking the Cycle: *Die Another Day*, Post-Colonialism, and the James Bond Film Series," *ZAA: Zeitschrift und Amerikanistic* 52, no. 1 (2004): 63–77; John Schwetman, "'Ever Heard of Evel Knievel?' James Bond Meets the Rural Sheriff,'" *Cinema Journal* 6, no. 1 (2017): 95–118; James Chapman, *Licence to Thrill: A Cultural History of the James Bond Films* (London: I. B. Tauris, 2007), 143.
3. David Sibley, *Geographies of Exclusion: Society and Difference in the West* (London: Routledge, 1995), 1, 19.
4. Funnell and Dodds, *Geographies, Genders*, 6, 54, 55.
5. Chapman, *Licence to Thrill*, 138.
6. McClure, "Defining, Re-Defining," 291.
7. Eco, "Narrative Structures in Fleming," 36.
8. Sibley, *Geographies of Exclusion*, 33, 86, 32, 33, 69.
9. Richard Dyer, *The Matter of Images: Essays on Representation* (London: Routledge, 2002), 130.
10. Owen Robinson, "'The Head-Quarters of Death': Early Nineteenth-Century New Orleans as Gothic Nexus," in *Tropical Gothic in Literature and Culture*, ed. Justin Edwards and Sandra Guardini Vasconcelos (London: Routledge, 2016), 40–55, 40.

11. Tashel Bordere, "'To Look at Death Another Way': Black Teen Males' Perspectives on Second-Lines and Regular Funerals in New Orleans," *OMEGA* 58, no. 3 (2008): 213–32, 214. For Bordere, "Jazz/musical funerals or second-lines have special significance for African Americans in that they are rooted in ceremonies dating back to the time of slavery and maintain a West African influence in their extravagance."
12. McClure, "Defining, Re-Defining," 295.
13. Adam McGee, "Haitian Vodou and Voodoo: Imagined Religion and Popular Culture," *Studies in Religion* 41, no. 2 (2012): 231–56, 232.
14. Sibley, *Geographies of Exclusion*, 33.
15. Sibley, *Geographies of Exclusion*, 23.
16. Sibley, *Geographies of Exclusion*, 33.
17. Stuart Hall, "Cultural Identity and Diaspora," in *Colonial Discourses and Post-Colonial Theory: A Reader*, ed. Patrick Williams and Laura Chrisman (London: Harvester Wheatsheaf, 1994), 227–37, 226. Italics in original.

CHAPTER 9

"WE ALL GET OUR JOLLIES ONE WAY OR ANOTHER"

The Perversity and Pleasure of Christopher Lee in
The Man with the Golden Gun (1974)

JULIE LOBALZO WRIGHT

Leon Hunt writes that popular accounts of the 1970s generally view the decade as the one "that style/taste forgot" and "an object of pleasurable, kitsch entertainment."[1] Released in 1974, the ninth official film in the James Bond film series, *The Man with the Golden Gun* (hereafter *TMWTGG*), fits this description more than any other Bond film released that decade. Kitsch is visible in the film's first scene through the zooming close-up of assassin Francisco Scaramanga's (Christopher Lee) superfluous third nipple, coming after a dwarf servant carries champagne to his master's lounging spot on a deserted beach populated with wicker Papasan chairs and zebra-print pillows. This takes place *before* the audience sees the inside of Scaramanga's palatial home, with its featured funhouse filled with mirrors, surveillance equipment, and animatronics. The film's energy crisis storyline, a safari-suit-clad Roger Moore suckling on a dancer's bellybutton, and Scaramanga's peculiar home and lifestyle create a Bond film that is quintessentially reflective of the 1970s. As James Chapman has noted, the Bond series was "in transition" in the early 1970s from the return of Sean Connery for *Diamonds Are Forever* (1971) to the establishment of Roger Moore as the new Bond in *Live and Let Die* (1973). The relative success of *Live and Let Die* meant that the next Bond film was produced and released quickly, with many critics noting how "derivative" *TMWTGG* is of previous Bond films and other popular films of the period.[2]

While this positions the film as one that "taste forgot," the casting of Christopher Lee infuses *TMWTGG* with an importance that its kitschy veneer belies. Quite simply, this is one of the few films in the entire series to feature two culturally significant British actors sparring against one another. Lee's long career rivals that of Moore, who was already a star by the time he began portraying James Bond. Emerging from the horror films of Hammer, a studio and style of filmmaking that have been reclaimed by critics and audiences for their cultural value, Lee's acting reached an admirable new level in the final decades of his life, including his performance as Scaramanga.[3]

Villains have always played an essential role within the Bond series, but as Roy Pierce-Jones notes, they became even more important in the Moore years, as the "lightweight actor" portraying Bond necessitated villains who brought "gravitas" to the films.[4] Scaramanga is frequently included on "Best Bond Villain" lists, with the character cited as one of the bright spots within an otherwise forgettable film in the franchise.[5] This chapter argues for the value of *TMWTGG* mainly through the pleasure of watching Lee. The actor's origins with Hammer horror films helped establish him as a psychosexual aristocratic villain, which legitimizes Scaramanga as the perfect foil to Moore's Bond. Furthermore, Lee's performance style assists with the film's insinuation that Scaramanga and Bond are equal foes.

TMWTGG begins on Scaramanga's island, located somewhere in Chinese seas, where he lives with his servant, Nick Nack (Hervé Villechaize), and mistress, Andrea Anders (Maud Adams). Scaramanga owns a golden gun and is known as one of the world's best assassins. After MI6 receives a golden bullet with "007" etched on it, Bond unofficially tries to find Scaramanga in Macau, Hong Kong, and finally Bangkok. There, he meets Andrea, who informs him that Scaramanga has a solar-powered energy beam that he intends to sell. Bond eventually flies to Scaramanga's island, where he participates in a pistol duel, chasing Scaramanga into his funhouse and killing him. The solar plant is destroyed and Bond escapes on a sailing ship with his assistant, Mary Goodnight (Britt Ekland).

Christopher Lee's enduring career began in 1948, spanned seven decades, and included appearances in three of the biggest franchises in Hollywood history: the *Lord of the Rings* trilogy (2001–2003), the *Star Wars* series (1977–), and the Bond films. While appearing in over two hundred films, he is most known, outside of the franchises mentioned, for the British Hammer films he made between 1957 and 1976, beginning with *The Curse of Frankenstein* (1957). His performance as Count Dracula in *Dracula* (1958) is generally viewed as instrumental in altering the cinematic version of the famous vampire into a darkly sinister and sexual being with bloodstained fangs. Although Lee played other characters in Hammer productions, including Frankenstein's monster, Kharis (a mummified priest), and Sir Henry Baskerville, his portrayal of Dracula is most closely tied to his star image.[6] Hammer was founded in 1934, spending its first two decades as a production, then distribution company before relaunching productions after World War II. In the mid-1950s, the company found success with an adaptation of the BBC Television series *The Quatermass Experiment* (1953), leading to a prioritizing of horror filmmaking, and it became the most dominant horror producer in the business until the mid-1960s. According to biographer Peter Hutchings, the company was proficient in its productions, with "considerable experience of turning round films quickly on small budgets and with limited resources" while also retaining key personnel that worked on numerous productions, offering the films a sense of "continuity."[7]

Continuity is habitually part of the star image through consistency gained in a body of work. This can be achieved by portraying characters that belong to a similar social type or set of types, remaining consistent with previous roles.[8] Some stars appear in a wide variety of genres, whereas others may be associated with a "particular genre at a particular stage of his/her career."[9] Throughout his life, Lee argued that he appeared in many different types of films and genres, suggesting that he was no longer "typecast" after his performance in Billy Wilder's *The Private Life of Sherlock Holmes* (1970).[10] However, the Hammer horror films loom large over Lee's career, leading to a perception that he always portrayed villains.

Part of this stems from genre and star expectations associated with the Hammer films. As film historian Wheeler Winston Dixon puts it, "when an audience sat down to watch a Hammer film, they knew exactly what to expect: a violent, vivid, boldly executed film that pushed the acceptable limits of graphic representationalism, coupled with high production gloss and the presence of the studio's signature stars, Lee and [Peter] Cushing."[11] Repetition is also a component of the Bond film series, with audiences "familiar with the stories, character types and narrative situations of the films, and, moreover, expect[ing] them to recur in each new film."[12] Hammer is a brand, one that, as Matt Hills argues, focuses on nostalgia for the era when Lee worked and on modernization, especially through the rebirth of the company in the mid-2000s.[13] Parallels can again be drawn to the Bond series, with its reliance on familiarity and difference and its desire throughout the series to be both nostalgic and progressive.[14]

Notably, the Moore Bond years have been characterized by Tony Bennett and Janet Woollacott as exploiting a "double referential structure" whereby the films were "renegotiated by referring to new tendencies and developments within popular culture, especially the cinema." Bennett and Woollacott write that by "playing on popular memory by referring to the earlier Bond films and to the more general figure of Bond associated with the 1960s, essentially by means of parody, they [the production team] also selectively activated the established currency of Bond and, in so doing, reorganised its cultural associations by referring to more influential genres within the contemporary cinema—the police fiction movies in *The Man with the Golden Gun*."[15] Therefore, *TMWTGG* features familiar Bond locations, established in the 1960s, such as casinos (in

Casino de Macau), beaches (Scaramanga's beach location in Phang Nga Bay, Thailand, now referred to as "James Bond Island"), and luxury hotels (the Peninsula Hong Kong; the Oriental Hotel). It also references contemporary popular genres, especially kung fu/martial arts (Bruce Lee's films were at their popular peak at this time), and recalls earlier Bond films, markedly observed with the incorporation of Sheriff J. W. Pepper (Clifton James) from *Live and Let Die*, who is, curiously, vacationing in Thailand.

The "double referential structure" can be extended to the casting of Christopher Lee. Pierce-Jones notes that Albert "Cubby" Broccoli's partner Harry Saltzman "knew better than most of the benefit in casting the right actors in the Bond films. Whoever plays Bond is always indebted to the quality of the cast around him."[16] Lee functions within dual expectations in the film as both a Bond villain *and* a horror legend. Bond villains operate as types that help "the reader/viewer disseminate information quickly," with this information relating to both the villain and to Bond himself.[17] The opening of *TMWTGG* establishes Scaramanga's sexual deviancy through the already mentioned zooming shot of his third nipple and the close-up of Andrea, drying his leg with a towel. Andrea demonstrates clear sexual desire for Scaramanga even as she fears him. The deviancy of Bond villains frequently extends to their sexuality, but Lee's horror background intensifies Scaramanga's eroticism. Hammer horror, as Andrew Mangravite suggests, had a "tremendous sense of style" through "psychological and sexual mechanisms at work" in their films.[18] *Dracula* established Lee's psychosexual image through a visual performance that emphasized his costume, tall frame (six feet, five inches), and expressive eyes. Lee's stature meant that Dracula would glide elegantly into a room with his oversized flowing cape accentuating his deliberate movements and easily consume his victims. These are erotically charged scenes that imply women desire Dracula even as he terrifies them.

A similar moment takes place in *TMWTGG* when Scaramanga returns to his sailing ship from the "Bottoms Up" club. He opens the door to the bedroom where Andrea is waiting, naked, under the sheets. Wordlessly, Scaramanga sits on the bed, pulls out his golden gun, points it at Andrea's face, and then moves it toward her bare chest (figure 9.1). She pulls the bedsheet toward her body, looking away in disgust. There is a cut to a close-up of Lee's face, where his expression changes from glee to disappointment, and then a medium close-up of the gun forcefully rubbing Andrea's lips. The score assists the short scene by alternating between romantic string flourishes and more pronounced baritone notes of the theme, exhibiting Scaramanga's conflicting eroticism.

According to Caroline Langhorst, beginning with Lee, Hammer sold its stars as sex symbols owing to their "roguishly villainous" roles that "evoked a mixture of attraction and repulsion in the audience."[19] It was noted by Lee on many occasions how unusual it was, at that point in the series, to portray a Bond

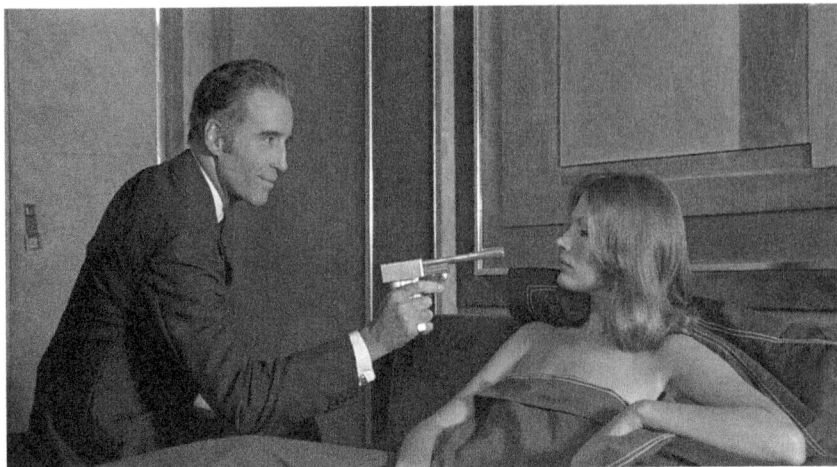

Figure 9.1 An erotically charged moment between Scaramanga (Christopher Lee) and Andrea Anders (Maud Adams). *The Man with the Golden Gun* (1974).

villain who was menacing *and* desirable. This interplay is also present in the aforementioned scene on Scaramanga's ship. When Lee appeared on the British magazine program *Pebble Mill* in 1996, he stated that Scaramanga could be "amusing. He could be entertaining, even to the ladies . . . At the same time, totally lethal."[20] The same can be said, and has been, about James Bond. A connection can be made to villains and James Chapman's argument that the films present "competitive masculinity" through the two extremes of Bond—his puritanism of hard work and his playboy indulgences.[21] Villains generally present the evil side of the good-vs-evil divide, with Bond and his Britishness on the virtuous side. What makes Scaramanga different is his half-English heritage, presenting him as closer to Bond than many previous foes who were broadly marked as "foreign." The Bond series has cast many admired British actors, including Judi Dench and Ralph Fiennes, who both portrayed M in the Daniel Craig films, but British-defined villains are less common, with Jonathan Pryce (*Tomorrow Never Dies* [1997]) and Sean Bean (*Goldeneye* [1995]) being exceptions. Alec Trevelyan, portrayed by Bean, is a worthy adversary for Bond, a former "oo" and friend. However, Scaramanga differs through his unconventional upbringing and the distinction he emphasizes between their two lines of work: Bond's is for "Her Majesty the Queen and a pittance of a pension" while Scaramanga does it for money and pleasure. But, at lunch on his island with Bond, Scaramanga is quick to add, "apart from that, we are the same."

It is evident that Scaramanga admires Bond and "sees himself and Bond as professional equals," even telling Bond that theirs is one of the loneliest professions.[22] Lee's outsized smile and giddy steps as he greets Moore on the beach illustrate that Scaramanga views this visit as a pleasurable one, even though he plans to eventually kill Bond. Both men kill as part of their job, but they also share an enjoyment of the finer things in life. Scaramanga is a gentleman, as evidenced when he pulls out Goodnight's chair for her as they sit down to a lunch served on sterling silver pieces. Sean Connery's working-class background added a roughness to the Bond character, whereas Moore situated the character back into a "comforting national stereotype" of Englishness.[23] This was achieved through Moore's success on the television series *The Saint* (ITV 1962–1968), which established his image as a charming British adventurer known for his quips and fashion style, overlapping with the Bond character type. While he was not from an upper-class background, his speech and demeanor tended toward class connotations of education and privilege. Christopher Lee's family heritage can be traced back to Charles the Great, with his father a lieutenant colonel of the King's Royal Rifle Corps and his mother a countess.

Hammer also aligned Lee with aristocracy. Many of his films took place within grandiose castles and stately homes where characters spoke in the "King's English." Jon Burrows notes that Lee bestowed the Hammer films with "an aristocratic bearing and polished charm," traits also evident in *TMWTGG*.[24] The audience learns that Scaramanga was born into a travelling circus, where he developed as a marksman when he was young and became an assassin for hire in his teenage years. After a stint with the KGB, he left to become an independent assassin who is paid $1 million per kill. This background is not ranked highly within social classes; however, his comradery with Bond identifies Scaramanga as possessing a similar combination of determination and extravagance that has been gained not through family lineage, but hard graft. It is Goodnight who is most out of place during lunch, wearing a bikini and awkwardly attempting small talk while Scaramanga and Bond trade statements/insults. The evidence of Scaramanga's taste is everywhere, from his Le Cordon Bleu–trained servant to the expensive silverware and the wine: Bond remarks that the latter is reminiscent of another wine and Scaramanga insists he add it to his wine cellar.[25]

This is not the type of lunch that would take place between everyday heavies or, indeed, the gangster figures that populate Scaramanga's funhouse. Bond is not being held against his will but being asked to converse about shared experiences while enjoying good food and drink. It is notable that Scaramanga has already formulated how he will kill Bond, not through torture or lasers but in the traditional gentlemanly activity of a duel. Bond even comments that it sounds a "bit old fashioned. I mean, pistols at dawn and that sort of thing."

Scaramanga agrees, stating that this "remains the only true test for gentlemen" (figure 9.2). Robert Murphy writes that Lee's Dracula had more "in common with the sadistic aristocrats played by James Mason in the Gainsborough melodramas than he does with puffy, evil-eyed Bela Lugosi," the Hungarian-born actor who was typecast in classical Hollywood horror films as a villain.[26] Mason, an actor who moved between Britain and America in his career, epitomized in melodramas made at the Gainsborough studio what Adrian Garvey terms the "perverse patriarch," a "deeply transgressive authority figure" who is a charismatic, but dangerous individual.[27] This description accords with many of the Hammer characters Lee portrayed, especially Dracula, who begins *Dracula* as an ideal host, polite and accommodating, showing his guest to his room and even carrying his luggage upstairs. These details indicate good breeding, adhering to an upper-class sensibility for decorum, but there is transgression and perversion underneath this projection of gentility. Other Bond villains have also hosted Bond at a dinner table, but Scaramanga differs in his amiable demeanor, his comfort in the situation, and Bond's reactions to him, which includes the polite insistence that they finish the "delicious lunch" that Nick Nack has prepared for them.

Scaramanga carries himself as a gentleman, wearing an impeccable white suit when he meets Bond at the Thai boxing match and proceeds to coolly tell him, "Don't try to follow me," with an added "please" to this friendly command. The final outfit that Lee wears in *TMWTGG* (see figure 9.2) is, as noted by Llewella Chapman, a "pale blue tropical outfit made from a lightweight cotton fabric" that is "cut loose" in order to "drape over Lee's frame."[28] This clothing

Figure 9.2 "Pistols at dawn" between Scaramanga (Christopher Lee) and Bond (Roger Moore). *The Man with the Golden Gun* (1974).

further aligns Scaramanga with Bond, not only through the similar shapes to Bond's clothing in the film, but in that Scaramanga, like Bond, reflects contemporary taste in fashion. This final outfit mirrors the safari-style suit jackets and shirts Moore wears throughout the film (the first time the actor does so as Bond).[29] It is significant that many of the Bond villains are not fashionable, generally appearing in clothing that could be mistaken for uniforms, especially solid-colored Nehru jackets in tan, grey, or navy blue. Nehru jackets were popular in the 1960s and 1970s, but the patterned or brightly colored flourishes that made them popular with other pop-cultural figures in the 1960s, such as the Beatles, were removed for the Bond villains. The affluence and conspicuous consumption of 1960s Bond is echoed in Scaramanga's dandyism. Similar to Bond and Scaramanga, the dandy is a figure who is able to be well-dressed because of his "funds, taste and knowledge." The "golden gun" that Scaramanga uses is also representative of his good taste, as Monica Germanà points out, his gun is made from "gentleman's accessories": a pen, cufflinks, and cigarette case, all items Bond regularly uses, too.[30]

Sexuality is tied to the dandy and gentleman figures, with "effeminacy" brought into focus especially in the late nineteenth century through the figure of Oscar Wilde.[31] While the most recent portrayal of Bond by Daniel Craig can be viewed as bisexual or pansexual (as elegantly argued by Elizabeth J. Nielsen), Bond's sexuality is generally endorsed as heterosexual, with villains exhibiting more "queer" tendencies.[32] The novel by Ian Fleming hints that Scaramanga is homosexual, whereas the film removes any suggestions of homosexuality. However, there is a perversity to him that emerges from Lee's background in Hammer films and corresponds to the Bond series. By the 1970s there was, as Leon Hunt argues, a "trickle-down permissiveness" in British popular culture, exhibited through horror and sexploitation films and "youthsploitation" fiction.[33] The Bond films can be viewed through this lens because of the outlandishness of the Moore films. It would be difficult to argue that *TMWTGG* presents more indulgences or deviant behaviors than do other films in the franchise. However, it offers a concerted effort to move away from some of the "realism" of *Live and Let Die* exhibited through the New York City locations. Scaramanga's "funhouse" is an important space to illustrate that, while Scaramanga has transformed himself into a refined man through his wealth, he has not completely left his circus background behind. The "funhouse" bookends the film, presenting Scaramanga as not just a competitor driven by ego, but also a man who lives in a house with many mirrors, video cameras, and location sets. While this is unusual, the fact that he is watched by his servant through television screens adds voyeurism and perversity to the situation (as does Nick Nack's commentary when Scaramanga is in the "funhouse"). Furthermore, Andrea alludes to Scaramanga's peculiarities when Bond interrogates her in her hotel room, never quite verbalizing the type of relationship she has with him and

commenting that he is "not like other men" in an effort to describe his "distinctive" physical feature. Andrea later tells Bond that Scaramanga is a "monster."

Camp is also intertwined with both the Bond series and sexuality, especially
nonheteronormative representations of sexuality. While it is notoriously difficult to define "camp," *TMWTGG* can be viewed as camp through its seriousness and exaggeration, but also its "breezy quality." In fact, Rob Faunce argues
that "much is campy in the Bond film series."[34] The Moore films were, according to Robert Shail, presented as "escapist" films at a time when there were various social and economic declines as opposed to the aspirational Connery
films in the 1960s. The Moore films are self-deprecating, "self-conscious," and
"camp" through their "knowingness" and "jokiness."[35] I would add, however,
that while these terms are relevant to Bond/Moore, Scaramanga/Lee is deadly
serious.

Lee is part of a tradition of British male actors hired to portray villains in
Hollywood films and to do so seriously. Andrew Spicer has written about these
actors "acting nasty" and while it is debatable if we can consider the Bond films
as British or Hollywood products, Spicer's observations are relevant to Lee.[36] At
least to American ears, the upper-class English accent connotes arrogance, snobbery, emotional repression, and deviancy. Therefore, as Spicer argues, many
British male actors portray "troubled or damaged men with deep-seated emotional and psychological problems" that indicate "authority" and "gravitas."[37]
Scaramanga is an equal foe to Bond because of his marksmanship and Lee's
earnest portrayal, especially in contrast with Moore's smirks and quips. Building on his work at Hammer, Lee's performance style is not confined to purely
his voice, which was described by Moore as "operatic," but utilizes his entire
body.[38] There is, as Spicer notes, a broad way that Lee performs that incorporates
impactful gestures with a "regal presence" when he is onscreen.[39] Lee's size is
an asset, as are long flowing capes worn when portraying Dracula, Saruman in
the *Lord of the Rings* trilogy, or Count Dooku in the *Star Wars* series. *TMWTGG*
demonstrates how he is able to "dominate and control space" through movements that are emphasized as opposed to words, such as when he rubs the gun
on Andrea's face or the ease with which he moves around his plant, gleefully
flaunting his various contraptions to Bond.[40] His body is not hidden as was
the case with Blofeld in *From Russia with Love* (1963) and *Thunderball* (1965),
nor are Scaramanga's movements stilted like Doctor Julius No in *Dr. No* (1962)
or overly flamboyant as seen with Raoul Silva in *Skyfall* (2012). This is a performance that emerges from Lee's commitment to material and his ability to
elevate performances through his understated but dynamic style.

This performance style is interrelated with Lee's long career in cult *and*
mainstream films. Matt Hills has examined Lee's association with cult film
stardom, arguing that some films may be "cult" without its "lead actors becoming 'cult stars.'"[41] While Lee has achieved cult status through Hammer and his

performance as Lord Summerisle in *The Wicker Man* (1973), he is a mainstream star widely known for many of the films he appeared in the 2000s, including five Tim Burton features. This duality carries over to his role in *TMWTGG* as the dark side of Bond. Scaramanga is, as Tom Mankiewicz wrote in the first draft of the screenplay, "a super-villain of the stature of Bond himself."[42] In the Bond universe, it is possible to embody contradictions. In fact, Matthew Freeman notes that Bond media outside of the films frequently include narratives that contradict established Bond narratives.[43] Therefore, Scaramanga has refined taste but resides in a very tacky home. He is desired by women, even while they fear him. He is a skilled marksman, but one who insists on competition. He is a very tall man with a dwarf for a servant.

TMWTGG can also be seen as a complicated text—one that is never high on lists of the "Best Bond Films," but is also not one of the very worst. To admit to liking the film is to align yourself with a small group of others who also celebrate the film's excesses, echoing cult film fans. In truth, a Bond film cannot be a cult film owing to how mainstream the films have been for sixty years. However, I would argue that some Bond films are appreciated for their cinematic merit, others for their fidelity to the Bond universe, and others for perfectly capturing a cultural moment. *TMWTGG* is, to return to Hunt, "kitsch entertainment" that thoroughly represents the mid-1970s. It is not the highlight of the Moore tenure, nor is it the shoddiest. James Chapman has observed that Bond "can mean different things to different people at different moments."[44] As we move further away from the time period of the film, it becomes more evident that *TMWTGG* is unique in the Bond canon because of Lee's presence. He infuses the film with, as noted, sincerity, illustrating his Hammer experience of lifting mediocre material through faithful performances. Furthermore, Scaramanga is the series villain most like Bond—dashing, cultured, dangerous, and hired to kill.

In Roger Moore's book *Bond on Bond*, there is a photo from the set of the film where Lee and Moore are back to back with their respective guns in their hands, ready to begin the duel between their characters (similar to figure 9.2). In the caption, Moore writes, "In *The Man with the Golden Gun*, I faced up to my old friend Christopher Lee. Or did I back him up?"[45] This is the manner in which I would hope most viewers regard this film—as one where Moore and Lee jousted to the death. Aren't we all lucky that they did?

Notes

1. Leon Hunt, *British Low Culture: From Safari Suits to Sexploitation* (London: Routledge, 1998), 1.
2. James Chapman, *Licence to Thrill: A Cultural History of the James Bond Films* (New York: Columbia University Press, 2000), 149–77, 176.

3. Lee was appointed a CBE (Commander of the Order of the British Empire) in 2011, made a Knight in 2009, and named Commander of Ordre des Arts et des Lettres by the French government in 2011.

4. Roy Pierce-Jones, "The Men Who Played James Bond," in *James Bond in World and Popular Culture: The Films Are Not Enough*, ed. Robert G. Weiner, B. Lynn Whitfield, and Jack Becker (Newcastle upon Tyne, UK: Cambridge Scholars, 2011), 367–68.

5. See Matthew Jackson, "The 11 Best James Bond Movie Villains, Ranked," Syfy, November 16, 2021, www.syfy.com/syfy-wire/best-james-bond-villains-ranked, as one example.

6. Lee portrayed Dracula ten times (seven in Hammer productions).

7. Peter Hutchings, *Terence Fisher* (Manchester: Manchester University Press, 2001), 82.

8. Martin Shingler, *Star Studies: A Critical Guide* (London: BFI, 2012), 110.

9. Andrew Britton, "Stars and Genre," in *Stardom: Industry of Desire*, ed. Christine Gledhill (London: Routledge, 1991), 202.

10. Robert Sellers, "The Total Film Interview: Christopher Lee," Total Film, May 1, 2005, web.archive.org/web/20070612192345/http://www.totalfilm.com/features/the_total_film_interview__christopher_lee.

11. Wheeler Winston Dixon, "The End of Hammer," in *Seventies British Cinema*, ed. Robert Shail (London: BFI, 2002), 18.

12. Chapman, *Licence to Thrill*, 19.

13. Matt Hills, "Hammer 2.0: Legacy, Modernization, and Hammer as a Heritage Brand," in *Merchants of Menace: The Business of Horror Cinema*, ed. Richard Nowell (New York: Bloomsbury, 2014), 229–49.

14. See William Proctor for a discussion of continuity in the Bond film series. "The Many Lives of 007: Negotiating Continuity in the Official James Bond Film Series," in *Fan Phenomena: James Bond*, ed. Claire Hines (Bristol: Intellect, 2015), 10–19.

15. Tony Bennett and Janet Woollacott, "The Moments of Bond," in *The James Bond Phenomenon: A Critical Reader*, ed. Christoph Lindner (Manchester: Manchester University Press, 2003), 28–29.

16. Pierce-Jones, "Men Who Played James Bond," 362.

17. Steven Gerrard, "Blofeld," in *From Blofeld to Moneypenny: Gender in James Bond*, ed. Steven Gerrard (Bingley, UK: Emerald, 2020), 169.

18. Andrew Mangravite, "The House of Hammer," *Film Comment* 28, no. 3 (May–June 1992): 46.

19. Caroline Langhorst, "'Rebel Rebel?' Oliver Reed in the 1960s," in *Sixties British Cinema Reconsidered*, ed. Duncan Petrie, Melanie Williams, and Laura Mayne (Edinburgh: Edinburgh University Press, 2020), 32.

20. This interview was included on the Christopher Lee episode of the BBC's *Talking Pictures* (July 11, 2015).

21. James Chapman, "'Keeping the British End Up': James Bond and the Varieties of Britishness," in Gerrard, *From Blofeld to Moneypenny*, 14.

22. Chapman, *Licence to Thrill*, 174.

23. Sarah Street, *British National Cinema* (London: Routledge, 1997), 87.

24. Jon Burrows, "Lee, Christopher (1922–)," in *Journeys of Desire: European Actors in Hollywood: A Critical Companion*, ed. Alastair Phillips and Ginette Vincendeau (London: BFI, 2006), 335.

25. Lucy Bolton notes that fans are aware of Bond's "consummate knowledge of fine wines and other drinks." "The Phenomenology of James Bond," in Hines, *Fan Phenomena: James Bond*, 68.

26. Robert Murphy, *Sixties British Cinema* (London: BFI, 1992), 163.
27. Adrian Garvey, "Ageing Masculinity in the Films of James Mason," in *Lasting Screen Stars: Images That Fade and Personas That Endure*, ed. Lucy Bolton and Julie Lobalzo Wright (Basingstoke, UK: Palgrave Macmillan, 2016), 143.
28. Llewella Chapman, *Fashioning James Bond: Costume, Gender, and Identity in the World of 007* (London: Bloomsbury, 2022), 137.
29. Chapman, *Fashioning James Bond*, 135.
30. Monica Germanà, *Bond Girls: Body, Fashion, and Gender* (London: Bloomsbury, 2020), 30, 60.
31. Christine Berberich, *The Image of the English Gentleman in Twentieth-Century Literature: Englishness and Nostalgia* (New York: Routledge, 2016), 41.
32. See Elizabeth J. Nielsen, "'A Bloody Big Ship': Queering James Bond and the Rise of 00Q," in Hines, *Fan Phenomena: James Bond*, 136–45.
33. Hunt, *British Low Culture*, 2.
34. Rob Faunce, "'The Gay Bond' or 'Bond Goes Camping,'" in Weiner, Whitfield, and Becker, *James Bond in World and Popular Culture*, 403, 404.
35. Robert Shail, "'More, Much More . . . Roger Moore': A New Bond for a New Decade," in *Seventies British Cinema*, ed. Robert Shail (London: BFI, 2002), 154; Sue Harper and Justin Smith, *British Film Culture in the 1970s* (Edinburgh: Edinburgh University Press), 188.
36. Andrew Spicer, "Acting Nasty: British Male Actors in Contemporary Hollywood," in Phillips and Vincendeau, *Journeys of Desire*, 141–42.
37. Spicer, "Acting Nasty," 141.
38. Roger Moore, *My Word Is My Bond* (London: Michael O'Mara Books, 2008), 76.
39. Spicer, "Acting Nasty," 142.
40. Hutchings, *Terence Fisher*, 90.
41. Matt Hills, "Cult Movies with and without Cult Stars: Differentiating Discourses of Stardom," in *Cult Film Stardom: Offbeat Attractions and Processes of Cultification*, ed. Kate Egan and Sarah Thomas (Basingstoke, UK: Palgrave Macmillan, 2013), 21.
42. Michael Hann, "My Favourite Bond Film: *The Man with the Golden Gun*," *The Guardian*, October 3, 2012, www.theguardian.com/film/filmblog/2012/oct/03/favourite-bond-man-golden-gun.
43. Matthew Freeman, "James Bond as Transmedia Fan Anomaly," in Hines, *Fan Phenomena: James Bond*, 29.
44. Chapman, *Licence to Thrill*, 15.
45. Roger Moore with Gareth Owen, *Bond on Bond: The Ultimate Book on Over 50 Years of 007* (London: Michael O'Mara Books), 38.

CHAPTER 10

NOBODY DOES IT BETTER

"Keeping the British End Up" at a Time of National Crisis in
The Spy Who Loved Me (1977)

TERENCE MCSWEENEY

R oger Moore's third outing as James Bond, *The Spy Who Loved Me* (1977), contains more than a few of the most memorable moments in the long-running franchise, but there is one scene in particular that apparently caused audiences to leap to their feet at its London premiere on July 7, 1977, even King Charles III, then Prince of Wales, according to contemporary accounts.[1] Pursued by Soviet agents on skis across the vertiginous Austrian alps, Bond dispatches two of them before launching himself off a huge snowy peak, tumbling apparently to his death . . . only to pull a cord and deploy a Union Jack–emblazoned parachute at exactly the same moment as John Barry's Bond theme triumphantly resounds. It has undoubtedly become an iconic moment not just for the franchise, but also in British film history as a whole, one that is often returned to in retrospectives on the series, and it was hailed as the second-best moment from a Bond film ever according to a Sky poll in 2013.[2] It has also become one of the most widely parodied in the Bond canon, by the diverse likes of *American Dad* (Fox/TBS, 2005–), when a Bond-like British agent completes the same move except his parachute has a picture of Queen Elizabeth II on it, and in the episode "Never Say Alan Again" of *I'm Alan Partridge* (BBC Two, 1997–2002), where Alan (Steve Coogan) performs a one-man reenactment of the very same sequence for his bemused guests.

While audiences might have cheered in the cinema at the London premiere, for the British public at large there did not seem to be much else to cheer about in Britain in July 1977—as the titles of books like Andy Beckett's *When the Lights Went Out: What Really Happened to Britain in the Seventies* (2009) and

Alwyn W. Turner's *Crisis? What Crisis? Britain in the 1970s* (2013) testify; indeed, it is a decade Kenneth O. Morgan memorably described as "our unfinest hour."[3] This was the year after Britain was forced to borrow heavily from the International Monetary Fund and one in which the country was debilitated by strikes from all manner of professions, from firefighters to undertakers, that ultimately led to the "winter of discontent" in 1978. In these years IRA bombs were still detonating across London and foreign cars had started to outsell British ones domestically for the first time ever. Yet at exactly the same time as this, the release of *The Spy Who Loved Me* coincided with another event calculated to project a very particular idea of England in 1977: the Queen's Silver Jubilee, which celebrated the country's past, present, and future in ways closer to the vision offered in Bond films, both providing a very particular answer to what Christine Berberich has called "the question of England."[4]

The Spy Who Loved Me was a wish-fulfilment fantasy on the national scale at a very specific moment in British history. This is a recurring thematic motif in Bond studies, as many scholars have persuasively argued that the Fleming novels and their cinematic counterparts should be read as a prolonged attempt for England to negate its readily apparent declining imperial status and fantasize about continued preeminence in the international sphere, a thesis that finds its most pronounced articulation in Simon Winder's *The Man Who Saved Britain* (2006).[5] However, this study departs from preexisting iterations of the argument by presenting the Bond franchise in 1977 as very much aware of its status as an allohistorical fantasy in a year that pulled Britons between the poles of the Jubilee celebrations and the realities of a country wracked by political and economic turmoil. Bond is read here in a way similar to how scholars have engaged with iconic superheroes such as Superman, Iron Man, and Captain America, especially in recent decades, given the reemergence of the superhero film as the most commercially successful and culturally impactful genre of the modern era. It is in Moore's tenure in the role, after all, that the character becomes increasingly superhuman, less fallible, and less vulnerable than he ever was before, offering us parallels between James Bond and Jason Dittmer's understanding of superheroes in his *Captain America and the Nationalist Superhero: Metaphors, Narratives, and Geopolitics* (2012). Dittmer wrote that "superheroes are not reflections of, but are instead (along with many other elements) co-constitutive of the discourse popularly known as American exceptionalism."[6] What synechdochal figure of British national identity can rival Bond's enduring status in the years since *Dr. No* (1962)? He is a character who is not only a reflection of, but following Dittmer's template, has had a significant influence on complicated notions of British identity in the now more than sixty years since he first graced the screen. *The Spy Who Loved Me* provides us with a superlative example of this process, portraying Britain as secure in its identity as a superpower, continuing to innovate, dominate, and play a central role on the global stage as Bond becomes involved in a frequently ironic and self-referential adventure to save the world and seduces the Soviet Union's finest female agent—the beautiful XXX, aka Major Anya Amasova (Barbara Bach)—at a key moment of the Cold War era. Many viewers, including director Christopher Nolan and Roger Moore himself, regard this as the very best of the seven Bond films Moore starred in between 1973 and 1985.[7]

The film also marks an important moment in the evolution of the franchise, a continuation of what came before but also something of a departure. It was the first film that Albert "Cubby" Broccoli produced without his long-time partner Harry Saltzman, after the latter sold his half of the rights in 1975, with their nine previous films together establishing the essential parameters of the series. It was also the first Bond film to be an entirely original adventure, unconnected to the plot of any of the Fleming books, even though it takes its title from the 1962 novel of the same name, which was much more experimental than other books in the series. Finally, it was made after *The Man with the Golden Gun* earned a disappointing $97.6 million at the worldwide box office, making it, with the exception of *On Her Majesty's Secret Service* (1969), the lowest-earning film ever in the franchise when adjusted for inflation. In the face of pressure to downscale Bond's adventures, Broccoli instead did exactly the opposite, doubling the budget to a then-huge $14 million (nearly $2 million of which was spent on the construction of the "007 Stage," opened on December 5, 1976 by former prime minister Harold Wilson), making almost everything bigger, grander, and more spectacular than before. The final result was a successful one for Broccoli and the rest of the team: it made $185.4 million at the box office and was warmly received by critics and fans, arguably revivifying the franchise in the process.

The Spy Who Loved Me is as immersed in its sociopolitical moment as the Bond franchise has always been, enough to provide a frisson of relevance for contemporaneous audiences, although whether the films have anything of substance to say about their respective eras has, of course, been debated by Bond scholars for more than half a century. In this case, the plot follows the disappearance of two ballistic-missile submarines, one British and one Soviet, and it is this mystery that Bond spends most of the duration of the film attempting to solve. In the process, he is forced to work alongside an elite Soviet agent, the beautiful and formidable Major Anya Amasova or Agent XXX, a relationship made especially challenging due to their ideological and personal rivalry and the fact that Amasova learns that Bond had killed her lover, one of the skiing agents from the film's prologue. The film offers numerous parallels between the two opposing agents, both of whom are the very best their country has to offer, providing a striking and compelling characterization for Amasova in a series that has more often than not provided problematic depictions of women. They both discover that tycoon Karl Stromberg (Curd Jürgens) is responsible for the theft and plans to initiate World War Three between the United States and the Soviet Union, which will destroy the world, while leaving his own underwater city to thrive (figure 10.1).

By the time of the film's production, in the *real* world rather than the *reel* world, the Cold War was experiencing a period of détente, which is clearly manifested in the portrayal of the Soviet Union in a far less critical light than previous installments in the franchise, and those that it would pivot back toward in later Moore films.[8] This is even referenced explicitly twice in the film: once by General Gogol (Walter Gotell), the head of the KGB, who suggests "We have entered a new era of Anglo–Soviet cooperation," and later by Stromberg, who, on observing Bond's relationship with Amasova, remarks, "A British agent in love with a Russian agent . . . *Détente indeed.*" Thus, instead of the likes of the sociopathic Rosa Klebb (Lotte Lenya) in *From Russia with Love* (1963) or Lieutenant-General Orlov (Steven Berkoff) from *Octopussy* (1983), the film features Amasova and the much more sympathetic Gogol, who would appear in every film for the rest of Moore's tenure as Bond. Gogol is shown to be intelligent, reasonable, and very far from an antagonistic figure. Indeed, when Britain joins forces with the Soviet Union, their rivalry is seen almost as healthy competition, unlike in previous films, with only the assassination attempt on Bond at the start of the film offering a counterpoint to this. Gogol and Amasova are even invited into the top-secret British base under the Abu Simbel temple in Egypt, something that would have been unthinkable in previous films. This process was described by Janet Woollacott as an attempt to "de-politicise James Bond."[9] However, this is a reductive view of how popular culture texts are political, as the decision to portray the Soviet Union in less adversarial ways is not a retreat from the politics, rather even more evidence of how the Bond films have always functioned as something of a cultural barometer intrinsically

Figure 10.1 Neither shaken nor stirred: the indefatigable James Bond (Roger Moore) comes face to face with Karl Stromberg (Curt Jürgens) in *The Spy Who Loved Me* (1977).

connected to the sociopolitical tapestry of their times. Furthermore, just because Bond is not killing Soviet agents as frequently in *The Spy Who Loved Me* as he had done before and would do again does not mean that he is any less of an inherently political figure than he has been throughout the history of the series.

Just as important as the *presence* of the Soviet Union in *The Spy Who Loved Me* is the relative *absence*, for long stretches of the film, of the United States of America. By 1979 the nation had been the world's most formidable superpower for more than thirty years, with a nuclear arsenal exceeding the combined totals of the Soviet Union and Great Britain by a considerable margin, but in the world of *The Spy Who Loved Me* this is not apparent onscreen at all. Watching the film, audiences then and indeed now could be forgiven for thinking that, in actual fact, England was still a "great power" as defined by Hedley Bull around this time as "in the front rank in terms of military strength . . . recognised by others to have, and conceived by their own leaders and peoples to have, certain special rights and duties."[10] In the year before the film was released both the United States and the United Kingdom spent exactly the same portion of their gross domestic product on defense, 5.19 percent. The disparity between what that actually meant in real-world money is considerable, equating to $74.72 billion for the United States, compared to $10.7 billion in the United Kingdom. Representatives of the United States do not show up until well into the second half of the film, and even then play a decidedly supporting and even comical role in Bond's mission to rescue Amasova after she has been kidnapped by Stromberg.

The film demonstrates Britain's status as a great power in a range of ways: through its lingering shots of high-tech British submarines filmed in Faslane, the real UK submarine base, and numerous mentions of its large arsenal of Polaris missiles. It can also be seen in the frequent displays of advanced British technology such as infrared heat sensors, high-tech watches, satellite tracking, and even the iconic underwater car built by the British Lotus Cars Limited, all of which would have seemed incredibly futuristic for audiences in 1977, the same year *Star Wars* was released.

However, as one might expect, it is in the figure of Bond himself that England's significance and supremacy is most clearly demonstrated, as it has been throughout the history of the franchise. Jason Dittmer observes that Captain America and Superman function as "icon[s] of American technological innovation and the hierarchies of domination it permits" in ways that could easily be applied to Bond in terms of his physical and mental superiority, his ingenuity, and of course his sexual prowess, all of which are frequently explicitly connected to Bond's own national identity.[11] Bond does not quite wear the flag (or its colors) on his body as many American superheroes do, although, as seen in the opening scene with the parachute, at times he comes very close to doing so. In its nostalgic and very conservative evocation of traditional British ideals and values, the film might be read as comparable to Richard Donner's *Superman* (1978), released just the year after, at a historical moment when, as many have suggested, "the US was in the throes of an existential crisis."[12] In *Superman* the eponymous character, played by Christopher Reeve, states, "I'm here to fight for truth and justice and the American way." *The Spy Who Loves Me* makes it very clear that Bond does something similar for his own country, and just as Superman is representative of the preeminence of the United States, so too is Bond of Great Britain.

For Bond, this is apparent as early as when he is attacked by Soviet agents in Austria. Even though he is outnumbered, as he often will be, he outwits and defeats his enemies. Not only is his skiing better than that of those who are supposed to be his counterparts, but, as the film progresses he will be shown to have superior fighting and driving skills to anyone he faces, surpassing their intellect, knowledge, ingenuity, and wit. Even some of his jokes are designed to disparage other nationalities, whether their barbs target Egyptian builders or Russian politics. In the film's finale, it is Bond who disarms the bomb that would have killed hundreds, he who reprograms the nuclear missiles that would have started World War Three, and he who, as he has always done, saves the world.

This superiority is placed sharply in view when he is considered alongside the film's two antagonists, both of whom are explicitly offered as distorted mirror images of Bond, as has often been the case in the franchise: the primary villain, Stromberg, and his metal-toothed henchman, Jaws (Richard Kiel). Both are shown as decidedly lacking in comparison to Bond, whether that might be in their intellect, ability, or attractiveness to women. As previously mentioned, Stromberg was the first primary antagonist not to be taken from the Fleming novels, but his plans to destroy the world and rebuild humanity underwater are heavily reminiscent of those of Ernst Stavro Blofeld, and indeed the character actually *was* Blofeld in previous versions of the script until Kevin McClory's widely publicized legal battle with Eon Productions prevented the company from using the character until the issue was resolved in 2013. Like Blofeld, Stromberg is clearly an elitist figure, evocative of the old world and old money, the very things Bonds *seems* to stand against, but actually very clearly is representative of himself. The franchise has paradoxically always asked audiences to cheer for Bond's snobbishness and praise his refined palate while deeming Stromberg and others like him effete and unmasculine for having very similar traits and tastes. A similar process is discernible with Jaws, who in *The Spy Who Loved Me* is a much darker presence than the comedic figure he would become, and perhaps be remembered as, in *Moonraker* (1979). In his memoir, *James Bond, The Spy I Loved* (2006), screenwriter Christopher Wood described Jaws as both "a figure of unmitigated evil" and "monstrous."[13] Jaws is even introduced with what would later be called a jump scare on the train to Sardinia, replete with klaxon sound and snap zoom, in a film made after *Carrie* (1976) but before *Friday the Thirteenth* (1980), two of many that would make the technique a perennial part of genre cinema in the years after. Even though Jaws is obviously the stronger man, Bond uses his ingenuity to defeat him when they come face to face, first by placing an electric lamp on his metallic teeth, then, at the climax of the film, by using a magnet to drop him into shark-infested waters. Both Stromberg and Jaws have a vaguely sexual air about them, with Jaws biting his victims and Stromberg's kidnapping of Amasova framed as a desire to possess something that belongs to Bond. Bond's final words to Stromberg after the villainous tycoon has tried to kill him, in a scene that contains some incredibly phallic imagery, are "You've shot your bolt, Stromberg. Now it's my turn!"

Bond's status as a sex symbol with remarkable carnal prowess had been long consolidated by the time of *The Spy Who Loved Me* and continues unabashed, with the character's sexual profligacy having emerged as one of the defining hallmarks of the Moore era. Rather than this being only superficial titillation, many scholars have persuasively argued that the Moore films in particular "directly linked Britain's strength to Bond's virility."[14] This is evident throughout the film, often quite explicitly, and begins as early as Bond's initial appearance, when, in the first of many double entendres, M (Bernard Lee) orders Moneypenny (Lois Maxwell) to "Tell him [Bond] to *pull out* immediately," which cuts to a shot of Bond in bed in the chalet in Switzerland with the first of the film's parade of beautiful, sexually available young women, referred to in the credits only as "Log Cabin Girl" (Sue Vanner). Bond's sexual aptitude is so extraordinary that she sighs, "Ah James . . . I cannot find the words." When he attempts to leave, she pleads with him, "But James, I *need* you," to which he replies, "*So does England.*" All through the film almost every woman Bond meets will be shown to be attracted to him, with many killed as a direct result of their interactions or even by his hand. Unlike later iterations featuring Pierce Brosnan and Daniel Craig, where these deaths will be integrated into Bond's characterization, this remains entirely uncommented on in *The Spy Who Loved Me*, as Bond moves from one encounter to the next without a thought for the numerous bodies, male and female, that are left in his wake.[15]

All of these aspects are most evident in the half an hour, more than a quarter of the film's running time, that it spends in Egypt. These scenes perpetuate stereotypes of an exotic, backward, and mysterious country and the superiority of white Western males that have been repeated in Hollywood and British film since the birth of the medium.[16] In these scenes, Bond is reintroduced riding a camel (which also uses Maurice Jarre's *Lawrence of Arabia* [1962] theme), then demonstrates that he speaks "fluent" Arabic by interacting with a Bedouin tribesman. He meets Sheikh Hossein (Edward de Souza), who is revealed to be an old Cambridge friend in possession of a harem containing several scantily clad women ("We don't only have oil, you know . . ." he reminds Bond). James initially declines an invitation to spend the night, but when Hossein offers him one of the women (Dawn Rodrigues)—yet another female character never provided with a name in the film, only one of several referred to collectively in the credits as "Arab Beauties"—he replies, "When one is in Egypt one should delve *deeply* into its treasures." In the very next scene, in Cairo, connected to the previous one by, of all things, a sound bridge that uses the Adhan, the Islamic call to prayer, he is introduced to the beautiful Felicca (Olga Bisera) who tells him, "Mr. Fekkesh asked me to *entertain* you while you are waiting," before passionately kissing the man she has known for just moments. Bond tells her, "I had lunch, but I seem to have missed *dessert*." When she notices an assassin hidden above in one of the panels of the room, the following sequence of shots is cut so rapidly that it is hard to determine whether she is hit accidentally or Bond purposely spins her in the way of the bullet, reminiscent of the death of Fiona Volpe (Luciana Paluzzi) in *Thunderball* (1965). What is clear is that Bond drops her lifeless body to the floor as he sprints after the assassin to the roof and proceeds to kill him even though he gives up the information Bond needs. The film will never mention Felicca again. The ambiguity surrounding her death (and indeed that of Volpe) means that Bond scholars and fans have debated ever since if either one is the first woman to be *actually killed* by Bond in the franchise. Yet if Bond was not responsible for the deaths of Volpe or Felicca, he certainly kills the character of Naomi (Caroline Munro), Stromberg's pilot, who flirts with him and then tries to kill him, only to have her helicopter destroyed by one of Bond's missiles shot from the Lotus.

It is in Egypt where Bond meets XXX, the film's "Bond girl," a figure who both contributes to and complicates many of the ideas this chapter has been exploring, certainly to the benefit of *The Spy Who Loved Me*. By the time of the tenth film in the series, Broccoli, director Lewis Gilbert, and writers Christopher Wood and Richard Maibaum were well aware of the expectations fans had of those inhabiting the role of the "Bond girl." Although there had undeniably been some formidable female characters in the nine films prior to *The Spy Who Loved Me*, Moore's tenure had thus far only delivered Solitaire (Jane Seymour) and Mary Goodnight (Britt Ekland), not exactly high points for the representation of women in the series and perhaps two of those Christopher Lindner had in mind when he described "Bond girls" as "generic, interchangeable, [and] dependent." [17] However, as Gilbert comments in the BBC documentary *The Making of "The Spy Who Loved Me,"* "Most Bond girls have been kind of, perhaps with the exception of one or two, they've been kind of passive, and I mean he's, you know, kind of anti-women's lib in a way, but in this case [with the character of XXX] I think women's lib would be rather proud of her because she is his equal in every way and matches him all the way through the picture." [18] While this is not entirely true, Amasova is indeed a compelling figure from the moment she is introduced on the screen (figure 10.2). Several Bond scholars have asserted that her characterization is, as Jeremy Black writes in *The Politics of James Bond* (2005), "a reaction to claims that the early Bond films were sexist and also to the growing feminist current from the 1960s."[19]

The film introduces her with an act of legerdemain, as Gogol is heard to ask on the radio, "Where is Agent XXX?" as the camera smoothly glides over an attractive couple kissing on a bed, with the handsome and muscular man, Sergei Barzov (Michael Billington), prioritized within the frame, leading audiences to naturally assume that *he* is XXX. As Gogol continues, "Agent XXX, acknowledge and identify," the man gets up wearily as if reacting, but it is the woman who answers: "This is XXX. Message received and understood." Amasova will show herself to be a capable fighter, even saving Bond's life. She knows as much about Bond as he does about her and had seen the blueprints of the Lotus two years before. Her intellect certainly rivals his. She even bests him by resisting his advances on the small Egyptian boat before knocking him out with her own cigarette lighter gadget. But the film is Bond's, after all, so while it frequently demonstrates what a good agent she is, it also demeans her at the same time by having her fall asleep on Bond's shoulder, showing her as lacking driving skills compared to his (which leads to his jibe "women drivers!"), and revealing her to be jealous of other women after they begin their relationship.[20]

The film climaxes with Bond saving the world, killing Stromberg, and rescuing Amasova as they both escape his underwater craft *Atlantis* in a luxurious capsule. It is only then that she pulls a gun on him, intending to get her revenge for Bond killing her former partner. But he has saved her life and this can only mean one thing in the Bond universe, at least during the Moore era:

Figure 10.2 James Bond (Roger Moore) in Egypt with Major Anya Amasova (Barbara Bach) in *The Spy Who Loved Me* (1977). Agent XXX is formidable, but the film belongs to Bond.

that he will be rewarded with sex (as he had been rewarded earlier when he saved her from Jaws on the train). When their superiors arrive, both from MI6 and the KGB, they find the two agents naked. "What do you think you're doing?" demands Bond's superior. Bond's answer, the film's final line of dialogue, is "Keeping the British end up, Sir!" accompanied by a brief instrumental musical hall rendition of Carly Simon's "Nobody Does It Better" (1977), evocative of the long-running *Carry On* franchise (1958–1992).

The film has shown that, in the world of Bond, nobody *does* do it better: neither Egyptians, Russians, nor Americans. This understanding of Bond is similar to how iconic U.S. heroes have been able to "connect the political projects of American nationalism, internal order, and foreign policy (all formulated at the national or global scale) with the scale of the individual or body. The character of Captain America connects these scales by literally embodying American identity, presenting for readers a hero both of, and for, the nation."[21] By replacing *Captain America* with *James Bond* and *American* with *British*, Dittmer provides a useful framework with which to approach the enduring popularity of the Bond series. In *The Spy Who Loved Me* Bond, and the world he inhabits, are projections of how the country wished to see itself on the global stage at a time of crisis, but, given the vivid irony that permeates the film, there is a very real sense that the producers are distinctly aware that it is all a fantasy, one that continued to grow even further into the realms of parody as Moore's tenure progressed. Yet this embrace of Bond as a manifestation of "the best of British" even while acknowledging its status as an ironic text also helps to explain why the franchise has resonated so profoundly in the more than sixty years since 1962.

Notes

1. See Stevan Riley, *Everything or Nothing: The Untold Story of 007,* documentary film, Passion Pictures/Red Box Films, 2012.
2. See Matilda Battersby, "Showdown Between Goldfinger and Sean Connery Voted Greatest James Bond Moment," *Independent,* January 2, 2013, www.independent.co.uk /arts-entertainment/films/news/no-mr-bond-i-expect-you-die-showdown-between -goldfinger-and-sean-connery-voted-greatest-james-bond-moment-8435196.html.
3. Alwyn W. Turner, *Crisis? What Crisis? Britain in the 1970s* (London: Aurum, 2013); Andy Beckett, *When the Lights Went Out: What Really Happened to Britain in the Seventies* (London: Faber and Faber, 2009); Kenneth O. Morgan, "Britain in the Seventies— Our Unfinest Hour?," *Revue Française de Civilisation Britannique* 22 (2017), journals .openedition.org/rfcb/1662.
4. Christine Berberich, "Putting England Back on Top? Ian Fleming, James Bond, and the Question of England," *Yearbook of English Studies* 42 (2012): 13–29.
5. Simon Winder, *The Man Who Saved Britain* (London: Picador, 2006).
6. Jason Dittmer, *Captain America and the Nationalist Superhero: Metaphors, Narratives, and Geopolitics* (Philadelphia: Temple University Press, 2012), 10.

7. Jack Shepherd and Matt Maytum, "Christopher Nolan on Bond's The Spy Who Loved Me: "I've spent a lot of my career trying to get back to that feeling," Games Radar, August 26, 2020, www.gamesradar.com/christopher-nolan-james-bond-tenet-spy-who-loved-me/.

8. Thomas J. Price, "The Changing Image of the Soviets in the Bond Saga: From Bond Villains to Acceptable Role Partners," *Journal of Popular Culture* 26, no. 1 (1992): 17–37.

9. Janet Woollacott, "The James Bond Films: Conditions of Production," in *The James Bond Phenomenon: A Critical Reader*, ed. Christoph Lindner (Manchester: Manchester University Press, 2003), 99–117; 108.

10. Hedley Bull, *The Anarchical Society: A Study of Order in World Politics* (Basingstoke, UK: Macmillan, 1977), 201–2.

11. Jason Dittmer, "American Exceptionalism, Visual Effects, and the Post-9/11 Cinematic Superhero Boom," *Environment and Planning D: Society and Space* 29 (2010): 114–30; 122.

12. Jane Salminen, "Superman on the Silver Screen: The Political Ideology of The Man of Tomorrow on Film," *Widerscreen* 20, no. 3 (2017), widerscreen.fi/numerot/2017-3/superman-silver-screen-political-ideology-man-tomorrow-film/.

13. Christopher Wood, *James Bond, the Spy I Loved* (Tunbridge Wells: Twenty First Century, 2006), 55, 77.

14. Jeremy Black, *The Politics of James Bond: From Fleming's Novels to the Big Screen* (Westport, CT: Praeger, 2005), 137.

15. For example, in *GoldenEye* (1995), Alec Trevelyan (Sean Bean) asks Bond, "I might as well ask if all those vodka martinis silence the screams of all the men you've killed . . . or if you've found forgiveness in the arms of all those willing women for the dead ones you failed to protect?"

16. See Jack Shaheen, *Reel Bad Arabs: How Hollywood Vilifies a People* (New York: Olive Branch Press, 2009).

17. Christopher Lindner, "Foreword," in *For His Eyes Only: The Women of James Bond*, ed. Lisa Funnell (New York: Wallflower, 2015), xvii.

18. *The Making of "The Spy Who Loved Me,"* documentary film, BBC and Open University, 1977, www.youtube.com/watch?v=4eZ6YOZHMPs.

19. Black, *Politics of James Bond*, 137.

20. See Stephanie Jones, "Women Drivers!" The Changing Role of the Bond Girl in Vehicle Chases," in Funnell, *For His Eyes Only*, 205–13.

21. Jason Dittmer, "Captain America's Empire: Reflections on Identity, Popular Culture, and Post-9/11 Geopolitics," *Annals of the Association of American Geographers* 95, no. 3 (2005): 626–43; 627.

CHAPTER 11

MOONRAKER (1979) AND THE CANVAS OF ESCAPISM

STEVEN GERRARD

The opening of *Moonraker* (1979), the eleventh film in the James Bond franchise, is a memorable one that encompasses in just a few minutes all the reasons why fans revere or revile the film. Britain's top super-secret agent, James Bond (Roger Moore), is pushed out of a private jet without a parachute as it hurtles through the sky. As 007 plummets to the ground, he successfully manages to chase the plane's parachute-wearing pilot, who had escaped the craft moments earlier. Finally reaching him, Bond wrestles the man's parachute off his back and frantically clips the canopy safely to himself. Then, from the crashing plane emerges Jaws (Richard Kiel), a seven-foot-tall, metallic-toothed assassin hell-bent on killing Bond. As the two men tussle, with the ground hurtling toward them, Bond pulls his ripcord and the parachute opens, propelling him skyward. Jaws attempts to do the same, but his ripcord snaps. Seeing a circus tent some miles away, he flaps his arms and heads for it. As Bond escapes into the distance, Jaws slams into the circus tent, collapsing it. Cue drum roll. Cue the film's opening credits. *Moonraker* has begun.

Often regarded as one of the lesser Bond films in the Eon canon, *Moonraker* remains an important addition to the series up to and beyond its release in 1979. It marked Roger Moore's fourth outing as James Bond and, while Sean Connery's 007 had almost ventured into space in *You Only Live Twice* (1967), *Moonraker* took the secret agent beyond the confines of Earth. Escapism has always proved a vital component of Bond's adventures, and *Moonraker* takes its audience from the Cold War of the era to the coldness of outer space, clearly paving the way for the more outlandish elements of an invisible car in *Die Another Day* (2002) and *No Time to Die*'s (2021) magnetic bodysuit that stops falling people crashing into the floor. *Moonraker*, with its outlandish plot, a suave agent battling a smoothly villainous megalomaniac, a tough no-nonsense female lead, and spectacular use of locations, offered to the British filmgoing public a chance to escape—even if for only two hours—from a country that was undergoing social and cultural upheaval. Recognition that Bond can provide such a sense of escapism is not new, but by discussing the film's positioning on the cinematic plain while also examining the changing cultural climate during its production, it becomes clear that *Moonraker* remains arguably the most escapist Bond film of the canon.

Escapism is certainly a human trait, a vital part of the psychological processes that we undergo when placed in times of anxiety. The concept was introduced in the 1950s as an explanation for the masses' use of entertainment. According to Matthias R. Hastall's arguments, "people use media to actively disengage themselves from troubling thoughts and unpleasant mood states caused by challenging life situations."[1] In this respect, cinema forms a part of mass media consumption, alongside television, radio, newspapers, and now the internet. As such, when discussing a film like *Moonraker* and the Bond canon in more general terms, it becomes clear that, through their often-outlandish plots and scenarios, they produce a genuine sense of escapism for their consumer. It is very easy to dismiss escapism as a form of trivial pastime whereby, according to the philosophical approach of Yi-Fu Tuan, "'Escapism' has a somewhat negative meaning in our society and perhaps in all societies. It suggests an inability to face facts—the real world. We speak of escapist literature, for instance, and we tend to judge as escapist places such as mega-shopping malls, fancy resorts, theme parks, or even picture-perfect suburbs."[2] While humans are the only creature on Earth to be able to conceive of the more philosophical meanings of escaping (rather than the physical running away from danger, etc.), Tuan posits the idea that we can "ponder the nature of a threat rather than confront it directly." If this is the case, then this pondering allows us to create thought and from that thought comes ideas of culture. As he writes, "Culture is more closely linked to the human tendency not to face facts, our ability to *escape* by one means or another"[3]

Cinema appears to offer an ideal chance to escape through a cultural lens away from our humdrum existences toward an idealized state. That idealized area is, naturally, predisposed toward an individual's own tendencies: some people like musicals for their flamboyant music, singing, and dance sequences; others like horror films for the cathartic release that these bring. According to John Longeway,

"Escapist" entertainment's essential purpose is to draw us away from our every-day troubles, and, sometimes, to help us to fantasise ourselves as better, more important, and better off than we really are. Indulgence in such entertainment helps us avoid, temporarily, unpleasant truths that we must live with, and it is this escape from unpleasant reality that gives us the terms "escapist" and "escapism."[4]

While both Longeway and Tuan offer philosophical ideas about escape and escapism, Christoph Klimmt argues that the original interpretation and under-standing of the word was "rooted in the assumption that people in western mass societies were alienated and suffered from poor life satisfaction."[5] Cin-ema does offer a sense of escapism for its audience. For two hours, they can be taken on a journey into a narrative that could be funny, exciting, horrible, cel-ebratory, or fantastic. As a reminder, the 1970s in the United Kingdom saw such society-impacting elements as the rise in unemployment, strike action, the near-collapse of the Labour Party, and high inflation. Films offered a genuine respite from those troubling times.

By the time that the film *Moonraker* was released in 1979, James Bond was even more escapist than ever. Ian Fleming's stories had been written and filmed when Britain had undergone massive social change. The country had come through the ravages of war, and the postwar period had seen the country enter a period of austerity. However, with the move into the 1960s came a colorful and vibrant energy that found its way into such cultural areas as music, art, theatre, television, and cinema. By the Seventies, the downturn in the coun-try's fortunes was evident, as seen in daily strikes and protest marches up and down the land. However, Bond's adventures provided a respite from this and helped their readers and viewers to escape into a realm of fantasy that removed them from the hardships of the decade.

On a smaller scale, Bond's appetite for food moved into the realms of gourmet-escapism for many during a period in which Britain was still—up until 1954—in rationing. His eating of foie gras and cold rock lobster, swilled down with Campari, Cinzano, and soda water are clearly at odds with what the British public had been used to. In the 1953 novel *Casino Royale*, Bond says, "I take a ridiculous pleasure in what I eat" before polishing off caviar, tournedos, arti-choke heart, and half an avocado—all swilled down with Taittinger cham-pagne.[6] In the first film, *Dr. No* (1962), Bond has numerous cocktails and Red Stripe beer and eats from a well-stocked breakfast trolley. When Honey Ryder (Ursula Andress) asks, "How can you eat at a time like this?" Bond's reply of "Because I'm hungry. We don't know when we'll get the chance to eat again" clearly indicates two things: the first is that he had seen deprivation during the war years and knows the value of food; the second, that the filmmakers knew these items were out of almost all of the public's grasp. While the food and drink serve as a gourmet accoutrement to Bond's adventures, they offered up the exotic for a British public used to chips and beer, not caviar and champagne. Bond drove modern, expensive cars such as the British Bentley or Aston Martin DB5, which were out of the price range of most ordinary citizens. Bond's globetrotting took him and his readers/viewers to exotic places like Jamaica, Japan and the Bahamas; meanwhile, British audiences were mostly living in terraced streets surrounded by the soot and grime of the era. In the novel of *Moonraker* (1955), Bond's adventures take him only to his gentlemen's club, Blades, and areas on the southeast coast of England. However, the film moves to locations including Rio de Janeiro, California, Venice, and outer space. With such exotic locales, the British moviegoing public were offered the chance to be "removed" from their country to be presented with wonderful vistas of places that were usually not affordable to visit. If one considers that the Development of Tourism Act 1969 gained Royal Assent, leading to the formulation of the British Tourist Authority that encouraged visitors to come to the United Kingdom, here was Bond leading the way as both an export of the UK *and* promoting the world to his homegrown audience.

On the wider scale, Bond's original adventures navigated their way through such events as the Suez Crisis in 1956, the fracturing of the British Empire into the Commonwealth, Ghana's independence, decimalization, and joining the European Economic Community. It must be remembered that the novels were set in the postwar era. This was when Britain's role on the world stage was decreasing. Therefore, when Bond battles despots from around the world, he "maintain[s] the myth of British . . . superiority." This comes through in the way that he overcomes his villains (who are often foreign), but arguably more through Bond himself. Christine Berberich argues that Bond demonstrates both his English gentleman persona (despite the character's being of both Scottish and French heritage) and a "particular English superiority."[7] In the opening titles of *On Her Majesty's Secret Service* (1969), through the image of sand slipping through an hourglass, we see Bond's adventures play out with the figure of Britannia and Union Jacks as a backdrop. This feeling of Bond-as-Britain comes through the films of the Moore era: Bond fights against voodoo-using Bahamian drug lords, a Cuban-descended British assassin, a German industrialist, and, in *Moonraker*, a French megalomaniac. They are Other and must be conquered if Britain is to remain a stable and controlling power on the world stage.

Moore's interpretation of Bond may have been considered more lightweight than both Connery's or George Lazenby's but this helps his tenure negotiate an era in which the United Kingdom saw violence (Bloody Sunday, 1972), strikes, three-day weeks, humiliation (Britain borrowed money from the International Monetary Fund, 1976), celebration (Queen Elizabeth II's Silver Jubilee in 1977),

the Winter of Discontent, and the polarization of politics, culminating in the
return to Conservative rule in the year of *Moonraker's* release. Set between the
Swinging Sixties and the divisive Eighties, Britain's 1970s were somber at best:

> Recollections of the seventies are coloured by memories of a public blackout,
> reminiscent of the second world war during the blitz, without the compensat-
> ing feeling of national heroism and historic endurance. The earlier years of the
> decade featured not only many strikes by the engineers and electrical work-
> ers, but Edward Heath's catastrophic three-day week in response to the min-
> ers' strike of 1974 when London's major thoroughfares were cast into darkness,
> shops and restaurants were unlit and gloomy, public television services were
> suspended for several nights a week, and suburban families ate their sombre
> dinners at home not very romantically with the light of such spare candles as
> shopkeepers still had available.[8]

Moore's Bond was a return to the "older, more class-ridden paradigm" of Britain's past, arguably from a public that wanted to return to a place of escapist-
nostalgia as a removal from the seemingly unending turmoil that the country
was undergoing.[9] On the cinematic plain, Britain was not only committed to
producing socially aware films that reflected the nation-state, but also produced
wide-ranging, escapist genre fare. Notable examples include Hammer Films,
especially their gothic horrors, and producer Peter Rogers' comedic *Carry On*
series (1958–1992), which used both parody and a sense of absurdist realism.
Bond was seen as a part of this genre fare. What was noticeable in these movies is that, while the move into the 1970s saw both Hammer and *Carry On* running out of steam (both in terms of creativity *and* box office appeal), the Bond
films appeared at roughly one every two years, and to box office success. It was
clear that the public *wanted* Bond adventures that removed the audience from
their everyday lives into one of pure escapism. The characters were often as
exotic as the locales, and while the narratives were outlandish in their extremes
(despite displaying often-conservative values), they offered a serious respite
from the mundanities of life in Britain.

   At the end of *The Spy Who Loved Me* the end titles had proclaimed that
"James Bond will return in *For Your Eyes Only*." However, when *Star Wars* (1977)
was released to massive box office success, Eon looked at *Moonraker* for Bond's
next adventure. It already had a title with built-in appeal for cinemagoers
hooked on science fiction, despite the film's owing very little to its source material. While *Star Wars* certainly pushed Eon toward making a genuine James
Bond science fiction movie, the year of its release also saw such blockbuster productions as *Alien, Star Trek: The Motion Picture*, and *The Black Hole* sitting
alongside more-artistic fare such as *Stalker* and *Quintet*. It is evident that science fiction cinema offered viewers a chance to escape from the mundanities

Figure 11.1 On a hovercraft gondola in Venice. This eleventh entry in the film franchise embraces the escapist fantasy that would define the Moore era. *Moonraker* (1979).

of "real life" and experience the *fantastique*. Indeed, this melding of the world of spy espionage to out-and-out science fiction proved a winning formula for Eon, and provided more escapism for the viewer. While *Moonraker* does have its fair share of bona fide spy film elements, it is arguably most impressive when the science fiction aspects come to the fore: Bond's watch-cum-pellet-gun, his flying speedboat, the hovercraft gondola (figure 11.1), the Moonraker Shuttle, the space station, and the space suits. For Eon, the move toward science fiction was inevitable—not just because of *Star Wars*, but from the logical push from their own past canon, where *Thunderball* (1965) saw the world being threatened by nuclear war, *You Only Live Twice* (1967) had SPECTRE's rocket program on show, and Scaramanga's (Christopher Lee) flying car whisked him to his idyllic hideaway in *The Man with the Golden Gun* (1974).

Such was the producers' attempt at (escapist) realism that they promoted their space technology as based on that used by NASA. Space technology author Eric Burgess writes that most space operas "ignored physical laws but appealed to popular imagination" and that "*Moonraker* attempted to achieve space reality." The film's space suits, its Skylab-like propulsion units, and Drax's space station all follow designs similar to those in use in national space programs; they had to not only "reach new heights of realism" but to be "aesthetically pleasing, functional and visually suitable for various camera angles and viewpoints."[10] The film's release was to coincide with NASA's own space shuttle launch, but that was delayed, while the film's release was not. For Eon, it was evident that Fleming had rewarded them with a title alone that could sell tickets:

The public wanted outer-space adventure and Broccoli felt that in MOONRAKER—Ian Fleming's 1955 novel about an early nuclear-tipped

ICBM aimed at London—he had a story and a title that were ripe for the times. Using sections of Fleming's plot about a private industrialist who bankrolls building rockets, Christopher Wood constructed a narrative that had one key element already firmly in place—the film would feature James Bond travelling into space.[11]

Moonraker's plot slavishly follows the pattern and other elements of *The Spy Who Loved Me*, including the returning henchman, Jaws. This isn't surprising, as its scriptwriter, Christopher Wood, mostly known for the creation of young, sexually inexperienced Timmy Lea in the *Confessions of . . .* movies (1974–1979), had also written the previous Bond film. Tim Pulleine's *Monthly Film Bulletin* review said as much: "[T]he latest instalment looks like nothing so much as a remake of *The Spy Who Loved Me*."[12] The plot is simple: Bond is sent on a mission to retrieve a stolen space shuttle—Moonraker—owned by French entrepreneur Hugo Drax (Michael Lonsdale). His adventures take him to the United States, Venice, the Amazon, Rio de Janeiro, and finally Drax's space station. It is from there that Drax intends to use biological warfare to destroy humankind before repopulating the planet with his master race. Production was moved to Paris, with special effects work taking place on the 007 soundstage at Pinewood Studios. The budget was set at $14 million, and the film's production values are (as always) on the screen; the incredible parachute chase pre-title sequence "proved to be jaw-droppingly amazing because it was clearly not faked . . . The fact that anyone could do this type of action was enough to induce gasping disbelief among viewers."[13]

As the series had become so reliant on the more spectacular elements, *Moonraker*'s action sequences, a staple of all Bond films (despite some awful back-projection on occasion) are flamboyant. Bond's Venetian gondola becomes a hovercraft, his Amazonian speedboat a hang glider. He battles Jaws on a cable car overlooking Rio de Janeiro. Drax's space station is impressively destroyed during a space battle. This out-and-out escapism is evident, but the film's parodic intertextuality from inside and outside the Bond canon reaches a high point in *Moonraker*: Jaws' return and indestructability showed he was a fan favorite; the beach drunk from *The Spy Who Loved Me* returns in Venice as a pigeon does a double-take on seeing Bond's gondola float across St. Mark's Square; the signature tune from *Close Encounters of the Third Kind* (1977) forms a musical key to a laboratory door; and, Bond's ride on horseback is accompanied by Elmer Bernstein's score to *The Magnificent Seven* (1960). This playful bricolage demonstrates that the film is just that—a film. But it also shows that the production team's willingness to bring in these elements both supplements the rehashed plot from *The Spy Who Loved Me* and concedes that these were escapist adventures to enjoy. This knowingness defined the film, which, while arguably postmodern in this approach, offers the idea that perhaps here the canvas of escapism overtakes the fundamental seriousness of the narrative. That is, the film becomes such a panoply of different intertextual components that the audience is completely aware of what they are watching: a movie in which their hero can withstand any amount of physical punishment, is suave and sophisticated, ruthless and deadly, and has a sense of ironic detachment from his surroundings. In other words, Bond offered the audience a purely escapist and masculine fantasy role model for certain demographics of his audience, while also providing spectacular entertainment along the way.

Moore's interpretation of Bond was radically different from Connery's and Lazenby's. His lightweight charm did, however, display a sometimes-ruthlessness, and, while the actor was self-deprecating about his acting, this often-lighter approach, verbalized through sarcasm and one-liners, clearly illustrates Bond as an indestructible character, whereby no "real" harm can come to him. It is this very indestructability that offers up ideas about the character's being completely escapist himself.[14] This is displayed in *Moonraker* in numerous ways. On the one hand, Bond takes a beating from Jaws, who hauls him off the floor during a fistfight. But he also employs laconic dialogue (when he escapes from Drax's python: "He had a crush on me"; upon seeing one of Q's agents using bolas: "Balls, Q?"; admiring Q's dart gun: "Very novel, Q. Must get them in the stores for Christmas"; after tossing Drax into space: "He had to fly"; when suspended from a cable car and Holly Goodhead [Lois Chiles] tells him to hang on, a withering "The thought *had* occurred to me"). This only reflects that Moore and the filmmakers are knowing about the way that this incarnation of 007 is to be portrayed: the spoof elements tell the audience that, despite the cataclysmic events happening around him, Bond remains a steadfastly escapist, masculine fantasy role model.

If one takes into account Elihu Katz and David Foulkes writing that "Escapist worlds . . . are made of unreal or improbable people who are very good or very bad (or very good-bad) and whose successes and failures conveniently cater to the supposed wishes of the audience," it becomes clear that, upon close analysis, *Moonraker* does succeed in offering up ideas of escapism in two ways.[15] The first is through the adventure itself, and the backdrop of exotic vistas that house the narrative. More importantly, Moore follows both Connery and Lazenby in some aspects of his Bond portrayal—the casual meting out of violence, the laconic quips—but simultaneously moves away from them in a rather lighter way. Therefore, Moore's interpretation becomes a vessel through which certain audience demographics can not only *become* Bond through identification (where the individual can experience fistfights, adventures, bedding beautiful women), but also offers a respite from the realist cinema and television approaches for which Britain was celebrated.

This removal from the realist is there to see all through the film. Bond's first appearance involves being pushed out of a private jet in flight. The sequence is breathlessly executed. There are extreme wide shots of Bond and his assailant hurtling across the skies, close-ups of the two men wrestling for the parachute, and, when Bond kicks the man in the face, the pilot screams as he disappears into the distance. To then emphasize the danger of the situation, the image cuts to Bond struggling to put the harness belt securely into place. Even though the sequence is spectacular and utterly fantastical, the fact that it is stuntmen *physically* doing the stunts, and with some obvious shots where Bond is not Roger Moore, the escapist "reality" is evident. Despite the audience being fully aware that Bond will survive, it is serious, it isn't tongue in cheek, until the end of the sequence when Jaws "flaps," birdlike, before crashing into a circus tent after Bond escapes. This incredulous feeling of Bond's indestructibility is then questioned and negated by Miss Moneypenny, who, when told by Bond, "I fell out of an airplane without a parachute . . . You don't believe me, do you?" answers with, "No. And you should go right in." It becomes obvious that the filmmakers are bordering on and facilitating between notions of the serious and the unbelievable.

This unbelievability threads its way through the narrative's set pieces. Bond is almost killed in a G-Force simulator, kills Drax's Chinese henchman by throwing him from a high window into a grand piano, jumps from a crashing cable car onto a patch of grass that breaks his fall, careers down a steep hill on an ambulance gurney, and flies a space shuttle. If we return to Katz and Foulkes' ideas about escapist worlds and unreal people, *Moonraker* becomes not just a potentially cathartic release into escapism for the cinema-going public, but also cements its mix of seriousness and silliness through this escapist lens.

This mix especially comes through toward the end of the movie. When discussing Drax's plans to repopulate the Earth, Bond, standing next to Jaws, says, "Leaving you on your flying stud farm leading your new master race . . . And, of course, anyone not measuring up to your . . . *standards* . . . of physical perfection will be exterminated? Interesting" (figure 11.2). Here, there is no laughter. Bond has used these words with precision, looking at Jaws (with his metal teeth) and the henchman's short-sighted girlfriend Dolly (Blanche Ravalec) as a symbol of what is wrong with Drax's plans. At this moment, Bond has used his guile, not his charm, to aid him. In this respect, his actions and words are dealt with seriously. When Jaws realizes the consequences of Bond's questioning, he turns on Drax and begins to beat up the station's armed guards. The scene moves from seriousness towards the obvious silliness of the premise: Jaws is an assassin, paid for his duties, and has tried to kill Bond on numerous occasions. But with just one sentence from his enemy, he does an about- turn.

With Moore's interpretation of the role heavily reliant on gags, any seriousness is dissipated by the charm of Moore-the-actor and Bond-the-comic. This approach to Bond is jarring, and the fight and action sequences from which Bond escapes make him an unbelievable hero. His quips and one-liners clearly

Figure 11.2 Reaching for the final frontier: James Bond (Roger Moore) goes to space. *Moonraker* (1979).

show he can rise above any danger, and the audience knows this, resulting in the filmmakers pushing Bond closer to parody than before. That this becomes so broad in its playing positions the hero as an impossibility. Yet moments of seriousness do come through and it is *those* moments that make Moore's performance/role in *Moonraker* demonstrate just how important his interpretation of Bond is. The broad playing and fantastically escapist character that Bond has become, where the agent goes *into space* and fires a laser canon from a spaceship while simultaneously fending off an army of henchmen, places him into the more fantastical adventures of *Star Trek*'s Captain Kirk rather than the pen-pushing Harry Palmer in *The Ipcress File* (1965).

The year 1979 was a strong one for science fiction cinema: alongside *Moonraker*, other science fiction movies included *Time After Time*, *The Brood*, and hybrids like *Mad Max* and *Phantasm*. These were fantastic escapist fare. However, for many British individuals, the Seventies was an era in which strikes were commonplace and high taxation was a reality for the majority. While the Queen celebrated her Silver Jubilee, James Callaghan's Labour Party were in turmoil. By 1979, the Conservative Party had come to power, with their right-wing polemic of destroying mining communities on the domestic front and attempts to apply their agenda to Britain's relationships with other countries. Their leader, Margaret Thatcher, had stated in a 1978 interview on Granada Television's *World in Action* that the people of the United Kingdom were worried that they would "be swamped by people of a different culture," clearly indicating where her views lay on areas such as immigration.[16] This polarization seems to indicate a natural conclusion to a decade embroiled in turmoil. This is where a film like

Moonraker offered respite from these destructive elements, despite its heavy leanings toward the right-wing politics of the era.

This was the apex of escapism in Eon's canon of Bond films. James Bond had had adventures around the globe: he had been to Jamaica, Japan, America. He had battled criminal masterminds hell-bent on raising the price of gold to destroy Western markets; he had rid the world of maniacal despots; he had rescued nuclear warheads from the sea, had been on a fictitious moonscape, had destroyed opium manufacturing and distribution. The film's escapism is abundant. While the overuse of product placement is in evidence (Bond's escape from an ambulance alone sees him pass advertisements for Seiko watches, Marlboro cigarettes, 7 Up, and British Airways), and the back projection is at odds with terrific effects, the film is at its most successful in the way that it navigates between the boundaries of seriousness and silliness, and this is done through the lens of escapism.

The movies' outlandish moments are there to see. The serious tone is there too, albeit hidden under a throwaway line, one of Moore's raised eyebrows, or Drax's deadpan delivery. Yet it remains a film that not only exhibits the outlandish mixed with seriousness, but clearly expanded upon the excesses of *You Only Live Twice*, moving on from the smaller scope of some of its predecessors and cementing the tone for the remainder of Moore's tenure. This, in turn, led to the flamboyant excesses of *Die Another Day* and *No Time to Die*. On the one hand, it has elements of pure escapism. On the other, just as importantly for the Briton of 1979, *Moonraker* took its audience away from the streets of the United Kingdom, where strikes and violence were offered up on nightly news programs, to the beauty of Venice and the Amazon. *Moonraker*'s (and, therefore, *our*) Bond narrative offers a chance of negotiation between the audience and the filmmakers to enter into the realms of purely escapist fantasy from the confines of the real world. While other Bond movies may have had a grittier "edge" to them, the facts that *Moonraker* does have some nastier elements and that it allowed opportunities to facilitate changing tastes for its audience, clearly shows that as it riffed off the science fiction boom started with *Star Wars*, the film negotiated a path between realist and fantasy cinema. After all, this was the Bond film that took the hero, and his audience, to outer space.

Notes

1. Matthias R. Hastall, "Escapism," in *The International Encyclopedia of Media Effects*, ed. Patrick Rössler, Cynthia A. Hoffner, and Liesbet van Zoonen (Oxford: Wiley & Sons 2017), 524.
2. Yi-Fu Tuan, *Escapism* (Baltimore, MD: John Hopkins University Press, 1998), 5.

3. Yi-Fu Tuan, "Escapism," Archis, June 1, 2002, archis.org/volume/escapism/. Emphasis added to second quotation.

4. John L. Longeway, "The Rationality of Escapism and Self-Deception," in *Behavior and Philosophy* 18, no. 2 (1990): 1.

5. Christoph Klimmt, "Escapism," in *The Concise Encyclopedia of Communication*, ed. Wolfgang Donsbach (Oxford: Wiley Blackwell, 2015), 178.

6. Ian Fleming, *Casino Royale* (London: Jonathan Cape, 1953), 55.

7. See Christine Berberich, "Putting England Back on Top? Ian Fleming, James Bond, and the Question of England," *Yearbook of English Studies* 42 (2012): 13–29; 14, 24.

8. Kenneth O. Morgan, "Britain in the Seventies—Our Unfinest Hour?," *Revue Française de Civilisation Britannique/French Journal of British Studies* 22 (2017), special issue: 1.

9. Michael Denning, "Licensed to Look: James Bond and the Heroism of Consumption," in *The James Bond Phenomenon: A Critical Reader*, ed. Christoph Lindner (Manchester: Manchester University Press, 2003), 58.

10. Eric Burgess, "The Making of *Moonraker*," *New Scientist*, June 21, 1979, 984; quoted in James Chapman, *Licence to Thrill: A Cultural History of the James Bond Films* (London: I. B. Tauris, 2007), 166–67.

11. John Cork and Brian Scivally, *James Bond: The Legacy* (London: Boxtree, 2002), 177–83; 177.

12. Tim Pulleine, "Moonraker," *Monthly Film Bulletin*, August 1979, 180.

13. Cork and Scivally, *James Bond*, 178.

14. Roger Moore, quoted in Lynne Caffrey, " 'Witty, T***y, Sex!' Wicked Humour behind Roger Moore's Dapper Demeanour," Extra.ie, May 24, 2017, extra.ie/2017/05/24/news /extraordinary/classic-roger-moore-quotes.

15. Elihu Katz and David Foulkes, "On the Use of the Mass Media as 'Escape': Clarification of a Concept," *Public Opinion Quarterly* 26 (1962): 377–88; 382.

16. Margaret Thatcher, interview by Gordon Burns for *World in Action* on January 27, 1978, www.margaretthatcher.org/document/103485.

CHAPTER 12

THE SPECTRE OF DEATH

Revenge and Retribution in *For Your Eyes Only* (1981)

STUART JOY

T he continuity across Ian Fleming's novels about the British spy
James Bond has largely been overlooked in cinematic adaptations
of the series. However, the death of 007's wife, Tracy di Vicenzo
(Diana Rigg), during the finale of *On Her Majesty's Secret Service* (1969) rever-
berates across five decades of Bond's history in print and on screen. In the film's
follow-up, for example, Sean Connery's 007 embarks upon a personal vendetta
to hunt down Ernst Stavro Blofeld (Telly Savalas), the man responsible for
orchestrating Tracy's death. Elsewhere, in *The Spy Who Loved Me* (1977), Roger
Moore's iteration of Bond pointedly interrupts a KGB agent (Barbara Bach)
when she attempts to broach the topic of his short-lived marriage. Several years
later, in *Licence to Kill* (1989), we are reminded that Timothy Dalton's 007 was
"married once . . . a long time ago," and it is the ensuing murder of a friend's
wife that becomes the catalyst for his own violent brand of retributive justice.
In *The World Is Not Enough* (1999), Pierce Brosnan's Bond simply sidesteps a
question about whether he has ever lost a loved one by refusing to answer it.
Even though references to the character of Tracy di Vicenzo are not present
in the subsequent rebooting of the franchise, her death looms large over the
women with whom Daniel Craig's 007 is romantically involved. The tragic loss
of Vesper Lynd (Eva Green) in *Casino Royale* (2006) and the ending of *Spectre*
(2015), for instance, both evoke the haunting conclusion of *On Her Majesty's
Secret Service*, while *No Time to Die* (2021) is perhaps the most overt paean to
Bond's defining personal relationship.

Prior to this, the most explicit acknowledgment of Bond's trauma occurred during the pre-credit sequence of *For Your Eyes Only* (1981), in which 007 pays a somber visit to the cemetery where his wife is buried. As he approaches her grave, a bouquet of red roses in hand, we clearly see the inscription on the headstone which states: "TERESA BOND. 1943–1969. Beloved Wife of JAMES BOND," along with the phrase "We have all the time in the world." The engraving unambiguously recalls Bond's final words to Tracy at the denouement of *On Her Majesty's Secret Service* as he cradled her lifeless body in his arms. In *For Your Eyes Only*, Bond's momentary melancholic introspection provides a glimpse of the underlying fragility at the core of his action-hero identity. Nonetheless, in line with most mainstream films that tend to overlook bereavement in favor of preserving plot momentum, there is no time for Bond to grieve.[1] Instead, his fleeting emotional vulnerability is interrupted by a helicopter that has been sent by MI6 to collect him for his next mission. However, it quickly becomes apparent that Bond's long-time adversary Blofeld, who for legal reasons could not be named in the film, has remotely hijacked the vehicle. As the helicopter soars over London, Bond succeeds in retaking control of the aircraft and impales "Blofeld's" motorized wheelchair on one of the helicopter's landing skids. Bond then hoists him into the air before unceremoniously dumping him down a disused industrial-scale chimney to his apparent "death."

As Lisa Funnell and Klaus Dodds point out in *Geographies, Genders and Geopolitics of James Bond* (2017), by connecting this sequence to Bond's grieving at the cemetery, the opening of *For Your Eyes Only* depicts his actions as revenge for his late wife.[2] In doing so, it highlights what Lynette S. Moran labels a noticeably "masculine experience of grief" frequently articulated in popular culture: i.e., that even in mourning, men at any age can use action-based plots of thrill and adventure to reconcile their past traumas.[3] These portrayals of vengeful men contribute to hegemonic norms of masculinity within mainstream media and to cultural understandings of grief. Such depictions frame the experience of bereavement through the prism of distinctly gendered emotional displays. In *For Your Eyes Only*, for example, the death of "Blofeld" during the climax of the opening sequence seeks to draw a metaphorical line under Bond's loss by equating his (masculine) retribution with a gratifying sense of closure. For the remainder of the film, however, it is Melina Havelock (Carole Bouquet), the grieving daughter of murdered marine archaeologists, who drives the narrative forward in her pursuit of personal vengeance. The film shows Havelock to be an active woman who, unlike most other "Bond girls," embraces her raw anger and aggression in ways typically reserved exclusively for Bond and other male protagonists. Indeed, her quest for revenge takes precedence over her personal relationship with Bond and it underpins the emotional core of the film.[4] In doing so, it exposes some of the stereotypes and contradictions inherent in the complex interrelationship between revenge and gender otherwise lacking in mainstream cinema. Thus, the film raises questions about how revenge narratives have an impact on wider perceptions of gender; whether such narratives reinforce traditional gender roles, interrogate "masculine" values, or establish new ways of conceptualizing women and men. But despite its perceived feminist credentials, *For Your Eyes Only* may not truly abandon the Bond franchise's legacy of female subjugation through its revision of women's relationship to violence.[5]

Revenge Is a Dish Best Served Male

The association between violent (male) revenge and retributive justice has long been a staple of Western art and culture that predates cinema.[7] In his study of revenge drama, literary scholar John Kerrigan even goes so far as to position revenge as one of the defining themes of narrative construction: "a building-block, the seed from which something larger can grow, since one man's vengeance being another man's injury . . . will breed others as blood calls for blood and the symmetries of action extend into plot."[8] As Kerrigan's distinctly gendered language indicates, violent revenge has historically been the purview of men. This is unsurprising given that study after study has shown that men are more prone than women to physical aggression.[8] However, research also shows that men and women do not fundamentally differ in the way they *experience* the emotions that commonly lead to violent behavior. This raises the question of what inhibits women from *expressing* such emotions; the answer may reside in a broader understanding of gender norms and the position of women in patriarchal societies that reserve power exclusively for boys and men.

Building on the work of Nancy Chodorow, feminist psychologist Leslie Brody proposed a comprehensive theoretical model to account for gendered differences in emotional displays between boys and girls.[9] She suggested that children are conditioned from an early age to internalize gender-appropriate emotional responses through complex interactions among a variety of factors, including biological differences, cultural pressures, family relationships, and peer interactions. For Brody, this process begins at birth depending on assigned sex and continues through differing socialization practices. These, in turn, influence the course of children's emotional expressiveness while preparing them for the successful completion of culturally determined gender roles. In line with these roles, Brody argues that "boys are shaped to minimize emotional expressions with some important exceptions: notably anger." By contrast, girls are taught to maximize emotions that promote empathic concern and prosocial behavior while minimizing expressions of aggression and anger. The beneficiaries of these "display rules" are, in most cases, boys and men. This is to say that the limitations placed upon the specific kinds of emotions that women can comfortably express function to maintain cultural gender roles as well as their accompanying status and privilege.[10]

Such gendered differences are not merely restricted to being informed by interpersonal relationships; television, films, literature, video games, and other forms of media play a significant role in fostering prescriptive stereotypes about what constitutes normative behavior. These texts not only reflect, but also shape expectations about emotional expression. For example, in 2018, Antonina Starzyzyńska and Magdalena Budziszewska analyzed sixty revenge narratives produced by major Hollywood studios in the twenty-first century. They concluded that these films perpetuate longstanding sociocultural traditions that teach women to fear their own aggression. For Starzyzyńska and Budziszewska, these films show women that any attempt to express such basic emotions as anger, even in the most extreme of cases, threatens to disintegrate their identity and marginalize them from the discourses of femininity. These films, they argue, embody antiquated values that linger in the shared consciousness of patriarchal societies. They go on to note that what is equally disturbing is that these stock narratives have strong formative effects on the youngest members of society. Girls, for example, "grow up in the narrative context that does not offer them heroic imagery and reduces them to the roles characterized by passivity and victimhood instead."[11] The dearth of positive onscreen role models for girls and women is a problem that extends beyond revenge narratives. In a study conducted by the Annenberg Inclusion Initiative examining inequality in 1,300 popular films from 2007 to 2019, the authors concluded that "the portrayal of gender roles still fall along stereotypical lines."[12] It is within this context that the women of the Bond franchise take on significance because they call attention to the representation of women in culture more generally.

For His Eyes Only

Women have undoubtedly been central to ensuring that James Bond has remained one of the most enduring icons of popular culture throughout the last sixty years. Christoph Lindner, writing in Lisa Funnell's essential anthology *For His Eyes Only: The Women of James Bond* (2015), notes that female characters play a significant role in framing our understanding of the protagonist: that "women in the 007 series have largely been defined by their relationship with Bond, just as Bond himself has often been defined by his relationship with women." The difference, he says, "is that Bond is named, identified, singularized, whereas women remain generic, interchangeable, dependent."[13] The fundamental issue regarding the perception of women and the problematic representational politics of the franchise is fueled, at least in part, by the undercurrent of sexism associated with the "Bond girl" label. This term, while widely adopted in popular and academic discourse to discuss the women of the series, illus-trates the gendered tensions about the role. Tony Bennett and Janet Woolla-cott, for example, assert that any discussion that engages with the terms of ref-erence suggested by the phrase "Bond girl" is committed to framing female gender identities and forms of sexuality through the lens of normative mascu-linity.[14] Along similar lines, in their study exploring the public perceptions of women in the franchise, Funnell and Taylor Johnson remark that the label "not only obscures the diversity notable in the representation of women across the series but also reduces their narrative importance by presenting them as func-tions of Bond (i.e., they are Bond's girl)." They go on to argue that "the use of the term 'girl' to describe and often patronize women infantilizes them and dimin-ishes their professional accomplishments while stressing their sexual avail-ability to Bond."[15] By contrast, Monica Germanà, the author of *Bond Girls: Body, Fashion, Gender* (2019), offers an alternative perspective on the negative con-notations inscribed in the gendered language of patriarchal societies. Speaking during an interview for the *James Bond Radio* podcast, she put forward a per-suasive argument for reclaiming the phrase "Bond girl," asserting that "there is nothing wrong with the term 'girl' per se. It's been used derogatively in sexist language, but that doesn't mean that it can't be reappropriated in a positive and self-assertive fashion."[16] It is this ongoing tension—between Bond girls as sexually subordinate objects versus the portrayal of female characters who pos-sess agency and choice—that is at the heart of the debate surrounding the use of the phrase "Bond girl" as well as the broader implications of her intersec-tion with feminine and feminist cultures.

How does one define a "Bond girl," then? In the collective consciousness of popular culture, these characters embody a potent cocktail of intelligence, beauty, athleticism, and skill.[17] While many viewers might still consider their attractiveness and physicality to be among their most defining characteristics, Bond girls are not merely objects for male pleasure. Rather, according to Ger-manà, these characters challenge accepted conventions about femininity and gender roles, as well as 007's own attitudes toward women. In her monograph, she asserts that: "Bond Girls and female villains twist the known paradigms of the male gaze, restoring power to its fetishized object." She also says that "Dead or alive, desired and desiring, rather than an assuaging strategy in support of the masculine ego, the unveiled phallicism of Bond female characters exposes the deep scars of Bond's wounded masculinity."[18] Moya Luckett argues that in addition to their textual function, Bond girls are often used to index over fifty years of popular assumptions about feminism and femininity.[19] It is within this context that Fernando Gabriel Pagnoni Berns positions *For Your Eyes Only* alongside *Octopussy* (1983) as being influenced by the radical feminist move-ment of the second wave and especially the emergence of female-only commu-nities that offered women a place to live beyond the reach of patriarchy.[20]

The Forgotten Bond Girl

Given *For Your Eyes Only*'s apparent connections to the radical feminist move-ment, it is perhaps unsurprising that references to Melina Havelock are largely absent from the vast majority of promotional material and international pub-licity that typically coincides with the release of each new entry in the Bond franchise; these journalistic discussions typically rank Bond Girls—from the most attractive or memorable to the best or worst or the most or least intelligent—and tend to favor sexualized images of women as objects of a dom-inant male look.[21] References to the character are also entirely absent from the Bond-related documentaries *Everything or Nothing: The Untold Story of 007* (2012) and *Bond Girls Are Forever* (2002).[22] Bennett and Woollacott similarly fail to acknowledge Havelock in their influential study *Bond and Beyond: The Political Career of a Popular Hero* (1987) and she is only a footnote in Funnell's work examining the heroic identity and transnational appeal of the Bond girl.[23] The most conspicuous omission is undoubtedly Roger Moore's book *Bond on Bond* (2015), which contains no reference to Havelock, even in a chapter dedi-cated to Bond girls.[24] The absence of both popular and critical discourses related to Melina Havelock is especially surprising given the perception of the charac-ter upon whom she is based from the short story *For Your Eyes Only*.[25] In *The World Is Not Enough: A Biography of Ian Fleming* (2020), Oliver Buckton notes that Havelock is positioned as Bond's "female equal," while James Chapman acknowledges that she possesses a narrative agency entirely independent of Bond.[26] Elsewhere, in *Ian Fleming & James Bond: The Cultural Politics of 007* (2005), Craig N. Owens goes so far as to assert that Havelock's power even arouses a figurative fear of castration in 007.[27]

Pagnoni Berns is one of only a few scholars to acknowledge the significance of Havelock in the history of the Bond franchise. Referring to the screen adap-tation of *For Your Eyes Only*, he says that Havelock is presented as "one of the strongest Bond Girls" in the franchise, who, like her literary counterpart, "is actually on par with Bond." He goes on to recognize that throughout the film she is shown to be competent and resourceful, dispatching her parents' assas-sin with a crossbow and demonstrating other skills that are commensurate with Bond's own. Unlike other Bond girls, Havelock is never captured or held hos-tage by the villain. In fact, in *For Your Eyes Only*, it is Havelock who saves Bond during their first encounter, when she shoots one of his pursuers with an arrow. Bond's subsequent attempts to reassert his masculinity are often short-lived and it is Havelock who frequently undermines traditional gender stereotypes. This is noticeably evident during the car chase, a feature that has become a staple of the Bond franchise over the years. During this sequence, it is Havelock who successfully guides Bond through enemy territory in her yellow Citroën 2 CV

Figure 12.1 Melina Havelock (Carole Bouquet) undermines a visibly dumbfounded Bond (Roger Moore) by forcibly retaking control of her Citroën 2CV. *For Your Eyes Only* (1981).

(figure 12.1). As Pagnoni Berns notes, "[T]he car is clearly different from the high technological gadgets he has access to as the male hero."[28] Nevertheless, Havelock ably drives Bond out of trouble until she inadvertently rolls the vehicle when *he* instructs her to change direction. Funnell and Dodds note that Bond's interactions with women in cars are clearly informed by a pronounced patriarchal ideology that conveys implicit messages about the intersection between gender and ability in the franchise. They remark, "the competency of women as heroic allies is often signaled, if not partially embodied, by their driving skills and those who do not measure up (in Bond's eyes) are deemed inferior agents and allies."[29] In *For Your Eyes Only*, Havelock's "mistake" necessitates that the characters switch places to reestablish a more traditional approach to gender roles. Moments later, however, Havelock undermines Bond's masculine authority once again by forcibly retaking control of the car when he briefly hesitates. Instances such as these are indicative of the way she disrupts gender roles, but it is her active pursuit of personal revenge and her disinterest in 007 that most clearly identifies her as being distinct among the history of Bond girls.

For Your Eyes Only: Confronting the Male Gaze

At the start of *For Your Eyes Only*, Havelock is first shown on board a small seaplane en route to visit her parents. In these initial moments, she is introduced reapplying her makeup, an act that for Pagnoni Berns emphasizes a frequent primary concern of the "Bond girl"—that is, an "aesthetic femininity."[30] However, in stark contrast to the opening frames of the film, the sequence concludes with an extreme close-up (ECU) of Havelock's eyes as she stares directly into the lens of the camera following the traumatic murder of her parents (figure 12.2). The significance of this final shot should not be understated; from a thematic perspective the moment emphasizes Havelock's agency as opposed to her beauty while conveying a complex and layered approach to her characterization; the tight framing communicates Havelock's anger, sadness, and confusion but, most of all, her desire for revenge. Indeed, the narrative importance subsequently accorded to Havelock's pursuit of personal revenge is such that it "takes precedence over the romance between Bond and herself," according to Chapman.[31] From a symbolic perspective, the ECU is also important as it is one of only a few moments in the franchise where a character other than Bond breaks the "fourth wall."[32]

In film history, moments such as these—when a character directly addresses the viewer—draw attention to the construction of the narrative by acknowledging the technology that produces it. Marc Vernet describes this technique as having a double effect: "It foregrounds the enunciative instance of the filmic text and attacks the spectator's voyeurism by putting the space of the film and the space of the movie theatre briefly into direct contact."[33] Vernet is right to emphasize the transgressive potential of the "look" and the power that it holds to disrupt the viewer's immersion in the fictional world. However, breaking the fourth wall also possesses the ability to increase character-based forms of engagement by intensifying our relationship with fictional characters.[34] In the Bond franchise, instances of self-consciousness are generally reserved exclusively for 007 and, as such, are indicative of the intimate relationship shared between the protagonist and the viewer.[35] Thus, the effect of breaking the fourth wall in *For Your Eyes Only* has gendered implications, as it enhances our engagement with a secondary character who, like Bond, resists objectification.[36] Rather than being subject to the male gaze, the use of direct address leaves the

Figure 12.2 Melina Havelock (Carole Bouquet) stares directly at the camera in a moment that disrupts the viewer's voyeuristic gaze. *For Your Eyes Only* (1981).

audience unable to distance themselves from Havelock's emotional experience of grief. Consequently, the traditional male gaze is disrupted.[37]

From this point forward, Havelock's desire for personal revenge becomes her defining characteristic as well as forming the basis of a significant subplot that drives the narrative forward. Significantly, this emphasis is largely out of step with the broader discourse of feminine violence offered by cinematic narratives about women who kill. According to Starzyzyńska and Budziszewska, for instance, revenge is frequently framed as a response to acts of physical abuse—almost always rape—inflicted upon female characters in these films.[38] Havelock's quest for personal revenge does not conform to the rape-revenge narrative structure that, as Yvonne Tasker argues, is heavily characterized by a problematic binding of eroticism to violence and vulnerability to invulnerability in the victimized violent women.[39] Instead, For Your Eyes Only is indebted to a long and storied cinematic history of (masculine) vengeful equivalence. In these narratives, masculine aggression is warranted by the death or suffering of loved ones and men's violence is framed as a righteous, justified, and necessary response that benefits the social order; violent retribution functions to reinstitute patriarchal law. Likewise, in For Your Eyes Only, Havelock's initial act of vengeance does not satiate her desire for retribution. Consequently, she attempts to pursue the man responsible for orchestrating her parents' deaths based on a logic of violent masculinity that seeks to restore order and balance the scales of justice.

Unfortunately, Havelock's gesture of defiance against the expected complicity of a "good girl" within a patriarchal system is eventually neutralized by the necessity within mainstream narratives for female subjugation. Annette Kuhn discusses this imperative in relation to classic Hollywood cinema in Women's Pictures (1994). She points out that these stories often involve a woman who motivates the plot through her "troublesome" presence, finally accepting a "normative" role in society.[40] This cinematic trend is notably evident at the climax of For Your Eyes Only, during which Havelock's agency is stripped from her when the opportunity to avenge her parents is taken by another man seeking his own revenge. Furthermore, in line with the traditional ending of a Bond film, Havelock—like so many women in the franchise before her—seemingly succumbs to 007's sexual advances, thereby reaffirming the patriarchal order.

On the one hand, the formulaic ending of For Your Eyes Only seems to undermine any claim that the film can be interpreted by adopting a feminist perspective. However, upon closer inspection, the final exchange between Havelock and Bond is indicative of the film's broader attempt to challenge gender norms by contesting traditionally defined "masculine" qualities.[41] The scene begins with a passionate kiss between the two, but it is Havelock who instigates their embrace; her subsequent question, "Do you know what I'd like?" (emphasis added), also suggests an inversion of traditional gender-based power dynamics in sexual relationships.[42] In the ensuing moments, Bond moves to undress Havelock but pauses momentarily before lowering her robe; it is *her* look and *her* words—"For your eyes only, darling"—that grant him the permission to continue. Even though these words are ostensibly rooted in the language of patriarchal possession, the context in which they are deployed speaks to the possibility of manipulating the way she is surveyed by Bond, becoming herself the one who controls the visual economy of desire. Melina Havelock's body may be for Bond's eyes only, but it is not forfeited at the expense of her own distinctive agency.[43]

Notes

1. See Lynette S. Moran, "Men in Mourning: Depictions of Masculinity in Young and Older Widowers in Contemporary Film," *Men and Masculinities* 19, no. 1 (2016): 4.
2. Lisa Funnell and Klaus Dodds, *Geographies, Genders and Geopolitics of James Bond* (London: Palgrave Macmillan, 2017), 36. Admittedly, the rather comical dispatch of Bond's archenemy was principally motivated by the ongoing litigation regarding the rights to the screen version of the character of Blofeld. See Robert Sellers, *The Battle for Bond*, 2nd ed. (Sheffield: Tomahawk Press, 2008).
3. Moran, "Men in Mourning," 14.
4. See Jeremy Black, *The Politics of James Bond: From Fleming's Novels to the Big Screen* (Westport, CT: Praeger, 2005), 142.
5. See Fernando Gabriel Pagnoni Berns, "Sisterhood as Resistance in *For Your Eyes Only* and *Octopussy*," in *For His Eyes Only: The Women of James Bond*, ed. Lisa Funnell (New York: Wallflower, 2015), 119–27.
6. Karina Schumann and Michael Ross, "The Benefits, Costs, and Paradox of Revenge," *Social and Personality Psychology Compass* 4, no. 12 (2010): 1193–1205.
7. John Kerrigan, *Tragedy: Aeschylus to Armageddon* (Oxford: Clarendon Press, 1996), 14.
8. See John Archer, "Sex Differences in Aggression in Real-World Settings: A Meta-Analytic Review," *Review of General Psychology* 8 (2004): 291–322.
9. Nancy Chodorow, *The Reproduction of Mothering: Psychoanalysis and the Sociology of Gender* (Berkeley: University of California Press, 1978); Leslie Brody, *Gender, Emotion, and the Family* (Cambridge, MA: Harvard University Press, 1999).
10. Brody, *Gender, Emotion, and the Family*, 4, 228.
11. Antonina Starzyzyńska and Magdalena Budziszewska, "Why Shouldn't She Spit on His Grave? Critical Discourse Analysis of the Revenge Narratives in American Popular Film from the Developmental Point of View," *Psychology of Language and Communication* 22, no.1 (2018): 304.
12. Annenberg Inclusion Initiative, *Inequality in 1,300 Popular Films: Examining Portrayals of Gender, Race/Ethnicity, LGBTQ & Disability from 2007 to 2019*, Annenberg Foundation and USC Annenberg Inclusion Institute, August 9, 2020, assets .uscannenberg.org/docs/aii-inequality_1300_popular_films_09-08-2020.pdf, 11.
13. Christopher Lindner, "Foreword," in Funnell, *For His Eyes Only*, xvii.
14. Tony Bennett and Janet Woollacott, *Bond and Beyond: The Political Career of a Popular Hero* (London: Macmillan, 1987), 241.

15. Lisa Funnell and Tyler Johnson, "Properties of a Lady: Public Perceptions of Women in the James Bond Franchise," *Participations: Journal of Audience and Reception Studies* 17, no. 2 (2020): 97.
16. Matthew Chernov, "Talking Fashion, Fetishism & Fleming with 'Bond Girls' Author Monica Germanà," *James Bond Radio*, November 11, 2019, jamesbondradio.com /talking-fashion-fetishism-fleming-with-bond-girls-author-monica-germana/
17. See Funnell and Johnson, "Properties of a Lady," 95–114.
18. Monica Germanà, *Bond Girls: Body, Fashion, Gender* (London: Bloomsbury, 2019), 201.
19. Moya Luckett, "Femininity, Seriality and Collectivity: Rethinking the Bond Girl," in *The Cultural Life of James Bond: Specters of 007*, ed. Jaap Verheul (Amsterdam: Amsterdam University Press, 2020), 149.
20. Pagnoni Berns, "Sisterhood as Resistance," 120.
21. See Claire Hines, "For His Eyes Only? Men's Magazines and the Curse of the Bond Girl," in *James Bond in World and Popular Culture: The Films Are Not Enough*, 2nd ed., ed. Robert G. Weiner, B. Lynn Whitfield, and Jack Becker (Newcastle upon Tyne, UK: Cambridge Scholars, 2011), 169–77; Claire Hines and Stephanie Jones, "Loaded Magazines: James Bond and British Men's Mags in the Brosnan Era," in *From Blofeld to Moneypenny: Gender in James Bond*, ed. Steven Gerrard (Bingley, UK: Emerald, 2020), 152–66; Radika Seth, "14 Bond Girls Who Overshadowed 007," *British Vogue*, September 25, 2021, www.vogue.co.uk/arts-and-lifestyle/gallery/best-bond-girls; Joshua Rich, "Countdown: The 10 Worst Bond Girls," *Entertainment Weekly*, November 13, 2006, ew.com/article/2006/11/13/countdown-10-worst-bond-girls/.
22. Bouquet's reluctance to appear in Bond-related retrospectives may partially be explained by her own dismissive attitude toward the role: "I wanted respect at least. I didn't want to be a bimbo. It's a great movie to look at and it's a great movie for special effects but [not] for actors who are trying to act. I was dreaming of Shakespeare which is absurd now but at the time it was important to me. I never intended to become just another Bond girl. I'm not simply a plastic doll like the rest of them." Quoted in Tim Greaves, *The Bond Women: 007 Style.* (N.p.: 1-Shot Publications, 2002), 60.
23. Funnell merely lists Havelock among "other notable characters." See Lisa Funnell, "From English Partner to American Action Hero: The Heroic Identity and Transnational Appeal of the Bond Girl," in *Heroes and Heroines: Embodiment, Symbolism, Narratives and Identity*, ed. Christopher Hart (Kingswinford, UK: Midrash, 2008), 61–80; 64.
24. See Roger Moore, *Bond on Bond: The Ultimate Book on Over 50 Years of 007* (London: Michael O'Mara Books, 2015). The absence of any reference to Moore's co-star Carole Bouquet (aside from one caption) may be connected to a "tactless" remark she made during the production of *For Your Eyes Only* that the fifty-three-year-old Moore reminded her of her father. See Matthew Field and Ajay Chowdhury, *Some Kind of Hero: The Remarkable Story of the James Bond Films* (Stroud, UK: The History Press, 2015).
25. Ian Fleming, *For Your Eyes Only* (London: Jonathan Cape, 1960).
26. Oliver Buckton, *The World Is Not Enough: A Biography of Ian Fleming* (Lanham, MD: Rowman & Littlefield, 2020), 198; James Chapman, "'Women Were for Recreation': The Gender Politics of Ian Fleming's James Bond," in Funnell, *For His Eyes Only*, 15.
27. Craig N. Owens, "The Bond Market," in *Ian Fleming & James Bond: The Cultural Politics of 007*, ed. Edward P. Comentale, Stephen Watt, and Skip Willman (Bloomington: Indiana University Press, 2005), 105–28; 115.
28. Pagnoni Berns, "Sisterhood as Resistance," 121.
29. Funnell and Dodds, *Geographies, Genders, and Geopolitics*, 184.

30. Pagnoni Berns, "Sisterhood as Resistance," 121.
31. James Chapman, *Licence to Thrill: A Cultural History of the James Bond Films* (London: I. B. Tauris., 2007), 177.
32. Another notable example occurs at the climax of *Live and Let Die* (1973), when Baron Samedi (Geoffrey Holder) breaks the fourth wall by raising his hat to the audience while laughing maniacally and staring straight into the lens of the camera.
33. Marc Vernet, "Look at the Camera," *Cinema Journal* 28, no. 2 (1989): 48.
34. See Jonathan Cohen, Mary Beth Oliver, and Helena Bilandzic, "The Differential Effects of Direct Address on Parasocial Experience and Identification: Empirical Evidence for Conceptual Difference," *Communication Research Reports* 36, no. 1 (2018): 78–83.
35. For example, during the final shot of the unofficial James Bond film *Never Say Never Again* (1983), Sean Connery's "007" slyly winks at the audience. At the end of the pre-title sequence of *On Her Majesty's Secret Service* (1969), George Lazenby's Bond looks directly at the camera and speaks to the audience with a self-reflexive quote referencing Connery's departure from the series. Elsewhere, in *Octopussy*, an Indian snake charmer briefly plays Monty Norman's "James Bond's Theme" in the midst of a performance.
36. Notable exceptions to this trend are the Bond films of the Daniel Craig era. See Lisa Funnell, "'I Know Where You Keep Your Gun': Daniel Craig as the Bond–Bond Girl Hybrid in *Casino Royale*," *Journal of Popular Culture* 44, no. 3 (2011): 455–72.
37. See Laura Mulvey, "Visual Pleasure and Narrative Cinema," *Screen* 16, no. 3 (1975): 6–18.
38. Starzyzyńska and Budziszewska, "Why Shouldn't She Spit on His Grave?," 300–301.
39. See Lisa Coulthard, "Killing Bill: Rethinking Feminism and Film Violence," in *Interrogating Postfeminism Gender and the Politics of Popular Culture*, ed. Diane Negra and Yvonne Tasker (London: Duke University Press, 2007), 153–75.
40. Annette Kuhn, *Women's Pictures: Feminism and Cinema* (London: Verso, 1994), 34.
41. See Pagnoni Berns, "Sisterhood as Resistance," 122.
42. See A. K. Blanc, "The Effect of Power in Sexual Relationships on Sexual and Reproductive Health: An Examination of the Evidence," *Studies in Family Planning* 32, no. 3: 189–213, 190.
43. Special thanks to Kierren Darke and Philip Joy for providing valuable feedback on early drafts of this chapter.

CHAPTER 13

THE (CLOWN) SUITED HERO

James Bond, Costume, Gender, and Disguise in *Octopussy* (1983)

CLAIRE HINES

To a significant extent, the familiar image of James Bond posing dressed in a midnight-blue, black, or sometimes ivory dinner jacket and trousers, accessorized by his gun and surrounded by women, defines both the character and the franchise, being used, for instance, on the glossy poster designs created as part of the films' publicity campaigns, almost without exception. This is the case with the posters for *Octopussy* (1983), with the tuxedo-clad and gun-wielding Roger Moore as Bond in the foreground, the female lead Octopussy (Maud Adams) and another six arms entangling him from behind. There is a strong "sexual grammar" to these and other Bond film posters, and emphasis is placed on the agent's virile masculinity, signified through his posture, confidence, attractiveness to women, and suave, well-dressed style, distinctly connoted by the dinner suit (or tuxedo).[1]

Yet although the *Octopussy* poster and publicity campaign use the tuxedo that is iconic of the Bond image, a motivation for this chapter is another outfit worn by Bond in the film that couldn't be more different, but in retrospect is no less (in)famous and therefore merits discussion. For now, Bond dressed as a clown is probably all that needs to be said to bring this controversial counter-image to mind. Like the film, this costumed image and the sequence during which Bond disarms a nuclear bomb in a crowded circus tent has polarized audiences, film critics, and commentators. But what might further analysis of this and other disguises used by Bond in *Octopussy* bring to our understanding of costume, gender, and Bond's image as the suited hero? This chapter adds to existing analyses of costume in the franchise, but shifts the focus of attention away from Bond's established association with tailoring and fashion to examine whether *Octopussy* might challenge aspects of the cinematic identity of the Bond character by unusually (over)emphasizing costume as disguise throughout.

For a number of reasons, Bond is not usually considered a man of disguise. However, in theory, surely, he should be. After all, a primary element of the spy's job description must be an ability to hide one's identity, change one's appearance, go undercover, and disguise oneself effectively to survive in the field. In a way, this also applies to the actor playing Bond on screen. It is important to get the relationship between the Bond character and actor right. What this means has changed over time, from Sean Connery through to Moore and beyond. Over the years, Bond has periodically been reinvented through casting, yet always remains himself: "Bond, James Bond."[2] To clarify, before going any further, the definition of disguise in this chapter differs from a cover or false identity, although there are inevitably connections and overlaps between these in the Bond films. Disguise here relates directly to appearance and refers to the use of costumes and accessories during missions to hide Bond's identity to some extent. In particular, I will explore that, in a significant departure for the famously stylish superspy, Bond wears several distinctive disguises during *Octopussy*, most memorably the horsey-gear-cum-military-uniform during the pre-credit sequence, a mechanical crocodile disguise, and a number of circus costumes that include the clown suit and a gorilla outfit.[3]

The plot of this disguise-heavy thirteenth installment in the film franchise is complicated, to say the least; however, broadly speaking, when Bond is assigned the mission to solve the murder of another British agent, he discovers a jewelry-smuggling scheme that he follows to India, which is actually a cover for a plan to detonate a nuclear bomb and destroy a US Air Force base in West Germany in the hope of tricking Europe into disarmament (in the belief that it was an American bomb detonated by accident, and leaving borders open to invasion). This was a highly topical reference in the 1980s, when the movement for nuclear disarmament had regained strength.[4] During the summer of 1983 *Octopussy* performed well at the box office, being among the highest-grossing films despite strong competition from the third film in the *Star Wars* series, *Return of the Jedi* (1983), and *Superman III* (1983).[5] Nevertheless, it has been observed that the film's critical reception was rather "muted."[6] "The Bond Wagon Crawls Along" headlined Richard Schickel's review for *Time*.[7] Pauline Kael of the *New York Times* considered "silliness" to be the "chief charm" of *Octopussy*, and like others she was accepting of (well, "resigned to") Moore in the Bond role, saying, "He may not be heroic, but he's game." Kael referred to *Octopussy* as "part parody and part travesty," an insightful assessment to which I later return to reflect on gender, costume, and the clown disguise.[8]

The Well-Dressed Spy

No matter what the actor who portrays Bond looks like, in the franchise the suit he wears can be understood to function as the opposite of a disguise, being definitive to the signification of the character and transformative for the actor in the role of Bond. It can be argued that in this respect the suit is, in fact, Bond's ultimate uniform. More than any other item of clothing in his wardrobe, the dinner suit is associated with his suave masculinity and iconic status. Indeed, in the illustrated coffee table book *Dressed to Kill* (1995), focused on the character's style and sartorial transformations and impact on male fashion, Bond is labelled *The Suited Hero*.[9] It is a subtitle that recognizes the enduring significance of his classic style of dress.

Clearly, there are scenes and costumes in *Octopussy* that fit comfortably with the well-dressed image expected of the Bond character. These include the elegant three-piece suit he wears during his usual briefing with M (Robert Brown) and the tropical suit and ivory dinner jacket he wears when in India on his mission.[10] During his stint in the role Moore developed his own take on Bond largely through performance, but aspects of dress are also highly influential on a sense of both change and continuity of the look of the character. In *Fashioning James Bond* (2022), Llewella Chapman examines the essential role that costume and fashion has played in the Bond franchise, with special attention to the agency of the wardrobe staff, director, producer, scriptwriter, and actor involved in designing and creating costumes over the years. In retrospect, the Moore era is especially judged (with some good reason) for some of Bond's clothing being of its time, particularly the safari suit, first worn in *The Man with the Golden Gun* (1974) and donned in other films, including *Octopussy*. Although Moore's reputation for safari suits has been joked about, in fact this fashion-conscious choice is reflective of how aspects of the all-important sartorial wardrobe associated with the Bond image might change to reflect the (agency of the) actor and the time of the film's release.[11]

Other scholarly and online writing on costume and the Bond films has largely focused on aspects of fashion and tailoring, especially the role of the suit in the wardrobe and signification of Bond.[12] Online, Matt Spaiser's *Bond Suits* blog extensively analyzes formal and casual menswear throughout the franchise. As he observes, "Bond usually dresses as himself, whether he's using his own name or an alias. He has a strong sartorial identity and dresses in an elegant manner with an eye for detail. On occasion he modifies his usual manner of dress to better fit in with a crowd, but it's usually only a slight alteration." However, Spaiser follows up this observation with the comment that by contrast, "*Octopussy* is the unusual Bond film where Bond spends half the film not dressing how we expect him to."[13] This remark is made in a post that catalogues many of the film's outfits used as disguises by Bond and others. By my calculation, the screen time that Bond spends disguised in *Octopussy* amounts to around thirty minutes out of the two-hour, eleven-minute run time, but the comment is especially interesting because of the case being made for the particular significance of disguise to Bond in this film.

A discussion of costume must extend beyond clothing to include some of the associated gadgetry. During the Connery era Q branch gadgets became a signature element of the Bond films, some of which the agent uses to conceal his identity or accessorize a disguise. Bond's gadgets, too, generally have a strong association with style, fashion, and gender. As Louis Markos observes, Bond's gadgets "are also *accessories* that the well-dressed gentleman simply cannot do without. . . . Bond, with the help of his gadgets, will always save the day and, it must be understood he will always look damn good while he's doing it."[14] *Octopussy* might be considered something of an exception to this statement, certainly when it comes to some of the less than fashionable costumes and gadgets that Bond must employ when doing his heroic world-saving. Before moving on to a closer analysis of some of his key disguises in *Octopussy*, it is first useful to consider some past functions of disguise in the world of Bond.

Bond and Disguise

While the focus on Bond's strong sartorial style related to his masculine image and heroic identity means that he is not thought of especially as wearing disguises, prior to *Octopussy* the character had already adopted them both in the films and in the Ian Fleming novels on which the earlier entries in the franchise are based. One notable example from the Connery era includes the pre-credit sequence of *Goldfinger* (1964), when Bond must infiltrate and destroy a secret facility in Latin America. The sequence begins with a seagull bobbing on the water, which an emerging Bond is revealed to be wearing on his head, along with scuba gear. After discarding the headgear, Bond enters the drug laboratory to plant explosives and then exits, removing his wetsuit, underneath which he is somehow inexplicably wearing an immaculate (dry) tuxedo. In a continuation of this visual joke, he then produces a perfect red carnation, casually pausing to position it in his buttonhole before entering a nightclub. A second, more problematic use of disguise occurs in *You Only Live Twice* (1967), adapted from Fleming's novel, where Bond goes undercover as a Japanese fisherman for his mission. In the film, Connery's eyebrows and eyes are changed, his skin is tinted, he wears a wig and kimono to "transform" the character's appearance.

Another example for consideration occurs in *On Her Majesty's Secret Service* (1969), where Bond impersonates genealogy expert Sir Hilary Bray. For this disguise, he dons a heavy, old-fashioned coat with an Inverness cape, a style closely associated with Sherlock Holmes, and later, at dinner, a tartan kilt, to infiltrate the villain's mountaintop lair in the Swiss Alps.[15] For some viewers, it might well be "hard to take [this Bond in disguise] completely seriously," given that this is also a film where the new Bond George Lazenby turns directly to the camera and comments, "This never happened to the other fellow."[16] Nevertheless, as Sir Hilary Bray, Lazenby's Bond uses his irresistible sexual allure on the women in residence at the lair, which is masquerading as a clinic, and thereby disrupts the villain's plan to use them as assassins. This is necessary in a story that otherwise sees Bond fall in love and get married to Tracy di Vicenzo (Diana Rigg), a potentially threatening departure from his reputation as a playboy bachelor.[17]

In their own ways, these examples are illustrative of the potential uses of Bond in disguise for comedy, action, and/or dramatic tension. The opening scenes in *Goldfinger* move between moments of visual humor and serious action. This self-contained pre-credit sequence is highly self-parodic and "at once demystifies and affirms the excess of gadgetry, action, style and sophistication associated with Bond by this time."[18] It must be said that Bond's "Japanese" disguise in *You Only Live Twice* is rightly viewed as very offensive. In *On Her Majesty's Secret Service*, Bond's innate sex appeal and success with women proves markedly stronger than his impersonated identity, and another form of ironic juxtaposition occurs in the use of this disguise to reinforce the masculine image of the character.

Bond in Disguise in *Octopussy*

Although the clown suit is remembered as "Bond's ultimate disguise" in *Octopussy*, the film and especially the later circus scenes afford many other opportunities for him to depart from his standard wardrobe and perhaps wear something impromptu.[19] To infiltrate the circus, these disguises range from a simple crew jacket to a red shirt and black leather waistcoat as worn by one of the twins from the knife-throwing act, to a hairy gorilla costume. The last of these clearly sends up the well-dressed Bond image but is also an example of his skill at improvisation and willingness to do anything for the mission's success. Bond resourcefully hides in the gorilla costume he finds on a costume rack in the circus train to evade capture. He is in danger of being discovered during the scene, which ends with the head of the costume being decapitated by a scimitar wielded by the primary henchman (Gobinda, played by Kabir Bedi), just as Bond escapes through a vent-hatch above. Yet the sight of Bond disguised in this costume is largely jokey, especially when, as villain Kamal Khan (Louis Jourdan) says, "The bomb will go off in two and a half hours," the agent, in his gorilla suit, conspicuously checks his watch for timings. According to director

John Glen, this quick glance was improvised by Moore during filming with a spontaneity that demonstrated his sense of humor, and further illustrates the impact of the actor playing Bond.[20]

The opening of *Octopussy* (like that of *Goldfinger*) starts off with Bond in a planned disguise, in a pre-credit sequence that has no relation to the rest of the film. The camera follows a Land Rover with a horse trailer in tow, being driven by Bond. In Chris Moore's serialized adaptation of *Octopussy* (based on the screen story and screenplay) for the *Evening Express* newspaper, Bond is described in this opening as "resplendent in tweed hacking jacket, yellow sweater and cheesecutter cap—the sort of outfit he would not normally be seen dead in."[21] This disguise allows Bond to be waved through the gates of the heavily guarded military base, shortly after which he reverses the outfit to make it a Latin American military uniform. Although humorous in effect, the visual transformation demonstrates exactly the attention to detail we would expect from Bond. The hacking jacket, for instance, is turned inside out to reveal an officer's tunic with insignia and rows of medal ribbons. When he pulls away the neck of the fake sweater, a shirt collar is revealed with a neatly made tie, and the cap can be reversed. He also wears a leather belt with a holster, carries a slim leather briefcase (which holds an explosive device), and, to complete the effect, his female accomplice presses a fake moustache into place, making him more closely resemble Colonel Luis Toro (Ken Norris), with whom he soon comes face to face.

Overall, this pre-credit sequence is action-oriented, as Bond's objective to sabotage an experimental plane leads to his capture and escape from the military base. Later in the sequence a less conventional element of Bond's first disguise proves vital to his escape using a mini-jet supplied by Q branch; when Bond pulls down the tailboard of the trailer, the rear end of the dummy horse lifts upward to reveal the jet plane. Another mechanical animal disguise built by Q branch is used by Bond during the film's Indian-set sequences to facilitate his infiltration of Octopussy's island home. Bond makes his way to the island in a crocodile submarine, a disguise that proves highly effective but hardly qualifies as the kind of gadget accessory to a well-dressed gentleman mentioned by Markos in the quote above. (Others do, though, including the modified Mont Blanc fountain pen and high-tech Seiko watch.) The camera first tracks what appears to be a crocodile gliding through the water, but its jaws open wide to show Bond at the controls (figure 13.1—cue laughter), then close again.

In an earlier scene, Bond has entered Q's (Desmond Llewelyn) temporary workshop, set up at only a day's notice in Udaipur, much to Q's annoyance. Typical of these scenes by this point in the franchise, the relationship between Bond and Q is gently antagonistic. The older gadget expert admonishes Bond for his "adolescent antics" while equipping him with devices he will later find

Figure 13.1 James Bond (Roger Moore) disguised as a crocodile. *Octopussy* (1983).

invaluable in the field. Although there is no sign of the crocodile disguise in this scene, there are plenty of experimental gadgets being worked on by technicians specifically for use in India. Here, the viewer must acknowledge the backward-looking imperialist associations and uncomfortable racial stereotyping that accompany this and other aspects of the film's "tourist view of India."[22] This would include the makeshift Q branch that is accessed through a crowded bazaar and the disguises and gadgetry of the snake charmer, rope trick, and exotic wildlife signified by the crocodile submarine. However, it must also be acknowledged that, while Bond might not exactly look good in the crocodile disguise supplied by Q, it still nevertheless facilitates both his mission and (over)confident masculinity.

Under cover of night Bond pilots the one-person submarine in the form of the crocodile to approach undetected and gain access to Octopussy's heavily guarded island palace and its inhabitants. Bond has previously learned about the island from his Indian contact Vijay (Vijay Amritraj), who told him that "I hear the island is full of beautiful women. No men allowed." Bond's response in hearing about the all-female island is "Really? Sexual discrimination. I'll definitely have to pay a visit." The crocodile submarine operates in this way like other gadgets, vehicles, and equipment in the franchise to demonstrate Bond's mastery and accessorize his heroic masculinity.[23] Furthermore, his ironic sexism and subsequent use of the crocodile submarine to access Octopussy's island may better be understood by analyzing the intersection between gender and Cold War politics:

> Bond will pay the women a visit and will inevitably disrupt and reposition them. Yet his means of doing so is so absurd as to be impossible to take seriously. The risible image of Bond infiltrating Octopussy's all-female island

fortress while disguised as a crocodile works to destabilize a largely feminist movement in much the same way as showing Bond deactivating a nuclear warhead while wearing a clown costume undermines the movement for disarmament.[24]

Like the crocodile disguise and other costumes discussed, the clown suit is more than just a visual joke, and its significance at this point in the bomb plot of *Octopussy* and in relationship to the Bond image is well worth attention.

"Just Clowning Around?"

Bond wears the clown suit at the circus on an American military base in Germany to change his appearance because those searching already have a description of him. The *Octopussy* serialization based on the screenplay describes Bond being given the idea by "a line of gaudily dressed clowns heading for the big top," after which in the film he enters their caravan and then exits in similar larger-than-life clown garb.[25] The Bond fantasy is obviously such that he can appear this way despite hastily putting on his own costume and makeup (figure 13.2). His new appearance is described as a clown with "checkered vest, baggy pants, floppy coat, enormous shoes. . . . [he has] white greasepaint on his face, painted clown lips, put on a bulbous red nose, orange wig and a bowler hat."[26] In the next scene, this outfit and makeup means that Bond has no trouble getting into the circus big top, though his deception is under threat because the guards realize he has stolen the clown costume.

In the film, the circus audience laughs as the clown Bond is mistaken for part of the entertainment, first entering the arena to the trumpet fanfare and

Figure 13.2 James Bond (Roger Moore) infiltrates the circus dressed as a clown. *Octopussy* (1983).

announcement for the "cannonball" performer, then getting in the way of the act in the lead-up to the stunt. (There is also surely an ironic reference being made to families watching the new Bond film together.) In desperation, Bond crosses the arena to approach a U.S. general and alert him to the bomb, breathlessly announcing himself (not for the first time) as not a clown but a British agent, pulling off the bowler, wig, and nose. "Great clown bit . . ." and "This man is either drunk or crazy," are some of the incredulous responses he draws on this occasion. It is noteworthy that earlier in *Octopussy* the British agent 009 (Andy Bradford) wore the same clown suit and similar makeup but the association was much darker: in fact, Bond is sent to investigate the circumstances around his death at the outset. Dressed as a clown, 009 is chased through dark woods and killed by the circus's knife-thrower twins (whom Bond later encounters and kills), before crashing through a window. In the script, 009's clown makeup is described as "grotesque," a term that could be used to describe the tone of this sequence and the "foreshadow[ing]" of Bond later appearing in the costume.[27]

Tension is also building during this later sequence because, like Bond, we are aware that precious minutes are ticking away on the hidden bomb. Moore plays the scenes inside the circus tent straight despite the costume. With the help of Octopussy, Bond exposes the bomb concealed in the giant cannon and the camera cuts between shots of the now-silent crowd, the threatening countdown of the digital timer, the concentration on his painted clown face, and his white, cloth-gloved hands carefully reaching to remove the detonator, which he does just in time. As the outline in these paragraphs highlights, the parodic effect shifts notably throughout different parts of this important sequence; from the opening laughs at Bond's appearance, his clumsy entrance into the arena (in the big clown shoes), and crossing paths with another identical clown, to his frantic attempts to reach the general, frustration at not being taken seriously when he says there is a bomb in the cannon, and, most significantly, as already observed, the ambivalence of this world-famous spy hero saving us from the "danger" of a nuclear armament by defusing a stolen bomb when dressed in a shaggy wig and big red nose.

However tense the scene, the image of Bond disguised in a clown suit routinely appears among "worst of" moments in the franchise as collated by the media and fans.[28] Unsurprisingly, it has also been noted by various commentators that this is a disguise that "needlessly reminds us that Moore's reign as Ian Fleming's master spy was characterised by humour."[29] Yet, like other disguises in this chapter, it can be argued that the parodic effect of this costume does not necessarily disrupt the Bond image, and other commentators emphasize that the sequence evokes suspense.[30] In one version of the script, it is interesting that, having stopped the bomb, Bond gathers himself just enough to deliver a "Just clowning around" punchline, overtly making light of the threat and his heroism.[31] This quip did not make it into the final film.

It is also notable that when Kael referred to the film as "part parody and part travesty" in her review, she expressed her disappointment at the roles for women in *Octopussy*.[32] While the crocodile submarine appears to seriously undercut the Bond image, I have discussed that it is a use of disguise that (akin to the example from *On Her Majesty's Secret Service*) facilitates his confident heroic masculinity and the "repositioning" of the Octopussy character from a strong and independent woman who rejects male authority to an ally and love interest for the spy hero.[33] As I have also discussed, the clown suit might be regarded instead as another "perfect disguise" with intertextual meaning and wider significance when understanding the important relationships among costume, gender, and Bond.[34] Looking forward, for instance, to the Daniel Craig era, the skeleton-themed Day of the Dead costume worn by Bond in the pre-credit sequence of *Spectre* (2015), set in Mexico City, is perhaps most in this tradition, albeit with a great deal more style than in *Octopussy*, using disguise to make Bond blend in but also stand out as "Bond. James Bond."[35] Moreover, similar to the *Goldfinger* example, for visual humor the *Spectre* opening involves Bond removing this outer disguise to reveal a suit underneath (and follow it with a casual shirt-cuff adjustment).

Finally, it is helpful to call on what literary critic Linda Hutcheon refers to as the ambivalent "doubleness" of parody, which subverts but also legitimizes the text (or image) being parodied.[36] Used in this instance, this explains the intertextual negotiation that exists between disguises like the absurdly unflattering clown costume in *Octopussy* and the tailored wardrobe that is central to the signification of Bond. Although the moment when the clown-suited Bond is under pressure to stop a bomb hidden in a cannon is not light-hearted, the topical reference to the threat of nuclear arms calls attention to another doubly-coded parodic function of the heroic superspy in disguise in this film. Read in this way, the disguises worn by Bond in *Octopussy* and in other films in the franchise may rely on and joke about but can also strengthen the audience's familiarity with his dominant cinematic identity as a masculine ideal and famously (not clown) suited hero to this day.

Notes

1. Tatiana Prorokova-Konrad, "The Sexual Grammar of the Cold War: The James Bond Film Posters," *International Journal of James Bond Studies* 5, no. 1 (2020).
2. Pam Cook and Claire Hines, "'Sean Connery *Is* James Bond': Re-Fashioning British Masculinity in the 1960s," in *Fashioning Film Stars: Dress, Culture, Identity*, ed. Rachel Moseley (London: BFI, 2005), 147.
3. Bond is certainly not the only character to use disguise in this or other Bond films. On disguise in *Octopussy*, see Matt Spaiser, "Bond in *Octopussy*: A Master of Disguise,"

Bond Suits (blog), July 13, 2020, www.bondsuits.com/bond-in-octopussy-a-master-of
-disguise/.

4. James Chapman, *Licence to Thrill: A Cultural History of the James Bond Films*, 2nd ed.
    (London: I. B. Tauris, 2007), 181.

5. Raymond Benson, *The James Bond Bedside Companion* (Hertford: Crossroad Press,
    2012), 97.

6. Chapman, *Licence to Thrill*, 184.

7. Richard Schickel, "The Bond Wagon Crawls Along," *Time*, June 27, 1983, 52.

8. Pauline Kael, "Review of *Octopussy* (directed by John Glen)," *New York Times*, June 27,
    1983, 93–94.

9. Jay McInerney, Nick Foulkes, Neil Norman, and Nick Sullivan, *Dressed to Kill: James
    Bond, the Suited Hero* (Paris: Flammarion, 1995).

10. See Llewella Chapman, *Fashioning James Bond: Costume, Gender and Identity in the
    World of 007* (London: Bloomsbury, 2022), 177–78.

11. Chapman, *Fashioning James Bond*, 284.

12. For instance, Cook and Hines, "Sean Connery *Is* James Bond," 147–59; Sarah Gilli-
    gan, "Branding the New Bond: Daniel Craig and Designer Fashion," in *James Bond in
    World and Popular Culture: The Films Are Not Enough*, ed. Robert G. Weiner, B. Lynn
    Whitfield, and Jack Becker (Newcastle upon Tyne, UK: Cambridge Scholars), 76–85.

13. Spaiser, "Bond in *Octopussy*."

14. Louis Markos, "Nobody Does It Better," in *James Bond in the 21st Century: Why We
    Still Need 007*, ed. Glen Yeffeth (Dallas: BenBella, 2009), 165.

15. Chapman, *Fashioning James Bond*, 86–87.

16. McInerney et al., *Dressed to Kill*, 86.

17. Stephen Nepa, "Secret Agent Nuptials: Marriage, Gender Roles, and the 'Different
    Bond Woman' in *On Her Majesty's Secret Service*," in *For His Eyes Only: The Women
    of Bond*, ed. Lisa Funnell (New York: Wallflower, 2015), 192.

18. Claire Hines, *The Playboy and James Bond: 007, Ian Fleming and* Playboy *Magazine*
    (Manchester: Manchester University Press, 2018), 166.

19. Spaiser, "Bond in *Octopussy*."

20. Qtd. in Mark A. Altman and Edward Gross, *Nobody Does It Better: The Complete,
    Uncensored, Unauthorized Oral History of James Bond* (New York: Tom Doherty Asso-
    ciates), 403–4.

21. Chris Moore, "Part 1—*Octopussy* Serialisation," *Evening Express*, July 18, 1983, 6.

22. Chapman, *Licence to Thrill*, 176.

23. For example, see Martin Willis, "Hard-wear: The Millennium, Technology and Bros-
    nan's Bond," in *The James Bond Phenomenon: A Critical Reader*, 2nd ed., ed. Chris-
    toph Lindner (Manchester: Manchester University Press, 2009), 169–83.

24. Stephanie Jones and Claire Hines, "'Like a Party Political Broadcast for You-Know-
    Who': Margaret Thatcher and the Reception of *Octopussy* (1983)," in *The Bondian Cold
    War*, ed. Muriel Blaive, Martin Brown, and Ron Granieri (Abingdon: Routledge, in
    press)

25. Chris Moore, "Part 5—*Octopussy* Serialisation," *Evening Express*, July 22, 1983, 6.

26. Richard Maibaum and Michael G. Wilson, *Octopussy*, screenplay, June 10, 1982, 119.

27. Maibaum and Wilson, *Octopussy*, 11; Spaiser, "Bond in *Octopussy*."

28. For example, David Berry, "The 10 Worst Moments in the History of James Bond on
    Film," National Post, November 5, 2015, nationalpost.com/entertainment/the-10-worst
    -moments-in-the-the-history-of-james-bond-on-film.

29. Brian W. Fairbanks, *Writings: Film Literature Music Society* (Morrisville, NC: Lulu, 2005), 256.
30. Rick Mayers quoted in Altman and Gross, *Nobody Does It Better*, 401.
31. Maibaum and Wilson, *Octopussy*, 124.
32. Kael, "Review of *Octopussy*," 177–78.
33. Tony Bennett and Janet Woollacott, *Bond and Beyond: The Political Career of a Popular Hero* (Basingstoke, UK: Macmillan Education, 1987), 117.
34. John Glen, quoted in Altman and Gross, *Nobody Does It Better*, 403.
35. Matt Spaiser, "The Day of the Dead Costume in Spectre," *Bond Suits*, October 31, 2006, www.bondsuits.com/day-dead-costume-spectre/.
36. Linda Hutcheon, "The Politics of Postmodernism: Parody and History," *Cultural Critique* 5 (1986): 179–207.

CHAPTER 14

SCOWLS AND COWLS

Grace Jones, Costume Design, and *A View to a Kill* (1985)

RANDALL STEVENS

A *View to a Kill*, released in 1985, is a rather off-the-rack Bond film in many ways. There are the expected quips, action sequences, and megalomaniacal schemes. Like many other entries in the franchise, the film also attempts to ensure its success through several appeals to contemporary trends. From scenes of snowboarding (which grew in popularity across the 1970s and '80s and celebrated its first World Cup in 1985) to a plot revolving around Silicon Valley (where the first Apple computer, the Macintosh, had been constructed the year before) to James Bond's (Roger Moore) flair for making quiche (which a bestselling, tongue-in-cheek book of 1982 claimed "real men" never did), the film wears its era of production quite heavily.[1] This is no more visible than its appeal to MTV, which started broadcasting in 1981. Pop stars Duran Duran recorded a high-energy, radio-friendly theme song, the only Bond single to make number one on the U.S. *Billboard* chart. And it was only after seeking rock stars David Bowie and then Mick Jagger to play villain Max Zorin that the producers eventually settled for Christopher Walken—whom they styled to look like Bowie in his mid-'70s Thin White Duke phase.

The presence of Grace Jones in the film is clearly part of this MTV-inflected strategy. While she had recently appeared in *Conan the Destroyer* (1984), Jones was far more widely known as a musician and model than an actor, thanks to her breakthrough album *Warm Leatherette* (1980) and its follow-up, *Nightclubbing* (1981), as well as her work with photographer and graphic designer Jean-Paul Goude. Her presence in the film as action hero and duplicitous

henchwoman May Day can be considered stunt casting, an attempt to capital-
ize on a hot commodity to extend viewership beyond the normal fan base of
the spy franchise. The result might be thought of as less a character and more
a featured icon. Indeed, action film scholar Yvonne Tasker suggests that in
both *A View to a Kill* and *Conan the Destroyer*, Jones "performs a parody of her
own sexualised public persona" and little more.[2]

Yet this public persona is considerably complex and does not fit neatly into
the Bond template. Scholars generally agree that Jones troubles established binaries and hierarchies around gender and race, with her performances—whether
as model, singer, or film actor—often functioning as confrontational commen-
taries on normativity.[3] Witness her appearance at the start of *A One Man
Show* (1982) in a gorilla suit and a grass skirt, playing bongos, an image that
Francesca T. Royster offers as an example of Jones's twisting of conventional
sexual, racial, and colonial tropes into unreadability.[4] These challenges to normative models were particularly important to Jones in the early 1980s, when,
as post-cinema theorist Steven Shaviro argues, "Jones *embodied* an all-too-
familiar racist and sexist iconography with such vicious, sarcastic excess as to
blow it apart. At the same time, she crossed the boundaries separating men from
women not with a cozy androgyny, nor even with the 'glam rock' stylizations
of the period, but by displaying a cold and forbidding, more-than-masculine,
and ultimately ungenderable hardbody."[5] Such a description is utterly alien to
any other significant female Bond actor, before or since.

This distinction is further amplified by the way in which Jones is dressed in
A View to a Kill.[6] Jones was the first "Bond Girl" to take a hand in developing
and designing her own character costumes, a project she undertook with the
help of her collaborator and friend, fashion designer Azzedine Alaïa. In press
and publicity material, Jones is keen to emphasize that many of May Day's outfits were inspired by or copied from outfits in her own personal wardrobe.
These outlandish and highly notable outfits therefore blur the line between
Jones's transgressive public image as a performance artist and May Day's idiosyncratic brashness, and further pull Jones away from the rest of the cast in
terms of look and characterization. In what follows, this chapter will unpick
the place of Grace Jones within the film, considering how her presence is more
than just a collection of scowls and cowls. Through this work, the aim is to
reveal the unexpected layers of this oft-disregarded character.

Boundaries, Boldness, Betrayals: Playing May Day

In many ways, May Day adheres to expectations regarding similar characters in the Bond franchise. She is, for instance, one of many female characters
who sleeps with Bond but does not make it to the end credits because she

troubles the moral and sexual universe of the films.[7] Charles Burnetts accordingly groups May Day with other "fluffer" characters (as he labels them): women who keep Bond aroused until he can find more permanent union with the Bond Girl of any given film.[8] May Day resembles Helga Brandt (Karin Dor) in *You Only Live Twice* (1967) or Xenia Onatopp (Famke Janssen) in *GoldenEye* (1995): all are manipulative dissemblers who use sex, cunning, and physical strength in their attempts to best Bond, but also end up violently dispatched.

And yet, even as she adheres to some standard tropes, the character of May Day is also atypical in many ways, both in terms of her narrative positioning and Jones's performance choices. Take, to begin with, issues of gender and representation. Related to Jones's willfully androgynous qualities, the character of May Day possesses a muscular physicality unmatched by many other women encountered by Bond. Whether lifting unsuspecting foes high above her head or single-handedly hauling a heavy bomb on a train cart, she undertakes physical feats that are explicitly beyond Bond's abilities. As Lisa Funnell states, through these immense acts the character "subverts gender binaries," and indeed, her closest comparison in the Moore years is probably Jaws (Richard Kiel), the indestructible henchman of earlier outings *The Spy Who Loved Me* (1977) and *Moonraker* (1979).[9] Part Bond Girl and part hypermuscular henchperson, May Day is a strange hybrid. Echoing Shaviro's comments above, Funnell argues that the filmmakers of *A View to a Kill* "struggled to adjust Jones's star image to meet the gendered expectations of the franchise while still satisfying her fan base; as a consequence, the film does not establish any definite boundaries for her character."[10] If both Jones and May Day lack boundaries, then this is particularly challenging in the context of the Bond franchise, a series of films with—to put it mildly—often rather clear-cut and conservative gender politics.

Jones is also one of only a handful of black female actors to play a significant role in the Bond films, alongside, most notably, Naomie Harris in several Craig installments, as well as Gloria Hendry in *Live and Let Die* (1973), Halle Berry in *Die Another Day* (2002), and Lashana Lynch in *No Time to Die* (2021). While May Day is unlike Hendry's earlier character Rosie Carver in that she is clearly not spatially or ideologically associated with a black community, Jones's blackness is nonetheless still seen by many film scholars as key to interpreting the role. Both Charles Burnetts and Travis Wagner, for instance, see in May Day the performance of a defiant colonial subject whose body and fate are controlled by Bond and Zorin, the white men at the film's center.[11] As a female character in a Bond film, her options are already curtailed; as a black woman, even more so. She may be able to "challenge" Bond's "power and privilege" through certain actions, but she is not exactly "a revolutionary character" thanks to her minimal dialogue and her death.[12]

Yet Jones's performance and physicality push against this "subaltern" positioning.[13] She stands tall and proud throughout the film, her stature augmenting the character's narrative role as assassin. (After all, it is she, not Zorin, who does the most killing, including three of Bond's male allies and a corporate partner of Zorin's who is weighed down with too many scruples.) In her autobiography, Jones highlights the intense glare that she wears throughout the film, a look that says "if you messed with her, she was going to kill you."[14] A more intense glare compared to the slightly insouciant confrontation offered on the cover of her album *Nightclubbing*, May Day's glower was a studied performance choice. Jones describes how the look was a conscious emulation of her abusive step-grandfather "Mas P," who scowled disapprovingly at her when she was a child as a form of control. As Jones describes, she consciously turned this look into something else:

> [Mas P] taught me something about how to demand attention, but I could turn it into a cartoon, which takes the sting out of it for me. I can see it in old pictures of him, this force in the eyes that I use in various ways as a performer. . . . He tried to intimidate me, a vulnerable little girl, keeping me in check. That was my way of dealing with this monster—turn it into something he would have been horrified by.[15]

In two of her early scenes, Jones deploys this glare to interrupt Bond's spying on the film's other female lead, Stacey Sutton (Tanya Roberts). Stepping into frame, she faces down Bond with a cool, innate confidence, forcing him to redirect his attention (figure 14.1).

But Jones also (and perhaps surprisingly) mocks the intensity of this studied glare at other points in the film. After an assassination at the Eiffel Tower and a car chase on the streets below, May Day escapes the hapless Bond thanks

Figure 14.1 May Day (Grace Jones). *A View to a Kill* (1985).

to Zorin's timely arrival in a speedboat. Removing her mask (of which more below), she nods to Zorin in stern satisfaction at a job well done. Then her cool suddenly breaks, her face slipping into a wide grin and a hearty laugh ripping loose. She even slaps herself playfully across the cheek as she cackles. This is not a one-note emotionless killer, but someone more complicated.

Later, a sparring scene trades in a form of unbridled animality that Jones had long called on in her stage performances.[16] Pinned by an insouciant Walken, she strains and bites at him as he moves closer. She continues visibly struggling as he forcefully kisses her, but then Zorin leaps from her as he is called away. Left on the floor, Jones gives May Day an irritable eye-roll: is this disappointment at losing a contest, or frustration at the interruption of foreplay? Shortly thereafter, she finds Bond unexpectedly in her bed (where he has decided to flee to avoid detection elsewhere). Although initially shocked, she slips under the covers with him, asking only the rhetorical, "What else is there to say?"

Anna Everett argues, "Bond's sexual couplings with women of color do not signify tender and romantic encounters as much as they naturalize Bond's masculine prerogative of accepting these women's lusty hypersexual offerings to him."[17] If so, is that the case here? Charles Burnetts complicates reading this as such an "offering" by suggesting that May Day's dialogue frames the encounter "as an overdetermined conquest between historic colonizer and oppressed."[18] The line is, after all, stated defiantly and purposefully, rather than as surrender or romance, and after saying it May Day immediately wrestles her way on top of Bond by grabbing his neck. This act of aggression and control is hardly diffused by Moore's own eye-roll at the scene's climax, meaning that Bond's "masculine prerogative," while certainly performed, also seems undermined and even mocked. Spurned by Zorin, May Day seizes her chance to exercise her own prerogative in terms of aggressive sexual play.

The trope of the female villain character shifting allegiances thanks to Bond's bedroom prowess was established enough to be acknowledged in the dialogue of the fourth film of the franchise, *Thunderball* (1965), but while May Day changes sides near the end of *A View to a Kill*, this moral reclamation is not prompted by sexual contact with Bond. Instead, it arises through her discovery of Zorin's betrayal and his cold-hearted murder of fellow henchwomen Jenny Flex (Alison Doody) and Pan Ho (Papillon Soo Soo). This turn leads to May Day's heroic death wheeling a bomb away from a mine full of dynamite in Silicon Valley, a fate that does not resolve the transgressive currents generated by Jones's performance. She is, after all, "never contained or punished for her violent and sexual exploits," a fact that perhaps makes her death at once paradigmatic of the franchise's treatment of black female characters and a kind of vengeful self-liberation.[19]

The latter is certainly how Jones plays it. When Zorin floods the mine, Bond and May Day struggle to survive, and in the aftermath she leans exhausted on his shoulder. But shortly after this she returns to her former hardness, barking orders in Bond's face with no hesitation as they realize the gravity of the situation. Literally doing all the heavy lifting, May Day viscerally wrestles with weighty machine cranks and heaves against an overloaded handcar. Bond helps out, and the two briefly work together with slick aptitude, a strong contrast to the much more farcical adventures the British spy has had with Stacey Sutton across the preceding hour of the film.

Though she carries the bomb from the mine (saving San Francisco), May Day must sacrifice herself in the process. As the handcar reaches a safe distance and she realizes her fate, she shows no fear, but uses these final moments to laugh openly and with relish, as she did after the Eiffel Tower chase. But this is not quite the full story. Zorin appears in his airship and he and May Day lock eyes, prompting her to switch from glee back to her hard and unflinching stare. It is this expression that is eradicated by the explosion, leaving Zorin and the viewer with a powerful sense of the character's unshakable resolve. Compare this with Walken's Zorin a few minutes later, when his memorable final moments find him giggling incredulously as he begins the fall to his death from the Golden Gate Bridge. Where Jones finds room for stature in her character's final moments, Walken expresses only nihilistic abandon.

In all these ways, Jones's performance augments and further complicates a role that is already straining at some of the boundaries set by the franchise. She is neither a female Jaws nor exactly a "Bond Girl." Jones's "ungenderable hardbody" is clearly present and celebrated, and her performance choices present us with a hungry sexual animal, a mute sociopathic killer, and a fun-loving girl-on-the-run, sometimes all in the space of a single scene. Like much of her other work, Jones turns May Day into a hard-to-classify bundle of tropes and contradictions. But this is not just about the work performed by Jones. Royster suggests that by "viewing Jones as a performer rather than as produced media spectacle, we are allowed to think of her as an agent always in collaboration with an audience."[20] This concept of collaboration is key, extending beyond just audiences and into Jones's work with other creative personnel, most significantly couturier Azzedine Alaïa.

Costume, Couture, Collaboration: Dressing May Day

In Hollywood cinema, costume design is often considered to play a subordinate role to the demands of storytelling. In the words of designer Anthea Sylbert, one "must not leave a movie whistling the clothes."[21] Yet clothes are central to the construction of May Day (just as, we will see, May Day and Jones are central to the construction of these clothes). To explore this, it is first necessary to consider the differences between film costume, couture, and everyday dress. In terms of the social world, dress can be a gendered practice, a mode of communication, a means of achieving conformity, a way for individuals to accumulate and perform cultural capital, or a way for subcultural movements to define themselves in opposition to the mainstream. By contrast, in cinema dress occupies a quite different function as one element of storytelling among many. Although Hollywood has greatly influenced trends in everyday dress throughout the twentieth century, cinematic "costume" stands apart from the social world.

In Classical Hollywood cinema, elements of film form such as mise-en-scène, editing, sound, and performance tend to play supporting roles to the true star of the picture: narrative continuity. This preoccupation with the all-encompassing demands of narrative might go some way toward explaining the curious lack of intersection between Hollywood costume history and the cycles and trends of the twentieth-century fashion industry. Certainly, it has been one of the key reasons why leading fashion designers have rarely lent their skills to designing for Hollywood productions (with notable exceptions, such as Coco Chanel's short-lived collaborations with Samuel Goldwyn Productions in the 1930s). Couture garments make an iconic statement and are often considered to be works of art on their own terms, while costume should be unobtrusive and not seek to disrupt. Couture, therefore, occupies an uneasy place in the context of narrative cinema because, while costume tells a story, the point of couture is to speak for itself.[22] While the leading fashion houses set the annual template for what might eventually become *everyday dress*, couture as a rarefied form of fashion has always been the preserve of the rich. Couture is not costume, and although there was once a relationship between the two, Hollywood producers of the 1920s found that being led by Parisian couture houses was, from an industrial perspective, impractical and disempowering.

In her book *Undressing Cinema* (1997), Stella Bruzzi lingers on the debate about "whether clothes should perform a spectacular as opposed to a subservient visual role in film," that is, to stand out rather than meeting the demands of the narrative.[23] May Day's outfits are so spectacular that they are at times "intrusive" (to use Bruzzi's wording) in the way that they draw the eye. However, the spectacle of her couture also serves the film's narrative progression because of the role these outfits play in positioning this character as the archetypal female villain. May Day is powerful, overtly sexual, and at times threatening, an unknown quantity who defies easy categorization and becomes less knowable with every outlandish costume change. It is precisely May Day's role as the "Bond Girl" archetype that allows for the space to experiment with these more disruptive abstractions that are the preserve of couture rather than costume. This effect is arguably heightened by Jones's star persona and her place as a well-known transgressive figure in the performing arts.

Stardom, clothing, and commodification are, of course, bound together. Pam Cook and Claire Hines discuss the tension between stardom and character in the Bond franchise in relation to the character of Bond and those actors hired to play him, particularly referring to paratextual material used to market the films and sell tie-in merchandise.[24] Put simply, they argue, it is Bond who is the star of the show, not the actor who plays him. It is Bond, not Pierce Brosnan, who poses with an Omega watch in glossy magazine advertisements, and it is ultimately Bond, not Brosnan, who sells the product. The stereotypical behaviors associated with the franchise's leading characters have relatedly taken on an element of caricature, of being larger than life (and, as such, they are often parodied in popular culture).

Like Bond and his villainous counterparts, the "Bond Girl" has become something of a caricature, as Grace Jones noted when she discussed her approach to developing the character of May Day, whom she perceived to be almost cartoonish in her villainy and whom she compared to the kind of fantasy character that might be at home in a classic Disney film. If Jones had a very clear sense of who she wanted May Day to be, then she was keen that this should be reflected in the character's costumes:

> I was way ahead of the game. I looked at Disney colors, because I figured being a Bond girl was like being in a cartoon. I picked out every piece of fabric. I took in tips I had learned from Issey [Miyake] and Kenzo [Takada], and had direct input from one of my other favourite designers who became a friend, Azzedine Alaïa, but Bowie and Jagger were right in thinking that you have trouble operating with any kind of soul, or intimate energy, inside such an industrial production.[25]

Jones and Alaïa collaborated with costume designer Emma Porteous to create May Day's distinctive outfits. This highlights another key reason why couturiers rarely lend their skills to Hollywood: their working practices are often at odds with the practical demands of shooting a major studio production. For example, the scene where May Day parachutes from the Eiffel Tower was performed not by Jones, but by a stunt double, and the nature of this stunt as well as the need for multiple takes meant that several copies of the black mediaeval-inspired outfit May Day wears had to be created and held in reserve—a time-consuming process that was the responsibility of the costume department, regardless of how involved Jones and Alaïa may have been in the creative process.

Jones had previously modelled for Alaïa and promoted his clothing lines, and throughout the 1980s Alaïa continued to design some of Jones's most iconic outfits. Alaïa specialized in sculpting soft fabrics into shapes that signified power and toughness (and, indeed, before moving into fashion design he originally trained as a sculptor). He was famed for his experiments with the texture and weight of textiles, and he specialized in making stiff fabrics like leather soft and flowing so that they draped sensually on the female form, even though "he seldom used internal structures such as boning or petticoats, instead exploring the qualities of the fabrics themselves to achieve deceptively complex shapes that float weightlessly around the body." This weightlessness was not timid, however, and he was known in particular for making chiffon (a traditionally soft and sheer material associated with feminine styles) into "a fabric with a hard, predatory sex appeal."[26] This makes his clothes almost paradoxically well suited to filmmaking.

Fashion sociologist Joanne Entwistle argues that dress cannot be understood without the "living, breathing, moving body it adorns," and notes the alienating experience of seeing clothes that are without a body (such as in an exhibition context), describing how they seem to lose a sense of vitality.[27] The movement and shape of the female body are absolutely integral to Alaïa's designs, which do not generally retain their shape, cut, or identity when viewed on the hanger. Lycra clings to May Day's body; while this emphasizes her femininity and sexuality, it also makes visible the muscular contours of her thighs and upper arms. Particularly notable in A View to a Kill is a labial hooded pink ensemble evocative of a confident and active female sexuality, which provides a point of contrast to the sculptural shoulder-emphasizing black leather outfits so emblematic of the 1980s "power dressing" silhouette.

Jones, then, performs May Day as someone very much aware of the power of these clothes, as someone owning the persona they create. At the end of the scene in which May Day intervenes in Bond's first meeting with Stacey, Jones uses her outfit's lengths of purple fabric to shoot an aggressive gesture in Moore's direction: grabbing the ample hem, she flicks it away from Bond's direction, a subtle but pointed use of the costume to challenge his authority and show her disdain.

Meanwhile, the flow and undulation of Alaïa's designs are not only displayed, but embodied and put in motion in the action sequences. May Day's appearance at the Eiffel Tower codes her as a cross between a ninja and a knight. Wearing a loose-fitting jumpsuit of black cloth, with a black cape fluttering behind her, she runs up the exposed staircases. Her face is covered by a mask, which evokes a mediaeval helmet (known as a "great helm") thanks to the thin, rectangular eye slits. She even attacks Bond with a fishing rod in the manner of a sword, nearly throwing him from the tower. Bond has to wrestle with fishing thread, which now entangles his legs, a clumsy act that throws into relief May Day's confident leaps over railings and banisters, movements also heightened and dramatized by the billowing cape and the sharp but undulating silhouette of the jumpsuit (figure 14.2). She may pointedly remove the cape before the parachute jump, but the way it flutters foreshadows the gliding movements of May

Figure 14.2 May Day (Grace Jones) and Bond (Roger Moore). *A View to a Kill* (1985).

Day over Paris, in comparison to Bond's brutish and awkward car chase on the streets below.

Finally, in the Silicon Valley mine near the end of the film, Jones is dressed in leather boots that reach high over the knee, beneath a grey shawl-type dress. As May Day chases Bond and Stacey through the tunnels, a close-up shows the wind slightly billowing another of her signature hoods, communicating that she is on the trail of her targets, who are themselves following signs of breeze to find their way to the exit of the mine. After the shaft floods thanks to Zorin's duplicity and May Day changes allegiance to Bond, she ditches the dress, revealing beneath it a tailored black vest and skirt. These allow her muscular arms and legs to be visible during her exertions twisting pulleys and cranking levers.

Alaïa's by-turns sculptural, clinging, tough, and feminine designs work to develop May Day as a complex, unknowable, and contradictory character. In turn, May Day's physicality and movement bring vitality to Alaïa's designs, which retain their shape only as they cling to the body. *A View to a Kill* also presents us with a rare instance of couture costumes working both with and against narrative progression. If we follow the film studies model of classical continuity vs spectacle as outlined by Bruzzi, the costuming of May Day seems to offer a simultaneous sense of narrative continuity (in constructing the "Bond Girl" archetype) and disruption (the garments stand out as couture creations). Furthermore, the garments themselves have come to stand apart from the Bond franchise as emblematic of Alaïa's profound influence on late twentieth-century fashion design history. The dresses May Day wears have been shown at fashion exhibitions, and particular pieces (such as her hooded pink jersey ball gown) have retained an influential afterlife in popular culture.

A View to Kill For

What is Grace Jones doing in *A View to a Kill*? She is expanding the audience for a Bond film, certainly, but perhaps more interestingly she is finding a space for her distinctive confrontational persona within this corporate production. She is also providing an opportunity for the display of couture fashion in ways that reveal its cinematic possibilities and dangers. Undressing the roles of both Grace Jones and Azzedine Alaïa in the creation of May Day's actions and look has revealed how couture amplifies her unusualness as a character, both in terms of making her visually distinctive and in the way these designs allow and even encourage certain performance choices on Jones's part. Jones in the film, without doubt, presents a view to kill for, but this close analysis has demonstrated how this is not just a case of a few spectacular, out-of-place garments drawing our attention, like couture fashion found unexpectedly on a high-street rack. Rather, this is a more intriguing ensemble of character and clothing, in which the very distinctiveness of the couture approach helps to build and develop a character who is already a striking addition to the franchise.

Notes

The author would like to acknowledge the contribution made to this chapter by an uncredited co-author.

1. Bruce Feirstein, *Real Men Don't Eat Quiche* (New York: Pocket Books, 1982). Feirstein would go on to cowrite several Pierce Brosnan Bond films in the 1990s.
2. Yvonne Tasker, *Spectacular Bodies: Gender, Genre and the Action Cinema* (London: Routledge, 1993), 27.
3. Miriam Kershaw, "Postcolonialism and Androgyny: The Performance Art of Grace Jones," *Art Journal* 56, no. 4 (1997): 19–25; Francesca T. Royster, "'Feeling Like a Woman, Looking Like a Man, Sounding Like a No-No': Grace Jones and the Performance of Strangé in the Post-Soul Moment," *Women & Performance: A Journal of Feminist Theory* 19, no. 1 (2009): 77–94; Abigail Gardner, "Framing Grace: Shock and Awe at the Ageless Black Body," in *Rock On: Women, Ageing and Popular Music*, ed. Ros Jennings and Abigail Gardner (Farnham, UK: Ashgate, 2012), 65–86.
4. Royster, "Feeling," 79.
5. Steven Shaviro, *Post-Cinematic Affect* (Winchester: Zero Books, 2010), 19. Emphasis in original.
6. See also Llewella Chapman, *Fashioning James Bond: Costume, Gender, and Identity in the World of 007* (London: Bloomsbury, 2022), 187–88.
7. Lisa Funnell and Klaus Dodds, *Geographies, Genders and Geopolitics of James Bond* (London: Palgrave Macmillan, 2017), 29.
8. Charles Burnetts, "Bond's Bit on the Side: Race, Exoticism and the Bond 'Fluffer' Character," in *For His Eyes Only: The Women of James Bond*, ed. Lisa Funnell (New York: Wallflower, 2015), 60–69.

9. Lisa Funnell, "Negotiating Shifts in Feminism: The 'Bad' Girls of James Bond," in *Women on Screen: Feminism and Femininity in Visual Culture*, ed. Melanie Waters (Basingstoke, UK: Palgrave Macmillan, 2011), 199–212, 206.

10. Funnell, "Negotiating," 206.

11. Burnetts, "Bond's Bit on the Side"; Travis L Wagner, "'The Old Ways Are Best': The Colonization of Women of Color in Bond Films," in Funnell, *For His Eyes Only*, 51–59.

12. Wagner, "'The Old Ways Are Best,'" 56.

13. Wagner, "'The Old Ways Are Best,'" 56.

14. Grace Jones, *I'll Never Write My Memoirs* (New York: Simon and Schuster, 2015), loc. 4428.

15. Jones, *I'll Never*, loc. 4428.

16. See Royster, "Feeling."

17. Anna Everett, "Shaken, Not Stirred Britishness: James Bond, Race, and the Transnational Imaginary," in *The Cultural Life of James Bond: Specters of 007*, ed. Jaap Verheul (Amsterdam: Amsterdam University Press, 2020), 187–206, 196.

18. Burnetts, "Bond's Bit on the Side," 65.

19. Funnell, "Negotiating," 206; see also Monica Germanà, *Bond Girls: Body, Fashion and Gender* (London: Bloomsbury, 2020), 91.

20. Royster, "Feeling," 85.

21. Quoted in Robin Blaetz, "The Auteur Renaissance, 1968–1980," in *Costume, Makeup and Hair*, ed. Adrienne L. McLean (New Brunswick, NJ: Rutgers University Press, 2016), 99–121, 108.

22. Stella Bruzzi, *Undressing Cinema: Clothing and Identity in the Movies* (London: Routledge, 1997).

23. Bruzzi, *Undressing*, 8.

24. Pam Cook and Claire Hines, "'Sean Connery is James Bond:' Refashioning British Masculinity in the 1960s," in *Fashioning Film Stars: Dress, Culture, Identity*, ed. Rachel Moseley (London: British Film Institute, 2005), 147–59.

25. Jones, *I'll Never*, loc. 4468.

26. "Azzedine Alaïa: The Couturier: Teacher Notes," The Design Museum, n.d., fashion-docbox.com/89495146-Fashion/Azzedine-Alaia-the-couturier-teacher-notes.html, accessed June 21, 2022.

27. Joanne Entwhistle, *The Fashioned Body: Fashion, Dress and Modern Social Theory*, 2nd ed. (Cambridge: Polity Press, 2015), 9.

CHAPTER 15

"A TIME WHEN INDISCRIMINATING BED-HOPPING IS DEFINITELY NOT ADVISABLE"

Safe-Sex References in the UK Press Reception of
The Living Daylights (1987)

STEPHANIE JONES

I t should come as no surprise that official publicity materials for *The Living Daylights* (1987) made no mention of HIV or AIDS. Yet mainstream UK newspapers made numerous references in their film review columns to safe-sex campaigns designed to tackle the spread of HIV. It was common for critics at the time to employ references to current affairs so that they might "link a film to significant contemporary issues." Reviewing practices were designed to remind readers of the relevance of film reviews by elaborating on how films connected to the culture around them.[1] *The Living Daylights* provided critics with a chance to connect the film to a health crisis that loomed large in the public consciousness in 1987. Crucially, the choice of topical references in the film's reception emphasized how ideas about masculinity were (and were understood to be) changing in the mid-to-late 1980s. Reflecting on Fleet Street press reviews, this chapter illustrates the extent to which the primary purpose of a James Bond film review in the '80s UK press was to register and explore anxieties around change.

The Living Daylights' press reception registered two main types of change, which were connected to gender in different ways. First, the actor playing James Bond changed from Roger Moore to Timothy Dalton. Accordingly, the series switched from a popular comic actor to a serious "Shakespearean" stage player. In doing so, one iteration of a masculine archetype was replaced with another. Second, reviews of *The Living Daylights* made heavy use of "topical practices" in the form of references to safe-sex campaigns designed to tackle the spread of HIV and AIDS.[2] Such practices illustrate how a Bond film's press reception can record contemporary anxieties about sex and gender and connect these to the mythical masculinities found in the series. In turn, a focus on reception offers up a different set of priorities when reading *The Living Daylights* compared with approaches that focus on, or start with, analyzing the film.

"Governments Change . . . The Lies Stay the Same"

As James Chapman notes, in the second half of the 1980s the Bond franchise offered a blend of continuity and change. This allowed the films to operate as a long-running series that maintained traditions and offered novel elements at the same time.[3] According to Cary Edwards, the mood of *The Living Daylights* differed from the heavily comic tone found in the previous installment, *A View to a Kill* (1985), starring Roger Moore.[4] Mixing comic set pieces (such as tobogganing across an international border on a cello case, figure 15.1) with gritty depictions of war and suffering in Afghanistan, *The Living Daylights'* plot begins in Europe. KGB machinations around defections and assassinations bring Bond into contact with a cellist called Kara Milovy (the film's main female lead, played by Maryam d'Abo). The action moves to Tangier and then on to Afghanistan, where Bond crushes an arms and opium deal before returning to Tangier to kill the main villain, Brad Whitaker (Joe Don Baker). The plot loops back to Central Europe, where Bond is reunited with Kara. Many of the conventions of the Bond films remained in place for *The Living Daylights*. Maurice Binder's titles, John Barry's music, a gadget-enhanced Aston Martin all adhered to series traditions. Importantly for critics, the film's central romance between Bond and Kara progressed much more slowly compared to other Bond films and is tied up separately from the rest of the plot at the end.

An understanding of continuity and change is not only part of the academic discourse on Bond: it also informed popular critical discourse at the time of

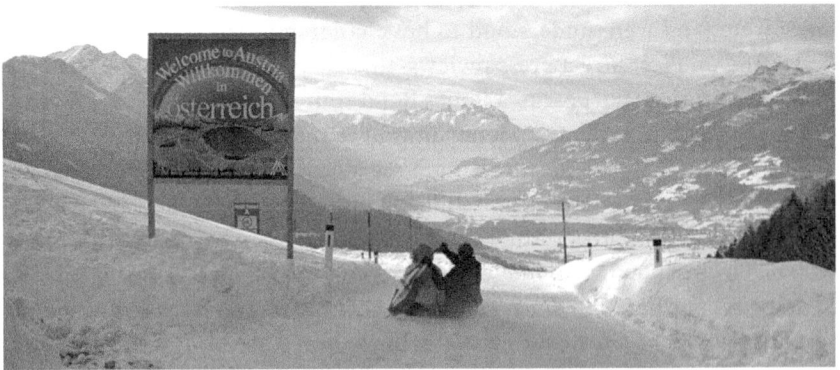

Figure 15.1 Crossing the Austrian border on a cello case. *The Living Daylights* (1987).

The Living Daylights' release. In other words, press critics understood changes in the context of Bond traditions, too. To return to academic theory, following Tony Bennett and Janet Woollacott, we might think of this mechanism as a way of maintaining "popular consent" to the ideologies within Bond.[5] Adjustments to the formula can be seen as adjustments to the series' ideological positions on imperialism, technology, women, and other issues.[6] An appreciation of this method of understanding Bond can also be seen in the way reviews weigh up changes in the formula, make connections to topical events, and deliberate on what changes mean for future installments.

Academic debates have, in addition, focused on the ways that *The Living Daylights* resonates with contemporaneous geopolitical issues. Klaus Dodds and Lisa Funnell claim that Bond films of the détente Cold War period are distinguished more by Cold War geopolitics than representational and identity politics.[7] I want to argue that the reverse is true: that press responses to the film show that personal politics were more significant than geopolitics in the film's UK reception. For example, one of the most significant changes for critics was the reduction in the number of Bond's sexual partners. Raymond Benson notes that "the AIDS epidemic was changing everyone's outlook, and motion pictures and television were only just beginning to reflect the new attitudes."[8] However, Chapman is skeptical that this is the reason why Bond takes fewer lovers in 1987 compared to 1985. His alternative explanation is that *The Living Daylights* returns to Fleming, where (as Kingsley Amis observes) Bond "acquires" only one girl per foreign trip.[9]

Both Chapman's and Dodds and Funnell's claims point to the significance of scope and method in determining what is meaningful or significant about *The Living Daylights*. While it is entirely possible to make Dodds and Funnell's reading based on connecting textual evidence to geopolitics, reception evidence points in a different direction: the politics of personal identities were very important for critics who reviewed the film in the UK press. Taking a less text-centric approach, Chapman draws on the UK press responses but does so in a way that merges a contextual framing of reviews and marketing materials with a close reading of the film. A deeper analysis of press responses, focusing on the way they frame the film, offers a snapshot of how *The Living Daylights* was understood in terms of very specific topical concerns—ones that point to significant tensions for those receiving the film at the time of its release.

"Be Careful, 007. It's Just Had a New Coat of Paint"

As one might expect, the exhibitors' campaign book for *The Living Daylights* makes no reference to AIDS or the safe-sex campaigns that were prevalent in the public consciousness in 1987. It is more surprising, perhaps, that it also makes little mention of Dalton as a novelty in the Bond formula. One or two references to "the new James Bond" can be found, particularly in the promotional poster, but overall, the campaign book's strategy is to connect Dalton with continuity and tradition rather than novelty or change. It depicts the Bond phenomenon as an institution that (as of 1987) is fifteen films long and twenty-five years old. Accordingly, the book frames many aspects of Bond films in terms of a recipe: the films have an agreed-upon template with variation in elements such as locations, cars, and girls. The press book emphasizes the novelties in *The Living Daylights* yet firmly places these elements within a well-articulated framework of tradition. Most contemporary critics made several corresponding assumptions about their readers, whom they expected to be very familiar with the Bond character, the films' conventions, and the series' historical significance. Critics also assumed that the reader knew Roger Moore had retired and Dalton was the new Bond.

Critics tended to structure their reviews using the idea of a formula; each reported to their readers what the new ingredients brought. Dalton was a novelty for critics and reviews were organized around a discussion of Dalton as the most important new element. Other ingredients that were repeatedly mentioned were villains, action sequences, gadgets, girls, and locations. The plot tended to be recounted only briefly. Two Fleet Street critics (Shaun Usher in the *Daily Mail* and Sheila Johnston in the *Independent*) readily admitted to not following the plot or finding it very important when evaluating the film.[10] In other words, the reception materials pointed to different priorities than do academic works, which have focused on the plot. The tone of the reviews was conversational and focused on how well the key innovations or differences worked. One significant difference was Bond's sexual relationships, particularly his relationship with Kara. This provided the forum for AIDS and safe-sex references as a means to make reviews more topical. Yet the way the references were used varied considerably in terms of how they revealed a position on the AIDS crisis and its potential impact on the Bond formula.

The campaign book did not provide much fanfare for Dalton as a new element in the Bond formula. Instead, it used a strategy that is reflected in press responses to *The Living Daylights*—the idea of returning to Fleming. In an interview with Dalton on page six, the actor tells a story that places him further back in the Bond films series than 1987, about being approached to play Bond when he was aged about twenty-five (1971 or thereabouts). This was followed by further appeals to Bond traditions, including Dalton's discourse on the acting craft, specifically that he went back to Fleming and began "analysing" what was on the page. What Fleming represents in this context is somewhat ahistorical. The author is no longer associated with "sex, snobbery and sadism" (following Paul Johnson's review in the *New Statesman* in 1958).[11] By 1987, Ian Fleming was a respectable literary figure, shorn of associations with sexual deviance and credited with the enduring success of the film series. This is important for how AIDS references operate in the reviews.

"Not Tonight . . . Something with a Second Bedroom": AIDS References in Reviews

Following the AIDS crisis, the perceived impact of sexual health messages on the Bond formula was a key source of topical references in reviews of *The Living Daylights*. Bond having only one sexual relationship in the film is understood in terms of a substantial contemporary concern about the dangers of casual sex.[12] These references fit in with several other recurring concerns in the reviews: the casting of a new actor who looked the part, his professional credentials as a serious actor with a classical lineage, and finally a sense in which AIDS (and campaigns to tackle the spread of the disease by reducing one's number of sexual partners) had changed the sexual practices of James Bond, signalling an end to the permissive society. Dalton's persona helped critics to articulate a move from Bond as a "sexual" figure to a more "romantic" one. For this move to make sense, it was important to acknowledge Fleming's literary persona with something less sexualized and more old-fashioned than "sex, snobbery and sadism." Topical references to AIDS were also very complex and nuanced in their commentary on sexual health campaigns and moral scares. Critics deployed their references in a way that requires a deeper exploration of the broader history of AIDS reporting in the UK press.

Jeffrey Weeks notes that AIDS provided an opportunity in the 1980s for the "moral Right" to promote values of chastity before marriage and fidelity within marriage, as well as the exclusion and condemnation of sexual deviance.[13] HIV's position as a (for the most part) sexually transmitted disease allowed moral campaigners to argue for rolling back on the sexual revolution. Medical and media historian Virginia Berridge has divided UK media responses to AIDS during the 1980s and '90s into four periods. Press responses to *The Living Daylights* bear hallmarks of the third "national emergency" period from 1986–1987 and foreshadow the subsequent "backlash" of 1988. The period 1981–1983 was characterized by "gay plague" narratives in the press that saw AIDS as a "disease of others," an attitude that continued until about 1986. Media attention broadened out in 1983–1985 to include heterosexuals. *The Living Daylights* was marketed and released at a time of "wartime national emergency." This period was different in character and was led by television. Berridge notes that messaging at this time was marked by a liberal discourse: "official consensus formed around 'safe sex' and 'harm minimization,' not around quarantine or anti-gay propaganda."[14] Others, such as Weeks, have summarized Secretary of State for Health Norman Fowler's message as "Stick to one partner; if you don't, use a condom."[15] Indeed, the *Don't Die of Ignorance* leaflet, sent to every household in the UK, conveyed the message "It is safest to stick to one faithful partner. Unless you are sure of your partner, always use a condom."[16] According to Berridge, from 1988 onward came a backlash against moralizing. The *Sunday Times* claimed that "the supposed epidemic was being used as a threat to reassert family values and to deny the young the joys of sexual liberation."[17] Topical references to AIDS in reviews of *The Living Daylights* focused on Bond's reduced number of partners for heterosexual sex and offered some commentary on using condoms, but also noted an end to a time of sexual freedom (of which James Bond is understood to be emblematic).

The review for the *Morning Star* is instructive in that it sets out the landscape for AIDS references in press reviews generally. Critic David E. Morgan notes: "What we are presented with is a post sex Bond for the age of Aids [*sic*] scares and the moral backlash. Previously known for his sexual promiscuity, Bond is now a one woman man—a remarkable transformation!"[18] Bond is no longer "promiscuous," and this is a result of the AIDS crisis. The Bond series could have directly addressed safe sex as a way for the agent to keep his "permissive" sex life while protecting himself and his partners from STIs (if not being unceremoniously killed by the villain). Instead, in the words of the review's headline, "Bond adjusts" to reduce the number of sexual partners to one, echoing campaigns for sexual fidelity. For Morgan, "post sex Bond" is understood as a symbol of the moral backlash; the alternative "safe sex" Bond is conspicuous by his absence.

References to AIDS and safe sex varied in terms of their directness. *The Guardian* was notable for directly mentioning condoms. The headline "Kiss Kiss, no bang bang" plays on a nickname for James Bond (Mr. Kiss Kiss Bang Bang) to make the reference to Bond's having fewer sexual relationships in *The Living Daylights*. Derek Malcolm notes a change to the Bond formula to accommodate Dalton and to "take suitable cognisance of the post-permissive society," suggesting the end of an era. For the critic, Bond's sex life is reined in to just one partner because Dalton portrays him as a square who is "unlikely to ask Q for a fool-proof condom for the Aids-era [*sic*]." Malcolm is the most explicit of all reviewers in addressing the idea that *The Living Daylights* could not show Bond using a condom and so has Bond stick to one partner instead. But he is ambivalent about what this means for the future of the franchise: "007 has at last grown less like a predatory little boy," but whether fans of the series will take to the change is "anybody's guess."[19] In any case, this adjustment is understood to be a significant one that has profoundly transformed an icon.

The *Morning Star* also develops a distinction between "romantic" and "sexual" iterations of Bond. Here, Dalton's pedigree as a "Shakespearean" actor (who had recently portrayed Heathcliff and Rochester, too) is important to that sense of being "romantic." In other words, the idea of a romantic Bond is more complex than simply a one-woman Bond; faithful Bond takes on additional resonances to do with literary classics and a simpler time gone by. Ultimately, Morgan concludes that the Bond series is a robust social force that will continue to "transmit messages" and a "flawed vision" about the wider world.[20] Clive Hirschhorn's review in the *Sunday Express* explores the opposite position. The review celebrates a family values approach to controlling AIDS and does not see the adjustment as a major negative change to the film series: "at a time when indiscriminating bed-hopping is definitely not advisable, Bond is wisely given just one playmate," which elides an alternative where the agent has multiple partners but uses condoms.[21]

Phillip French identifies and sends up *The Living Daylights'* "stick to one partner" response to AIDS in his review in the *Observer*. He indicates that the Bond films have overreacted to the AIDS crisis: "The former playboy hero of the western world now has a sex life only slightly more adventurous than Squadron leader Bigglesworth." Instead, says French, Bond displays more "chivalric love" toward Kara and goes on a "romantic quest" to rescue her, further building a distinction between "romance" and "sex." The critic is optimistic about the future of the series but seizes the opportunity to take another swipe at Bond's permissiveness at the review's close: "[*The Living Daylights*] should ensure the future of the series—provided 007 doesn't feel obliged to marry Kara and settle down in Chiswick."[22]

Shaun Usher's review in the *Daily Mail* illustrates the way in which safe sex references, Dalton, and the romantic Bond are connected. The review is headlined "Now Bond is No No Seven!" and is subtitled with the line "Dalton plays him as the spy for the Safe Sex era":

> There's every reason to suspect a Smersh coup, swapping the sexually predatory James of yore for his macho but priggish twin brother Horace. For this is No-No Seven, likelier to pass on passion than make passes at the heroine, whom he treats with the romantic diffidence of a management trainee escorting the boss's daughter to the firm's annual dance. Well, the cinema version of Bond is a quarter-century old. So perhaps it's time he grew up. Especially since the social climate is against the brand image of a licence-to-ladykill stud. Certainly, Shakespearian actor Dalton looks the part. Typecast to creator Ian Fleming's vision of a saturnine, cruelly handsome achiever. But my word, after Connery's feral drive and Moore's caddish mischief, this Bond for the Safe Sex era seems a bit subdued.[23]

This long quotation illustrates that Dalton marks a break with the franchise's past (which is viewed quite favorably) and that there is a general sorrow that an era is over. The review implicates the "Safe Sex era" in changing Dalton's Bond into someone who looks the part, particularly in connecting to Fleming's character description, but is prevented from acting the part with a long list of sexual conquests.

By contrast, a review in the *Independent* (a new broadsheet launched in 1986) also makes a topical reference to safe sex, yet is clearly more conscious of the future of the series and more tolerant of contemporary concerns being addressed by the new installment, and displays greater negativity about the past:

> Dalton . . . projects a pleasant old-fashion romanticism, he has curbed his character's satyric impulses, The usual bevy of bikini beauties (as publicists like to call them) clusters around the villain, while Bond limits himself to a single liaison, signalled discreetly with a breathy, off-screen "Oh James!" Living "on the edge" while committed to safe sex and conspicuous consumption, he has secured his place (and the longevity of the series) as a mythical hero tailored for modern anxieties.[24]

Sheila Johnston is critical of Moore's Bond. As the review goes through its key critical motions, it touches on Dalton—the new actor—as a romantic rather than "satyric" figure who provides a break with the past and a suitable type of heroism for the changed moral landscape (figure 15.2).

Dalton's Bond persona stands in for a reversal from certain concepts that critics align with Roger Moore's portrayal (bad acting, the tastelessness of the 1970s, a playful outlook on seduction, and being far removed from Fleming's version of the character). Dalton was seen, by contrast, as indicative of the 1980s (sophisticated, good at acting, romantic rather than seductive, and, somewhat paradoxically, closer to Fleming). As Usher's review suggests, critics were persuaded that he looked the part. Reviews offered a wealth of physical descriptions of Dalton, focusing on his looks and particularly his face. He was, for example, described by French in the *Observer* as "like the Bond on the covers

Figure 15.2 A romantic interlude between Bond (Timothy Dalton) and Kara Milovy (Maryam d'Abo) on a Vienna Ferris wheel. *The Living Daylights* (1987).

of the 1950s Pan paperbacks."[25] Critics made links to the literary character through the physical descriptions in the books and their illustrations. Dalton's acting heritage also helped to layer in additional meanings to Bond as a "romantic." This developed his Bond as a more serious iteration of the character. He was described as a "Shakespearean actor" in publications as varied as the *Daily Mail*, the *Daily Telegraph*, and the *Morning Star*.[26] There were also references to his time with the Royal Academy of Dramatic Arts in the *Times* and the *Sunday Telegraph*.[27]

Victoria Mather's review in the *Daily Telegraph* connected the serious, grown-up, romantic Bond with the era: "Gone is the dreadful schoolboy humour purveyed by Mr Moore; Mr Dalton is as dry as his Martinis and, post-Aids [sic], contents himself with falling in love with the girl rather than taking her to bed." The review suggests a positive outcome for the "family values" moral response to the AIDS crisis and a celebration of Dalton's mature, romantic Bond who is much better than Moore's. Mather claims that *The Living Daylights* pulls the character back to the era of the gentleman spy: "Dalton has restored a vital element to 007—the very best of British, the amateur gentleman who is better than any professional."[28] This is a curious and highly selective way of reading the character, whose appeal is generally taken to be located in a meritocratic and sexually permissive moment very different to that of the amateur gentleman spy.[29] Mather feels that the film is a success because Dalton marks both a return to Fleming and to the era of the chaste or married Edwardian gentleman spy. Any differences between Fleming's kind of spy and the Edwardian kind are dissolved through positioning Dalton's Bond as a romantic figure anchored in a simpler past (and very much prefigured by the press campaign book).

Tom Hutchinson in the *Mail on Sunday* uses his AIDS reference in a hyperbolic account of the changes Dalton's Bond brings. The review laments the loss of "the bold, carefree character built up over 14 previous films" and states that "it is sad that Timothy Dalton's debut as James Bond should be in a movie dedicated to dismantling the legend." The turns in the review's wording indicate a backlash against the "stay faithful" approach to the AIDS crisis through topical reference: "As though in post-Aids [sic] panic, the once-lecherous agent is faithful to cellist Kara." This—along with the seriousness of the film—is like "taking an axe to the Albert Memorial."[30]

"Whoever She Was, It Must Have Scared the Living Daylights Out of Her"

Topical references are a way for critics to make film criticism relevant to readers. AIDS references in UK press reviews of *The Living Daylights* show an unexpected impact of the prevailing messages to prevent the spread of HIV on the way the film was read. The government message summarized by Jeffrey Weeks as "Stick to one partner; if you don't, use a condom" presented critics with a way to make their criticism of the new Bond film relevant to their readers. The topical reference facilitated interpretations of James Bond's faithfulness to one "Bond girl," Kara Milovy, and a reduction of other sexual partners as a significant change in the formula. This coincided with other changes in the Bond series, notably that Dalton had replaced Moore and would, in all likelihood, go onto to star in many more films, thereby setting up new traditions where Bond was more serious, romantic, and grown up and less emblematic of the sexual revolution. Some critics saw this as the end of an era while others emphasized the beginning of a new one. Topical practices revealed critics' views on Bond's role as an icon of swinging sexual permissiveness but also on the moral issues that informed responses to the AIDS crisis. Dalton's persona as Bond layered in extra meanings to this issue. In particular, his pedigree as a serious actor helped to build a distinction between the old "sexual" Bond and the newer "romantic" Bond for those critics who wanted to celebrate the potential of this new era rather than to lament the passing of the old one.

What is surprising is that the implicit or assumed predictions—that Timothy Dalton would make many more films, that AIDS had changed the Bond formula forever—did not pan out. Dalton made one more film, *Licence to Kill* (1989), before the series went into a hiatus until 1995. The franchise returned with a new actor, Pierce Brosnan, as Bond. By 1995, the West's relationship with HIV/AIDS was very different. In the United Kingdom, the national emergency and backlash periods were over and the press generally treated HIV and AIDS with a newer set of political associations. (The global picture was very different, of course.) The reception approach reveals that personal politics is important for *The Living Daylights*. Looking at the topical references of film reviews offers a snapshot of how a film lands in a particular time and place and how a film such as *The Living Daylights* bears out interpretations that are unexpected when one thinks only about its formal characteristics.

Notes

1. Ernest Mathijs, "AIDS References in the Critical Reception of David Cronenberg: 'It May Not Be Such a Bad Disease After All,'" *Cinema Journal* 42, no. 4 (2003): 29–45; 30.
2. Mathijs, "AIDS References," 30.
3. James Chapman, *Licence to Thrill: A Cultural History of the James Bond Films* (London: I. B. Tauris, 2007), 196.
4. Cary Edwards, *He Disagreed with Something That Ate Him: Reading "The Living Daylights" and "Licence to Kill"* (London: CreateSpace, 2018), 28.
5. Tony Bennett and Janet Woollacott, *Bond and Beyond: The Political Career of a Popular Hero* (New York: Methuen, 1987), 278.

6. Bennett and Woollacott, *Bond and Beyond*, 281.
7. Klaus Dodds and Lisa Funnell, "Going Atmospheric and Elemental: Roger Moore's and Timothy Dalton's James Bond and Cold War Geo-Politics," in *Media and the Cold War in the 1980s*, ed. Henrik G. Bastiansen, Martin Klimke, and Rolf Werenskjold (Cham: Palgrave Macmillan, 2019), 63–85, 83.
8. Raymond Benson, *The James Bond Bedside Companion* (London: Boxtree, 1988), 247.
9. Chapman, *Licence to Thrill*, citing Kingsley Amis, *The James Bond Dossier* (London: Pan Books, 1966), 46.
10. Shaun Usher, "Now Bond Is No No Seven," *Daily Mail*, June 30, 1987; Sheila Johnston, "James Bond: For Your Eyes Mainly," *The Independent*, July 2, 1987.
11. Paul Johnson, "Sex, Snobbery and Sadism," *New Statesman*, April 5, 1958.
12. Critics are divided on whether Bond and Kara share a sexual relationship. It is also debatable whether Bond has sex with the woman on the yacht in the pre-credit sequence, but reviewers tended not to notice or count this.
13. Jeffrey Weeks, "Love in a Cold Climate," *Marxism Today*, January 1987, 12–17, 13.
14. Virginia Berridge, "AIDS, the Media and Health Policy," in *AIDS: Rights, Risk and Reason*, ed. Peter Aggleton, Peter Davies, and Graham Hart (London: CRC, 1992), 13–24; 16, 15, 23.
15. Weeks, "Love in a Cold Climate," 12.
16. Department of Health and Social Security, *Don't Die of Ignorance* (London: H.M.S.O., 1986), booklet, accessed at: wellcomecollection.org/works/kx943x59.
17. *Sunday Times*, cited in Berridge, "AIDS, the Media," 17.
18. David E. Morgan, "Bond Adjusts," *Morning Star*, July 3, 1987, 8.
19. The name "Mr. Kiss Kiss Bang Bang" purportedly comes from an Italian journalist in 1962 and found its way to becoming a potential name for the soundtrack to *Thunderball* (1966). Derek Malcolm, "Kiss Kiss, No Bang Bang," *The Guardian*, July 2, 1987, 15.
20. Morgan, "Bond Adjusts."
21. Clive Hirschhorn, "Dalton's Bond . . . Better Than Plonk," *Sunday Express*, July 5, 1987, 18.
22. Philip French, "Bond and Bondage," *Observer*, July 5, 1987, 19.
23. Usher, "Now Bond Is No No Seven."
24. Johnston, "James Bond: For Your Eyes Mainly."
25. French, "Bond and Bondage."
26. Usher, "Now Bond Is No No Seven"; Victoria Mather, "The Resurrection of a Gentleman's Bond," *Daily Telegraph*, June, 30, 1987; Morgan, "Bond Adjusts."
27. David Robinson, "Bond Grows Up at Last," *Times*, June 30, 1987; Richard Mayne, "Old Spies Never Die," *Sunday Telegraph*, July 5, 1987, 17.
28. Mather, "Resurrection."
29. See, for example, Chapman, *Licence to Thrill*, 96.
30. Tom Hutchinson, "Wise Guy Bond Turns into Mr Nice Spy," *Mail on Sunday*, July 5, 1987.

CHAPTER 16

BOND IN THE NEW WORLD ORDERS

Licence to Kill (1989)

STACEY PEEBLES

W hen *Licence to Kill* premiered on July 10, 1989, it broke new ground in a number of ways—and not least of these was the film's rating. Released as PG-13 in the United States and 15 in the United Kingdom, it was the first James Bond film to go beyond the PG or simply "Approved" ratings of its predecessors. Though in the States, all subsequent films in the series have stayed at the PG-13 level, *Licence to Kill* remains the only Bond film to garner the U.K.'s 15 rating. And even that rating required some cutting: scenes of a whipping, a shark attack, and several violent deaths had to be altered for the British Board of Film Classification to approve its release, and the Motion Picture Association of America trimmed scenes in order to avoid an R rating in the States.[1]

This was, the ratings suggested, a darker, more intense version of Bond, and the film's star reflected this as well. Timothy Dalton's two outings as 007, *The Living Daylights* (1987) and *Licence to Kill*, showcased a Bond who was notably more severe and less playful than previous iterations, particularly in the latter film. Caryn James titled her *New York Times* review "Dalton as a Brooding Bond in *Licence to Kill*" and called him "the first James Bond with angst, a moody spy for the fin de siècle." She goes on to call Dalton's performance "glowering," "moodier," and "an angry Bond," concluding that this as well as the story "makes him fit for the 90s."[2]

More recently, Daniel Craig has shepherded Bond through the two decades after 9/11, two "forever wars," and even a global pandemic that delayed his last film for almost two years—reasons enough, one assumes, for the more serious affect for which his performances are known. But what about Dalton's?

Released in 1989, *Licence to Kill* in particular was a turning point for James Bond, both politically and culturally. Most obviously, the fall of the Berlin Wall and the end of the Cold War meant a realigning of the agent's identity and purpose and a need to find new, sinister enemies to confront and take down. But he was also operating on the cusp of the third-wave feminist movement—another potential realignment of his raison d'être, the particular expression of masculinity that makes Bond Bond. *Licence to Kill* negotiates these turning points by representing ambivalence about new world orders—both political and cultural—an ambivalence that is most evident in Bond's encounters with a love interest and a villain who are uncomfortably similar to him. The villain can be overcome with reassertions of righteous and extreme violence (hence those ratings), but the woman is trickier. Bond's status in light of changing gender roles remains uncertain, a question that is asked but not answered in the film's final scene.

Licence to Kill opens with a classic Bond set piece. In Key West, Florida, on the wedding day of Bond's close friend Felix Leiter (David Hedison), the Drug Enforcement Administration intercepts the groom on the way to the ceremony. Powerful South American drug lord Franz Sanchez (Robert Davi) is nearby, and Felix, accompanied by Bond, dashes off to try and apprehend him. Sanchez's villainous status is confirmed when we see him discover his girlfriend Lupe Lamora (Talisa Soto) in bed with another man. He promptly has the man dragged off to be killed while he personally whips Lupe as punishment. Before the scene ends, a close-up of her anguished face emphasizes the brutality of his actions. As Felix's bride Della (Priscilla Barnes) waits anxiously at the church, Felix and Bond pursue Sanchez in an elaborate chase, culminating in Bond dramatically boarding Sanchez's plane in midair and attaching a cable from the DEA's helicopter. Bond and Felix are then able to skydive down to a tearful Della and walk right into the wedding in their morning suits, only slightly rumpled.

So far, so good—this is a Bond that we're familiar with, snappy and insouciant. But there are hints that this Bond will turn out to be a bit different. Felix and Della present him with a silver lighter engraved with the words "love always." When the bride offers to throw him her garter, he refuses, looking a bit shaken at her implicit suggestion that he be the next one to get married. She throws it to him anyway, and he catches it with a pensive expression, prompting her to ask Felix, "Did I say something wrong?" Felix answers that his friend had been married once, and that it was a long time ago—a reference to Bond's brief marriage in *On Her Majesty's Secret Service* (1969). In that film, Bond, as played only once by George Lazenby, falls in love with and marries Contessa Teresa di Vicenzo (Diana Rigg). It seems like a happy ending, until she is killed by Bond's nemesis Blofeld (Telly Savalas) in the final moments of the film. Dan Mills has argued that *On Her Majesty's Secret Service* is an outlier in the Bond canon, not least because both the film and Fleming's original novel "offer a significant departure from the typical treatment of women in the franchise," in that the female characters "play vital roles in the narrative and demonstrate considerable autonomy, which, at times, works to emasculate their male counterparts." Mills notes that "Lazenby's Bond proposes to di Vicenzo precisely because she rescues him: this is the gesture that makes him fall in love"— a remarkable reversal of the usual Bond formula, which dictates that *he* will rescue a woman and *she* will fall in love—and also that when Bond cries at her death, "this is the only time this occurs across a franchise that spans 23 films and 50 years."[3] (Mills was presumably writing before 2012's *Skyfall*, in which Bond does cry again, though that's a remarkable fifty-six-year gap between tears.)

Dalton's troubled expression at the suggestion of marriage in *Licence to Kill* seems to harken back to that earlier film, and a more complicated way of being in the world. The film's title refers not just to Bond's permission to use deadly violence as an agent of MI6, but the fact that this is revoked during the course of the plot, his resignation tendered. (The film's original title was *Licence Revoked*, but it was changed in order to avoid confusing American viewers who might understand this to be a driver's license.[4]) This is Bond, then, without his usual license—to devastate the ladies and his enemies alike. Instead, here he operates as a free agent, rendered vulnerable by that loss of status and an uncertain place in the new world orders. The dangers presented by a new kind of villain become apparent not long after the opening sequence, and the new kind of woman is not far behind.

Sanchez, it's revealed, escapes custody, and his henchmen confront Felix and Della on their honeymoon (figure 16.1). One of the men, played by a young Benicio del Toro, knocks Felix out. When he comes to, Felix asks where his wife is. As the henchman Dario, Del Toro responds with the disturbing and idiosyncratically delivered line, "Don't worry, we gave her a nice *honeymooooon*." Sanchez assures Felix that his actions are nothing personal—just business— before ordering him to be held over a shark tank and slowly lowered into it as he screams in pain and terror. It's a grisly scene, sharpened by Bond's clear anguish when he later finds Della dead, shot and slumped on her bed, and Felix wrapped in a bloody cloth nearby. He's still alive, but in critical condition, apparently missing one leg below the knee and with one severely damaged arm. Villains using violence for spectacular effect are nothing new to the Bond films, of course—one of the canon's most famous images is Shirley Eaton as Jill Masterson in *Goldfinger* (1964), covered in a coat of gold paint and left to die. But the context is a new one here, and both the degree and the effect of violence ratchets up as the film continues.

Figure 16.1 Robert Davi as Franz Sanchez and a young Benicio del Toro as Dario. *License to Kill* (1989).

After all, Sanchez is a different antagonist—he's neither Soviet nor exploiting Cold War tensions for his own profit, as in Timothy Dalton's previous Bond film, *The Living Daylights*, from 1987. "James Bond's obsession with Russia has long signaled Western discontent with its Soviet enemy of old," notes Ian Kinane. "[I]ndeed, the Bond franchise has always been at its most lewdly outlandish and political[ly] confrontational when it has Bond facing down Mother Russia." The Soviet or Russian bad guys were over the top but, Kinane continues, often rooted in real-world fears. "Beneath the hyperbole . . . lies Ian Fleming's deeply troubling concern with the operations of SMERSH, the umbrella counterintelligence organization of the Red Army, and the primary antagonists of Fleming's early Cold War Bond thrillers."[5] The Soviet Union would not dissolve until Mikhail Gorbachev's resignation in 1991, but in 1989, the signs were there.

America, and thus Hollywood, needed to find a new enemy. During his presidency, Ronald Reagan had been all about the Cold War, but in 1989, newly elected President George H. W. Bush was ready to step out from the shadow of his predecessor. In his first presidential address, on September 5, Bush held up a bag. "This," he said somberly, "is crack cocaine, seized a few days ago by Drug Enforcement Agents in a park just across the street from the White House." As it turned out, the back story of this particular prop was a bit more complicated. Rather than the product of a drug deal taking place in Lafayette Park—an implausible thing at best—it was a DEA setup with the specific purpose of confiscating something that Bush could gesture with on television. The true story broke a few weeks later, Dana Carvey parodied the moment on *Saturday Night Live*, and the bag of crack became famous as an ill-gotten but handy propagandistic accessory.[6] In the moment, however, the atmosphere was dead serious. "Drugs are a real and terribly dangerous threat to our neighborhoods, our friends, and our families," Bush insisted. "No one among us is out of harm's way." It was a war, he said, a war that must be won, with everything at stake. Anyone who used or sold drugs was contributing to the cataclysm, but Bush put particular emphasis on the danger of what he called "the cocaine cartels." "In Columbia alone," he noted in dismay, "cocaine killers have gunned down a leading statesman, murdered almost two hundred judges and seven members of their supreme court." Bush pledged money, resources, the military, prosecution, and even the death penalty for drug kingpins. "Our message to the drug cartels is this: the rules have changed."[7]

Whether or not the cartels were listening, Americans were. Just one week later, the *New York Times* reported that 64 percent of people polled cited drugs as the nation's most significant problem, up from 22 percent at the end of July: "The percentage was the highest recorded for any single issue since the Times/CBS News poll began in 1976 and is one of the highest registered by any major national survey."[8] Concerns about the Cold War and the economy had turned—or been turned—to this new enemy, and this new war on drugs.

Sanchez, then, embodies these concerns. But as a villain, he's not just about the dangers of a bag of crack. He's also about the particular dangers of what Bush called "the kingpin," the master of supply and demand, the dark success story. Sanchez is the leader of a drug cartel with international reach that he wants to extend even further. Later in the film, when he's enticing a group of Japanese businessmen to invest, he tells them that he has "an invisible empire from Chile to Alaska," and that "What I want to do, amigos, is to make you part of it. I want the Pacific to be our little puddle."

This is business, as he tells Felix—business built on violence and intimidation as much as narcotics production and distribution. Sanchez is an early depiction of a cartel boss, a character type that saw a great deal more nuance in later narratives such as *Traffic* (2000), *Sicario* (2015), *Narcos* (Netflix, 2015–2017), and *El Chapo* (Univison/Netflix, 2017–2018). In the 1980s, this was still a relatively new character type, represented perhaps most hyperbolically by Al Pacino as the Miami-based Cuban drug lord Tony Montana in *Scarface* (1983), a change in emphasis from the 1932 original, which focused on the Chicago-based Italian Tony Camonte (Paul Muni) as a gangster and bootlegger. Stereotypical though Sanchez may be, it's a notable shift in Bond bad guys, as this one represents effective, if ruthless, global capitalism rather than the evils of Soviet-era communism. As Misha Glenny has written, this makes Sanchez very much a man of his time, perfectly suited to his historical moment: "The post–World War II order began to crumble in the first half of the 1980s," she notes.

"The world was taking its first steps toward the liberalization of international financial and commodity markets . . . Then came the fall of Communism in 1989 . . . Out of ideas, short of money and beaten in the race for technological superiority, Communism fizzled out in days rather than years. This was a monumental event that fused with the process of globalization to trigger an exponential rise in the shadow economy."[9]

Writing about cartel violence in Mexico, Sayak Valencia coined the term "gore capitalism" to refer to the logical outgrowth of these shifts: "the transformation of First World capitalism through globalization." As she explains, "'gore capitalism' refers to the undisguised and unjustified bloodshed that is the price the Third World pays for adhering to the increasingly demanding logic of capitalism. It also refers to the many instances of dismembering and disembowelment, often tied up with organized crime, gender and the predatory uses of bodies. In general, this term posits these incredibly brutal kinds of violence as tools of *necroempowerment*." Money and success are the goals, violence the means. And that necroempowerment, as Valencia puts it, is appealing because in the depressed economies of nations like Mexico, it offers a way for young men to fulfill what they see as their role. "Due to a number of factors," she writes, "the use of direct violence is more and more popular among powerless populations. In many cases, it is seen as a response to the fear of demasculinization that haunts many men as a consequence of rising workplace precarity and their own subsequent inability to legitimately take on the role of male provider."[10] Violence legitimizes the cartel, and the cartel legitimizes masculinity.

Rather than a representative of the U.S.S.R., political and social antithesis to both Britain and the United States, Sanchez is the entrepreneur in extremis, playing and winning at the West's own game and doing so with a suave demeanor that even Bond would have to envy. As played by Robert Davi, Sanchez is a Pablo Escobar figure who physically resembles Manuel Noriega, an association underscored by Sanchez's residence in the fictional Republic of Isthmus, a clear corollary for Panama.[11] Noriega's history reads like that of an American hero gone bad—born to a poor family, education at the School of the Americas, a successful military career resulting in political leadership, alliance with the CIA, but a fall from grace after revelations about drug trafficking, racketeering, and authoritarian rule, culminating in a U.S. invasion of Panama in 1989, the same year of *Licence to Kill*'s release. Noriega was subsequently captured, tried, and sent to prison.

How, then, does Bond respond to such a threat? Sanchez is a powerfully masculine figure with the knowledge and wherewithal to build a global narcotics empire, a man savvy enough to hide his business behind the broadcasts and compound of a popular televangelist and quick to use perverse violence as a way of ensuring control. Bond, too, after all, has historically been characterized as powerfully masculine, resourceful, savvy, and without too many qualms about using violence creatively. Here, he might be outgunned in the figurative, literal, and Freudian senses. The mutilated body of Felix and the dead, likely violated body of Della signify something different: an apex capitalist predator. "For the violence specialists of gore capitalism," writes Valencia, "*the lacerated and violated body is itself the message.*"[12]

When Bond pushes for reprisal, the DEA tells him in Key West that Sanchez is now out of their jurisdiction, that they can't even get an extradition. "There are other ways," Bond replies, indicating that he, too, is willing to work outside the law and use violence as a message. After locating the warehouse where Felix was tortured, he commits his own perverse violence: he throws one henchman into a tank full of electric eels and locks another in a container full to the brim with maggots, snarling "bon appétit" as he does so. He knocks a third into the same shark tank used for Felix's dismemberment, tossing a suitcase full of money at him in disgust. In consequence, Bond is called on the carpet—and appropriately, it happens, at the historical house of Ernest Hemingway, paragon of masculinity. M (Robert Brown) disapproves of the agent's "private vendetta" and chastises him for neglecting his next mission. Bond pleads on behalf of Felix, but M is unmoved. "Spare me this sentimental rubbish," he says. "You have an assignment. And I expect you to carry it out objectively and professionally." "Then you have my resignation, sir," Bond responds. M then revokes his license to kill and demands his weapon. Bond won't give up the gun, and instead surprises the guards and bolts.

Bond and Sanchez are shadow figures of each other in many ways, a doubling that at first suggests the agent's darker side, a moral ambiguity stemming from the methods he uses in this unsanctioned quest for bloody revenge. Ultimately, however, the two men are distinguished by the contrast between Sanchez's single-minded pursuit of profit and Bond's dismissal of money in favor of loyalty, love, and friendship. Bond tosses that suitcase full of cash at one of Felix's attackers, betting that the man will let go of the crane above the shark tank to grab the money—which he does, and dies. Bond disdainfully watches the water fill with blood, bills floating in the mess, and his friend Sharkey (Frank McRae) remarks, "What a waste." Bond looks at him, and Sharkey clarifies: "The money." But Bond isn't interested—he leaves it behind. A few scenes later, he escapes a marine station in a small plane carrying large packages of Sanchez's cash. After he tosses out the pilot and is certain of his getaway, bills scatter throughout the plane and in its wake. Again, he doesn't care—one blows against his arm and he brushes it off, smiling at the absurdity of it, perhaps. *These bad guys and their precious money*, he seems to be thinking. Whatever violent means Bond is willing to use, the implication is that he's gunning for justice, not profit, and in the end, that gives him an edge. If, as Valencia writes, Bond is also someone responding to a fear of demasculinization due to rising workplace precarity, he does so with his own brand of necroempowerment and distinguishes himself from Sanchez in the motivations for and goals of that violence.

Bond's vengeance against Sanchez is finally achieved in appropriate fashion in the film's flashy finale. First a number of Sanchez's henchmen are gorily eliminated. Bond frames the manager of the marine station, whom Sanchez then locks in a decompression chamber and cuts the oxygen all at once. The man explodes and spatters blood all over the money that Bond had planted on him. (Bond leaves the money, but that's not Sanchez's way. "Launder it," he tells his men.) Later, in Sanchez's drug production base, Pam Bouvier (Carey Lowell) shoots Dario, who then falls into a shredder. And then everything blows up, quite literally. Bond ignites a laboratory in Sanchez's compound where workers are hiding cocaine in containers of gasoline for smuggling. The buildings explode into flames. Sanchez flees in a tanker truck with Bond in pursuit. The truck crashes, cocaine-laden gasoline leaking everywhere, and Sanchez prepares to kill Bond, brandishing a machete rather than a gun and admonishing him, "You could have had everything." Why, his comment suggests, did you give up on the chance for so much money, to be an apex capitalist predator? But again, Bond counters him. "Don't you want to know why?" he asks, and Sanchez pauses, perhaps indeed curious about his motivations. Bond pulls out the lighter given to him by Felix and Della, showing Sanchez its inscription from them a half second before he ignites it, engulfing Sanchez in flames as well as the tanker itself. Bond has metaphorically outgunned this new enemy and asserted his motivation for justice rather than the blood-spattered money of the cartel, of capitalism in extremis. Even a machete, it turns out, is no match for friendship, loyalty, and righteousness. This aspect of Bond's identity, then, has been restabilized, further confirmed by his reinstatement to MI6 by the end of the film.

Bond's other confrontation with a new world order doesn't end quite so definitively. Early in the film, Bond goes looking for an informant named P. Bouvier, a CIA contract pilot with information about Sanchez. Bond finds Bouvier at a bar in Bimiji, realizing upon his arrival that the pilot is a woman. "Well this is an unexpected pleasure," Bond remarks, though sarcastically, with none of the opportunistic flirting so common to the character. Bouvier, for her part, responds in kind, without smiling or openly appraising him. "Where's Leiter?" is her only comment. She's clearly used to being in control. When Dario, Del Toro's character, shows up along with several others of Sanchez's men, Bouvier asks Bond, "You carrying?" When he reveals his small, concealed pistol, she tsk-tsks her disapproval, giving him a glimpse of the large shotgun she has under the table, and tells him to just hit the deck when the shooting starts. Dario menaces Bouvier, prompting Bond to say, "Take your hands off her. She's with me." But Bouvier refuses to play the damsel. "He's with *me*," she counters, and shoves the barrel of the gun up against Dario. In the ensuing melee, she's adept at fighting, showing Bond-style improvisation when she uses her gun to shoot an enormous hole in the wall of the bar for them to escape through. A well-aimed bullet from Dario's gun doesn't even faze her, as, to Bond's surprise, she's wearing a bulletproof vest. Like Sanchez, Bouvier appears to be out-Bonding Bond—she's cool, collected, skilled with violence, and slips easily through a foe's hands. If Sanchez is representative of a new, post-Soviet kind of enemy, Bouvier is a new kind of woman, a vague prototype of the third-wave feminism that would begin in earnest with reactions to Anita Hill's testimony in 1991 and the riot grrrl subculture of the early '90s.

It's no surprise, then, that in their getaway boat, Bond and Bouvier bicker about who is in charge. He calls it lucky that she dodged Dario's bullet; she insists it was experience, not luck. "Look, I just saved your life back there," she points out. "*You* saved *my* life?" he responds incredulously. Bouvier, it seems, is too much like him for his taste. Bond tells her to leave this tough business to the professionals, to which she notes that she's been an Army pilot, flying in "the toughest hellholes in South America, and I will not have you lecture me about professionalism." The tension breaks a bit when the engine runs out of gas and Bond asks for her help in going after Sanchez in Isthmus City. As they negotiate what he would pay her to fly him there, she drives a hard bargain, stepping in closer and closer until the deal is sealed, and she kisses him. "Why don't you wait to be asked?" Bond comments, prompting her to reasonably reply, "Well, why don't you ask me?"

Bond would seem to have quite literally met his match, a cool-headed woman who doesn't hesitate to take the lead with either guns or sex (figure 16.2). But when they arrive in Isthmus City, differences between them become apparent, much to her frustration. They check into a large hotel, where Bond refers to her as his executive secretary, "Miss Kennedy." She's quick to question him as soon as the hotel staff leave the room. "It's *Ms.* Kennedy," first of all, and "Why can't you be *my* executive secretary?" Bond laughs and replies, "We're south of the border. It's a man's world." North of the border, things are changing, but in this story, Bond can still be Bond in Latin America.

Bond proceeds to attempt an assassination of Sanchez, and his absence turns Bouvier from confident operative to fretting, would-be girlfriend. She smokes a cigarette for the first time in five years, worrying about his safety, and is even more unsettled by the later revelation that he slept with Sanchez's girlfriend Lupe instead of leaving the country. "I'll be damned if I'll help him," she fumes, though Q (Desmond Llewelyn) brushes it off: "Look, don't judge him too harshly, my dear. Field operatives must often use every means at their disposal to achieve their objectives." "Bullshit!" she counters, and Q sighs at the burden of dealing with her emotions.

Bouvier's power has definitely been undercut and her similarities to Bond diminished, though in comparison with other "Bond girls," that power remains

Figure 16.2 Timothy Dalton as James Bond and Carey Lowell as pilot Pam Bouvier. *License to Kill* (1989).

impressive. Consider Pussy Galore (Honor Blackman) in *Goldfinger* (1964), arguably the first strong woman in the Bond film franchise. Like Bouvier, she's also a pilot. She plays an active role in the plot and defeats the villain's plans while Bond is held captive. "So why is Bond considered the hero of the story?" writes Tom McNeely. "Quite simply it is because he converts a lesbian . . . It isn't until Pussy is 'cured' of her lesbianism that she takes steps to save the world."[13] And, of course, there's the name. Even in films where the female characters have shared Bond's profession as an undercover agent, they often end up as helpless captives or, as McNeely notes, threatened with death by drowning, a situation that requires wet, clinging clothes and a resuscitating kiss to resolve. But Bouvier isn't like this—she is generically named, consistently competent, never in need of rescuing. McNeely argues, too, that even when she protests that Bond's assignation with Lupe is "bullshit!" she's at least being honest about her feelings and, as very few characters ever do, "indict[ing] Bond for his inexcusable promiscuity."[14]

And so Bond's final negotiations with Bouvier recover some of the more fluid gender and sexual dynamics that her character seems to have been written to convey. After Sanchez's death, Bond pauses for a moment in quiet grief, a reflection that is interrupted by the blaring of a truck's horn. Bouvier has arrived, commanding the shell of a tanker and barking, "What are you waiting for? Get in!" His response is relieved and slightly aggrieved: "Yes sir," he says, and she smiles as he submits to riding in the passenger seat. The two next appear at a swanky party where Lupe, dazzling in her diamonds, pulls Bond in for a passionate kiss. Bouvier watches and then runs off to cry by herself. "You could stay here with me," Lupe offers, but Bond is after the New Woman, not the old fashioned one. "I think you and El Presidente will make a perfect couple," he remarks, and leaps off the patio and into a swimming pool next to the distraught Bouvier. He pulls her in, and as they embrace, they repeat their lines from earlier in the film, but with a twist. "Why don't you wait until you're asked?" she says, stealing his admonishment. "So why don't you ask me?" he counters, as reasonably as she did before.

Bouvier demonstrates a level of feminine or feminist power that is both impressive and ultimately ambivalent. Whereas Bond's distinction from Sanchez's apex capitalist predator is finally made as clear as the writing on that lighter given to him by Felix and Della, how he should relate to Bouvier is much less so. Like him, she is tough, accomplished, and determined, but also blusters and cries over Bond's failure to show her the proper attention. She needs him to make the grand final gesture that leads to a happy kiss, but she also steals his line and implies his presumptuousness. Bond and Bouvier ask questions of each other and switch roles as they do so. Could Bond have a love interest who really does look more like him? Or would he inevitably reassert his dominance? When it comes to women, we can't know—at least not in this film, because in the end, those questions are never answered.

Licence to Kill takes Bond into new territory, though he returns to more familiar ground in the next Bond film, *GoldenEye*, in 1995, which stars Pierce Brosnan and features an enemy with Soviet roots and the femme fatale Xenia Onatopp (Famke Janssen), who enjoys killing people by choking them to death with her thighs. *Licence to Kill*, then, is a notable foray, released right on the edge of dramatic political and social realignments. Bond will always defeat the bad guy in whatever guise he appears, even if it would initially seem uncomfortably close to his own. But whether he can, or should, continue to "get the girl" and assert that possessive dominance, that traditional masculinity, remains to be seen at the end of the film. Because whose line is it, anyway?

Notes

1. "*Licence to Kill*: Alternate Versions," IMDb.com, www.imdb.com/title/tt0097742/alternateversions, March 11, 2022.
2. Caryn James, "Dalton as a Brooding Bond in *License to Kill*," *New York Times*, July 14, 1989.
3. Dan Mills, "'What Really Went on Up There James? Bond's Wife, Blofeld's Patients, and Empowered Bond Women," in *For His Eyes Only: The Women of James Bond*, ed. Lisa Funnell (New York: Wallflower, 2015), 110–11, 118.

4. MI6 Staff, "Title Change: How the Spelling of Timothy Dalton's Second Adventure Changed," MI6: The Home of James Bond 007, April 26, 2020, www.mi6-hq.com /sections/articles/licence-to-kill-title-change?id=04686#.

5. Quoted in Roxanne Roberts, "When Russia Was the Villain: How This Moment Echoes the Era of Cold War Spy Novels and *Rocky IV*," *Washington Post*, March 11, 2022, www .washingtonpost.com/lifestyle/2022/03/10/russia-cold-war-putin-villain/.

6. Michael Isikoff, "Drug Buy Set Up for Bush Speech: DEA Lured Seller to Lafayette Park," *Washington Post*, September 22, 1989, A1.

7. George H. W. Bush, "Presidential Address on National Drug Policy," September 5, 1989, www.c-span.org/video/?8921-1/president-bush-address-national-drug-policy.

8. Richard L. Berke, "Poll Finds Most in U.S. Back Bush Strategy on Drugs," *New York Times*, September 12, 1989, www.nytimes.com/1989/09/12/us/poll-finds-most-in-us -back-bush-strategy-on-drugs.html.

9. Misha Glenny, *McMafia: A Journey through the Global Criminal Underworld* (New York: Random House, 2008), xv–xvi.

10. Sayak Valencia, *Gore Capitalism*, trans. John Pluecker (South Pasadena, CA: Semiotext(e), 2018), 81, 19–20, 134.

11. The Noriega connections are noted briefly by Lisa Funnell and Klaus Dodds in *Geographies, Genders and Geopolitics of James Bond* (London: Palgrave Macmillan, 2017), 62, and Jeremy M. Black in *The Politics of James Bond: From Fleming's Novels to the Big Screen* (Westport, CT: Praeger, 2000), 151.

12. Valencia, *Gore Capitalism*, 163. Emphasis in original.

13. Tom L. McNeely, "Somebody Does It Better: Competent Women in the Bond Films," in *James Bond in World and Popular Culture: The Films Are Not Enough*, ed. Robert G. Weiner, B. Lynn Whitfield, and Jack Becker (Newcastle upon Tyne, UK: Cambridge Scholars, 2011), 179, 182.

14. McNeely, "Somebody," 182.

CHAPTER 17

COLD WAR NOSTALGIA, (GEO)POLITICAL PROGRESS, AND JAMES BOND IN *GOLDENEYE* (1995)

TATIANA KONRAD

Goldenеye (1995) was the seventeenth film in the James Bond series and the first to star Pierce Brosnan. It was also the first in the franchise to be made after the collapse of the Soviet Union. This makes it a curious example of James Bond cinema in terms of the politics that the film negotiates. On the one hand, there are numerous scenes that inform the viewer about significant geopolitical transformations in the world. On the other, the film continues to imagine the confrontation between the USSR and the Free World that existed during the Cold War. This chapter explores the film's hesitation to fully move beyond the Cold War and examines the scenes that overtly communicate the period's end. Additionally, it analyzes how the images of the Cold War and the film's explicit commentary on the (geo)political reorganization of the world shape James Bond as a new hero for the post–Cold War era.

Cold War Nostalgia

In *GoldenEye*, James Bond is on a mission to save the world from a nuclear electromagnetic orbital weapon called "GoldenEye" that was developed by the USSR. Beginning with a sequence set in 1986, it is a film about the Cold War. Yet, released in 1995, this is the first example of Bond cinema that tackles the Cold War during an actual post–Cold War era. As a result, the film is stuck between the two eras, making it difficult to classify straightforwardly as one or the other. Was James Bond viewed as a Cold War hero in the 1990s? Would the character lose his meaning once set outside the Cold War frame? Was the series unable to reflect the (geo)political changes in *GoldenEye*, thus projecting the real-existing hesitation and confusion that surrounded 1990s geopolitics? Was the Cold War setting a deliberate choice made to emphasize the cold relationship between post-Soviet Russia and the West that remained after the collapse of the Soviet Union? Or did the creators choose to be nostalgic and communicate the values of the Free World, foreground an easily recognizable hero (embodied by James Bond), and reinforce the security of the Cold War, when heroes and villains were defined in a clear-cut way? These questions make one meditate upon the role of the Cold War in *GoldenEye* and the way it affects the character of James Bond.

The Cold War as a theme has been raised in multiple cinematic productions in the post–Cold War era. Even after the collapse of the Soviet Union in 1991, it has often appeared on screen, as illustrated, for example, by the 2010s wave including Steven Spielberg's *Bridge of Spies* (2015), David Leitch's *Atomic Blonde* (2017), and Guillermo del Toro's *The Shape of Water* (2017).[1] These films negotiate contemporary political and cultural issues through the lens of the Cold War. James Bond's stagnation in the Cold War times in *GoldenEye* tells its viewers much about 1990s politics. The film oscillates between nostalgic references to the Cold War and progressive attempts to reimagine the world after the long-lasting confrontation between the Free World and the countries of the Eastern Bloc. The two perspectives, in fact, intertwine to such an extent that they create an aesthetic of their own, moving away from the Cold War imagery and reinforcing its significance at the same time. In his study *The Screen Is Red*, Bernard F. Dick singles out the most crucial and frequently reoccurring themes in Cold War cinema, among them the Bomb, science, communism, and espionage.[2] All of these appear in *GoldenEye* through the space-based nuclear weapon, the Severnaya research station, Russian characters, including Bond's ally Natalya Simonova (Izabella Scorupco), and, of course, spies. James Bond himself is identified as a man of the time by M (Judi Dench), who calls him "a sexist, misogynist dinosaur, *a relic of the Cold War.*" *GoldenEye* is nostalgic about the Cold War, not only perpetuating easily recognizable images and metaphors but also foregrounding the effectiveness of such tropes to communicate very precise messages to the audience.

Discussing the meaning of Cold War tropes in twenty-first-century cinema, Vesta Silva and Jon Wiebel accentuate the "certainty and stability" that the Cold War guaranteed, compared to post-9/11 upheavals and unrest. Such a perspective would have been perceived as paradoxical during the Cold War itself, when the arms race made the world fear a nuclear war and a possible end of the world, yet today this period is no longer considered the most complex or dangerous in global history—largely so, of course, because it is over and the major fears that existed then did not materialize. According to Silva and Wiebel, "Cold War nostalgia narratives are a way of resecuring a sense of American exceptionalism and victory in a time of uncertainty and fear. In other words, nostalgic Cold War narratives help reassure contemporary Americans that we are still the good guys (and gals) fighting on the right side to protect the world." This observation about the United States can be applied to the West at large, however, including the United Kingdom: nostalgic references to the Cold War resurrect fixed and easily recognizable images of heroes and villains, thereby helping the viewer understand the power dynamics in a certain film. *GoldenEye*'s Cold War, for example, reinforces the good nature of James Bond and the evil nature of communism, thereby helping Bond remain a hero in the post–Cold War era, when a division of characters into heroes and villains can be unclear. In this way, nostalgia in *GoldenEye* should not be seen as a wish to return to the past as such but rather an attempt to restore some recognizable narratives that characterize that past. Indeed, as Silva and Wiebel assert, "nostalgia is not and never can be a literal reconstruction of the past. Because nostalgia is always already linked to a particular interpretation of the past, it is necessarily a re-visioning of that past."[3]

Reading *GoldenEye* as a nostalgic narrative also helps audiences to understand the character of James Bond. The reference to Bond as a "relic of the Cold War," albeit in a negative context, signposts a specific kind of hero who was needed in the 1990s. To be precise, it illuminates the lack of such a hero and, in order to fill the vacant spot, resurrects the figure of James Bond from the past. This, in turn, reveals the absence of the new, post–Cold War James Bond. Silva and Wiebel argue that "nostalgic stories empty out much of the complexity of the past in order to position it clearly as an object of longing and desire."[4] However, while James Bond is described as a character from the past, this is not the James Bond who is needed in the 1990s, and M's negative characterization only helps to reinforce it. M's anger is a reaction to James Bond's inability to adjust and take on the role of a new, post–Cold War hero.

The aesthetics of *GoldenEye* re-create the atmosphere of the Cold War, too. In his analysis of the film *Red Sparrow* (2018), Ian Scott identifies "traditional Cold War imagery" that depicts Russia as "a typically gray, regimented society full of decaying housing blocks and regressive everyday clothing, a place where long crane shots follow lonely vehicles making their way to rural, secretive training schools designed in the Palladian style." Such and similar "visual and aural signifiers," according to Scott, have dominated Cold War cinema since 1945, turning "historical setting and events" into "symbol[s] and metaphor[s]."[5] *GoldenEye* is filled with details that resurrect the Cold War and its realities in a similar way. The Russians—through their military uniforms, accent, and obsession with nuclear weapons—effectively reflect the cinematic grammar of the Cold War that largely simplifies characters, dividing them exclusively into communists and members of the Free World, and thus making both immediately recognizable. Moreover, the film insists on how safe such an approach is through the references to chemical weapons. Lisa Funnell and Klaus Dodds note that the images of the weapons that open *GoldenEye* make the viewer reconsider the collapse of the Soviet Union as a positive outcome for the West and the world in general, foregrounding instability in a country that is filled with dangerous weapons.[6] Fashion is another aesthetic means through which a visual division of the characters is achieved. In her analysis of *GoldenEye*, Monica Germanà emphasizes visual discrepancies between Natalya Simonova and Xenia Onatopp (Famke Janssen) through references to their wardrobes. Simonova's clothes project "plain ordinariness" and Onatopp's "sartorial glamour." This visual element in the film also, in fact, tells the viewer something about the Soviet Union, namely that while the majority of the population were reduced to a grey mass, certain people had access to food, furniture, clothes, and other items that were produced in the Free World or in accordance with the fashion and standards that were popular there, which reflects the hypocrisy of the ruling elites and long tradition of corruption in (post-)Soviet states. Onatopp's "expensive fashion," in the words of Germanà, designates her as a member of such a "specific kind of elite," and precisely as a comrade of the corrupt General Ourumov (Gottfried John).[7]

Most powerfully, however, Cold War aesthetics are communicated via the opening credits in the film and the images that accompany the soundtrack performed by Tina Turner, as well as later, in the scene when Bond finds out that Janus—the main antagonist—is, in fact, his friend, agent 006 Alec Trevelyan (Sean Bean), who he assumed was dead. Both scenes largely rely on recognizable Soviet imagery: a sickle, a hammer, military stars, the Soviet flag, and the color red accompany the song (figure 17.1); statues of Soviet leaders appear both during the song and in the scene when Bond meets Trevelyan.

Figure 17.1 Cold War aesthetics are conveyed via recognizable Soviet imagery during the opening credits. *GoldenEye* (1995).

These images are ambiguous. On the one hand, they signify progress, for all these cinematic symbols are falling, flying away, breaking, or already broken; the color red is replaced with a panoply of colors—grey, yellow, orange, violet, and blue—to communicate the collapse of the Soviet Union as well as reinforce the multiplicity and diversity that is characteristic of the Free World. Yet, on the other hand, the presence of these elements makes the Cold War part of the post–Cold War reality. According to political writer Brink Lindsey, in the scene when James Bond walks through the vandalized monuments, "the soaring ambitions and ruthless power of the Soviet era have been reduced to kitsch . . . [but] the cruel gazes of the fallen leaders still cast a pall—still chill the soul with their inhuman, all-too-human arrogance. The past, though dead, still haunts."[8] Through these symbols, *GoldenEye* recognizes historical and political changes that characterize the post-Soviet/post–Cold War era, yet the film fails to reconstruct a new reality, thus reflecting the real-life confusion and hesitation that the world experienced in the first years after the end of the Cold War, having lived for decades in an environment with harsh yet clear rules.

The Post–Cold War Bond

GoldenEye, however, does not stagnate in and romanticize the Cold War era. The film emphasizes that progress and a shift from that time's way of thinking is necessary. Even M's description of Bond as a "a sexist, misogynist dinosaur, a relic of the Cold War" denotes a wish for progress. Bond's treatment of and attitudes toward women, which may have appeared charming and normative to patriarchs during the Cold War, are fully inappropriate in the new world. Funnell and Dodds argue that M despises Bond's habit of dominating and using women because this is "out of touch with the changing gender politics of the 1990s"; Bond, according to M, is "root[ed] . . . in the colonial/Cold War past rather than the modernizing present."[9] Yet, in line with Funnell and Dodds, I claim that while these details combine progress and stagnation—the world has been transforming but Bond remains the same—there is more to it than that. Bond is easily recognizable via the elements that make him a Cold War hero, which helps the audience identify him as a good guy, sustaining a vision of the world that is determined by its own rules. Yet the film also sees such a perpetuation of Cold War ideas and ideals as problematic. For example, Bond's anti-feminist attitudes are considered and foregrounded in the film itself, via M's famous line. According to James Chapman, "the film diffuses the obvious criticisms that could be made of the Bond character (that his attitude towards women is out of date in the 1990s) by voicing them itself through the agency of a female authority-figure."[10] In other words, the film wants to move away from the Cold War, yet fails to do so straightforwardly.

GoldenEye recognizes the limitations of the Cold War James Bond and fore-grounds how much the world has changed. The idea of change is communi-cated via various means. One is the appearance of a new M, played by Judi Dench. This change has been vigorously discussed by scholars and reviewers and ranges from postfeminist perspectives on the role and the place of women in the West to the questioning of such optimistic conclusions and false beliefs that gender equality has been achieved, as one might perceive through women in power like M.[11] Next, Valentin Zukovsky (Robbie Coltrane), a KGB agent dur-ing the Cold War, is now the head of a mafia group, which reflects the trans-formation that has been taking place in Soviet Russia, especially in the 1990s. Leningrad has reassumed the name St. Petersburg. The change of location from the USSR to Cuba that is depicted in some scenes in the film is also symbolic: the temperature shift, from a cold to hot climate, can be interpreted as a way to reflect the end of the Cold War and a symbolic warming of the relationship between the countries that used to be involved in the ideological war. Judith Roof also recognizes *GoldenEye* as the first film in the series that "separate[s]" the agent from the machine/technology, "anticipat[ing] in broad terms the ensu-ing systemic battles between humans and calculating machines that continue in future Bond films—as well as nostalgia for the former battles it rehearses yet again."[12] Even the music choices starkly differ from the ones made in the previous Bond films, turning *GoldenEye*, in the words of composer Eric Serra, into a "modern," perhaps even "too modern" film for its time.[13]

Moreover, Bond participates in (the formation of) the new geopolitical order, which suggests that he himself is ready to change. Funnell and Dodds single out different kinds of technology and vehicles that Bond uses in *GoldenEye*, including "secret communication machines, tanks, planes," which "convey geo-political meaning."[14] The key object, however, that not only re-creates the new geopolitical order but emphasizes both stagnation and the progress of James Bond himself is the tank. The key scene takes place as he is trying to rescue Natalya Simonova, who has been captured by General Ourumov. Bond finds the largest and most stable vehicle he can—a military tank—and maneuvers it through the streets of St. Petersburg (figure 17.2). Expectedly, Bond destroys everything on his way, from cars to buildings, which emphasizes the agent's power over his enemy, who appears rather small, sitting in a back seat of his car, nervously drinking from a flask and looking back and forth, hoping to be fast enough to escape Bond's lethal means of transportation. Funnell and Dodds single out an important moment in the scene:

> At one point, he [Bond] crashes through a monument at the center of town and the statue remains on the top of the tank as Bond drives on. The artifact is an ironic extrapolation of the Bronze Horseman statue of Peter the Great that is located in St. Petersburg. The addition of wings to the horse (to create a

Pegasus) transforms the statue into the emblem adopted by British Airborne Forces during World War II. Thus, the sight of this British symbol moving through the streets of St. Petersburg sends a message about Britain's access to a newly independent Russia after the Cold War.[15]

This observation emphasizes the powerful role of Britain in the new geopolitical order. Yet the scene as such conveys a much more important message. The tank is symbolic in the context of the Cold War and the collapse of the Soviet Union in particular. August 19, 1991, is an important date in the history of the U.S.S.R. On that day, a group of communist hardliners, many of whom were members of the State Committee on the State of Emergency (SCSE/GKChP) organized a coup against the first and only Soviet president, Mikhail Gorbachev. The coup lasted for two days and led to the collapse of the Soviet Union several months later, on December 26, 1991. On those two days in August, Moscow was filled with tanks. On August 19, Boris Yeltsin, the leader of the civil resistance, who would soon become the first post-Soviet Russian president, delivered his famous speech atop a tank, claiming that the violent taking of government power was illegal and issuing several decrees that recognized the actions of the SCSE/GKChP as a state crime.[16] There are many individuals, events, decisions, and things that Russians and other former Soviet nations associate with the end of the Cold War and the collapse of the Soviet Union, and tanks on Moscow streets in August 1991 are one of them. The choice to place James Bond on a tank and let him chase an evil Soviet military man in such a way is thus symbolic. James Bond mirrors Boris Yeltsin—as the politician was perceived in August 1991—projecting *change*: Russia has changed, having transformed from a Soviet state into a free one.

Figure 17.2 Depicted on a tank, James Bond (Pierce Brosnan) mirrors Boris Yeltsin, liberating the country from the ghosts of the Cold War and thus communicating change. *GoldenEye* (1995).

The location is symbolic, too: while the action does not take place in Moscow, St. Petersburg was an official capital of the Russian Empire from 1712 to 1918 and has always been viewed by Russians as a second capital. Thus, while the film preserves the national significance of the coup, re-creating the events in St. Petersburg helps move away from a more coded city, Moscow, whose buildings, streets, and monuments immediately prompt the viewer to think about the Cold War, something especially true in the 1990s, when the film was released. The new James Bond thus takes on the role of a liberator, akin to Boris Yeltsin, demonstrating that he is ready to get rid of the ghosts of the Cold War both by clearing the country of corrupt communist leaders and by transforming himself from a Cold War hero into a new action figure of the 1990s.

The tank scene effectively demonstrates how nostalgia works: borrowing elements from the past to outline the reality of the present. According to Silva and Wiebel,

> In one sense, nostalgia simplifies the past in order to make it instantly recognizable and desirable. In film especially, the symbols of the past must be familiar and must connect firmly to the particular emotions or understandings that are part of the dominant reading of the narrative. Feature films do not have much time to explore conflicted signifiers or nuanced expressions of political uncertainty.[17]

This is exactly what *GoldenEye* does using specific elements (a tank) or filming in certain locations (St. Petersburg) and thus deliberately connecting itself to the past in order to reenvision the present. The film employs those coded references to the Cold War to re-create the tension of the historical moment in which James Bond finds himself, being part of a film that is set in the time of the Cold War yet released shortly after the ideological conflict. Nevertheless, as Silva and Wiebel assert,

> nostalgia is not necessarily about a literal desire to return to the past—even a commercially romanticized one. . . . [P]art of what nostalgia gives us is the safety to dream about times that we cannot return to. Unlike depictions of other times and conflicts, Cold War narratives allow us to explore tensions and global conflicts with the comfort of knowing that American ideals will come out safely on the other side. Like a particularly good roller coaster, we can experience the anxiety and fear of being at risk without ever entering into any real moral or narrative danger.[18]

The tank in *GoldenEye* helps to link the immediate post–Cold War then-present to such events as the collapse of the Communist Party of the Soviet Union and of the country itself. To both British and Russian audiences, but also to the global viewer, the tank is a reminder about the turbulent times in the history of the Soviet Union and the Cold War that preceded the August Coup. But it also works to do exactly what Silva and Wiebel describe: remind the viewer that all these events are in the past and thus inevitably promise a better, safer future: "Rather than a literal return then, nostalgia gives us a sense of the past as a way of feeling better about the present. Nostalgic audiences do not necessarily think that such filmic representations are true, but truth is not the goal. The goal is recognizability and a recapturing of that which was admirable—particularly in times when such feelings or qualities seem lacking."[19] Standing for the collapse of the Soviet Union, the tank denotes progress: no longer will James Bond have to fight against Soviet communists; no longer will the fears of the Cold War haunt nations worldwide. But this also means that James Bond will no longer be a Cold War hero.

Toward a New Hero

Tony Bennett and Janet Woollacott describe James Bond as a "popular hero."[20] The seriality of the Bond narrative has also made him a hero across a large portion of the twentieth century, into the twenty-first. That the character inevitably changes, or has to change, depending on the geopolitical, cultural, and social events that take place in the global arena, is communicated in *GoldenEye*. The film does not present a new hero, but it overtly articulates that such a change must occur because James Bond himself largely depends on world politics. His character makes sense only within a specific historical context and concrete political choices. An easy transformation is almost impossible and *GoldenEye* demonstrates this through imagery that oscillates between Cold War stagnated reality and post–Cold War progress. Just as the world was confused after the end of the Cold War and the collapse of the Soviet Union, trying to grasp the meaning of the new world order, so is the first post–Cold War James Bond, who appears as an equivocal character, stuck somewhere in between. The Cold War has inevitably had an impact on cultural production, including cinema. According to Bryn Upton, "The Cold War influenced how films were made, which films were made, and how audiences understood the films they watched."[21] Films produced in that era, in the words of Cyril Buffet, "not only reflected the Cold War; they also projected it."[22] After the end of the Cold War, despite the remaining, large interest in the ideological conflict, cinematic images of the period have no longer performed the exact same function as they did at the time. Such images continue to communicate different political tensions and social and cultural values and to work to foreground the Otherness of some characters and even nations, but they are created in and affected by a different political reality. Funnell and Dodds argue that the collapse of the Soviet Union "effectively ended the formal cartographies of the Cold War (which was a consistent focus of the Bond franchise) and ushered in a new era of geopolitical exchange between Russia and Western nations."[23] *GoldenEye* reveals a transformation, or the need for one, that affects both the environments in which the action stories take place and the hero himself, who, while remaining nostalgic about the past, enters a new era of James Bond cinema.

Notes

1. See Tatiana Prorokova-Konrad, ed., *Cold War II: Hollywood's Renewed Obsession with Russia* (Jackson: University Press of Mississippi, 2020).
2. Bernard F. Dick, *The Screen Is Red: Hollywood, Communism, and the Cold War* (Jackson: University Press of Mississippi, 2016), 44–57, 58–76, 104–34, 192–209.
3. Vesta Silva and Jon Wiebel, "The Warm Glow of Cold War Nostalgia," in Prorokova-Konrad, *Cold War II*, 30, 35.
4. Silva and Wiebel, "Warm Glow," 36.
5. Ian Scott, "The Coldest City: Berlin and the Remapping of Cold War Movie Aesthetics," in Prorokova-Konrad, *Cold War II*, 96, 97.
6. Lisa Funnell and Klaus Dodds, *Geographies, Genders, and Geopolitics of James Bond* (London: Palgrave Macmillan, 2017), 86–87.
7. Monica Germanà, *Bond Girls: Body, Fashion and Gender* (London: Bloomsbury, 2019), 107–8.
8. Brink Lindsey qtd. in Funnell and Dodds, *Geographies, Genders*, 89.
9. Funnell and Dodds, *Geographies, Genders*, 41–42.
10. James Chapman, *Licence to Thrill: A Cultural History of the James Bond Films* (London: I. B. Tauris, 1999), 257.
11. Peter C. Kunze, "From Masculine Mastermind to Maternal Martyr: Judi Dench's M, *Skyfall*, and the Patriarchal Logic of James Bond Films," in *For His Eyes Only: The Women of James Bond*, ed. Lisa Funnell (New York: Wallflower, 2015), 237.
12. Judith Roof, "Physiques/Physics over Figures: Some Thoughts on James Bond's Nostalgia," *International Journal of James Bond Studies* 3, no. 1 (2020): 5.
13. Eric Serra qtd. in Jon Burlingame, *The Music of James Bond* (Oxford: Oxford University Press, 2012), 206.
14. Funnell and Dodds, *Geographies, Genders*, 78.
15. Funnell and Dodds, *Geographies, Genders*, 168.
16. Boris Yeltsin was elected as the first president of the Russian republic in the USSR on June 12, 1991. On the evening of December 25, 1991, with the collapse of the USSR, he became the first president of Russia.
17. Silva and Wiebel, "Warm Glow," 36.
18. Silva and Wiebel, "Warm Glow," 36.
19. Silva and Wiebel, "Warm Glow," 36.
20. Tony Bennett and Janet Woollacott, *Bond and Beyond: The Political Career of a Popular Hero* (London: Macmillan Education, 1987), 13.
21. Bryn Upton, *Hollywood and the End of the Cold War: Signs of Cinematic Change* (Lanham, MD: Rowman & Littlefield, 2014), 1.
22. Cyril Buffet, "Preface: Visual Reflection of the Cold War," in *Cinema in the Cold War: Political Projections*, ed. Cyril Buffet (London: Routledge, 2016), xi.
23. Funnell and Dodds, *Geographies, Genders*, 86.

CHAPTER 18

BOND BY THE NUMBERS

Tomorrow Never Dies (1997)

LLEWELLA CHAPMAN

Following on from the commercial success of *GoldenEye* (1995), *Tomorrow Never Dies* (1997) not only cemented Pierce Brosnan in the role of James Bond, but also was the first film of the Eon Productions franchise not to be overseen by Albert R. "Cubby" Broccoli, who died before the start of production. Thus, "Bond 18" was important, not only to prove that coproducers Barbara Broccoli and Michael G. Wilson were able to carry the mantle of the Bond films, but also to present the character as still relevant, topical, and of interest to audiences and critics alike for a franchise that, at the time of the release of *Tomorrow Never Dies*, had spanned eighteen films produced over thirty-five years.

By this time, writers for the Bond films were attempting to produce original material and characters while drawing upon successful tropes and "Bondian" formulas included in the previous films, owing to Ian Fleming's novels having been thoroughly mined for material, minus *Casino Royale* (1953). Janet Woollacott explains that "Bondian" was the term used by Albert Broccoli and Harry Saltzman to mean "in the spirit of James Bond."[1] Lewis Gilbert defines the formula as including: "An unknown leading lady. All the people who are well known like M and Miss Moneypenny. The character of Bond, you couldn't change . . . but you can change his attitude to a certain extent." Woollacott outlines the other parts of the formula, namely what she terms "Bondian effects," such as "the importance of the sets, the gadgets, the foreign locations, the threatening character of the villains (which must incorporate both a physical threat and an intellectual threat to the hero), Bond's relationship with the girl in the story, the jokes and the form of the crucial pre-credits sequence." As British critic Philip French observed, by the time of *Tomorrow Never Dies* "The form of an 007 picture is as rigid as the haiku that Bond learned to write in *You Only Live Twice.*" Todd McCarthy, writing for the American trade paper *Variety*, concurred, believing the released film to be formulaic and "a solid but somewhat by-the-numbers entry" to the franchise.[2]

Therefore, my chapter will analyze Bruce Feirstein's first draft for "Bond 18," dated August 23, 1996, in relation to the Bond formula and previous films of the franchise that the writer drew upon, as well as the social, political, and cultural contexts that occurred during the script's development. As argued by Sue Harper, released films "are simply the traces left by the struggles for dominance during the production process—by the contest for creative control."[3] *Tomorrow Never Dies* demonstrates this, especially in relation to the early "Bond 18" project to the final film.

As Matthew Field and Ajay Chowdhury outline, the "Bond 18" project was greenlit in May 1995 following positive reaction from American audiences to the teaser trailer for *GoldenEye*, prompting the senior vice president of United Artists, Jeff Kleeman, to "seek stories and writers . . . it was worth spending $200,000 to get a script moving."[4] United Artists requested that mystery novelist Donald E. Westlake produce a treatment for the film, which he delivered in August 1995, followed by a second, shorter treatment in October. Kleeman recalled that Westlake's ideas included a pre-title sequence set in Transylvania and the "flooding" of Hong Kong. Separately, Feirstein, who had cowritten the script for *GoldenEye* with Jeffrey Caine, was tasked with developing his version of "Bond 18," having pitched it to Broccoli in March 1996 before the producer died, and following conversations with Wilson. Feirstein envisaged the villain as a "media mogul," inspired by his work as a journalist and his understanding of how the same news story can be reported from different points of view: "I had worked for all the prototypes of this character. I had written for magazines owned by Rupert Murdoch, I had been on CNN."[5] Feirstein was insistent that he was not inspired by Westlake's treatments, but rather that both writers had separately considered setting the film in Hong Kong: the island was hugely newsworthy at the time due to the impending transfer of the colony from British to Chinese rule in accordance with the 1984 Sino-British Joint Declaration. As recognized by Lisa Funnell and Klaus Dodds, during Brosnan's tenure as Bond "the contrasting depiction of East and South East/Southeast Asian cities conveys important messages about shifting geopolitical relations in the 1990s and early 2000s."[6] Feirstein's first draft also includes references to Fleming's work, particularly *Moonraker* (1955), as well as the Bond films *Goldfinger* (1964), *Thunderball* (1965), *On Her Majesty's Secret Service* (1969), and *For Your Eyes Only* (1981), some of which were carried across to the film.

Feirstein's draft script begins with Bond having been sent on a mission to the Khyber Pass to report back to MI6 and the Royal Navy on a secret military airbase, perhaps in reference to Timothy Dalton's Bond visiting Afghanistan during *The Living Daylights* (1987). Bond discovers the presence of terrorists Gustav Meinholtz ("Neo-Nazi, former East German STASI agent"), Vilko Barkoviac ("Bosnian war criminal"), Sitoshi Isagura ("Japanese religious fanatic") and Kim Dae Yung ("North Korean nuclear specialist") handling a range of weapons procured from the United States, Chile, China, France, and Russia. Following the credits, Bond next appears in Professor Jenny Wu's accommodation at the University of Oxford, "brushing up on a little Chinese," before being interrupted by Moneypenny, who requests that Bond attend MI6 at 4 p.m., telling him, "Don't be late," in a humorous allusion to Sean Connery's Bond and Sylvia Trench (Eunice Gayson) reuniting over a riverside picnic in *From Russia with Love* (1963).[7]

On arrival at MI6, Bond is debriefed by Colonel Dominique Everhart, employed by the North Atlantic Treaty Organization (NATO), on his Khyber Pass mission, where it is revealed that the terrorists were attempting to smuggle enriched uranium to produce nuclear devices. In reference to Hong Kong and the geopolitical and colonial inspiration behind Feirstein's script, the character of Rendera Sikrahm (Anglo translation: Richard Stamper) is recognized as having been present during the events at the Khyber Pass base, and is described by Everhart:

> His father was from Nepal—a Gurkha warrior—conscripted by the British government to fight in China during World War II—after which the family settled in Hong Kong, where the young Stamper was undoubtedly treated like a second class citizen by both the Hong Kong Chinese and the local British. (beat, aside:) We've all read about the signs at the British swimming pools in Hong Kong that said [*sic*] "No Ghurka's allowed."[8]

To this, Bond dryly responds: "Nothing like a little imperialism to promote loyalty among the faithful." Stamper's background is similar to Alec Trevelyan's (Sean Bean) in *GoldenEye*. Following the debrief, Everhart questions whether Bond is married, to which he answers in the negative, with the script directing: "For an instant, something crosses Bond's face: Bittersweetness? Remorse?" in reference to his being a widower from *On Her Majesty's Secret Service*.[9]

There are other notable references and "Bondian" formula elements in Feirstein's work. It is on entering M's office, for example, that Bond is asked what the secret agent knows of Sir Elliot Harmsway, in a slight reference to Fleming's *Moonraker* when M asks what Bond knows of Sir Hugo Drax. Bond outlines his knowledge of Harmsway: "British media mogul. Born in Hong Kong; controls newspapers, TV, radio, cable, satellites; books, magazines, movies, computer software. Theme parks . . .'Able to topple governments with a single story'—as he says in his press," referring to Harmsway owning the newspaper *Tomorrow*.[10] Harmsway's surname invites direct comparison between the character and Alfred Harmsworth, 1st Viscount Northcliffe, a British newspaper and publishing magnate. Owner of the *Daily Mail* and the *Daily Mirror*, Lord Northcliffe held vast influence over popular opinion in the Edwardian era.

M reveals that MI6 believes Harmsway to be involved with Stamper and Yung, information that has been withheld from NATO, and that MI6 investigated him in 1988, owing to his "being furious at the British plan to return Hong Kong, and supposedly started his own negotiations with the Chinese government."[11] M sends Bond on a mission to Venice to determine Harmsway's involvement with the uranium smuggling operation and "stop him," informing Bond that he is to wear a Venetian carnival mask and wait to be contacted by MI6's informant. According to Feirstein, the inclusion of Venice was at Wilson's suggestion.[12]

In the draft script, the informant is Paris, a woman with whom Bond has had a previous relationship:

PARIS

Don't you even miss me? Didn't I mean *anything* to you?

BOND

Nothing.[13]

Although Bond remains cold and suspicious toward Paris, going so far as to slap her across the face after she becomes hysterical and begs Bond to protect her from Harmsway, she nevertheless informs him that the uranium is being held on Harmsway's yacht, the *Sea Dolphin II*, and that the tycoon intends to host a press conference there the following morning. The yacht is included for two reasons: first, it is a Bond villain trope, used in both *From Russia with Love* and *Thunderball*, and second, Robert Maxwell, the disgraced British media proprietor, had drowned in the Atlantic Ocean in 1991 after falling from his yacht, the *Lady Ghislaine*.

Bond arranges with an Italian intelligence official, Franco DiGiacomo, to investigate Harmsway's yacht if Bond determines the presence of uranium. On Bond's boarding the *Sea Dolphin II*, Feirstein describes Harmsway as "a man with an EVIL EUPHORIA—showing off all the charm and charisma that's made him one of the world's most powerful media tycoons," before Bond discovers the uranium in a red box and notifies DiGiacomo.[14] Following the conference, Harmsway introduces Bond to his wife, revealed to be Paris. After DiGiacomo arrives to arrest Harmsway, Bond sends her to his hotel room for safety. The uranium in the box is found to have been switched with the depleted variety, and thus Harmsway gains the upper hand over Bond, warning him: "A piece of advice, Mr. Bond: Don't screw with the man who buys ink by the ton. (beat). It's deadlier than uranium . . . Aren't you late for a meeting?"[15] Bond realizes that Harmsway is alluding to Paris. On arriving at his hotel room and looking through the balcony window, he discovers Paris's body floating in the Grand Canal.

In reference to Ernst Stavro Blofeld and the SPECTRE organization, as well as contemporary geopolitical figures, Harmsway proceeds to hold a conference with his subordinates in "a room that looks as if it could only exist in, well, a James Bond movie: Slick, stark, sterile. Steel, glass, chrome," based at his Scottish manor house.[16] The employee called "Number One" reports on the "entertainment division." Number Two, "looking remarkably like Bill Gates," reports on the "software division" and the development of a new operating system, "Gates '99," which is "deliberately filled with bugs," as an ironic acknowledgment to Y2K.[17] Number Five reports on the U.S. presidential election and explains that "the Democrat" is ahead by nine points, to which Harmsway suggests: "Maybe it's time to publish that story about his sex life. Even things up. A close race is always better for our TV ratings," in an implicit reference to Bill Clinton. Number Three reports that Saddam Hussain is "demanding a bonus" for his role in the Gulf War, which makes Harmsway suspicious enough to arrange for Number Three's removal from the meeting. Harmsway then moves on to reveal to the other members present: "In exactly thirty-six hours, we are going to initiate phase one of the world's most perfect crime: The biggest theft in the history of mankind . . . In the Strait of Malacca," echoing the plot of *Goldfinger*. Harmsway arranges for Number Three to be killed by Arab spies by revealing him to be an Israeli agent via a report printed in *Tomorrow*. This is consistent with the demise of other SPECTRE agents in previous Bond films: for example, Kronsteen (Vladek Sheybal) in *From Russia with Love*, Helga Brandt (Karin Dor) in *You Only Live Twice* (1967), and Karl Stromberg's unnamed assistant (Marilyn Galsworthy) in *The Spy Who Loved Me* (1977).

Echoing the sinking of the British information-gathering vessel *St Georges* at the beginning of *For Your Eyes Only*, the script also has Harmsway arrange to sink HMS *Indomitable* in the Strait of Malacca so as to mine it for the gold reserves it is transporting from Hong Kong to Britain prior to the handover of the territory to China. After the frigate has been wrongly reported as missing south of Kuala Lumpur, owing to Harmsway having manipulated the vessel's GPS system, Bond is sent as an "observer" on a Royal Navy mission to recover the gold. Bond privately reveals to M that he believes the frigate to have been sabotaged, with M agreeing and ordering Bond: "I want you to find that gold, and secure it."[18] Bond makes mention of Harmsway's headquarters having recently moved to Kuala Lumpur. M is unimpressed and, in a similar allusion to *On Her Majesty's Secret Service*, tells Bond:

Contrary to what you may believe, 007, the world *is not* filled with mad-men who can hollow out volcanoes, stock them with big-breasted women, and threaten the world with nuclear annihilation . . . The case is closed. The Italian authorities ruled the girl a suicide. We had enough trouble keeping your name out of the media. For everyone's sake—(beat) Your job is to find the gold. Not settle some personal score with Elliot Harmsway.[19]

A direct connection is also made to *GoldenEye*. When Bond arrives in Malacca, he teams up with Jack Wade, a CIA operative who had previously assisted Bond to investigate the Janus Syndicate.[20] It is while the pair are exploring the strait that they first meet an unnamed woman captaining a "sleek launch." She is later revealed to be Sidney Winch, "about 32, tough, smart, and (here's a surprise,) beautiful," owner of a marine salvage company. Winch later refers to Harmsway as her "uncle," owing to his friendship with her father, when Bond meets her again in the Kuala Lumpur Yacht Club, inclusive of the obligatory casino scene.[21] It transpires that Winch is also trying to obtain the gold from the frigate wreckage for mercenary gain, and there is a reference to an enemy agent in *Dr. No* (1962) in that her bodyguard is named "Taro." That evening, Bond discovers HMS *Indomitable* and a damaged gold bar that has been left alongside a "broken uranium grinding tooth."[22] Sidney captures Bond and Wade, having tracked their fishing boat, and takes both items. On his return to Kuala Lumpur, Bond is contacted by Harmsway via his car telephone, requesting that they meet at his offices at Harmsway Towers. Not realizing that Harmsway was behind the frigate sinking, Sidney inadvertently reveals the gold bar and uranium tooth, after which Harmsway attempts to kill both her and Bond:

SIDNEY

Uncle Elliot: How could you do this to me?

HARMSWAY

Oh, please, Sidney. There's a hundred billion dollars at stake.
  (*beat*)
Besides, I never really liked your father that much. He cheated at cards.

Harmsway's last line ironically alludes to M's suspicions of Drax cheating at bridge in Fleming's *Moonraker*. When Bond questions whether Harmsway's guards are going to kill "a helpless girl," Harmsway offers a reply inspired by colonialism: "My guards are from South Africa, Mr. Bond. This is their chance to get even with the formerly 'Great' Britain."[23]

The remaining portion of the script that follows replicates the plot of *Goldfinger*, which the Bond producers deemed to be a blueprint for the successful "Bondian" formula. Bond and Sidney attempt to escape Harmsway Towers in

Bond's modified (unnamed, four-wheel drive) car but crash into the closed garage door in the car park, leaving the pair unconscious. Harmsway takes Bond and Sidney hostage, and on breaking into the Aberdeen Harbour Nuclear Power Plant in Hong Kong, explains his motivation behind wanting to destroy the territory in a nuclear meltdown: "A hundred and fifty years ago, my ancestors took this island—a barren, lifeless rock—and turned it into the greatest city known to civilization . . . And now that I'm being forced to give it back, I intend to return it in exactly the same condition: A barren, lifeless rock."[24] As is typical of previous megalomaniacs in the Bond films, Harmsway goes on to outline his plan and how it connects to the gold reserves he stole: "To save the economy, I'll let the new British government—*my* British government—announce that the gold was irradiated in Hong Kong—where no one will be able to touch it for a hundred years."[25]

Taking Sidney with him, Harmsway traps Bond in an airlock before leaving on the *Sea Dolphin II*, stationed outside the harbor. Bond uses his plastic-explosive shoelaces to escape the airlock and battles with Yung before escaping the nuclear plant by helicopter. Once aboard, Bond fights Stamper before holding Harmsway underwater as the yacht sinks. Bond is reunited with Sidney, who has escaped using scuba-diving equipment, and together they float away from the wreckage in a dinghy, with the script ending:

493. RETURN ON THE DINGHY
Bond and Sidney break off a kiss. She lies nestled in his arms.

SIDNEY

James . . . Is this *really* what a typical day is like for you?

Bond replies with a wry smile:

BOND

Yes . . .
(*pause*)
But some days . . . Are longer than others.

And with this, he reaches up over his head, and pulls a tarp over the two of them . . .
And the camera pulls back, and up, rising into the air to reveal:
The entire British Navy closing in on them from all points of the compass.[26]

This ending is similar to those of *Dr. No, You Only Live Twice,* and *The Spy Who Loved Me,* all of which include the presence of the Royal Navy.[27] Feirstein includes a further reference to Maxwell, with M dictating Harmsway's obituary to Moneypenny: "At present, local authorities believe the media mogul committed suicide."[28]

Following the delivery of Feirstein's draft script, Eon Productions hired Roger Spottiswoode as the film's director in September 1996. United Artists sent the script to the consulting firm Kissinger Associates, as they did not want a situation "like we had on *GoldenEye* where we [were] a few days into shooting in Russia and the Militsiya comes out and we have to go back to London," Kleeman explained. Kissinger Associates advised against using Hong Kong as the geopolitical backdrop of the film, as Spottiswoode recalled: "Nobody really knew whether it would be a peaceful handover. To come up with a fantasised version of an event that was only a few months old, did not seem a very wise choice."[29] This led to Spottiswoode employing a team of writers to work on redrafting the script, including Robert Collector, David Campbell Wilson, Leslie Dixon, Nicholas Meyer, Tom Ropelewski, and Kurt Wimmer. Various ideas were suggested regarding possible stunts, including a motorbike chase in both a Vietnamese shantytown and along the Great Wall of China, and Meyer offered an alternative motive for the media mogul villain, namely a war between China and India as a form of population control.[30] Daniel Petrie Jr. was also employed, and suggested the character of a German assassin, "Dr. Kaufman," who came to be included in the final film.

The accumulation of these ideas led to Petrie Jr. producing a script dated March 13, 1997, two days after it had been announced by the British press that Jonathan Pryce had been cast as Bond's unnamed nemesis (figure 18.1). Alison Boshoff reported: "Instead of stroking cats or carrying out contract killings, [the villain's] prime concern is increasing stock values and his weapons are news broadcasts and front pages."[31] Boshoff queried whether Murdoch was the inspiration. A spokesman for the production company denied this, explaining:

Figure 18.1 Jonathan Pryce as media mogul Elliot Carver. *Tomorrow Never Dies* (1997).

"We don't have anyone particular in mind . . . Any resemblance to real characters is entirely coincidental," ignoring the clear influence of Harmsworth and
Maxwell in Feirstein's characterization, perhaps owing to the ongoing script
revisions and to protect themselves legally.[32] Boshoff described the film's plot
as per Feirstein's first draft, including the pre-title sequence of the Khyber Pass,
a "show down" in Hong Kong and "an attempt to blow up a nuclear reactor."

Although Petrie wrote on the title page of the script, "Please note that this
is the final shooting script," Brosnan was unimpressed with it, with the star
reportedly declaring: "It's s***," later clarifying: "It was not articulate and cohe-
sive enough. We should have had that script up and ready the moment the
cash register started ringing after *GoldenEye* two years ago. I let my feelings be
known."[33] This led to Barbara Broccoli and Wilson turning back to Feirstein,
who reflected: "I knew having started this journey that I wanted to finish it. I
also knew that when a studio calls you and says we would like you to come back,
then it's an emergency."[34] The writer submitted a "second draft" script that
included moving the plot and action sequences from Hong Kong to Ho Chi
Minh City, Vietnam, and changing the "Bond girl" from Sidney to a "Chinese
female agent," originally named Yin Pow but later changed to Colonel Wai Lin
at the request of Michelle Yeoh following her casting in the role (figure 18.2).[35]

Feirstein explained that this version, which would be the basis of the shooting script, "pretty much outlines a lot—but not everything—that you see in the
final film," with the writer given "thirty days to fix" the script, owing to principal photography having already begun on April 1, 1997. Although the villain
remained a media mogul, Harmsway's surname was changed to Carver. The
motivation was adapted from Harmsway wanting revenge over the return of
Hong Kong to Carver wanting to provoke war between Britain and China in
order to obtain exclusive broadcasting rights in China. Instead of sinking a

Figure 18.2 Michelle Yeoh as Colonel Wai Lin. *Tomorrow Never Dies* (1997).

frigate to steal gold, Carver sinks the HMS *Devonshire* to steal a missile that he intends to launch at Beijing in order to destroy the Chinese government and replace it with one of his own, with the corrupt General Chang at its head. Carver's heritage was changed from British to Hong Kong–German. Rather than Bond drowning the villain, Carver is killed by a Sea-Vac drill that Bond ignites, although M dictates the same obituary of suicide by drowning. The characters of Carver's wife Paris and his henchman Stamper remained, albeit Stamper's ancestry was changed from Nepalese to German, with Kaufman included as his mentor.

Issues with the script continued during filming, with *The Guardian* reporting: "Battles are waging as disagreements between director, Roger Spottiswoode, and scriptwriter, Bruce Feirstein, threaten to destroy the film" and that Pryce and Judi Dench, returning in her role as M, were particularly annoyed over the continuous and ongoing script rewrites. *The Guardian* elucidated: "The poor luvs are having to learn their new lines the night before filming . . . there's not a lot of bonding behind the scenes. If the acrimony and the expense don't kill the script, the timing will. Feirstein's busy re-writing it on a daily basis."[36] Pryce was later quoted as having said: "I have never encountered anything that has changed so radically . . . I will make sure in the future that it is written in the contract that the script I agree to will be the script we use."[37] Dench allegedly complained to Spottiswoode: "You know, it was very off-putting indeed to have learnt the script, and at a quarter-to-ten the night before to get a loud knocking on the door by the courier with a new script. That's not fair."[38] The final shooting script is dated August 18, 1997, but included revisions made between April 1 and September 2. Around eight white pages remained from Petrie's script, with Feirstein's revision pages colored pink, blue, yellow, gold, buff, salmon, lilac, grey, ivory, and orange.[39] Cast and crew members purportedly referred to it as the "rainbow script."[40] Following the release of *Tomorrow Never Dies*, Brosnan reflected that "it was a difficult movie for all concerned," and that, although there "were problems with the script to start with . . . we overcame that as we went along."[41] In an interview with Neil Norman, the director was asked whether he would consider directing another Bond film, at which a "brief, embittered," off-the-record "burst of venom" followed: "It is enough to put off any filmmaker directing any Bond film ever again. There is, after all, only so much fun a man can take."[42]

The British critics were somewhat divided over the film, in part owing to the issues over the changing script and its numerous rewrites. Geoff Brown believed *Tomorrow Never Dies* to be "fun at first . . . but boredom sets in," questioning whether it was because the film "became swamped by the script's lame and juvenile jokes" and referring to Feirstein as the author of *Real Men Don't Eat Quiche* (1982).[43] Alexander Walker was somewhat damning in his assessment, stating that "the new Bond is a shambles. Made in admitted haste and chaos, the eighteenth in the series looks that way too . . . when the script hands [Spottiswoode] a joke or two, they're stale ones," although he praised Carver as "a combination of Rupert Murdoch's overreaching ambition and Robert Maxwell's underhand deviousness."[44] Ryan Gilbey was similarly unimpressed, opining that the film "is one of the most clumsy and uninvolving episodes in the Bond series" and the script "feels as if it was conceived to counter accusations that the Bond series doesn't engage with the real world . . . When the real world starts muscling in on entertainment, it's the latter that comes off looking battered and bruised."[45]

However, Quentin Curtis believed: "Bond plots have become so dull at late . . . That *Tomorrow Never Dies*'s premise comes over as startlingly fresh, even pertinent . . . Feirstein's script works the familiar Bond genre elements—the flip humour and the teasing sexuality, not to say sexism—for all they are worth." He felt, similarly to Brown, that the plot "fizzle[s] out so miserably. After its promising and amusing start, the movie is little more than a series of sequences" and that the scripting process is "visible upon the screen," although Spottiswoode "does well to paper over the cracks."[46] James Cameron-Wilson praised Feirstein for managing "to whip up a topical, ingenious and bitingly satirical confection pumped with some real wit."[47] Perhaps the most balanced review was provided by José Arroyo, who referred to the film as "responsibly formulaic . . . like a photocopy collage of previous Bonds," and stated: "The film is better than the general run of action/spectacle movies . . . But it is far from premium Bond."[48] Nonetheless, *Tomorrow Never Dies* would "pull in the crowds," as Brown acknowledged, despite the issues over the script and its rewrites. It grossed $125.3 million in the United States and $210 million in the international market.[49] As Carver mused in Fleming-esque fashion in the film: "The distance between insanity and genius is measured only by success."

Notes

1. Janet Woollacott, "The James Bond Films: Conditions of Production," in *British Cinema History*, ed. James Curran and Vincent Porter (London: Weidenfeld and Nicolson, 1983), 210.
2. Woollacott, "James Bond Films," 211; Philip French, "Oh, Put It Away, James," *Observer*, December 14, 1997, 12; Todd McCarthy, "*Tomorrow Never Dies*," *Variety*, December 14, 1997.
3. Sue Harper, *Women in British Cinema: Mad, Bad, and Dangerous to Know* (London: Continuum, 2000), 3.
4. Matthew Field and Ajay Chowdhury, *Some Kind of Hero: The Remarkable Story of the James Bond Films.* (Stroud, UK: History Press, 2015), 468.
5. Field and Chowdhury, *Some Kind of Hero*, 469.
6. Lisa Funnell and Klaus Dodds, *Geographies, Genders, and Geopolitics of James Bond* (London: Palgrave Macmillan, 2017), 120.

7. Bruce Feirstein, *Bond 18*, first draft screenplay, August 23 1996, 14.

8. Feirstein, *Bond 18*, 17.

9. Feirstein, *Bond 18*, 18. This was omitted from the later scripts, meaning that the only Bond films to date that make reference to the character's being a widower are *The Spy Who Loved Me*, *For Your Eyes Only*, and *Licence to Kill*.

10. Feirstein, *Bond 18*, 21.

11. Feirstein, *Bond 18*, 22.

12. Field and Chowdhury, *Some Kind of Hero*, 469.

13. Feirstein, *Bond 18*, 29. Emphasis in original.

14. Feirstein, *Bond 18*, 38. Emphasis in original.

15. Feirstein, *Bond 18*, 46–47.

16. Feirstein, *Bond 18*, 51.

17. As New Year's Day of 2000 approached, rumors abounded that the simultaneous date shifts on the world's computers would result in anything from inability to access files on home PCs to meltdowns at nuclear reactors.

18. Feirstein, *Bond 18*, 73.

19. Feirstein, *Bond 18*, 74.

20. Feirstein also included a cameo role for *GoldenEye*'s Valentin Zukovsky during Harmsway's press conference, and Bond explains to Wade that Natalya Simonova "married a hockey player," in reference to Isabella Scorupco's marriage to Mariusz Czerkawski, a Polish hockey player.

21. Feirstein, *Bond 18*, 85.

22. Feirstein, *Bond 18*, 93.

23. Feirstein, *Bond 18*, 129.

24. Feirstein, *Bond 18*, 138.

25. Feirstein, *Bond 18*, 139. Emphasis in original.

26. Feirstein, *Bond 18*, 157. Emphasis in original.

27. It is also in *You Only Live Twice* and *The Spy Who Loved Me* that Bond wears Royal Navy uniform, in reference to his being a Commander of the Royal Navy.

28. Feirstein, *Bond 18*, 157.

29. Field and Chowdhury, *Some Kind of Hero*, 470.

30. Field and Chowdhury, *Some Kind of Hero*, 471.

31. Alison Boshoff, "Bond to Fight Media War with a Mogul," *Daily Telegraph*, March 11, 1997, 3.

32. Dan Glaister, "Bond Stirred and Shaken," *The Guardian*, March 11, 1997, 9.

33. Garth Pearce, *The Making of* Tomorrow Never Dies (London: Boxtree, 1997), 25; Garth Pearce, "Shaken But Not Deterred," *Sunday Times*, November 30, 1997, 4.

34. Pearce, "Shaken but Not Deterred," 5.

35. Field and Chowdhury, *Some Kind of Hero*, 472.

36. "Pass Notes," *The Guardian*, Section 2, May 28, 1997, 3.

37. Pearce, "Shaken But Not Deterred," 5.

38. Field and Chowdhury, *Some Kind of Hero*, 475.

39. The page calculation is based on viewing a digitized copy of the final shooting script in the author's possession. Other sources claim that only three white pages remained.

40. Danny Greydon, "*Tomorrow Never Dies*," in *The James Bond Archives*, ed. Paul Duncan (Cologne: Taschen, 2015), 462.

41. Martyn Palmer, "Oh, Oh . . . So Compassionate," *Times*, December 11, 1997, 36.

42. Neil Norman, "Just a Bit of Fun . . .," *Evening Standard*, December 15, 1997, 48.

43. Geoff Brown, "*Tomorrow Never Dies*," *Times*, December 11, 1997, 37.

44. Alexander Walker, "Unshaken and Totally Unstirred," *Evening Standard*, December 11, 1997, 26.

45. Ryan Gilbey, "*Tomorrow* Barely Stirs," *The Independent*, December 12, 1997, 8.

46. Quentin Curtis, "Will Bond Ever Grow Up?," *Daily Telegraph*, December 12, 1997, 28.

47. James Cameron-Wilson, "*Tomorrow Never Dies*," *Film Review*, February 1998, 18.

48. José Arroyo, "*Tomorrow Never Dies*," *Sight and Sound*, February 1998, 53.

49. "007: In Numbers," *Screen International*, November 24, 2006, 32.

CHAPTER 19

BOND AT THE CROSSROADS

The World Is Not Enough (1999)

TOBIAS HOCHSCHERF

A rguably more than any other fictional character, James Bond is the subject of intense press coverage outside of the publicity cycles expected for new installments in franchise film productions. The months before the opening of the nineteenth official Bond film were no exception. The *New York Times*, for example, published a long feature by Michael Sragow on how Bond films faced the challenge of being able to "stay fresh" at the time of the new millennium when the franchise had already existed for more than forty years. The article concluded that "in its present state, the series, however lucrative, is functioning in reverse. Instead of catalyzing fresh fantasies, it encourages us to take one more ride on a whirligig or to repave memory lane. Either way, it leaves us shaken, not stirred."[1] This did not change fundamentally after the film's release, despite the fact that Michael Apted's *The World Is Not Enough* (1999, hereafter *TWINE*) includes all the expected ingredients of a successful Bond adventure: a debonair gentleman spy, resourceful villains threatening the world economy, exotic locations, spectacular stunt scenes, and a prominent international cast. Why were the critics and audiences not altogether pleased with the final result? And why is it regarded by many as a lesser film in the Bond canon? This chapter seeks to answer these questions by way of contextualizing the film, taking consideration of how its creators sought to update the franchise to keep it relevant while remaining aware of what fans looked for in a Bond adventure. The resulting film demonstrates that the producers of the franchise were not entirely sure how Bond's adventures should be framed as the twentieth century turned into the twenty-first, but it nevertheless remains an intriguing entry into the series of Bond adventures.

TWINE begins with the killing of Sir Robert King (David Calder), a British industrialist and friend of M (Judi Dench), by a bomb at the MI6 headquarters in London. James Bond's (Pierce Brosnan) subsequent mission is to safeguard King's daughter and heiress, Elektra (Sophie Marceau), while she oversees the construction of an important oil pipeline in Azerbaijan. Elektra is very reluctant to cooperate with the British Secret Service because of its role when she was abducted by terrorist and former KGB agent Renard (Robert Carlyle) prior to her father's death. With the help of American nuclear physicist Dr. Christmas Jones (Denise Richards), Bond reveals a plot to manipulate energy prices by sabotaging vital Russian oil supplies in an attempt to enhance the value of King's own pipeline as the only remaining option to transport oil to Europe. The villains behind this plot are Elektra and her former kidnapper Renard. Elektra's motive, which is only revealed more than halfway through the film, is revenge.[2] She personally blames M for having advised her father not to pay the ransom demand by her abductors. She also strongly opposes the way Western oil companies—including her father's firm—have been exploiting beautiful countries like Azerbaijan for their fossil fuels without regard to the countries' cultural heritage, inhabitants, or natural environment.

Before Bond can get to Elektra and Renard, they manage to take M hostage and bring her to the iconic Byzantine Maiden's Tower in Istanbul, from where they try to implement their plan by causing a nuclear explosion, notwithstanding the possible loss of many lives in and around the Bosporus metropolis. Once Bond eventually tries to free M, Elektra captures and tortures him. When he eventually manages to free himself with the help of one of Elektra's former helpers, Russian gangster boss Valentin Zukovsky (Robbie Coltrane), Bond kills Elektra and Renard. Evoking several previous Bond adventures, the final scenes show the British agent on the Istanbul rooftops with Dr. Jones in a romantic liaison captured by British thermal surveillance satellites.

Shot in numerous countries, including Spain, England, Scotland, Wales, France, Turkey, and the Bahamas, there was a real danger that *TWINE*'s transnational locations and its plot could be accused of a lack of cultural specificity and to use marketing jargon—product differentiation. The way that the film actually tries to counter such possible criticism is through its self-referential approach to the long-running franchise. Apart from numerous narrative and aesthetic allusions to earlier Bond films—including puns, banter, references to Bond's sexual prowess, and recurring characters such as M and Q (Desmond Llewelyn)—the title of *TWINE* itself is also homage to earlier adventures. It is the Bond family motto, revealed as part of the family crest in the George Lazenby film *On Her Majesty's Secret Service* (1969). While this allusion, as well as the several other references to the Roger Moore and Lazenby Bonds, seems to tie in with the stylized and humorous portrayals of the 1960s and 1970s, this is but one characteristic of *TWINE*. The film, too, contains an attempt to portray a tougher, more serious Bond grounded in the gritty realities of contemporary geopolitics and asymmetrical threats that characterized the afteryears of the Cold War. In this respect, *TWINE* is in many ways a Bond adventure at the crossroads. It seeks approval of the global and loyal fan base by adhering to Bondian elements and by offering references to previous films, but it also tries to attract a new generation of cinemagoers for whom Bond is only one of many action heroes. With *TWINE,* the Bond films still shy away from the idea of a reboot, which would be attempted with Daniel Craig less than a decade later, but demonstrate a willingness to adapt to contemporary expectations of the genre that were, indeed, changing.[3]

An Updated Bond Formula at Work:
The World Is Not Enough as Transitional Bond

Trying hard to adjust Bond to current expectations by way of updates and additions to the well-known Bondian elements, producing partners Barbara Broccoli and Michael G. Wilson at Eon also had to conquer criticism that, although Brosnan was widely seen as a worthy actor to play 007, he was not considered to possess the gravitas required for the darker side of the character to emerge. One could say that the role has an impact on Brosnan, rather than Brosnan's leaving a mark on Bond. As Sragow puts it in the aforementioned article for the *New York Times*: "in 'Goldeneye' and in 'Tomorrow Never Dies' (1997), Mr. Brosnan is less a model Bond than a model of Bond. He gets through poker-faced gags, lightning clinches and vehicular mayhem without leaving any gritty residue." Sragow finishes his negative résumé of the previous Brosnan outings by formulating an expectation directed at Eon: "Let's hope 'The World Is Not Enough' . . . gives him a chance to reveal what he's learned. The series needs an actor who can fill the part to bursting, and a production team willing to stick with him as he grows."[4]

Although the acting of Brosnan is at the center of the *New York Times* criticism, it is perhaps as much directed at his films themselves. Having an impact on the role through performance, after all, is only possible if the script opens up opportunities for just that. Months before the above article appeared, Eon had already reacted to the common desire to give the role of Bond—and with it its star—more room for character development by contracting new scriptwriters Neal Purvis and Robert Wade for the original screenplay. Their job, as they understood it, was, among other things, to "delve deeper into Bond's character and to make a new film a little bit Hitchcockian."[5] Their draft script, including the idea of a female villain, was then passed on to Dana Stevens—the first woman to work as a James Bond script consultant since *From Russia with Love* (1963)—who restructured the Elektra King character; Bruce Feirstein was also contracted for finishing touches at the end of the preproduction phase, with a focus on the character of Bond.[6]

According to James Chapman, the overall strategy worked quite well when the film was finally released. He argues that *TWINE* "is one of the better of the original screen stories for the Bond series in so far as it gives the impression of having been more carefully constructed," yet he qualifies his judgment a little bit by stating that "in marked contrast to *Tomorrow Never Dies,* the first half of the film at least seems more than a succession of set pieces laid end to end (though this criticism may be fairly levelled against the second half)."[7] The script, including several complex characters, significant twists, and subplots, certainly is multilayered and ambitious.

Eon's decisions, however, seem to have worked well financially. With worldwide grosses of $353 million, *TWINE* reaffirmed the commercial success of the Bond franchise with Brosnan.[8] The film did more than prove very profitable at the box office: international critical reception at the time was on the whole also rather positive. Particularly often, reviews mention the fast-paced fifteen-minute pre-title opening sequence, the new depth of Bond's character and, perhaps above all, the role and casting of the female villain Elektra. The *Chicago Sun-Times*'s influential critic, Roger Ebert, asserted that " 'The World Is Not Enough' is a splendid comic thriller, exciting and graceful, endlessly inventive. Because it is also the 19th James Bond movie, it comes with so much history that one reviews it like wine, comparing it to earlier famous vintages; I guess that's part of the fun. This is a good one."[9] And in his short review for the British *Radio Times,* Alan Jones gives the film four out of five stars, claiming that "this 19th James Bond adventure effortlessly juggles a hard-hitting story with all the expected 'super spy' embellishments and keeps everything in diamond-cut focus for maximum suspense and thrills" and concluding that "the world's greatest secret agent entered the new millennium in fine blockbuster form."[10] In a review by Janet Maslin for the *New York Times,* the attempt to give Bond's character more space for development is particularly appreciated: "Pierce Brosnan [now] bears noticeably more resemblance to a real human being. He shows signs of emotion, cuts back on the lame puns and makes lifelike conversation with fellow characters. Should he ever stop posing mannequinlike with left hand in trouser pocket, or engage in a clinch without appearing to be promoting his wristwatch, Mr. Brosnan's Bond will have entered the land of the living."[11]

TWINE, however, did not meet with unanimous praise. Claudius Seidl, in the German broadsheet *Süddeutsche Zeitung,* explicitly criticizes the mediocrity of Brosnan's Bond, who he writes seemed to have lost his glamour and inimitability: "The suit is by Brioni, the car a BMW—James Bond acts like he wants to win an election; he is a consensus man: a hero of the new middle class." Seidl, however, acknowledges that Elektra is "the most interesting woman Bond has met in a long time. Sophie Marceau seduces Bond and the audience and her appearance as a villainess is what is good about Michael Apted's film."[12] In a similar vein, Todd McCarthy, in the trade magazine *Variety*, also positively mentions the spectacular opening sequence, Brosnan's performance, and the role of Elektra, expressing that Her Majesty's secret service had now acquired a more nuanced character and a new vulnerability while the female villain was certainly a worthy opponent. Yet for him, the script writers wanted too much at the same time: "Daft, over-crammed plotting is a shame . . . There is a palpable sense of strain in the script to come up with new set piece ideas, and one of the problems is that there are too many of them. . . . While Bond buffs had widely speculated what a name director like Michael Apted might add to the proceedings, the answer is: very little."[13] Although *TWINE* could well be said to be ambitious but too overloaded, the most significant defining aspect of the film is how it tries to juggle a general commitment to change and at the same time conserve the very concepts that had made the series so very successful in the past.

Progressive Gender Politics and Misogynist Puns: Elektra King and Dr. Christmas Jones

As much as *TWINE* seeks to update the Bond formula for contemporary tastes, it also clings to many character traits that have been part of the Bond films for decades. Arguably above all, this is visible through the representation of gender. Talking about this topic in *TWINE*, James Chapman writes: "The promotional discourse of *The World is Not Enough* once again stressed the role of female agency and asserted the 'strong' roles for women in the film. On this occasion the claim was, perhaps, at least partially justified."[14] Elektra is not just the side-kick to a Bond villain, as had often been the case for women in the franchise, but plays the role of primary antagonist, an evil mastermind in her own right. In this sense, Elektra bears some resemblance to Melina Havelock (Carole Bouquet) in *For Your Eyes Only* (1981) in the way she is prepared to use violence in her desire for personal revenge. Chapman explains that the strong role owes as much to the script as it does to the casting of Bond's resourceful adversary: "Elektra is certainly one of the strongest-written parts of the series since the 1960s and the performance of Sophie Marceau, an accomplished French actress who had come to the attention of Anglo-American audiences following her role in Mel Gibson's *Braveheart* (1995), is undoubtedly the best by a 'Bond girl' since Diana Rigg in *OHMSS*."[15]

What Chapman does not mention in the above quote about the decision to cast Marceau is that the actress came with a large fan base owing to her immense success as a teenage star with the romantic comedies *La Boum* (*The Party or Ready for Love*, 1980) and its sequel from 1982, both of which were not only box-office hits in French-speaking countries but also successful throughout Europe and other mainly non-English-speaking countries. This strategy of casting continental European stars in more or less prominent female roles, which has been part of the franchise in almost all Bond films to date, is also apparent in the significant pre-title sequence of *TWINE* in which one of Renard's helpers tries to assassinate Bond in London. The killer is played by Italian actress Maria Grazia Cucinotta, who had made herself known internationally through her modelling career and her performance in the critically acclaimed adaptation *Il Postino* (*The Postman*, 1994).

Despite such continuities and new developments, many critics indicated that the role of Dr. Christmas Jones in the film constituted an unfortunate rollback to the misogynist characteristics of previous decades, clearly for marketing purposes.[16] Not only does this character easily succumb to Bond's sexual attractiveness, but it seems to unintentionally mock cinematic representations of eroticized female scientists. Her role and the decision to cast American model and actress Denise Richards seem to be informed more by the fictional character Lara Croft of the popular 1990s computer game franchise *Tomb Raider* than by the changing attitude toward female protagonists in the Bond series (figure 19.1).

The costume designs for Richards by Lindy Hemming, who joined the Bond production team with Brosnan's first outing in *GoldenEye* (1995), evoked the connections explicitly: "Nuclear de-commissioning underground [costume] aka Laura [*sic*] Croft."[17] Yet there is a dramaturgical difference between Croft and Jones: while Lara Croft is certainly an object of sexual desire, she cannot

Figure 19.1 Dr. Christmas Jones (Denise Richards) was modelled consciously after video game character Lara Croft. The Bond films followed the popular zeitgeist of the late 1990s to expand their appeal to younger audiences. *The World Is Not Enough* (1999).

be reduced to this role and clearly challenges the patriarchal order in many ways. Jones, however, seems more concurrent with Janet Woollacott's assessment of women in Ian Fleming's books, despite her alleged scientific expertise and academic merits:

> The narrative pattern of the Bond novels establishes the women as in some manner sexually and ideologically "out of place;" too aggressive (Vesper Lynd in *Casino Royale*), frigid (Gala Brand in *Moonraker*), damaged by rape (Tiffany Case in *Diamonds are Forever* and Honeychile Rider in *Dr No*), or lesbian (Tilly Masterton and Pussy Galore in *Goldfinger*). Such women are "out of place" in relation to men, as represented by Bond . . . Such a girl represents a challenge to the traditional sexual order, and Bond's answer is that of "putting her back in place beneath him (both literally and metaphorically)."[18]

Above and beyond narrative and dramaturgical roles, many of the interchanges between Bond and Jones in *TWINE* are reminiscent of Fleming's misogynist puns of the novels and the early films. The following conversation, filmed against a very artificial-looking evening sky with proverbial fireworks at the ending of the film, clearly reaffirms Bond's effect on women:

JAMES BOND
I've always wanted to have Christmas in Turkey.
DR CHRISTMAS JONES
Was that a Christmas joke?
JAMES BOND
From me? No. Never.
DR CHRISTMAS JONES:
So isn't it time you unwrapped your present?

And a little later in bed:

JAMES BOND
I was wrong about you.
DR CHRISTMAS JONES
Yeah? How so?
JAMES BOND
I thought Christmas only comes once a year.

While the depiction of Jones was uniformly criticized as sexist and stereotypical, not everyone agreed that Elektra and M were positive additions to female characters across the Bond canon. M is captured during one of her rare appearances in the field, only to be freed by Bond at the last minute, and

Elektra is eventually killed by Bond to reestablish his (male) dominance. Looking more closely at gender relations in the Brosnan Bond films, Lisa Funnell and Klaus Dodds argue that male and female representation are not at all equal:

> Spy work in the Brosnan era is coded or defined particularly through gender: while men are field-based agents, women do signals intelligence gathering. This taps into broader gendered conventions in the Brosnan era in which M, Bond's boss, is not only presented as a woman but is also characterized repeatedly as a bureaucrat or "bean counter." The films present a clear contrast between M's strategic calculation of risk and Bond's instinct-driven field work. In the end, Bond's hand-on approach always brings about the best results. This leads to the perception that intelligence gathering, which is coded as feminine, is not as effective as taking action, which is coded as masculine.[19]

Another aspect that is often overlooked in the critical responses to *TWINE* is the explicit xenophobia the film shares with many if not most previous Bond adventures. Bond, as the narrative pattern goes, is sent to fend off the threats posed by foreign villains such as Renard to reinstate the international peace order and protect British interests. While accented villains from abroad are usually easily recognized and thus pose less of a serious threat, villains who only seem to be British are a more serious matter. In this way, the British-Azerbaijani Elektra, who tries to defend her foreign mother's cultural heritage against British economic interests, is comparable to the traitor Alec Trevelyan (Sean Bean) in *GoldenEye*, who seeks to avenge his parents' death because of British foreign policy decisions. Alec, who is an MI6 agent just like Bond, is later discovered to be the British-educated son of Lienz Cossack parents who were betrayed when they were denied their promised repatriation after the Second World War. The killings of Alec and Elektra might be justified or even necessary because of their actions, yet there remains an uneasy feeling that the British interests Bond so actively defend are not always justified or in everybody's best interest.

Technology, Contemporary Realism, and Geopolitical Contexts

TWINE furthers the idea of a technologically savvy James Bond, a development that would be taken to the extreme with *Die Another Day* (2002). In his essay on Brosnan's portrayal of Bond in *GoldenEye*, *Tomorrow Never Dies*, and *TWINE*, Martin Willis argues that never before had James Bond possessed such an understanding of techno/cyber culture. While gadgets and the constant hassle between Bond and the MI6 Quartermaster (Q) had been a hallmark of the Moore and, to a lesser degree, also the Timothy Dalton Bonds, they are now an essential part of a secret agent around the new millennium, picking up and responding to the network society and contemporary anxieties of asymmetrical threats of technological domination. Or, as Willis puts it, "*GoldenEye, Tomorrow Never Dies,* and *The World Is Not Enough* portray a Bond of unlimited technological ability whose expert knowledge of applied science maintains a Western stronghold on political, economic, and cultural power in an Information Age wrought by fears of millennium catastrophe." While Willis's argument that the villain Renard has a cyber-body because a bullet has penetrated his head and made him immune to pain might be somewhat far-fetched, all of Brosnan's Bond films nevertheless prove that "information and communication [become] a key battleground between the British nation-state and global crime."[20]

The conflicts of the film are just as connected to the real world as previous entrants to the franchise had been, perhaps even more. And even if the role of 007 in 1999 remained remarkably stable, the geopolitical contexts had already shifted in the years since *GoldenEye*. One element where this change is noticeable is the locations, which arguably emerge as central to the narrative rather than travelogue backgrounds as in previous films.[21] The setting is often very specific rather than exemplary, as the problems in and around the former Soviet Union are actual rather than imaginary conflicts. In contrast to the cover-up name of Universal Export, MI6, moreover, is now officially and, through recurring long shots of the iconic MI6 headquarters in London, explicitly part of the Bond world. The franchise thus took into account that with the Intelligence Service Act, Britain in 1994, for the first time, publicly acknowledged the existence of MI6.[22] Another change is the very realistic storyline revolving around the environmental and economic causes of fossil fuel supplies (figure 19.2). The plot of *TWINE*, indeed, seems to offer much potential owing to how it handles

Figure 19.2 Fossil fuel for the West: far-sighted notions of contemporary geopolitics as a 007 film plot device. *The World Is Not Enough* (1999).

upcoming geopolitical conflicts over energy supplies and the threats posed by Russia and its border regions.

The film is remarkably visionary, as it seems to anticipate the dispute over the Baltic Sea gas pipeline North Stream 2 and the (armed) conflicts between Russia and other former Soviet states.[23] Russia in *TWINE* is not itself a rogue nation but portrayed as a victim of a cunning plot by Elektra, who plans to sabotage a Russian-owned pipeline in Istanbul. Bond is acting in the interest of the West as well as Russia in the film, as Funnell and Dodds argue: "By stopping King and her partner/lover Renard, Bond reestablishes the conventional geopolitical order in order to ensure that oil continues to flow to the West, and protects the interest of newly independent Russia."[24]

The political contexts of *TWINE*, as James Chapman argues, "are intriguing in that the conspiracy posits an alliance between international terrorism and corporate capitalism." For him, the renegade and tragic figure of Renard very much follows the zeitgeist after the collapse of the Soviet Union and the Warsaw Pact:

> Renard represents the forces of chaos and anarchy that have emerged following the end of the Cold War: according to MI6 intelligence he has worked in Moscow, North Korea, Afghanistan, Bosnia, Iraq, Iran, Beirut and Cambodia ("All the romantic vacation spots"). Renard is associated with what President Clinton had described in 1998 as an "unholy alliance of terrorists, drug traffickers and organised international criminals" who threatened to be the "predators of the twenty-first century."[25]

The new post–Cold War world order cannot adequately be described by the good West fighting the renegade rogues. In this sense, *TWINE* both confirms and frustrates Clinton's assessment of contemporary global threats.

Interestingly, there are but a few Bond films in which contemporary geopolitical conflicts over fossil energy are used as a plot device, despite the crucial role of oil and gas for the world economy: this was most notably the case in *The Man with the Golden Gun* (1974) and a later film starring Daniel Craig, *Quantum of Solace* (2008). *TWINE* is rooted in actual geopolitical conflicts rather than unlikely fictional scenarios, as was pointed out by Jeremy Black in 2001: "The politics of the film relates very much to the real world, both its setting in a volatile part of the world, the Caucasus, and in its plot: control over oil and its movements. The conflation of geopolitics and resources is handled deftly."[26] Yet rather than being sent to a mission in a faraway land to defend Britain's interests abroad, *TWINE* brings the threat home to London, where the MI6 headquarters is directly attacked and badly damaged. As a clear ramification of a globalized world, Britain has become more vulnerable than ever to outside threats. What aggravates the situation is the absence of help from Felix Leiter and the special British–American relationship or assistance from the European partners. The United Kingdom seems increasingly alone in the world. *TWINE*, according to such a reading, reassures audiences that British intelligence alone can overcome such challenges. In this way, *TWINE* captured a growing sentiment against international integration in Britain that found perhaps its most fertile breeding ground in the growing Euroskepticism that eventually contributed to the withdrawal of the United Kingdom from the European Union about twenty years after the film's release.

The Millennial Bond as Interlude

Looking back at the Brosnan films on the occasion of the series' fiftieth anniversary in 2012, when Daniel Craig had already successfully taken over playing Bond, film critic Peter Debruge argued, as this chapter does, that *TWINE* alludes to various previous installments of the franchise but also offers some rather unfortunate puns and light-hearted conversations:

> Brosnan's showy yet hollow third outing, "The World Is Not Enough," presents a conflicted persona torn between the corny antics of the Roger Moore era and the grim seriousness of where things would eventually go under Daniel Craig's tenure. It also contains a dose of Timothy Dalton-esque toughness . . . But so much of what made Brosnan such a great Bond is thrust into the backseat by lame jokes and a premature attempt to mix up the formula. He's stuck making sexist puns (to the shapely accountant who asks, "Would you like to check my figures?:" "Oh, I'm sure they're perfectly rounded.") and out-of-touch groaners (to a henchman with a gold-plated grill: "I see you put your money where your mouth is."). The new Q (John Cleese) is similarly introduced as an object of comedy. Even the villain (Robert Carlyle) can't help dropping pitiful wisecracks (e.g. "Welcome to my nuclear family," as he dramatically inserts the firing pin into a nuclear device).[27]

This is why *TWINE* should be understood as a Bond at the crossroads. Some elements were convincingly updated while other aspects arguably needed the more thorough reconsideration that Craig's films would bring about. The mixed coverage in newspapers and magazines demonstrates how several critics remained skeptical as to whether the producers did manage to modernize the series in an appropriate way. Or, to put it less diplomatically, *TWINE* is trying hard to please everyone, but really pleases no one. A more drastic—and ultimately convincing—attempt for change and development was only possible with Craig and the subsequent reboot of the franchise. It is only with Craig that the series becomes more transgressive in that it seriously challenges many of its established codes, its largely noncontinuous narratives and supposed certainties. Such an approach is sometimes hinted at in *TWINE*, but it seems the franchise was not yet ready to make the changes it was to make a few years later in *Casino Royale* (2006).

Notes

1. Michael Sragow, "Marketing Bonds: A Franchise Tries to Stay Fresh," *New York Times*, Section 2, September 12, 1999, 38.
2. This alludes, of course, to the story from Greek mythology in which Electra conspires with her brother to kill their mother.
3. Tobias Hochscherf, "Bond in the Age of Global Crises: 007 in the Daniel Craig Era," *Journal of British Cinema and Television* 10, no. 2 (2013): 298–320.
4. Sragow, "Marketing Bonds."
5. York Membery, "No, Mr Bond, I Want You to Live," *Sunday Times*, S2, February 21, 1999: 4.
6. Llewella Chapman, *Fashioning James Bond: Costume, Gender, and Identity in the World of 007* (New York: Bloomsbury Academic, 2022), 221.
7. James Chapman, *Licence to Thrill: A Cultural History of the James Bond Films,* 2nd rev. ed. (London: I. B. Tauris, 2007), 228.
8. Chapman, *Licence to Thrill*, 212.
9. Roger Ebert, "The World Is Not Enough," November 19, 1999, www.rogerebert.com/reviews/the-world-is-not-enough-1999, accessed March 17, 2022.
10. Alan Jones, "The World Is Not Enough," *Radio Times*, www.radiotimes.com/movie-guide/b-2h6fr6/the-world-is-not-enough/, accessed March 17, 2022.
11. Janet Maslin, "Submarines, Balloons and a Guy Named Bond," review, *New York Times*, Section E, November 19, 1999: 20.
12. Claudius Seidl, "Ein Held der neuen Mitte" (A Hero for the New Middle Class), *Süddeutsche Zeitung*, December 9, 1999, 19.
13. Todd McCarthy, "The World Is Not Enough," *Variety*, November 14, 1999, variety.com/1999/film/reviews/the-world-is-not-enough-1200459720/, accessed March 17, 2022.
14. Chapman, *Licence to Thrill*, 230.
15. Chapman, *Licence to Thrill*, 230.
16. On marketing strategies and *TWINE*, including the casting of Richards, see Corie Brown and Jeff Giles, "Bond—Stirred, Not Shaken," *Newsweek*, November 22, 1999, 80.
17. Llewella Chapman, *Fashioning James Bond*, 224.
18. Janet Woollacott, "The James Bond Films: Conditions of Production," in *The James Bond Phenomenon: A Critical Reader*, ed. Christoph Lindner, 2nd ed. (Manchester: Manchester University Press, 2014), 117–35; 128.
19. Lisa Funnell and Klaus Dodds, *Geographies, Genders, and Geopolitics of James Bond* (London: Palgrave Macmillan, 2017), 67.
20. Martin Willis, "Hard-wear: The Millennium, Technology, and Brosnan's Bond," in Lindner, *James Bond Phenomenon*, 169–70, 171, 178.
21. Chapman, *Licence to Thrill*, 231.
22. Funnell and Dodds, *Geographies, Genders*, 199.
23. Funnell and Dodds, *Geographies, Genders*, 151–153.

24. Funnell and Dodds, *Geographies, Genders*, 152.
25. Chapman, *Licence to Thrill*, 229.
26. Jeremy Black, *The Politics of James Bond: From Fleming's Novels to the Big Screen* (Westport, CT: Praeger, 2001), 168.
27. Peter Debruge, "Revisiting 1999's 'The World Is Not Enough,'" *Variety*, October 19, 2012, variety.com/2012/film/reviews/revisiting-1999-s-the-world-is-not-enough-11180 61197/, accessed March 26, 2022.

CHAPTER 20

THE DIGITAL DOMAIN OF
DIE ANOTHER DAY (2002)

CHRISTOPHER HOLLIDAY

[The film] might have been written by Jean Baudrillard. For here there are surfaces without depth, and signifiers with nothing signified; everything is so situational, contingent and temporary that Die Another Day seems more like the simulacrum of a movie; and if ever Oscars were handed out for postmodernism, this film would surely sweep the board. Pastiche, parody, bricolage, irony, ambiguity, reflexivity and self-consciousness: Die Another Day has these in computer-generated spades.

—Philip Kerr, *New Statesman*, November 25, 2002

So where is this cutting-edge stuff?

—James Bond to Q, *Die Another Day* (2002)

Released as an anniversary feature to mark forty years since the premiere of *Dr. No* (1962), the twentieth official James Bond film, *Die Another Day* (2002), has come to occupy a curious position within the 007 big-screen series. Despite a largely positive critical response among the U.K. and U.S. popular and trade press upon its original theatrical run in November 2002, the film has evolved a less than favorable reputation in the intervening two decades.[1] As Pierce Brosnan's final appearance in the role of 007, *Die Another Day* is firmly implicated in the series' rolling phases of production, which are marshalled by the steady cycle of Bond actors who have assumed the role of queen and country's best secret agent. *Die Another Day*'s status as an "end point" culminating Brosnan's four-film tenure as 007—coupled with the origin story narrative and stylistic revisionism made to the franchise by Daniel Craig's debut as Bond in *Casino Royale* (2006)—has retroactively strengthened the view that *Die Another Day* marked a ruinous distortion of the "Bondian" formula that has traditionally supported the "production ideology" and generic expectations that structure the series.[2] As Tony Bennett and Janet Woollacott argued following the release of *The Spy Who Loved Me* (1977), "Bondian" was regularly used across industrial and popular discourses to define the "spirit" of Bond films and their routinized pleasures as "a distinctive formula, [and] a specific genre of film."[3] While *Die Another Day* attracted geopolitical controversy among North and South Korean audiences (prompting "anti-007 boycotts" of the film and its removal from theatrical circulation after four weeks), particularly central to the perceived disruption made by Brosnan's final appearance to the "Bondian" formula was the identification of its anomalous involvement with Computer Generated Imagery (CGI).[4]

The film's shift toward CGI across a number of action sequences rebelled against the series' longstanding tradition of practical effects, models, and miniatures and *Casino Royale*'s subsequent adoption of a "new action realist" aesthetic of intensified proximity, immediacy, and claustrophobic verisimilitude, which many commentators argued better served the anxieties and trauma experienced across post-9/11 American culture.[5] *Variety*'s Todd McCarthy was certainly not alone in reporting how *Die Another Day* "pushes 007 into CGI-driven, quasi-sci-fi territory," noting that despite its production values being "up to series standard," a "windsurfing escape by Bond from an ice avalanche that is so patently absurd and so blatantly a CGI concoction . . . that it proves a total turn-off."[6] Frequent charges (both then and in the years since) have aggressively been levelled at *Die Another Day*'s overinvestment in visual effects (VFX) technologies and strongly "computerized feel," with a clumsy visibility to its CGI reflecting nothing more than the acceleration of computer processing across postmillennial Hollywood filmmaking. This chapter seeks to explore the form and function of *Die Another Day*'s digital imagery by arguing that the franchise's application of CGI was strongly indebted to several industrial shifts and market forces that would come to rapidly shape the history of VFX technologies within popular cinema. The film's wide-ranging use of computer graphics usefully sites Brosnan's final appearance firmly within Hollywood's industrial landscape of the early 2000s, with its 2002 release fully capturing the upward trajectory of VFX production and the mainstreaming of digital technology within commercial filmmaking practices. By examining *Die Another Day* as more than just a capitulation to the increasing computer processing of the period, this chapter argues that the film stands as an important blueprint for— and exploration of—the creative possibilities of CGI at a time when digital effects imagery in Hollywood was itself hardening into new aesthetic horizons.

Bond Goes Bluescreen

In June 2015, *Time Out* magazine ran an online feature documenting the "10 Worst CGI Special Effects in Movie History," which took simultaneous aim at "egregiously awful examples" of digital technology within popular blockbuster cinema and Hollywood's progressive industrial shift away from practical effects traditions. In a list that featured a cluster of Hollywood action blockbusters released at the turn of the millennium, including *Deep Blue Sea* (1999), *The Mummy Returns* (2001), *Hulk* (2003), and *The Matrix Reloaded* (2004)—as well as the digitally remastered 1997 rerelease of *Star Wars* (1977) with new CG visual effects from Industrial Light & Magic—the magazine listed Bond's "parasurf-ing over a fake CGI tsunami and crumbling ice glacier" in *Die Another Day* in an unfavorable first place.[7] Coming over a decade after the film's initial release, such responses to its digital VFX were not limited to retrospective accounts that critiqued its seemingly outdated technology. Rather, the *Time Out* article served to rehearse the kinds of ambivalent critical responses evident at the time regard-ing the film's unconvincing postproduction processing. Despite praising the film as the best since *The Spy Who Loved Me*, A. O. Scott in the *New York Times* none-theless reported in his 2002 review, "In one especially dreadful sequence, Bond windsurfs through a churning Icelandic Sea dotted with what seem to be huge chunks of digital meringue."[8] The film's use of CGI was also termed "dodgy" in the earlier 2002 print edition of *Time Out London*, while the series' "new reliance on blue screens and computer graphics" was a "let-down," "artificial," and highly "underwhelming."[9] Although many reviewers ultimately praised elements of *Die Another Day*'s nostalgic evocation of 007 big-screen history (particularly in the film's reflexive inclusion of gadgets and weapons from the previous nine-teen feature films), it was the prominence of its digital imagery and "comput-erised stunts" that defined the majority of the sustained critical derision.[10]

    As the many accounts of *Die Another Day* as the series' "absolute nadir" make clear, the film remains an important footnote in the franchise's ambiva-lent involvement with computer technologies.[11] Indeed, the application of com-puter graphics for its action sequences and stunt work functioned as "the unruly culmination" of several creative experiments and "embryonic explora-tions into CGI" made by the Bond series throughout the Brosnan era during the 1990s.[12] At the same time, *Die Another Day* also evidences how far com-puter graphics had begun to affect wider mainstream film production in the postmillennial period, if not define the kinds of digitally enhanced block-buster films against which 007 was now having to compete. Writing for the *Times* in November 2002, Ian Nathan argued that *Die Another Day* "has had to drag the series into the CG (computer graphics)-dominated modern world. The Bond films of the past have prided themselves on doing it for real."[13] In the Eon production notes released to accompany the film, director Lee Tama-hori similarly discussed the progressive integration of digital technology into *Die Another Day* as a departure, while citing Bond's relationship to the rheto-ric of authenticity that has conventionally restated the series' practical in-camera effects technologies:

> I put in a massive big-action piece that has never been seen before involving
> an enormous amount of special effects and CGI effects. It has created some
> nervousness only because the Bond movies are reality based stunt-wise. His-
> torically, everything has been done for real. There's usually not a lot of mod-
> ern Matrix type CGI stuff, but we are embarking on one in this that is pretty
> massive only because it can't be done as a real stunt. . . . It involves a resolu-
> tion to a chase on a glacier involving gigantic action, millions of tonnes of ice
> and tidal waves and, because you can't put people into that, it has to be done
> digitally.[14]

Tamahori's comments concerning the film's deviation from the "reality-based" stunt-work via CG-crafted action sequences familiar from *The Matrix* (1999) marks a notable reversal from the prerelease material of *The World Is Not Enough* (1999), where special effects supervisor John Richardson had champi-oned the film's steadfast use of practical effects imagery in defiance of Bond's Hollywood contemporaries. Richardson noted, "Film-making has moved more into the realm of computers over the past few years but we like to use traditional methods as much as possible. . . . Whilst the computer has many wonderful advantages, so do some of the proven traditional methods."[15]

The origins of the Bond series' "digital turn" can, of course, be traced as far back as the Roger Moore era (1973–1985), produced against the backdrop of a new Hollywood cinema increasingly invested in the spectacle of technology as part of its blockbuster economics. Following 1970s Bond cinema's generic inter-ventions (if not postclassical Hollywood's weakening of genre boundaries more broadly)—including the evocation of blaxploitation cinema in *Live and Let Die* (1973) and the martial arts genre for *The Man with the Golden Gun* (1974)—the release of *Moonraker* (1979) followed in the wake of science-fiction features *Star Wars* and *Close Encounters of the Third Kind* (1977) by marking the Bond franchise's first substantial involvement with digital processing. A June 1979 issue of *New Scientist* magazine identified how *Moonraker*'s optical effects unit, headed by optical effects cameraman Robin Browne, developed new techniques in front and back projection alongside "complex optical bench installations" replete with digital controls to integrate "stars, explosions, and lasers" into live-action and miniature/modelled scenes. As part of *Moonraker*'s digitized production, Eon hired "William Hansard, a top US front projection expert, [who] brought modern optical technology into play" in the design of Hugo Drax's command satellite and its array of consoles, control/communications panels, and television monitors. The climactic laser gun battle also involved the integration of "optically-produced simulated lasers" together with plastic scale models and human performers and organized via a "digitally-controlled system." Each individual laser "was inserted separately frame-by-frame," while matte paintings, optical printing, full-scale and model sets, and front/back projection all combined to provide *Moonraker* with its zero-gravity spectacle.[16]

Since the 1970s and throughout the information technology age, the Bond franchise has evolved an altogether more "chaotic oil-and-water" relationship to digital technology and computer animation, a connection that has been sharpened by the stylistic disparities between *Die Another Day* and *Casino Royale*.[17] In fact, the enduring cultural and industrial narrative framing Craig's debut has often leaned on its sidelining of the kinds of digital intermediaries that populated *Die Another Day*, with the revisionist credentials of Craig's five-film tenure conventionally anchored to its rejection of digital effects imagery as a match to its broader thematic occlusion of technology and gadgets. Daniel Ferreras Savoye notes that the "uneasiness created by the apparent artificiality of *Die Another Day*" ultimately paved the way for the "very positive public and critical receptions" of its successor *Casino Royale*, particularly given *Die Another Day*'s "extreme degree of independence" from Ian Fleming's source texts that was quickly followed by "the re-initialization of the series," which showed "a deliberate intention to return to the textual source."[18] Ahead of *Casino Royale*'s 2006 release, reviewer Daya Alberge similarly noted, "The makers of the new James Bond film admitted yesterday that they relied too heavily on computer-generated images for the spectacular stunts in their last two 007 movies. . . . [T]hey are going back to the old-fashioned way of making action thrillers and restoring the risk."[19]

Despite extensive—yet seamlessly invisible—digital VFX technologies involved in the production of *Casino Royale*, *Quantum of Solace* (2008), *Skyfall* (2012), *Spectre* (2015), and *No Time to Die* (2021), it is *Die Another Day* that has assumed the role of a messy "CGI fandango" whose spectacular digital "excess" would lead directly to "the dawn of a pared down, gritty Bond era."[20] An issue of VFX journal *Cinefantastique* published in 2002 outlined the many VFX studios across Europe and the United States that were contracted for *Die Another Day*'s armory of digital special effects, models, compositing, and video graphics for Brosnan's final performance as agent 007: Cinesite, Double

Negative (DNEG), The Moving Picture Company, and Framestore/CFC (who also produced the opening title sequence).[21] The short "Digital Grading" featurette packaged on the 2003 special edition DVD of *Die Another Day* also documented the role of computer-executed color processes and high-resolution light/shadow correction achieved in the digital grading suite, which scanned the film to transform it into computer data that could then have digital graders applied to provide visual continuity among location, studio, and digitized footage. The film's 680 CGI shots (almost three times the 250 used for *The World Is Not Enough*) included a photorealistic digital bullet that accompanied the opening gun barrel sequence; the pre-credits flame-thrower fight between Bond and Colonel Moon (Will Yun Lee); the descent by Jinx (Halle Berry) into the ocean following her escape from the DNA replacement therapy clinic housed on the fictional Isla de los Organos in Cuba (achieved via bluescreen and digital animation); the tsunami surfing sequence, which shows Bond targeted by the beams of the Icarus satellite only to escape by impossibly floating over the melting ice caps and rolling waves (figure 20.1); and the climactic destruction of Gustav Graves' (Toby Stephens) cargo plane as it passes through the weaponized satellite's energy beam.

As part of its extensive digital VFX, *Die Another* Day combined "A plethora of digital visual-effects practices such as CGI, 'universal-capture' techniques, digital color grading, digital wire removal, and blue-screen" to animate the collapse of the computer-generated icebergs and water sprays in the much-derided tsunami sequence.[22] However, the standard bearer of its intensified and incongruous digital VFX practices was the invisible car (the Aston Martin Vanquish model, renamed by Q [John Cleese] in the film as the "Vanish"). Johannes Binotto argues that despite Bond's increased framing throughout the Brosnan era as a hero for the electronic age, "The absurdity to which such a faith in technology will lead can be seen in the inane *Die Another Day* when

Figure 20.1 Bond's (Pierce Brosnan) windsurfing escape. *Die Another Day* (2002).

Bond is provided with an invisible car."[23] The targeting of the Aston Martin Vanquish as metonymically encapsulating the film's muddled application of CG technology can therefore be offset against 007's progressive digital mastery in an increasing techno-culture, but made commensurate with a Hollywood cinema that itself found digital imagery both aesthetically feasible and highly lucrative. Indeed, if the tone sounded by the contemporaneous 007 parodies *Austin Powers: International Man of Mystery* (1997) and its 1999 and 2003 sequels—alongside action film *xXx* (2000), which opened with the "symbolic" murder of a tuxedoed secret agent—had initially problematized Bond's viability in the media landscape, then Hollywood's aggressive turn to digital imagery in the early 2000s provided clear obstacles and opportunities for the Bond filmmakers.

"It's Called the Future—Get Used to It"

Pointing to the influence of the ever-expanding technological parameters of Hollywood cinema on the Bond franchise in the 1970s, André Millard suggests that not only was *Moonraker* "produced under the shadow of *Star Wars*," but the industry's broader "digital revolution" meant the Bond series had to follow "technological developments in both space travel and motion picture special effects."[24] *Die Another Day* was certainly no less a symptom of the wondrous possibilities and new audiovisual experiences engendered by new digital imaging technologies and computer graphics, which had initially held a fluctuating and creative relationship to mimeticism, simulation, and verisimilitude in the early period between 1989 and 1995 that Michele Pierson has termed the "wonder years" of digital VFX production.[25] Falling exactly in the intervening years between consecutive Bond films *Licence to Kill* (1989) and *GoldenEye* (1995), the "wonder years" in Hollywood were, for Pierson, a period where the plasticity of computer-generated effects solidified into a pervasive science-fiction electronic "technofuturist" style that supported the spectacle of digital illusionism. This hyperreal aesthetic would, as the 1990s progressed, ultimately give way to a more naturalistic "simulationist" register that Stephen Prince termed "perceptual realism."[26] With *GoldenEye*, the first Bond film to utilize computer-generated imagery via greenscreen image processing, the "wonder years" period into which Bond entered was therefore crucial in establishing the aesthetic possibilities of computer graphics. At the same time, the "flurry of mass media attention" that accompanied the competition and differentiation between digital VFX blockbusters throughout the 1990s would provide a vital context for understanding how 007 might adapt and integrate into Hollywood's growing multimedia culture.[27]

It comes as little surprise, then, that *Die Another Day* would ultimately appear so "excessively dependent on CGI technologies," given the sustained place of digital imaging within Hollywood's postmillennial industrial landscape and the computer's role as an anchoring force for the spectacle and fantasy of the Hollywood blockbuster.[28] As Tamahori's comments regarding the film's adoption of "modern Matrix type CGI stuff" make clear, *Die Another Day* was sold to international audiences based on its increased engagement with the kinds of CGI effects imagery and technologies popular across Hollywood filmmaking, just as the shifting brutality of *Casino Royale*'s visual style would later be connected to the gradual emergence of a post-9/11 "intensified" film style across U.S. cinema rooted in a chaotic freneticism, handheld camera work, and rapid editing patterns.[29] Tanine Allison argues, "Since 2000, visual effects have gained prominence not only through the progressive innovation of digital technologies, but also through the predominant business paradigm of Hollywood."[30] The first few years of the new millennium were pivotal in the industry and visibility of digital effects technologies, from developments in digital "wirework" and slow-motion bullet-time technologies (pioneered in the kung-fu stylings of *The Matrix* and broader assimilation of a Hong Kong fighting style within Hollywood action cinema) to motion-capture and the persuasive rendering of three-dimensional virtual bodies. The rise of the computer-animated feature film following the release of *Toy Story* (1995) also accelerated the presence of persuasive digital "synthespians" and computer-generated avatars across North American animation.[31] For Julia Moszkowicz, computer-animated films such as *Toy Story 2* (1999) and *Shrek* (2001) pushed the photorealistic credentials of computer graphics toward "persuasive" and "breathtaking" levels of naturalism, to the extent that it was "often easy to lose sense of CGI as a product of arts and scientific practice."[32] Such was the emergence of computer-mediated humanity in an increasingly digitized Hollywood that *Variety*'s Marc Graser argued if the rise of computer-generated characters had been a long-held promise for Hollywood's VFX sector and a signal of technological veracity, then "that time came in 2002."[33] The previous summer, feature films *A.I. Artificial Intelligence* (2001) and *Final Fantasy: The Spirits Within* (2001) had already narrativized the uncanny proliferation of digital humans that had begun to populate U.S. cinema during the preceding decade. Yet only three months before *Die Another Day*'s November 2002 release, it was another feature—the dystopian *Simone* (2002), telling the story of the world's first synthetic celebrity and the ethics of digital stardom—that replaced family-friendly Android narratives of human–machine coexistence (such as the 1999 Robin Williams star vehicle *Bicentennial Man*), with emergent technophobic stories of artificial intelligence that explicitly traded in the crisis of digital cyborgs, avatars, and robots. As computer-generated imagery therefore "became a more persistent and wide-ranging presence onscreen" in the early 2000s, the targeting of *Die Another Day*'s digital VFX sequences by reviewers and audiences seemed to coincide with a notably more cautionary phase in how modern Hollywood was understanding the consciousness of androids as much as the potential impact of digitally animated screen bodies.[34]

Despite protestations about its clumsy VFX imagery and boycotts across East Asia, *Die Another Day* was the sixth-top-grossing film of 2002, making $431,971,116 worldwide and becoming—until *Casino Royale*—the most commercially successfully Bond film at both the domestic and global box offices.[35] A closer look at the Top Ten highest-grossing films of 2002 further secures the industrial prominence of CG technology in this era, the commercial power of effects-driven blockbusters, and the genres (fantasy, science-fiction, superhero) in which digital animation had found an expressive home. In October 2001, *Variety* predicted that in the aftermath of 9/11 and amid these "anxious times," Hollywood would return the following summer to "action-prone normalcy" and that—due to an increased investment in the distraction provided by fantasy from political, social, and cultural trauma—"CGI creatures will abound."[36] Indeed, *Die Another Day* sat in the Top 10 alongside a number of VFX-heavy films that were central to the evolution and design of convincing digital monsters, aliens, and abject others in postmillennial fantasy cinema:

1. *The Lord of the Rings: The Two Towers* (2002) ($936,689,735)
2. *Harry Potter and the Chamber of Secrets* (2002) ($878,979,634)
3. *Spider-Man* (2002) ($821,708,551)
4. *Star Wars Episode II: Attack of the Clones* (2002) ($645,256,452)
5. *Men in Black II* (2002) ($441,818,803)
6. *Die Another Day* (2002) ($431,971,116)
7. *Signs* (2002) ($408,247,917)
8. *Ice Age* (2002) ($383,257,136)
9. *My Big Fat Greek Wedding* (2002) ($368,744,044)
10. *Minority Report* (2002) ($358,372,926)

As part of the longest-running film franchise in cinema history, *Die Another Day*'s place on this list also exemplifies the dominance of film series and cycles that would equally come to define contemporary Hollywood production. As Allison notes, such is the interplay between intensified franchise production aimed at preexisting markets and VFX imagery in post-2000 filmmaking that any list of the former "is nearly identical to a list of the most prominent visual-effects films since the turn of the millennium."[37] This history includes not only the 2002 Top 10 series *Lord of the Rings* and *Harry Potter*, but the franchise films *Spider-Man, Star Wars Episode II: Attack of the Clones, Men in Black II,* and *Ice Age*, which indicate the complex interplay between seriality and effects technologies in the immediate post-2000 period.[38]

Beyond the "multiple digital techniques" and computer-generated elements involved in the production of Tamahori's film, which collectively marked a "significant transformation in the aesthetics of the series," *Die Another Day* equally folds the spectacle of digital technology and computerized image processing into its narrative organization.[39] Alongside the Aston Martin "Vanish" that fictionalizes CG "adaptive camouflage" to explore the spectacle of persuasive digital illusionism, the film also interrogates the immersive and experiential properties of virtual reality (VR). A theme commonplace throughout Hollywood cinema of the late 1990s and early 2000s—from *The Matrix* and *The Thirteenth Floor* (1999) to *eXistenZ* (1999) and *The Cell* (2000)—the construction of cyberspace and experience of simulated audiovisual phenomena onscreen was matched by the growing application of bluescreen/greenscreen processing to create 3D digital environments for big-budget Hollywood productions. The term "virtual backlot" was coined the same year as *Die Another Day* by California-based Stargate Studios to define a type of digital production "created by composing the footage of actors with computer-generated sets and other visuals." *Sky Captain and the World of Tomorrow* (2004) was the first blockbuster feature to use entirely virtual backlot sets, the same year *The Polar Express* (2004) became the first full motion-capture film.[40] *Die Another Day*'s acknowledgement of VR onscreen certainly reflects an industrial interest in modes of holographic technology and the construction of virtual space. However, Tamahori's film also recalls the kinds of virtual/augmented reality technologies and simulation-based systems being used at the time as part of U.S. military training, in which conflict scenarios were designed and modelled

Figure 20.2 The virtual reality sequences borrow from first-person shooter video game styles and perspectives. *Die Another Day* (2002).

Figure 20.3a and b The virtual reality training exercise. *Die Another Day* (2002).

entirely within virtual spaces to test the participants' skills in combat, weapons assembly, pilot training, and even medical instruction.[41]

The first of *Die Another Day*'s VR sequences gestures to precisely this virtual combat training application by siting Bond inside a digital training facsimile constructed by Q to test 007's "rusty" shooting skills after his incarceration in North Korea. Briefly incorporating the slow-motion "bullet-time" aesthetic pioneered in *The Matrix*, the style of the VR scene also owes a debt to the first-person shooter (FPS) style of videogame, a media format popularized in the mid-1990s due in part to the commercial success of the 007 tie-in videogame *GoldenEye 007* (1997) for the Nintendo 64 console. With commercial cinema's own convergence with videogames intensifying in the early 2000s, the release of numerous film adaptations and anthology Bond video games leading up to *Die Another Day* provides a clear computer context for the film's exploration of weapon-based combat and perspective in 3-D virtual space, among them the FPS *The World Is Not Enough* (2000), *James Bond 007: Agent Under*

Fire (2001), and *James Bond 007: Nightfire* (2002), all for the Playstation.[42] Indeed, the rapid point-of-view changes and shifting camerawork as Bond moves through the digital corridors of MI6 in *Die Another Day*'s computer training simulation test recall the stylistic repertoire of these FPS games, which trade in the optical navigations and limitations of first-person subjective narration (figure 20.2). It is only when Q interrupts the virtual simulation by walking through the digital image that the illusion is suddenly broken, and *Die Another Day*'s identity as "more like the [Baudrillardian] simulacrum of a movie" in its "reflexivity and self-consciousness" is confirmed (figures 20.3a and b).[43] As the shot disintegrates in ways that confuse its own spatio-temporal logic, *Die Another Day* appears to momentarily replace its fictional reality with a perfect—and typically "Bondian"—simulacrum.

Rethinking 007's Reset

A consequence of its involvement with computer graphics, *Die Another Day*'s departure from—and heightened self-reflexivity with—the "Bondian" blueprint seemingly provided both the industrial and aesthetic conditions under which *Casino Royale* was required to function as a necessary reset for the series. For Christoph Lindner, the release of *Casino Royale* and the controversial casting of Craig worked "not just [as] a revising of 007, it is also a reimagining, a reintroduction, a re-evaluation, a reinvention and a renewal."[44] However, if "the tension created between innovation and convention, between departure and arrival, motion and stasis, beginning and ending" is what makes *Casino Royale* "such an interesting and unusual addition to the ever-expanding Bond canon," then such relationships regarding repetition and difference held in strain across the franchise are likewise what make *Die Another Day* so significant to the trajectory of contemporary 007 cinema.[45] Both films might be understood as incorporating intensified formulaic adjustment, with their contact to the "Bondian" generic profile simply a difference of degree rather than kind. Yet whereas *Die Another Day*'s processes of revisionism have been understood as technologically motivated deviations from an established template, those made by *Casino Royale* are conversely defined as requisite correctives against the nonconformity of its predecessor, showing at once the historical contingency of the Bond formula and its continual flexibility. However, the pleasures of *Die Another Day* can perhaps be found in how it sits squarely in the crosshairs of several digital intermediaries, processes, and techniques developed in service of pristine photorealistic representation during the early 2000s. Just as Bond cinema returned in the mid-1990s with *GoldenEye* at the culmination of the "wonder years" era of digital VFX exploration, *Die Another Day* stylistically bears out postmillennial Hollywood's growing fascination with and economic investment in computer graphics. The 9/11 terror attacks would, inevitably, alter the trajectory of commercial cinema and its constructions of heroic masculinity, violence, paranoia, and terrorism, with a darkness in tone that presented the digital spectacle of *Die Another Day* as increasingly incongruous with U.S. cinema's "new action realist" preoccupations with visual restriction, "claustrophobic immediacy" and stylistic disjuncture.[46] Yet with Tamahori's film now past its twentieth anniversary, its display of "cutting-edge stuff" functions not simply as evidence of 007 finally breaking under the weight of technological innovation, but instead as an intriguing reminder (and remainder) of how Hollywood and its audiences were shaping and reacting to industrial and aesthetic redefinitions of the blockbuster's fundamental ingredients.

Notes

The epigraph is taken from Philip Kerr, "Never Say Die Another Day," *New Statesman*, November 25, 2002, 45.

1. Commercially, *Die Another Day* was the highest grossing Bond film, taking in approximately $60 million more than its predecessor, *The World Is Not Enough* (1999).

2. James Chapman, *Licence to Thrill: A Cultural History of the James Bond Films* (London: I. B. Tauris, 2007), 19.

3. Tony Bennett and Janet Woollacott, *Bond and Beyond: The Political Career of a Popular Hero* (Basingstoke, UK: Macmillan, 1987), 179.

4. See Hye Seung Chung, "From 'Die Another Day' to 'Another Day': The South Korean Anti-007 Movement and Regional Nationalism in Post–Cold War Asia," *Spectator* 27, no. 2 (Fall 2007): 64–78.

5. See Vincent M. Gaine, "New Action Realism: Claustrophobia, Immediacy, and Mediation in the Films of Kathryn Bigelow, Paul Greengrass, and Michael Mann," in *A Companion to the Action Film*, ed. James Kendrick (Oxford: Wiley Blackwell, 2019), 289–306.

6. Todd McCarthy, "The Accent's on F/X as Brosnan & Berry Bond," *Variety*, November 18–24, 2002, 23, 26.

7. Joshua Rothkopf and David Ehrlich, "The 10 Worst CGI Special Effects in Movie History," *Time Out*, June 9, 2015, www.timeout.com/film/the-10-worst-cgi-special-effects-in-movie-history.

8. A. O. Scott, "Bang! Splat! Kapow! Must Be That 007," *New York Times*, November 22, 2002, E-1.

9. John O'Connell, "Die Another Day," *Time Out London*, November 20–27, 2002, 85; Nicholas Barber, "Nobody Does It Better? Not on the Strength of This, Old Boy," *Independent on Sunday*, Arts section, November 24, 2002, 10.

10. Anthony Quinn, "Beyond Salvation," *Independent*, review, November 22, 2002, 8.

11. Rothkopf and Ehrlich, "10 Worst CGI."

12. Christopher Holliday, "'Old Dog, New Tricks': James Bond's Digital Chaos," *International Journal of James Bond Studies* 4, no. 1 (2021): 8.

13. Ian Nathan, "Living Another Day," *The Times*, section 2, November 4, 2002, 17.

14. Quoted in *"Die Another Day*: Final Production Notes," British Film Institute collections, 2002, 83.

15. Quoted in "*The World Is Not Enough*: Production Notes," British Film Institute collections, 1999, 73.
16. Eric Burgess, "The Making of *Moonraker*," *New Scientist*, June 1, 1979, 987, 986, 987.
17. Holliday, "Old Dog, New Tricks," 4.
18. Daniel Ferreras Savoye, *The Signs of James Bond: Semiotic Explorations in the World of 007* (Jefferson, NC: McFarland, 2013), 125.
19. Daya Alberge, "Fake Stunts Banished as New Bond Keeps It Real," *Times*, March 14, 2006, 22.
20. Lucy Bolton, "The Phenomenology of James Bond," in *Fan Phenomena: James Bond*, ed. Claire Hines (Chicago: Intellect, 2015), 73.
21. Alan Jones, "Die Another Day," *Cinefantastique*, June 2002, 6–7.
22. Orit Fussfeld Cohen, "The Digital Action Image of James Bond," *Quarterly Review of Film and Video* 33, no. 2 (2016): 108.
23. Johannes Binotto, "Bond Rerouted: 007 and the Internal Conflict in/of Digital Media," *SPELL: Swiss Papers in English Language and Literature* (Zurich Open Repository Archive) 29 (2013): 60.
24. André Millard, *Equipping James Bond—Guns, Gadgets, and Technological Enthusiasm* (Baltimore, MD: Johns Hopkins University Press, 2018), 183.
25. Michele Pierson, *Special Effects: Still in Search of Wonder* (New York: Columbia University Press, 2002), 96–97.
26. Pierson, *Special Effects*, 101; Stephen Prince, "True Lies: Perceptual Realism, Digital Images, and Film Theory," *Film Quarterly* 49, no. 3 (1996): 27–37.
27. Pierson, *Special Effects*, 93.
28. Klaus Dodds and Lisa Funnell, "From *Casino Royale* to *Spectre*: Daniel Craig's James Bond," *Journal of Popular Film and Television* 46, no. 1 (2018): 2–10, 2.
29. See David Bordwell, "Intensified Continuity: Visual Style in Contemporary American Film," *Film Quarterly* (Spring 2002): 16–28.
30. Tanine Allison, "The Modern Entertainment Marketplace, 2000–Present: Special/Visual Effects," in *Editing and Special/Visual Effects*, ed. Charlie Keil and Kristen Whissel (New Brunswick, NJ: Rutgers University Press, 2016), 173.
31. See Christopher Holliday, *The Computer-Animated Film: Industry, Style and Genre* (Edinburgh: Edinburgh University Press, 2018).
32. Julia Moszkowicz, "To Infinity and Beyond: Assessing the Technological Imperative in Computer Animation," *Screen*, Autumn 2002, 300.
33. Quoted in Jonathan Burston, "Synthespians Among Us: Rethinking the Actor in Media Work and Media Theory," in *Media and Cultural Theory*, ed. James Curran and David Morley (London: Routledge, 2006), 250.
34. Lisa Purse, *Digital Imaging in Popular Cinema* (Edinburgh: Edinburgh University Press, 2013), 24.
35. "Die Another Day," Box Office Mojo, www.boxofficemojo.com/release/rl2974778881/.
36. Dade Hayes, "Betting the Store," *Variety*, October 29–November 4, 2001, 43.
37. Allison, "Modern Entertainment Marketplace," 173.
38. *Die Another Day* shares with *Star Wars Episode II: Attack of the Clones* a cinematographer in David Tattersall.
39. Cohen, "Digital Action," 108.
40. Lev Manovich, *Software Takes Command* (New York: Bloomsbury, 2013), 259.
41. See Robert J. Stone and Philip Barker, "Serious Gaming: A New Generation of Virtual Simulation Technologies for Defence Medicine & Surgery," *International Review of the Armed Forces Medical Services* (June 2006): 120–28.

42. See Robert Alan Brookey, *Hollywood Gamers: Digital Convergence in the Film and Video Game Industries* (Bloomington: Indiana University Press, 2010).

43. Kerr, "Never," 45.

44. Christoph Lindner, "Introduction: Revisioning 007," in *Revisioning 007: James Bond and Casino Royale*, ed. Christoph Lindner (London: Wallflower, 2009), 7.

45. Lindner, "Introduction: Revisioning 007," 7.

46. Gaine, "New Action Realism," 296.

CHAPTER 21

WHAT MATTERS MORE

Hierarchies of Value in *Casino Royale* (2006)

CHRISTINE MULLER

(Re)Introducing James Bond

Casino Royale (2006) begins in Prague in black-and-white, a setting and look that evokes the Cold War, with its film noir aesthetic (figure 21.1). The Cold War served, in reality and in fiction, as an overarching context for the

Figure 21.1 Bond (Daniel Craig) assassinates a corrupt fellow agent on M's (Judi Dench) orders. This helps him to earn the authority to kill at his own discretion while on mission. *Casino Royale* (2006).

motivations, objectives, and obstacles for Western intelligence operatives. For James Bond, this context had long sufficed to rationalize his choices, however violent, for audiences—that is, the broader historical and political circumstances shaped and justified who Bond was, what he did, and why. Yet *Casino Royale* is set decades after the Cold War ended, with a more diffuse global threat environment in its place. As the next scene switches to color, a look indicative of the "present day" in film time, so too must viewers' understanding of Bond: What now? Without the compellingly stark "good guy/bad guy" framework of the Cold War, what does it mean to be a character who embodies the blunt force of national power against its miscellaneous adversaries?[1] As this chapter will explore, these questions echo those raised at the inception of the War on Terror, the Cold War's successor in dominating Western foreign policy, not just a backdrop against which the Daniel Craig era of Bond is set, but one that influences the films profoundly.

The Gloves Come Off

In the wake of Al Qaeda's September 11, 2001, attacks on the United States, analysis turned to why the U.S. security apparatus had not detected and thwarted the covert operation in advance. While plenty of blame made the rounds, former president Bill Clinton sustained specific criticism for failing to neutralize the threat of Al Qaeda leader Osama bin Laden when he had the chance. The 2004 *9/11 Commission Report* assessed these claims, identifying as many as nine missed opportunities to capture or kill bin Laden during the 1990s. The commission's review, evaluating decisions on whether and how to eliminate a shadowy adversary by clandestine means, illuminated the priorities that inhibited aggressive action, including "fear of civilian casualties, uncertainty in the intelligence, diplomatic fallout, bureaucratic inertia"—all this at a time when bin Laden had yet to be fully understood by the media and ordinary Americans as an acute danger to the United States. Moreover, President Clinton himself seemed to have favored capture over kill, a more complex objective to achieve.[2] In the end, then, an array of both practical and ideological considerations informed the conclusion each time that targeting bin Laden was not worth the risk. Perhaps it had been possible for the Clinton administration to remove bin Laden as a national security concern, but his removal was not the only concern, and others had taken precedence.

On a broad level, this weighing of multiple competing commitments reflected a kind of interregnum of orientation in U.S. foreign policy, between a Cold War environment in which a single recognizable priority—to counter and contain the Soviet Union—had shaped all others and the single-minded focus that would characterize what would come next: the War on Terror. On September 16,

2001, in the immediate aftermath of the September 11 attacks, U.S. Vice President Dick Cheney described for journalist Tim Russert the new attitude that he thought the United States needed to confront Al Qaeda, explaining,

> We also have to work, though, sort of the dark side, if you will. We've got to spend time in the shadows in the intelligence world. A lot of what needs to be done here will have to be done quietly, without any discussion, using sources and methods that are available to our intelligence agencies, if we're going to be successful. That's the world these folks operate in, and so it's going to be vital for us to use any means at our disposal, basically, to achieve our objective.[3]

The "dark side" and "shadows" that the vice president invoked augured an era for the United States of controversially violent intelligence-gathering techniques, all directed at the primary aim of protecting the homeland from a foreign terrorist menace, regardless of the potential for adjacent consequences that had constrained action in the previous decade. Cheney envisioned mission-dedicated operatives taking extreme risks and measures in the service of their country. In 2004, detainee photos made public from the Abu Ghraib U.S. military prison in Iraq presented a sample of some of the extreme measures taken against suspected enemies of the United States.[4] The pictures triggered rebukes to halt and make amends for the psychological and physical abuse, but in documenting the fact of it, this visual record incorporated into the layperson's conception of national defense a raw and sobering insight. Such would have been viewers' revised perspective by the time of *Casino Royale*'s release in 2006: a rebooted understanding of the world in which perils, values, and methods appeared very different from those of the Cold War backdrop for the majority of earlier Bond films.[5]

To match viewers' reset expectations, *Casino Royale* would offer a reset James Bond,[6] someone who could operate plausibly within what viewers now conceived as the torturous and merciless prerogatives of contemporary international espionage.[7] By providing an origin story, chronicling how the long-familiar fictional character of Bond first becomes and learns to serve as an MI6 secret agent with a license to kill, the film establishes a clean slate from whatever viewers once knew.[8] In effect, *Casino Royale* formally reintroduces Bond, tracing how a protagonist conventionally known for sexual promiscuity, conspicuous tastes, state-of-the-art gadgetry, and relatively sanitized conflict comes to embody a profession that requires emotional detachment, surreptitious infiltration, substantial investment of state resources, and the capacity for judicious brutality. Along the way, viewers witness how becoming James Bond involves a series of choices as Bond negotiates the tensions between his needs and desires as an individual and concerns beyond himself. Ultimately, he develops from someone whose impulses result in short-term personal satisfaction but long-term complications for the British national interest to someone whose purposeful decisions yield personal losses but advance the broader national interest. In the end, in keeping with the "gloves come off" ethos of the War on Terror, the movie suggests that, while many people and things might matter, some matter more. And Bond comes to decide, in light of the big picture, that duty matters above all else.

To Kill and (Possibly) Be Killed

In the film's first scene, Daniel Craig's James Bond is in the middle of earning oo status, or the ability to kill on his own authority while on assignment, a moment in the character's life that, for movie viewers, had always been an accomplished part of his past. To earn this status, viewers learn, he needs to kill two people. Flashbacks show the inglorious first kill in a nondescript bathroom, where Bond uses all means at his disposal, including an attempted drowning in a sink, in a ferocious, close-quarters struggle with the man (Darwin Shaw) who has led him to his second target. This second kill proceeds more seamlessly: on orders from the head of MI6, M (Judi Dench), from a small distance Bond simply shoots the man, the corrupt MI6 Prague section chief Dryden (Malcolm Sinclair). Next, viewers see the agent on a visceral foot chase of a bomb-maker, Mollaka (Sebastien Foucan), that ends with Bond, frustrated by Mollaka's apparent eluding of him, shooting the man in broad daylight. Soon, viewers also see Bond create a needed diversion at a hotel by damaging the expensive car of a stranger who had mistaken him for a valet earlier in the day. At that same hotel, Bond initiates a liaison with a married woman, Solange (Caterina Murino), to gather information on her husband, suspicious contractor Alex Dimitrios (Simon Abkarian). As soon as Bond gets the information he wants, he leaves her, mid-tryst, putting the mission above his personal gratification. In sum, *Casino Royale* introduces a Bond who is loyal to M and the nation they both serve, tenacious and single-minded when on a mission, capable of using—and sometimes even killing—others, merely as instruments of his own objectives, and a little spiteful after a loss or even a slight. Whether this mix of character traits suits a man with a license to kill would seem a valid question.

Indeed, early in the film, M criticizes Bond for shooting Mollaka, a killing that takes place at an embassy in front of many witnesses and is recorded on camera, provoking an international incident and critical press that angers Parliament. M chides Bond because he is "supposed to display some kind of judgment" rather than act as merely a "blunt instrument" and advises him that "arrogance and self-awareness seldom go hand-in-hand." Bond tells M that he felt eliminating the bomb-maker was worthwhile, but she retorts, "One bomb maker is hardly the big picture." It would seem that while Bond is able to sustain a laser focus on a specific task, he is not yet able to recognize and adequately assess varying, sometimes competing, priorities. Such are the stakes not only of the film, but also of the intelligence-gathering profession: how to operate in threatening environments, in the service of national interests—interests greater than one's own—as an individual with particular quirks, shortcomings, and attitudes toward other human beings, as well as with the capacity to wield lethal force. In the War on Terror era of which contemporary viewers were a part, such stakes would be understood to be real, a part of the ongoing public debate about the means by which clandestine perils can be discovered and disrupted.

In the real world, scholars and practitioners in the intelligence community have closely considered these issues that are at the center of *Casino Royale*. Arthur S. Hulnick and David W. Mattausch assert that the state has a duty to protect its people.[9] However, Jan Goldman notes a tension between "doing what's right" in terms of one's job—what one is supposed to accomplish—and "doing 'the right thing'" ethically.[10] To that end, Joel H. Rosenthal has argued, "Institutional design is . . . decisive in producing morally favorable results." At the same time, though, "hiring and promoting people of integrity in the profession—men and women with a strong moral compass—will encourage morally favorable outcomes at the level of personal decision-making."[11] After all, as R. V. Jones points out, given the scale of intelligence operations conducted in secrecy with the potential for malpractice, it would be difficult to monitor such operations publicly, so the "only safeguard is a firm sense of ethics among its operators."[12] Hulnick and Mattausch note specifically that honesty within an intelligence organization is crucial because the work is often performed without direct supervision.[13] Indeed, J. E. Drexel Godfrey quotes the U.S. Central Intelligence Agency's (CIA) motto "And the Truth Shall Make You Free" to underscore how truth, as a mode and an object of investigation, is articulated as an institutional mission.[14] In effect, both professional structures and personal prudence work together, guided by and aimed at truth, to generate successful results in life-and-death scenarios, an approach evoked when M admonishes Bond for poor judgment.

Where Trust Falls

It is clear, then, that trust and trustworthiness are foundational for service—including the fictional Bond's service—in a clandestine profession. Sociologist Anthony Giddens has considered the role that trust plays within the conditions of modernity more broadly. He argues that "*All* trust is in a certain sense blind trust" because "trust is only demanded where there is ignorance." Moreover,

trust is "bound up . . . with contingency," in that "trust in persons is psychologically consequential for the individual who trusts: a moral hostage to fortune is given." After all, "to trust is also . . . to face the possibility of loss."[15]
Though Giddens writes about a much broader context, his framework is
especially apt for espionage, a profession that, as discussed in the previous section, involves people acting in secret, trying to learn the secrets of others, with
potentially global ramifications for what those secrets might conceal or reveal.
The prominence of secrecy and the unknown within spycraft underscores the
preciousness and precarity of trust. The questions of whom to trust and how
to be trusted, while determining what is true, are critical for the successful work
and even survival of real-world intelligence operatives, as well as the fictional
Bond character.

Indeed, such questions are central to *Casino Royale*. The film's opening scene
shows what happens when trust is betrayed: On M's orders, Bond kills a fellow
agent who had been selling secrets. Also early in the story, he works in the field
with a colleague, Carter (Joseph Millson), who, at the very least, is unreliable;
his ineptitude complicates a mission. Later, when expressing concerns about
Bond's judgment in the field, M ties her concerns explicitly to trust. She urges
Bond to "take your ego out of the equation and judge the situation dispassion-
ately. I have to know that I can trust you and that you know who to trust."[16] As
the plot unfolds, viewers follow a Bond who does come to trust his life to two
people, Vesper Lynd (Eva Green) and René Mathis (Giancarlo Giannini). By
film's end, though, Lynd has betrayed him and he believes Mathis has as well.
As he tells Lynd, "I thought he had my back. But there you go. Lesson learned."
This disillusionment is echoed later when M asks Bond, "You don't trust anyone, do you James?" He answers, "No," to which she responds, "Then you've
learned your lesson. Get back as soon as you can. We need you." This lesson—
not to trust others—implicitly excludes M, for Bond remains under her command without any stated qualms, leaving intact an intelligence officer loyally
serving his nation. At the same time, presumably, Bond is himself trusted more
because his professional service comes with no personal strings attached. But,
apart from his newly affirmed suspicion of others, how has Bond exhibited the
kind of judgment that M prizes?

What Bond Does Not Seem to Value

The question of judgment, of determining what matters more when faced with
multiple commitments and enticements, sits at the center of *Casino Royale*'s
plot. After Bond's killing of Mollaka on camera creates an international scandal, M tells Bond that Parliament doesn't "care what we do. They care what we
get photographed doing." Although policy-makers remain at a remove from

Bond's day-to-day activities, mediated through comments such as these by M, such remarks frame the government for which Bond works as interested more in image than substance—very much the opposite of the interests he exhibited at the time he shot the bomb-maker. Still, when killing Mollaka, Bond was not simply motivated by mission necessity; losing the chance to remove what he considered a threat also meant that an objective had eluded him, a personal defeat that, as M points out, affronted his ego. Lynd later infers something similar. As Bond plays a high-stakes game of poker against terrorist financier Le Chiffre (Mads Mikkelsen), risking—as Lynd puts it—innocent lives on a game of luck, as their loss at the table would mean that Le Chiffre won funding for terrorism, she observes that Bond seems to be playing more for himself than for the greater good. Like M, Lynd questions the purity of Bond's motives; they both doubt, as M cautions at the outset, that he values the "big picture" as much as his own pride.

Importantly, though, while M and Lynd question Bond's judgment, they never question his integrity. From Dryden to Dimitrios to Le Chiffre, personal profit trumps other motivations. Dryden forsakes his country for money, Dimitrios—according to M—gets his livelihood from anyone willing to pay, and Le Chiffre's wealth depends on capitalizing on the violence of others. After all, Le Chiffre comes to M's attention, and then to Bond's, when he is connected to the short-selling of airline stocks, knowing that a terrorist bombing will reward his bet. To the contrary, while Bond shows a burgeoning signature affinity for expensive things, he never compromises his duty in order to secure them. Even more crucially, while torturing Bond to regain access to the money he lost gambling, Le Chiffre threatens to castrate the agent if he doesn't surrender the desired information. In effect, perceiving that Bond is willing to endure harm to his body rather than betray his nation and enable harm to innocent others, Le Chiffre tells Bond, "I'll feed you what you seem not to value." Still, Bond endures, indeed seeming not to value his own body as much as loyalty and service to his country (figure 21.2).

To be fair, viewers do see Bond from the start prioritizing objectives beyond short-term personal and professional interests. Certainly, he pushes against and even breaks through boundaries, including M's home and her computer. But his personal compulsions to do so are still in the service of the greater good of national security. Even when seemingly pursuing personal gratification, such as his seduction of Solange, he immediately turns back to the mission as soon as that seduction yields actionable intelligence. In fact, when Solange is tortured and murdered in retaliation for Bond's incursion into the criminal network with which her husband is involved, Bond seems unfazed by her fate. In an extended shot, only the barest trace of an altered facial expression hints that he might register anything other than pure indifference. Observing his reaction, or apparent lack of one, M comments, "I would ask you if you could remain

Figure 21.2 Bond (Daniel Craig) endures Le Chiffre's (Mads Mikkelsen) torture and threats in an unwavering commitment to his mission. *Casino Royale* (2006).

emotionally detached. But I don't think that's your problem, is it?" Lynd later infers this emotional detachment when she presents her first impression of Bond, telling him that "MI6 looks for maladjusted young men who'd give little thought to sacrificing others in order to protect queen and country" and that, to Bond, women are "disposable pleasures rather than meaningful pursuits." It would seem, then, that Bond begins this story as the person readers and movie audiences had already known him to be: an intelligence operative who treats sexual partners as diversions or opportunities, but ultimately prioritizes the mission over any personal attachments. However, Bond's relationship with Lynd complicates this shallow commitment to duty alone.

The Big Picture: What Bond Values More

Soon after they meet, Bond tells Lynd that she is not his type because he thinks she is single; he prefers women who are unavailable for a genuinely intimate and committed relationship. As the fate of Solange suggests, this detachment enables Bond to focus on his mission—and might enable women to stay safe from any collateral effects of his work. In fact, when Lynd asks whether killing bothers him, he responds no, explaining that he would not be good at his job if it did, an exchange indicating why emotional disengagement has been a central feature of the Bond character. Nevertheless, intimacy develops between them. While on a shared mission, they share risks and mortal endangerment, connections forged under duress that require close collaboration and trust and cultivate more of the same. After they both nearly die, Bond shows tenderness when comforting a traumatized Lynd, and after Bond learns that Mathis might be a double agent and Lynd might be in danger, he rushes to try to save her. By the time their mission ends, Bond and Lynd are in a genuinely intimate and committed relationship. In fact, Bond sends M his resignation from MI6 so that he and Lynd can be together—and he can retain his soul through this turn to love over duty.

Unfortunately for both Bond and Lynd, she is actually a double agent who returns the money won from Le Chiffre to Mr. White's (Jesper Christensen) shadowy organization. This is a betrayal for Bond on multiple levels. He loses trust in someone he loved, and therefore it is a betrayal of that love; he loses money belonging to his government, and therefore it is a betrayal of his duty to that government; and he loses in general—he does not accomplish what he aimed to achieve—and therefore it is a betrayal of the ego so integral to his character. In his fury, when an adversary threatens to kill Lynd if Bond does not retreat from their fight, Bond responds, "Allow me." Later, in words infamously echoing Ian Fleming's novel, Bond reports to M, "The job is done. The bitch is dead." By the end of the film, it seems that as Bond affirms his commitment to duty first, he has not simply resumed his emotional detachment toward women: he now also harbors an edge of contempt toward them and the vulnerability that had briefly distracted him from a more compelling responsibility.

Forging James Bond

By the end of *Casino Royale*, James Bond has become the man audiences have known all along: an emotionally unavailable, polished professional capable of using strategic violence in service to country. For sure, throughout this film, he persists steadfastly in his MI6 service under M. Yet, much like Bond's faint trace of unsettlement after Solange's death, his actions after Lynd's drowning belie the contempt he has expressed about her. After all, when Lynd is trapped under water, Bond hazards his own life to save her, even when it is clear that she is actively choosing to die. When M informs Bond that Lynd had actually sacrificed herself for him, the news registers with him, albeit subtly. Bond might have explicitly embraced his duty in this film as that which matters most, but traces of his relationship with Lynd seem poised to linger. Even though she is dead by the end of the film, his relationship with her is undoubtedly the most important relationship Craig's Bond has with a woman, and her shadow looms over the rest of his tenure as the character.

While torturing Bond, Le Chiffre reminds him that he is expendable, that his government would be willing to let him die if it meant that Le Chiffre remained available to provide intelligence on a dangerous criminal network. This humbles Bond, who recognizes this potential scenario as the "big picture," in which he plays as instrumental a role as any person he himself has used to obtain a grander objective. Nevertheless, his refusal to compromise a state secret evidences that, indeed, he seems not to value anything else, not even his own fate, as much as he values his duty. So begins the Daniel Craig era in the James Bond narrative arc, one nestled deep in the murky War on Terror context of risking all manner of collateral damage in pursuit of whatever is deemed the paramount ambition.

Notes

1. For how Daniel Craig's approach to James Bond lays bare the constructedness of the character's persona, creating space for critique, see Sarah Thomas, "The New Brutalism: Agency, Embodiment, and Performance in Daniel Craig's 007," *Journal of Popular Film and Television* 46, no. 1 (2018): 34–45.
2. Glenn Kessler, "Bill Clinton and the Missed Opportunities to Kill Osama bin Laden," *Washington Post*, February 16, 2016, www.washingtonpost.com/news/fact-checker/wp/2016/02/16/bill-clinton-and-the-missed-opportunities-to-kill-osama-bin-laden/.
3. Dick Cheney, "The Vice President Appears on *Meet the Press* with Tim Russert," The White House, September 16, 2001, georgewbush-whitehouse.archives.gov/vicepresident/news-speeches/speeches/vp20010916.html.
4. Seymour M. Hersh, "Torture at Abu Ghraib," *New Yorker*, April 30, 2004, www.newyorker.com/magazine/2004/05/10/torture-at-abu-ghraib.
5. For the relationships between Ian Fleming's novels, the Broccoli family's Eon Productions movies, and the Cold War, see Christine Berberich, "Putting England Back on Top? Ian Fleming, James Bond, and the Question of England," *Yearbook of English Studies* 42 (2012): 13–29; Jeremy Black, "The Geopolitics of James Bond," *Intelligence and National Security* 19, no. 2 (2004): 290–303; James Chapman, "Bond and Britishness," in *Ian Fleming and James Bond: The Cultural Politics of 007*, ed. Edward P. Comentale, Stephen Watt, and Skip Willman (Bloomington: Indiana University Press, 2005), 129–43; and Edward P. Comentale, Stephen Watt, and Skip Willman, "Introduction," in *Ian Fleming and James Bond*, xi–xxiii. For the film's post-9/11, War on Terror context, see Klaus Dodds and Lisa Funnell, "From *Casino Royale* to *Spectre*: Daniel Craig's James Bond," *Journal of Popular Film and Television* 46, no. 1 (2018): 2–10. For how *Casino Royale* reflects its time of production and reception, see Will Scheibel, "The History of *Casino Royale* on (and off) Screen," in *Revisioning 007: James Bond and Casino Royale*, ed. Christopher Lindner (London: Wallflower, 2009), 11–32.
6. See Douglas L. Howard, "'Do I Look Like I Give a Damn?' What's Right about Getting It Wrong in *Casino Royale*," in Lindner, *Revisioning 007*, 33–49 for how

filmmaking choices distinguish what he characterizes as the rebuilt Bond of *Casino Royale*. These revise the opening, Bond's level of sophistication, the use of gadgets and torture, the role of women, and what it means to be a spy.

7. See Trevor McCrisken and Christopher Moran, "James Bond, Ian Fleming and Intelligence: Breaking Down the Boundary between the 'Real' and the 'Imagined,'" *Intelligence and National Security* 33, no. 6 (2018): 804–21. McCrisken and Moran view the Bond stories, both fiction and film, as engaging not only with broad cultural and political trends, but also assumptions about the specific work of actual intelligence officers.

8. For how *Casino Royale* serves as a superhero origin story, see Robert P. Arnett, "*Casino Royale* and Franchise Remix: James Bond as Superhero," *Film Criticism* 33, no. 3 (2009): 1–16.

9. Arthur S. Hulnick and David W. Mattausch, "Ethics and Morality in U.S. Secret Intelligence," in *Ethics of Spying: A Reader for the Intelligence Professional*, ed. Jan Goldman (Lanham, MD: Scarecrow Press, 2006), 40.

10. Jan Goldman, "Preface," in Goldman, *Ethics of Spying*, xi.

11. Joel H. Rosenthal, "Foreword," in Goldman, *Ethics of Spying*, x.

12. R. V. Jones, "Intelligence Ethics," in Goldman, *Ethics of Spying*, 18.

13. Hulnick and Mattausch, "Ethics and Morality," 47–48.

14. J. E. Drexel Godfrey, "Ethics and Intelligence," in Goldman, *Ethics of Spying*, 2.

15. Anthony Giddens, *The Consequences of Modernity* (Stanford, CA: Stanford University Press, 1990), 33, 89, 33; idem, *Modernity and Self-Identity: Self and Society in the Late Modern Age* (Stanford, CA: Stanford University Press, 1991), 41.

16. Unfortunately for Le Chiffre, his shadowy criminal facilitator and eventual murderer Mr. White (Jesper Christensen) tells him, in an echo of what M tells Bond, "Money isn't as valuable to our organization as knowing who to trust."

CHAPTER 22

<hr style="width:15%;border-top:3px solid black;" />

"LIKE A BULLET . . ."

Speed, Economy, and Canonical Continuity in
Quantum of Solace (2008)

ESTELLA TINCKNELL

Although routinely regarded as a disappointing follow-up to 2006's successful reboot of the James Bond franchise with *Casino Royale*, *Quantum of Solace* (2008) actually distills many of the qualities found in its more expansive precursor into 106 minutes of fast-paced action and narrative urgency. This is particularly interesting given that *Quantum of Solace*, unlike earlier films in the series, is explicitly positioned as a sequel, starting as it does—in the world of the film—just fifteen minutes after *Casino Royale*'s ending, with the captured Mr. White (Jesper Christensen) stuffed into the boot of James Bond's (Daniel Craig) car as it streaks through an Italian mountain pass. *Quantum of Solace* condenses aspects of both narrative and action from *Casino Royale* and from the Bond universe into a hyper-intensified tour of the canon, complete with references to Ken Adam's iconic 1960s production design for the franchise and a villain whose ambition to dominate the world is given a topical environmental twist.

A Quantum of Disappointment

Quantum of Solace was certainly the least critically successful of the Craig-led films in the Bond franchise. Although it did respectably at the box office (outpacing *Casino Royale* in the United Kingdom and United States), it disappointed many reviewers.[1] The somewhat cryptic title was itself even used to capture the sense that the film had not quite delivered on the expectations set up by Craig's first outing.[2] *Quantum of Solace* undeniably lacks the verbal wit of its predecessor, with some exceptions such as Bond's sly subversion of his cover in Bolivia, favoring a largely somber tone and dialogue that rarely interferes with the action.[3] The theme song, "Another Way to Die" by Jack White and Alicia Keys, was also seen as something of a disappointment, but not until audiences heard Adele's Shirley Bassey–like powerhouse ballad for *Skyfall* in 2012. This is despite the pedigree of its composer-performers and a smooth accompanying title sequence by MK12 that does justice to the franchise's reputation for compelling openers in its thematic visualization of dunes and bullets. Nevertheless, *Rolling Stone* magazine's comment that "White and Keys' voices fit together like 007 and celibacy" is cruelly apt.[4] In fact, *Quantum of Solace* had a troubled production history. It was caught up in the 2007–2008 Writers Guild of America strike, which meant that the barely finished script could not be added to by professional screenwriters once production had started. Daniel Craig stated that he and director Marc Forster were permitted to "work on scenes together" without the help of a writer, but that this led to a relatively improvisatory filming environment.[5] Although the title was taken from Ian Fleming, the story was new, developed independently by coproducer Michael G. Wilson together with Forster and regular Bond scriptwriters Paul Haggis and Neal Purvis. The highly topical environmentalist theme was, according to Wilson, partly inspired by the California "water wars" plot of *Chinatown* (1974).[6] This was then tied into a more conventional Bond story encompassing a South American political coup involving a villain, Dominic Greene (Mathieu Amalric), whose supposedly ethical reforestation company is a front for the international Quantum conspiracy.

The twitchy Greene is a more conventionally plausible villain than many in the Bond canon; gratuitous physical deformity is here replaced by a nervy smile signifying the character's underlying tension. It is his cruelty toward his erstwhile girlfriend and the film's nominal "Bond Girl," Camille Montes (Olga Kurylenko), including trading her with impunity to the despotic Bolivian General Medrano (Joaquin Cosio), that initially confirms Greene's villainy. His eventual and ironic fate, once defeated, is to be abandoned by Bond to die in the very desert where his schemes to monopolize Bolivia's water supply have been hatched. Yet while eminently satisfying and poetically resonant, this outcome reduces political complexities to individual actions. In fact, the environmental theme is not fully realized. The effects of water shortages on already impoverished communities are signalled only halfway through the film, for example, so that the revelation that the precious resource at the heart of the conflict is water, not oil, is never fully exploited. Furthermore, by setting this ostensibly environmentally aware plot within a more conventional scenario featuring a mustachioed Latino bent on dictatorship, the film struggles to incorporate the two strands into the familiar Bond landscape. These lacunae presumably arose due to the difficult production conditions and the concomitant pressure to get the film completed.

But, as Steven W. Thomas argues, Bond movies cannot in any case seriously address the unequal power relations of international politics (whether environmental or economic), for the films are themselves part of the global order that produces them. They respond to and articulate contemporary issues through a "slanted representation" that "reconfirm[s] the ideology of maverick exceptionalism that has always driven the Anglo-American style of global capitalism and has always been Bond's signature ethos."[7] Bond is thus pitted against a series of individuals ("villains") whose ruthlessness in the service of profit and/or world domination is in many ways a distorted mirror image of his own behavior and values. *Quantum of Solace*'s concern with environmental degradation and exploitation is a plot point, not a manifesto.

Yet while they offer an ongoing fantasy of individualized potency and British agency in the figure of Bond, to sustain credible realism as spy thrillers the films have always engaged with shifts in global politics, ever since *Dr. No's* release in 1962 at the height of the Cold War. The early films were thoroughly immersed in the ideological battle for supremacy between the USA and USSR, with Bond working in alliance with the CIA, for example. Klaus Dodds and Lisa Funnell further point out that, as well as fantasy, audiences "want storylines that are attentive to changing geopolitical orders and reflective of real-world shifts from the Cold War to the War on Terror in films that remain mindful of Bond tradition as evinced through the manner in which 007 responds."[8] In *Quantum of Solace*, however, Britain is depicted as a very junior partner in the post-9/11 global system, in which, as Tobias Hochscherf argues, a complex intersection of "volatile markets, powerful global corporations and ephemeral political, economic and military alliances" are the new norm.[9] The film even foregrounds the extent to which transnational power is now supposedly contingent on such shadowy yet pervasive networks from the start: "The first thing you should know about us is that we have people everywhere," says Mr. White upon his capture. *Quantum of Solace* thus seemed to mark a low point in the franchise's long-nurtured fantasy of British political supremacy and, indeed, the "special relationship." M (Judi Dench) is kept in the dark about the CIA's intentions, which are personified in the shifty figure of Gregg Beam (David Harbour), its South America section chief, who colludes with Greene to secure access to what he believes are oil reserves. Such nods to realpolitik contribute to the film's dark tone.

Self-Reflexivity and Seriality

And yet, despite these caveats, *Quantum of Solace* remains a pivotal text in the transformation of the franchise in the Craig era into a serial narrative, complete with its own distinctive arc. Its economy of narrative and inventive locational shifts from Europe to the Caribbean, and thence to South America and back, make it a veritable speed tour of the Bond canon's habitual tourism. It is also replete with pleasurably knowing references to its predecessors, although *Quantum of Solace*'s pared-back style and absence of gadgets, gimmicks, and gizmos mean that these are contained within a relatively naturalistic diegesis. For example, Dennis Gassner's production design pays homage to the work of Ken Adam, the legendary art director who created the spectacular sets for *Dr. No* and *Thunderball* (1965). *Quantum of Solace* also "quotes" the brutal gold-painted death of Jill Masterson (Shirley Eaton) in *Goldfinger* (1964) when British agent Strawberry Fields (Gemma Arterton), MI6's Bolivian contact, is killed by being coated in "black gold": crude oil. The setting of scenes in Haiti further permits a passing reference to the (admittedly uncomfortably racist) voodoo themes of *Live and Let Die* (1973), while the stage set for the opera performance in Bregenza, discussed in more detail later, foregrounds a giant optic oddly reminiscent of *For Your Eyes Only* (1981).

The most obvious example of such continuities, however, is the fact that *Quantum of Solace* begins straight after Bond's ambush of Mr. White at the Lake Garda villa in *Casino Royale*'s final scene. Here, the open ending was perhaps partially obscured by Craig's long-anticipated utterance of the totemic phrase, "the name's Bond, James Bond," a moment that signalled his full assumption of Bond's mantle as well as the franchise's triumphant resurgence after a four-year hiatus, its drama underscored by the iconic James Bond theme finally being played in full. The fact that *Quantum* picks up the same story was, at that time, exceptional in a franchise that, despite a mythic textual universe constituted by recurrent and familiar elements, had been careful to present individual films as stand-alone narratives, enabling new and returning audiences equal opportunity to access Bond at any point in the series and in no particular order. However, Annette Pankratz and Svenja Bohm argue that the Craig films have increasingly blended the tropes of the classical self-contained episodic film *series*, exemplified by earlier Bond films, with a new *serial* format in which the interplay between past and present is central.[10] *Quantum of Solace*'s self-reflexive references to earlier films in the canon is one example of this increased intertextuality. Another is clearly its status as episode two of a connected and complex narrative arc that would only finally be completed in *No Time to Die* (2021), with references to the Ellipsis conspiracy and recurring secondary characters from *Casino Royale*, such as fellow agents René Mathis (Giancarlo Giannini) and Felix Leiter (Jeffrey Wright).

Solace, Suffering, Somberness

While *Quantum of Solace* sought to complete the transformation of Bond into an even leaner and more dispassionate action hero than was seen in *Casino*

Royale, the closure offered in the final moment when he symbolically abandons Vesper Lynd's (Eva Green) necklace is unusually poignant. Bond's romantic attachment to and betrayal by Lynd provides *Quantum of Solace*'s emotional undertow as well as aspects of the plot. It is, after all, the only Bond film in which the "Girl," Camille, remains unattached to our hero and whose romantic indifference is returned, even unto their final platonic kiss. Bond, we understand, is still too emotionally damaged to form anything other than a pragmatic alliance with her. Indeed, Lynd, like Tracy di Vicenzo (Diana Rigg) in *On Her Majesty's Secret Service* (1969), had already been figured as an exception to the fleeting liaisons embodied by other "Girls," and that is why her treachery and suicide are so wounding. Like Tracy, she "challenges [Bond] sexually and otherwise."[11] And like Tracy, she is dead and no longer poses a direct threat. Camille, by contrast, is an ally, not a sexual challenge.

Unlike the 1969 film, *Quantum of Solace* foregrounds the shift toward a more vulnerable and psychologically complex version of its hero through the Lynd narrative thread. This, and the inclusion of a putative origins story for Bond, clearly constituted a response to the successful *Bourne* series of spy thrillers (2002–), whose damaged protagonist unravels his own history alongside a government conspiracy, and to the emergent Marvel canon (2008–), with its emotionally conflicted superheroes. In effect, "[t]he producers remixed Bond within a corporate context that understood the modern superhero franchise."[12] Indeed, as Hochscherf points out, to retain his commercial and cultural power the character, alongside the films, has inevitably undergone cosmetic modernization over six decades, so that he "articulate[s] something in the general zeitgeist."[13] His reimagining as a troubled and volatile figure, whose toughness belies a latent vulnerability, leverages contemporary articulations of masculinity onto the Bond persona while retaining his heroic status. If anything, the origins narrative of Bond's orphaning and abandonment indicated in *Casino Royale*, which would become an important plot element in *Skyfall*, is even more powerfully condensed in *Quantum of Solace*'s emphasis on Bond's barely suppressed rage at the world. Although *Quantum of Solace*'s focus on spectacle leaves limited room for this to be narratively developed, it is thematically paramount.

However, it is notable that it also transfers ultimate responsibility for Bond's emotions onto a woman, Lynd, which implicitly legitimates his sexually exploitative behavior. Although *Quantum of Solace* is marked by its relative sexual restraint, it contains one significant reversion to the franchise's ideological norms of female disposability: Bond's seduction of agent Fields to ensure her complicity in his Bolivian adventure. As noted earlier, this leads directly to her sadistic murder. While Bond registers passing regret at this and M expresses maternal dismay at her wayward surrogate son's callousness, the film attributes his response to the emotional damage wrought by Lynd. While the ruthless way in which he disposes of Slate (Neil Jackson), the hired assassin encountered in

Port-au-Prince, suggests a habitual indifference to others' pain bordering on psychopathy, *Quantum of Solace* regularly reminds us of the reasons for Bond's emotional frigidity: inner torment caused by a woman's betrayal.

In the Craig era, these emotional modifications have also been accompanied by the intensification of naturalistically brutal action and by a new focus on the male body as the site of torment. Physical punishment is a key trope in *Quantum*, with Bond's body and face bearing the scars of successive beatings. Indeed, it packs more violence into its relatively short running time than any other film in the Bond canon. Yet Bond's suffering is, in theory, matched by Camille's. Like Bond, she is presented as on a mission of revenge due to a harrowing back story: her family were murdered by General Medrano and she narrowly escaped incineration at his hands. However, this is not accorded the narrative weight given to Bond's experience; it is only revealed at a relatively late point in the film, and its significance is therefore subordinated to the privileging of male anguish.

Camille is, however, depicted as having physical and moral courage and therefore fulfils the basic function of the "true" Bond Girl as defined by Lisa Funnell insofar as she is "lead female protagonist, central to the plot of the film and instrumental to the mission of James Bond."[14] Her relative autonomy renders her an anomalous figure, compounded by the film's internal logic, which romanticizes Lynd's memory. While Funnell regards this as evidence of *Quantum*'s refreshing attitude toward its main female character, noting that it "ends on an empowering and even feminist note" as Camille walks away from Bond into her own future, it is perhaps a significant (if unspoken) factor in the film's perceived failings: she is no longer available as fantasy love object, in contrast to the "Girl's" traditional function.[15]

Elemental

Funnell also argues that, in any case, Bond and Camille are ultimately incompatible because they represent two opposed elements: Bond is water, while Camille is fire.[16] *Quantum*'s set-piece climax certainly features the latter, while *Casino Royale* had already established Bond's association with water through a range of key sequences, from Craig's erotically charged emergence from the sea in the Bahamas to the penultimate Venice-set scenes in which Lynd drowns in one of the city's canals. These elemental contrasts are further heightened in *Quantum* through heat and cold, with Bond's sadistic chilliness and repressed feeling contrasted with Camille's volatile anger. Such distinctions are not confined to the characters: they permeate the film's visual and discursive texture in numerous ways and here, again, a somber tone frequently dominates. Yet *Quantum*'s deployment of starkly different "hot" and "cold" landscapes to point up the film's emotional and narrative shifts is also one of its spectacular pleasures. As Marcia Citron observes, the film deploys a palette that emphasizes the contrasts between these "cold" and "hot" spaces, with greys, blues, and whites dominating the former in London, Bregenz, and Kazan and reds, ochres, and browns the latter.[17] The final confrontation with Greene and Medrano at the grotesquely brutalist hotel, La Perla de las Dunas, in the vast, shimmering Atacama Desert, is its climax (figure 22.1).[18]

The hotel building is a crude imposition on the red soil of its natural surroundings, an emphatically manmade structure in its modernism, wholly at odds with Greene's ostensible commitment to sustainability. Its exterior resembles a prison, a further visual affirmation of Greene's character. Inside, the vast, empty public rooms lined with gold-colored tiles and furnished in steel and glass with spiky metal trimmings are suffused with a yellowish tint that echoes the harshness and aridity of the desert landscape. Such an expressionistic mise-en-scène presents an apt homage to Ken Adam's production design for the early Bond films, with their extravagantly futuristic features. The hotel also acts as the backdrop to the spectacular penultimate set-piece. This features rapid cuts between two action-packed struggles as Camille fights off the predatory Medrano while Bond tackles Greene, culminating in a dramatic explosion when the building catches fire. Balls of flames hurtle along the floors and stairwells in tongues of scarlet and gold that echo the luminescent heat of the desert outside.

An equally striking visual contrast is produced earlier in the film through the sequential juxtaposition of the "hot," dusty Haitian airfield from which Greene's private jet takes off, the cobbled nighttime streetscapes of his destination, Bregenz, and the "cold" metallic grey skies and corridors of London's Whitehall. These backdrops are further contrasted with the final main location, the bleak snow-covered streets of Kazan, where Bond will confront Lynd's

Figure 22.1 Red hot: La Perla de las Dunas catches fire. *Quantum of Solace* (2008).

lover, Yusef Kabira (Simon Kassianides), also a Quantum agent. The humid rooms and bar of a cheap Port-au-Prince hotel, together with its potholed surrounding streets and pockmarked buildings, offer a further dramatic contrast with the soaring modernism of the Bregenz open-air opera house, whose gleaming foyers are apparently reserved for the global elite. Each of these locations provides, in a different way, a visual inflection of the film's underlying tone of emotional desolation.

Indeed, the opera house scene, with its well-dressed white patrons sipping champagne and nibbling canapés, having arrived by luxury yacht or limousine, is one of *Quantum of Solace*'s few and fleeting nods to the franchise's traditional commitment to the "wealth fantasy" in which action is combined with a high-end lifestyle and glamorous backdrops to Bond's seductions. Jonathan Murray argues that many of the settings favored by the Craig cycle are notable for their bleakness, and that Craig spends much of his time "navigating ruins"; even the La Paz mansion where Greene hosts a swanky party in *Quantum of Solace* is crumbling, signifying the ruinous nature of his project.[19] In Bregenz, however, the luxurious mise-en-scène carries additional momentum as the site of a significant turning point in the film's narrative.

The opera house is hosting a performance of Puccini's *Tosca*. This text's melodramatic plot, replete with scenes of political conspiracy, torture, execution, and self-sacrifice, is clearly apposite; its conclusion, with the tragic suicide of the heroine, even mirrors that of *Casino Royale*. The opera's highly futuristic staging featuring a giant ice-blue eyeball also chimes with the foregrounding of technology in *Quantum of Solace*'s action and its emphasis on Bond's emotional coolness. By stealing an earpiece from one of the Quantum conspirators, he accesses a clandestine conversation conducted between its board members, for whom attendance at the performance is a smokescreen. Opera is not the signifier of elevated feeling or transcendental experience in these scenes (unlike its function in, for example, 1990's *Pretty Woman*). Instead, the performance of *Tosca* seems intended to dramatize the disturbed pathology of the Quantum members. The giant optic stage set even reflects Bond's own all-seeing and dispassionate eyes as he uses digital technology to acquire a panoptical view of the various conspirators. As Citron says, this "heighten[s] the feeling of a detached . . . subjectivity" already central to *Quantum of Solace*'s discursive structure.[20] Such detachment is further emphasized by the coldly "frenetic montage" of action that rapidly follows, as *Tosca*'s own final dramatic scenes of assassination and suicide are intercut with a high-speed chase through backstage spaces. Bond crashes through doors and along walkways, flinging aside catering trolleys stacked with food, in pursuit of the rogue British Quantum member Guy Haines (Paul Ritter). One might even argue that the use of *Tosca*'s final aria here to underscore the action follows Phil Powrie's concept of the "crystal song:" a musical performance in a nonmusical film that serves to crystallize its central themes through an affective and pivotal display.[21] This sequence is certainly characteristic of *Quantum of Solace*'s extreme privileging of spectacle over narrative, its positioning of Bond as both detached and enraged, and its accelerated pace.

Speed and Spectacle: *Quantum of Solace*'s Cinematic Attractions

Memorably, Marc Forster said he wanted the film to be "like a bullet," an apt metaphor literally visualized in *Quantum of Solace*'s breathless prelude, which has all the familiar hallmarks of the Bond pre-credits opener, but in an intensified form: it is fast, furious, spectacular, visceral, and thrilling. Bond's Aston Martin DBS is shown in a dizzying race along the precarious alpine route of Strada delle Forre in the Tremosine pass, before plunging into the narrow passageways of medieval Siena, where the renowned Palio horse race is taking place. Once inside the gates, demonstrating a mastery of the city's geography that matches his driving skills, Bond steers the now-battered vehicle into an apparently secret tunnel where MI6 agents, including M, are waiting. The film's first line of dialogue, spoken after this fifteen-minute prelude, is Bond's, brusquely addressed to Mr. White who has (we now understand) been stowed in the boot of the car throughout the journey: "It's time to get out." Such brevity is of a piece with the speed and economy of the action preceding it (figure 22.2).

   This opening car chase also offers a series of stunningly picturesque backdrops against which the action is played out. Here, however, the pace of the shots and editing is so rapid it is almost impossible to fully process at first viewing. The sequence opens on a view of Lake Garda, with the pass and tunnels a distant image, just visible beneath the rocky mountainside. The camera zooms across the water to a long shot of the tunnel's external structure and then plunges

Figure 22.2 Fast and furious: the opening chase scene. *Quantum of Solace* (2008).

the viewer straight into the action. Bond's car slews along the mountain road, slaloming in and out of lanes and between honking eighteen-wheelers, while his pursuers (presumably White's henchmen) shoot at him from accompanying vehicles. At the entrance to the tunnel, Carabinieri see Bond's car and those of his antagonists heading for a nearby quarry and pursue them, although Bond manages to shake off both the law and the outlaws with predictable ease. This sets up what will follow. There is little in the way of exposition, and the story connections are subordinated to the thrill of a cinema of attractions. The fact that Siena is geographically distant from Tremosine, and that there is little narrative logic for MI6's presence there, is less important than that the Palio offers a dramatic visual contrast between the high-spec automobiles involved in the chase and the ritual of the medieval horse race.

Later, in Port-au-Prince, and notably without the conventional overtures that mark the arrival of the "Bond Girl" and set her up for a desiring gaze, Montes is introduced—right at the start of an equally frenetic action sequence. As Bond escapes the hotel where he has just killed his would-be assassin, Slate, she screeches to a halt in her Ford Ka and orders him, "Get in"—which he promptly does. (Bond Girls are permitted to issue instructions when their actions are ultimately supportive of our hero's, of course.) This initial encounter is the briefest of preludes to another spectacularly intense car chase, this time through the streets of the Haitian capital, initially pursued by another of Greene's associates whom Bond deals with as efficiently (if less brutally) as he has earlier antagonists. Criss-crossing junctions and lights, the little Ka darts in out of the stream of traffic, at one point causing a truck laden with elaborate coffins (knowingly signifying Haiti's death rate, as well as the country's attachment to funereal ritual) to overturn, its load scattered on the roadside.

Closure and Continuity: James Bond Will Return . . .

Quantum of Solace is exceptional in its use of the romance between Bond and Lynd as a major and haunting theme that connects the story to *Casino Royale*. This is especially important because it is the only counterpoint to the film's otherwise furious speed. A pivotal moment occurs after an explosive aerial dogfight with Bolivian fighter planes, when Bond and Camille shelter in a cave, leading to an interlude wherein they disclose their differing motives for seeking out Greene. As Bond hints at his melancholy, Vesper's lyrical leitmotif is heard on the soundtrack, a brief ostinato in a minor key and one that appears at other poignant moments in the story. This musical reference is long enough to register Vesper as an absent presence shaping Bond's emotional landscape. And yet it is also clear that Bond must abandon his attachment to Lynd if he is to fully reclaim his heroic status.

The leitmotif is heard again at the very end of the film after Bond has confronted Kabira. On this occasion he leaves the Quantum agent sufficiently alive to be interrogated, indicating a new maturity. As M approaches Bond outside Kabira's apartment, the Vesper leitmotif wells up on the soundtrack and the camera pans downward to the snow-covered ground. There, nestling in the whiteness, lies the Algerian love-knot necklace that Vesper wore; Bond has evidently been carrying it since her death and can now, finally, abandon it, having found closure. This permits the narrative to end and the Vesper story itself to be completed, a finality signalled by a significant shift in tone as, like *Casino Royale*, the "James Bond theme" finally plays in full, with the usual gun barrel sequence to underline its importance and the narrative's closure. Because *Quantum of Solace* has so effectively staged and then resolved Bond's despair, both in its emphasis on furiously frenetic action and in its emotionally desolate atmosphere, it paves the way for Bond to fully recover his equanimity, his status, and his virility in its sequels.

Notes

1. See, for example, Peter Bradshaw's review in *The Guardian*, October 18, 2008, www
.theguardian.com/film/2008/oct/18/jamesbond1 and Roger Ebert's online review,
November 11, 2008, www.rogerebert.com/reviews/quantum-of-solace-2008, although
Kim Newman in *Empire* appreciated its brevity and pace: August 2, 2008, www
.empireonline.com/movies/reviews/quantum-solace-review/.

2. See, for example, Jim Vejvoda's review for IGN, October 10, 2008, www.ign.com
/articles/2008/11/01/quantum-of-solace-review-5.

3. Having been told by his contact that their cover is that they are "teachers on sabbatical," Bond promptly abandons the allocated downmarket hotel and goes to the swankiest place in La Paz, where he announces this as fact, followed by "who have won the lottery," to a smirking receptionist.

4. David Ehrlich in *Rolling Stone*, November 2, 2015, www.rollingstone.com/music/music
-lists/james-bond-movie-theme-songs-ranked-worst-to-best-154927/.

5. Quoted in Matt Goldberg, "Daniel Craig Talks about the Script Problems on *Quantum of Solace*: Says Why He's Encouraged for *Skyfall*," Collider, December 7, 2011, collider.com/daniel-craig-quantum-of-solace-script-problems/.

6. Stax, "The Secrets of Quantum of Solace," IGN, April 4, 2008, web.archive.org/web
/20080410000608/http:/uk.movies.ign.com/articles/864/864542p1.html

7. Steven W. Thomas, "The New James Bond and Globalization Theory: Inside and Out,"
Cineaction 78, no. 78 (May 2009), 34.

8. Klaus Dodds and Lisa Funnell, "From *Casino Royale* to *Spectre*: Daniel Craig's James
Bond," *Journal of Popular Film and Television* 46, no. 1 (January 2018): 4.

9. Tobias Hochscherf, "Bond for the Age of Global Crises: 007 in the Daniel Craig Era,"
Journal of British Cinema and Television 10, no. 2 (April 2013): 306.

10. Annette Pankratz and Svenja Bohm, "Play It Again, James: Seriality in the Craig Bond
Films," *International Journal of James Bond Studies* 3, no. 1 (Spring 2020): 4.

11. Stephen Nepa, "Secret Agent Nuptials: Marriage, Gender Roles and the 'Different Bond Woman' in *On Her Majesty's Secret Service*," in *For His Eyes Only: The Women of James Bond*, ed. Lisa Funnell (New York: Wallflower, 2015), 192.

12. Robert P. Arnett, "*Casino Royale* and Franchise Remix: James Bond as Superhero," *Film Criticism* 33, no. 3 (Spring 2009): 2.

13. Hochscherf, "Bond for the Age of Global Crises," 300.

14. Lisa Funnell, "From English Partner to American Action Hero: The Heroic Identity and Transnational Appeal of the Bond Girl," in *Heroes and Heroines: Embodiment, Symbolism, Narratives and Identity*, ed. Christopher Hart (Kingswinford, UK: Midrash, 2008), 63.

15. Lisa Funnell, "Reworking the Bond Girl Concept in the Craig Era," *Journal of Popular Film and Television* 46, no. 1 (April 2018): 17.

16. Funnell, "Reworking the Bond Girl," 16.

17. Marcia J. Citron, "The Operatics of Detachment: *Tosca* in the James Bond Film *Quantum of Solace*," *19th-Century Music* 34, no. 3 (April 2011): 318.

18. The Brutalist exterior of the hotel was, in reality, the scientists' accommodation at the Paranol Observatory in Chile.

19. Jonathan Murray, "Containing the Spectre of the Past: The Evolution of the James Bond Franchise during the Daniel Craig Era," *Visual Culture in Britain* 18, no. 2 (July 2017): 6.

20. Citron, "Operatics of Detachment," 318.

21. Phil Powrie, *Music in Contemporary French Cinema: The Crystal-Song* (London: Palgrave Macmillan, 2017).

CHAPTER 23

"SOMETIMES THE OLD WAYS ARE THE BEST"

Technology and the Body in a Gothic Reading of
Sam Mendes's *Skyfall* (2012)

MONICA GERMANÀ

M arking the fiftieth anniversary of the James Bond franchise, Sam Mendes's *Skyfall* (2012) aptly explores the role of the ageing hero and MI6's "old-fashioned ways" in the modern world of espionage. After the Pierce Brosnan era, the casting of Daniel Craig to play James Bond in the adaptation of Ian Fleming's 1953 debut novel *Casino Royale* (2006) ushered in a new kind of Bond film, interested in exploring the hero's physical and psychological vulnerabilities. Building on the introspective emphasis placed on Bond's scarred body and traumatized psyche in both *Casino Royale* and *Quantum of Solace* (2008), in Craig's third film, *Skyfall*, Bond struggles as an ailing—and increasingly middle-aged—agent, M (Judi Dench) is encouraged to retire, and MI6 is accused of holding on to the traditional stratagems of "the golden age of espionage." Meanwhile, new blood in the forms of a youthful Q (Ben Wishaw) and Eve Moneypenny (Naomie Harris) appear to challenge Bond's heroic status and performance; as the newly appointed Chairman of the Intelligence and Security Committee, Gareth Mallory (Ralph Fiennes), puts it, "It's a young man's game."

The film channels its exploration of ageing through a thematic opposition between the cutting-edge technology at the service of the villain Raoul Silva (Javier Bardem) and MI6's obsolete strategies and equipment. In highlighting the challenges that new technologies pose to both Bond and MI6, the film's focus on cyberterrorism points to the natural/artificial, human/monster dichotomies that have been at the heart of Gothic science fiction since the publication of Mary Shelley's *Frankenstein* (1818), a novel with which, arguably, *Skyfall* establishes significant parallels. As Gothic narratives are both haunted by the past and unsettled by change ushered in by the future, similarly *Skyfall* sets out to excavate Bond's past traumas while it questions the future of technology.

Technology and the Bond Franchise

Before moving on to a detailed analysis of *Skyfall*, it is useful to reflect on technology's ambiguous function throughout the Bond franchise. From the threat of nuclear weapons in Bond's inaugural film, *Dr. No* (1962), to the deadly nanobots of *No Time to Die* (2021), technology has both been central to Bond's success and a controversial tool in the villain's grand plans for mass destruction. Bond's cars, all invariably equipped with concealed technological devices to aid his missions, have ranged from the iconic Aston Martin DB5, which debuted in *Goldfinger* (1964) and significantly returns in *Skyfall*, to the underwater Lotus driven by Roger Moore in *The Spy Who Loved Me* (1977), and Brosnan's invisible Aston Martin Vanquish in *Die Another Day* (2002).[1] Besides his enhanced vehicles, Bond's gadgets have included grenade pens, x-ray glasses, infrared film cameras, bug detectors and, of course, lethal guns.

If, on one hand, Bond appears to be perfectly in control of any technological device that is thrown his way, on the other, his mind remains resistant to the control that technology can exercise upon the human user. As Steven Zani suggests, "The danger of technology . . . is that we will always become that which we do." Influenced by Martin Heidegger, Zani returns to the Greek etymology of technology, "*Technê*," a term "associated with craftsmanship and artistic endeavor," to note that "[m]ore comprehensive than simply using tools, . . . technology is very closely related to *Wissen*, wisdom." It is this distinctly human wisdom that juxtaposes the villain's unregulated and hubristic love-affair with technology against Bond's human agency: "[I]n Bond, we see freedom rather than control, and a world where nature and technology help to define humanity, instead of consuming it."[2] Whereas Bond's wisdom succeeds in controlling technology, the villains' technological obsessions directly or indirectly cause their demises; thus, Dr. No (Joseph Wiseman) drowns in the radioactive water tank of his nuclear plant; a shot fired from his own golden gun kills Auric Goldfinger (Gert Fröbe); in *Tomorrow Never Dies* (1997), media tycoon Elliot Carver's (Jonathan Pryce) body is shredded by the same sea drill that he uses to sink HMS *Devonshire* in order to create highly profitable sensationalist headlines; computer programmer Boris Grishenko (Alan Cumming), henchman to Alex Trevelyan (Sean Bean), is killed by a vat of nitrogen in his own lab in *GoldenEye* (1995). "While the villains appear to be obsessively infatuated with their own technological dreams," as Keren Omry concludes, "for

Bond, technology remains an (external) object tool which serves to enhance his own powers as 007."[3]

While they warn against the dangers of technological excess at large, the Bond films also specifically address the most pressing issues raised by the cultural contexts in which they are situated. The earlier films therefore tie nuclear threats to Cold War politics, whereas Bond's more recent forays have shifted their emphasis to genetic engineering (*Die Another Day*), the environmental crisis (*Quantum of Solace*) and, presciently, the lethal power of a pandemic (*No Time to Die*). In the 1990s films—*GoldenEye, Tomorrow Never Dies,* and *The World Is Not Enough* (1999)—Brosnan's Bond showcases, as Martin Willis observes, "unlimited technological ability whose expert knowledge of applied science maintains a Western stranglehold on political, economic, and cultural power in an Information Age wrought by fears of millennium catastrophe."[4] In spite of his proven technical abilities, however, in these films Bond ultimately reaffirms faith in the human, exorcizing millennial anxieties about the rise of technocratic regimes and technological crime by placing the human subject in control of—and not at the mercy of—scientific and technological advances.

In a radical reaction to the SF technology of the 1990s, Craig's Bond launches, as Omry rightly notes, a "dramatic return to the body" and, simultaneously, a technophobic turn. Leaving behind the implausible gadgetry of the Brosnan era, *Casino Royale* places a more distinctly Gothic emphasis on the permeability of the human body to the threat of technology. From the start, *Casino Royale* displays the conflict between technology and Bond through an emphatic penetrative act when a tracking device "is literally inscribed on—and inserted into—his flesh." Bond's body literally bears "the scar of technology," a wound that speaks of his human physicality and resistance to the technocratic villains on one hand, and the concealed mechanics of digital technology on the other.[5] Although Bond can use digital technology to his own advantage in *Skyfall* and in *Quantum of Solace*, where identification imaging facilitates the traceability of suspects in real time, both films implicitly articulate the fear that "technology exerts a dehumanizing power that will kill us, or enslave us, or make us into mere nodes on a digital grid."[6] This is the "soft" threat of data technology: as cyberterrorism scholar Alan O'Day claims, "More than ever before, conflicts are about 'knowledge,' about who knows or can be kept from knowing what, when, where and why."[7] In other words, the new technological threats come from the invisible order of digital information, and this is conveyed through the multiple ghosts and hauntings of *Skyfall*.

Skyfall: "Old Dog, New Tricks"

It is the fear engendered by this most invisible and insidious side of technology, the fictional exploration of which was pioneered in William Gibson's cyberpunk novel *Neuromancer* (1984), that *Skyfall* investigates as it elevates the conflict between old and new technologies into the realm of global cybercrime. Silva's cyberattacks on MI6 and consequent publication of the confidential details of undercover agents on YouTube are driven by a personal revenge against M, who, on Silva's prior mission, handed him over in exchange for six agents held by the Chinese services, despite the fact that he was "a brilliant agent." Though it was triggered by M's betrayal, his assault displays the *modus operandi* of cyberterrorism, the remit of which reaches beyond the personal feud in order to cause extensive global damage. The "soft" power of global cyber-terrorism is, as Silva boasts in an attempt to shift Bond's loyalties, virtually limitless—"Destabilize a multinational by manipulating stocks? Easy. Interrupt transmissions from a spy satellite over Kabul? Done."—and seemingly effort-less: "Rig an election in Uganda? Just point and click." The film's treatment of cyberterrorism draws attention to the "overlap of cyberspace and terrorism," thus bringing together two significant modern fears: the fear of technology and the fear of terrorism."[8]

In contrast to the villain's technological sophistication, MI6 appears vulner-able and ill-equipped from the start of *Skyfall*, which begins with the theft of a hard drive containing sensitive information and Bond's attempt to retrieve it in Istanbul from Patrice (Ola Rapace), a "ghost" mercenary assassin who has "no known residence or country of origin." Back at the MI6 headquarters in Vauxhall, Tanner's (Rory Kinnear) frustration at technological failures—"We've lost tracking. We're blind here. What's going on? . . . Get me CCTV, satellite, anything!"—alludes to the agency's technological inadequacies against the invis-ible weapons of cyberterrorism. That MI6 is an anachronistic institution, out of touch with the more modern ways of intelligence, is made spectacularly clear when the headquarters, crumbled to the ground by Silva's computer-generated bomb attack, are declared "strategically vulnerable" and relocated to an under-ground section of Winston Churchill's old bunker, a fact that prompts Silva to gloat, "All that physical stuff . . . So dull, so dull. Chasing spies . . . so old-fashioned! . . . England. The Empire! MI6! You're living in a ruin as well. You just don't know it yet. At least here there are no old ladies giving orders and no little gadgets from those fools in Q-Branch." As Silva claims, the move reflects its clinging on to the old ways of "hard" intelligence and physical contact, defense strategies appropriate to the "old world" order, and an example of the ways in which Bond, MI6 and, in general, modern Britain are still haunted by the Empire.

Skyfall's discourse on technology is made more complicated by the film's concurrent exploration of the hero's ageing body and traumatized psyche. Significantly, Q's first meeting with Bond, who has been recently injured—albeit in error—by Moneypenny, is in front of Joseph Mallard William Turner's *The Fighting Temeraire, Tugged to Her Last Berth* (1839), a painting depicting an old warship's last journey to the scrap yard, delivering a melancholic reflection on ageing and "the implications of technological progress."[9] In response to Bond's comment that "youth is no guarantee of innovation," Q's awareness of the soft power of digital technology—"I'll hazard I can do more damage on my laptop sitting in my pyjamas before my first cup of Earl Grey than you can do in a year in the field"—seemingly equates youth with a willingness and ability to embrace new technologies. More specifically, Q's statement reinforces the notion that modern-day warfare has moved away from the battlefield and into cyberspace, replacing "hard" artillery with the "soft" weaponry of data and codes. "We do not go for exploding pens anymore," Q pronounces on presenting Bond with only a gun and a radio for his imminent mission.

Uncanny Technology

If old and new technologies register the generational divide between MI6's old and new guard, the real history of Hashima, the location of Silva's own head-quarters, is both haunting and haunted by the uncanny coexistence of old and new. A mining settlement established by the Mitsubishi Corporation in the 1890s, the island's population rapidly grew to reach five thousand people, when "giant, multi-storey concrete apartment blocks went up. Schools, bath houses, temples, restaurants, markets, even a graveyard, were built, all on a space the size of a football field."[10] As quickly as it sprang up, the community of Hashima suddenly vanished in 1974 when, as the coal ran out, Mitsubishi closed down the settlement and promised to offer jobs to the redundant work-ers back in mainland Japan on a first-come first-served basis.

The Gothic spectrality of Hashima's once-thriving community was poi-gnantly captured in the 2002 documentary *Hashima, Japan*, forty years after the mine closed down: "There are ghosts there for sure," claims the director Thomas Nordanstad, and "there is something not right about the place."[11] Accompanied by the haunting soundtrack of synthetic music and the whirring sounds of malfunctioning technology, the documentary's chilling shots of the dilapidated buildings, broken furniture, cooking utensils, and children's toys left behind as people hurriedly fled the island encapsulates the uncanny effects of technological "progress." As Fred Botting explains: "The uncanny, less a return from the past, becomes an effect of a disturbed present, a present affected by massive upheaval and transformation. It is less the revenance of a lost or sup-pressed human nature (against the artifices of modern culture) and more a prod-uct of scientific and technical innovation."[12] Rather than situated against the decadent backdrops and luxurious fittings of, for instance, Stromberg's (Curd Jürgens) and Hugo Drax's (Michael Lonsdale) lairs in *The Spy Who Loved Me* and *Moonraker* (1979), respectively, the ghost island of Hashima accommodates the death of old technologies and the rise of the new, providing a suitably Gothic background to the nebulous elusiveness of cybercrime and of the "shadows" and "ghosts" like Silva and Patrice who are enmeshed in its global dealings.

Underpinning the insidious mechanics of global capitalism and the uncanny adjacency of old and new technologies, Hashima becomes the place where the short-lived Bond Girl Sévérine (Bérénice Marlohe), a former Macau child prostitute and Silva's captive associate, is callously used as a shooting target and eventually executed. No longer a useful tool once her loyalty is compromised, Sévérine quickly becomes, as Silva suggests, "redundant" and, like a piece of obsolete technology, must be "eliminated." Nevertheless, the scene's soundtrack— Charles Trenet's 1938 hit "Boume," a song that ironically celebrates love and *joie de vivre*—and the fatal weapon, an antique pistol, ambiguously position Silva as oscillating between the future and the past. The implication, therefore, is that the villain is as haunted by his own past as Bond himself.

The Hero and the Monster

In one of the film's most compelling scenes, a confrontation in Hashima simultaneously blurs the hero/villain boundaries and emphasizes Silva's "strangeness" against Bond's "normality." Silva's cream-colored jacket, patterned shirt, and bleached blond hair stylize him outside the paradigms of straight masculinity, which Bond wears as effortlessly as his impeccably cut navy suit and white shirt, which Silva teasingly unbuttons to reveal Bond's scarred chest (figure 23.1). An inverted mirror to the Macau hotel room shaving scene when Bond attempts to unbutton Moneypenny's dress (figure 23.2), the overt homoerotic hints in Silva's flirtatious line ("There's a first time for everything") and Bond's response ("Who says it's my first time?") might look like a playful challenge to the agent's heteronormative masculinity. In fact, rather than sameness, the scene articulates otherness, as it highlights Silva's queerness. A trait frequently found in a Fleming Bond villain, who, as noted by Umberto Eco, "often appears monstrous and sexually impotent," sexual deviancy underpins the villain's "body monstrous—that is, frightening or ugly, abnormal or disgusting."[13] Inscribed on the villain's body is a kind of multilayered monstrosity that, as Jack Halberstam observes, marks the difference between "a pervert and a normal person, a foreigner and a native."[14] Indeed, as his name, accent, and demeanor convey, Silva is as queer as he is foreign, reproposing a familiar convergence of the franchise's complicated gender and colonial politics.[15]

Significantly, it is in the Gothic setting of MI6's subterranean prison that Silva's strangeness turns into horrific monstrosity, through the display of a facial deformity caused by an unsuccessful suicide attempt whilst in Chinese captivity. If the use of the prosthetic maxilla reminds us of the more comical figure of Jaws (Richard Kiel) in *The Spy Who Loved Me* and *Moonraker*, it is also much more problematic, as, rather than enhancing human strength with the addition of an extra weapon, it suggests physical damage and disability: as Silva poignantly puts it, "life clung to me like a disease." Moreover, as Silva's

Figure 23.1 Silva (Javier Bardem) confronts Bond (Daniel Craig). *Skyfall* (2012).

Figure 23.2 Bond (Daniel Craig) attempts to unbutton Moneypenny's (Naomie Harris) dress. *Skyfall* (2012).

final address to M—"Do you know what hydrogen cyanide does to you?"—reveals that the scars on Silva's body and mind are the direct result of MI6's inhuman procedures, the scene points to the ambiguous overlap of monster and victim, a trope frequently investigated, as Botting observes, in the Gothic: "Instead of being repulsive, monsters attract; instead of being destroyed, they must be loved. Repression is relocated: in identifying with outcasts and victims, those 'othered' and 'monstered' by repressive state apparatuses, they become charged with romantic rebelliousness."[16] Seen as a reaction to MI6's merciless exploitation of its own agents, Silva's cyber-attack points to the subversive politics of data hacking, a fact underscored by Silva's alleged resemblance with WikiLeaks hacker Julian Assange.[17] As "illegal" code-cracking juxtaposes "formal institutions . . . which were previously able to dominate access to information and . . . dissidents, who, with growing confidence, are able to circumvent traditional networks through technology," the film traces a fine line, arguably, between rebellious hackers and cyberterrorists.[18]

Raoul Silva was always "a slippery one," as M recalls. The meaning of the villain's name further complicates our understanding of his elusive identity and ambivalence toward Bond, M, and MI6. Meaning "forest" in Latin, "Silva" is evocative of the natural environment most associated, as Elizabeth Parker cogently argues, with the archetypal fear of that which remains "mysterious, shadowy, and just out of sight."[19] While "Bond villains" are typically "defined by how they take the natural world and mold it into their own image," the film points to Silva's monstrous behavior and "unnatural" body as the consequence of the British Secret Service's inhuman treatment of their own agents.[20] "Look upon your work, mother," Silva taunts M, branding her as the Frankensteinian creator of his monstrous body. Conversely, it is significant that M not only refuses to call Silva by his real name, Thiago Rodríguez, but also that she will have it erased from the MI6 memorial wall, adding that "soon your past will be as non-existent as your future." Just like Frankenstein's creature, Silva is relegated to the state of a nameless Other, a mere tool in the hands of an institution ready to dispose of him when he is no longer useful.

Surprisingly, this is where Bond and the villain's predicaments share common ground. As William McKinney notes, the franchise's distinction between James Bond (the individual) and 007 (MI6's tool) points to the use of code names instead of personal ones to privilege "function" over identity: "As 007, he [Bond] becomes precisely that which MI6 demands of its double-o agents—a weapon to be used, or discarded, as his superiors see fit."[21] As Silva points out while still in Hashima, this is exactly the kind of callous treatment M has also inflicted on Bond, by sending him back into the field in an unfit state: "Mummy was very bad," he concludes. Both Silva and Bond are, effectively, damaged goods and, in Silva's eyes, MI6 "has changed their nature." Like the rats forced by hunger to prey on each other in Silva's grandmother's story, both agents, whose ageing bodies and traumatized psyches are at risk of redundancy, embody a wounded kind of masculinity.

The characters' different answers to the questions of ageing and wounded heroism emerge in the film's treatment of technology. The theme is addressed emphatically by M, whose professional role and judgment have also been put into question since the data-leak incident. At the hearing with the Defence Minister, M's quote from the last lines of Tennyson's 1842 poem "Ulysses" significantly captures the vulnerability and courage of the ageing hero, and, simultaneously, justifies MI6's relevance in the fast-changing world of intelligence:

> We are not now that strength, which in old days
> Moved earth and heaven; that which we are, we are;
> One equal temper of heroic hearts,
> Made weak by time and fate, but strong in will.
> To strive, to seek, to find and not to yield.

While, arguably, both hero and villain could be described as "Made weak by time and fate, but strong in will," what sets Bond and Silva apart is their negotiation of their traumatic pasts, an act articulated by technology; whereas Silva's technology flashes forward to successfully embrace the connectivity of the global world, Bond confronts his past by holding on to what he knows. Silva's strategy is a subversive throw into the dark nebulousness of the future and a global centrifugal force against England and the Empire; Bond's unconditional loyalty to Queen and Country clings to the solidity of the past and reconnects him to his Scottish roots.

Bond's Revenants

The plot's move to Scotland, and, more precisely, to Bond's family home at Skyfall, in the heart of the Scottish Highlands, acts as a conduit for the agent's return to his personal past, a journey fittingly performed in his old Aston Martin DB5. It is here that the conflict between old and new, traditional and modern technologies is played out to Bond's benefit. Foreshadowed in the Gothic dilapidation of subterranean London and the uncanny spectrality of Hashima, the film depicts the Highlands as a different kind of haunted space, one that is personal and local rather than institutional and global, for in returning to Scotland, Bond reopens the wound of his parental loss. The architectural style of the house, its dark wood panelling and ghostly veils of cobwebs, all contribute to its reading as an eminently Gothic space: "Like all great ladies, she has her secrets," claims Kincade (Albert Finney), the old family gamekeeper.

The film's photography engages with a specific pictorial tradition of Scotland, exemplified by Edwin Henry Landseer's paintings of barren and moody Highland scenery, wilderness and wildlife; indeed, his iconic depiction of a majestic stag in *The Monarch of the Glen* (1851) is visibly mirrored in the sculpture at the entrance of Skyfall lodge. Such nineteenth-century pictorial construction of Scotland "as a wild and untamed environment, a rural periphery geographically distant" has had a long-lasting influence on cinematic representations, where it is not only a remote and desolate environment, but also, as Duncan Petrie observes, "far removed from the rules, conventions and certainties of contemporary metropolitan society."[22] The act of travelling, by Bond's admission, "back in time. Somewhere we'll have the advantage," conjures up the notion of a timeless past, with the Highlands conceived as an old, pre-technological world, where Bond believes Silva's own technological advantages will not work, although he will be fooled into using MI6's crypted track to get there. As the "real" Highlands—wind-swept and mist-enshrouded—superimposes the simulated map projected on Q's wall screen in London, Scotland, much like Hashima, becomes the space where the ghosts of the past and the specters of the future meet. Whereas Hashima is a postindustrial space irredeemably wounded by the rapacious logic of global capitalist technology, Skyfall is a space of personal trauma surrounded by a landscape constructed as "natural" and untouched by technological progress.

In choosing to face his demons, Bond reengages the human values he represents and takes a stance against the excesses of global technology that Silva embodies. On his "grand entrance," Silva's helicopter disrupts the eerie silence of the Highlands to the blaring sound of the Animals' 1964 cover of John Lee Hooker's "Boom! Boom!" (1961), a song, like Trenet's "Boume," about the "explosive" power of love and desire, and another throwback to the past. Against the sophisticated artillery and the numbers on Silva's side, Bond's defense is based on much simpler and homemade technology (with the exception of the machine guns concealed behind the Aston Martin's headlights). It is effectively facilitated by the topography of Skyfall, which, thanks to its underground passage, allows M to escape to the nearby chapel and Bond to leave the house unscathed, though not before having set up two gas tanks to blow it up. As Bond escapes through the priest hole where he hid as a young boy after his parents' death, there is a sense in which the burning of the house has a healing effect on his trauma: "I've always hated the place," Bond says to himself before the house explodes into a spectacular blaze. The notion of regeneration connects the explosion with the underwater scene that follows the attack from Silva's henchman, so that when a regalvanized Bond emerges from the frozen lake, he appears to be reborn to a new life before heading to the chapel to complete his mission.

The place that, more than any other, represents Bond's traumatic past and his haunting demons—the graves of both of his parents are in the adjacent churchyard—Skyfall's chapel is the backdrop to the film's climax. Within this self-consciously Gothic setting, the cause of the villain's demise is, appropriately, the most primitive of weapons, a simple dagger earlier handed over to Bond by Kincade. "If all else fails, sometimes the old ways are the best." The gamekeeper's prophetic words echo Moneypenny's line in the Macau close-shaving scene, where Bond's preference for a cut-throat razor—"I like to do some things the old-fashioned way," he tells her—underpins his attachment to tradition and, implicitly, his ambivalent stand on modernity. While, in the film's climactic ending, M's death could signify the end of the old guard, the victory of traditional combat over the virtual technologies of the present and near future define Bond's kind of heroism as unchanged and unchangeable through time.

In self-consciously addressing Bond's "midlife crisis," *Skyfall*'s emphasis on the power of the past does not, however, make the hero outdated. On the contrary: while the film's ambivalent preoccupations with technological advances expose Bond's complicated relationship with modernity, this is precisely what underscores the character's longevity fifty years from the start of the franchise. This side of the millennium, Bond's ability to renew himself while staying the same, much like the sartorial return of 1960s-style English suits in his wardrobe, frames him as a timeless classic, or, as Moneypenny concludes at the end of the shaving scene, "old dog, new tricks"; the image of the Union flag-draped bulldog figurine M playfully leaves Bond in her will perpetuates the same reassuring message of continuity both in relation to his career in the Service and the values of the Empire.[23] With its nods to Gothic tropes and its Victorian cultural references, *Skyfall* may be read in line not only with Shelley's *Frankenstein*, but also Robert Louis Stevenson's *Strange Case of Dr. Jekyll and Mr. Hyde* (1886), with which the film shares, on one hand, evident anxieties about the uncontrolled use of science and the hero's closeness to the monster, but also the hero's propensity for "resurrection," which Bond, wittily, claims as his own "hobby" at the start of the film. Like a revenant of himself, "James Bond will return."

Notes

1. As Sam Mendes explains, the choice of vehicle is a deliberate throwback to Bond's past: "It is a thematic thing . . ., it is about the old and the new, and there is something about the last part of the movie, which is deliberately, very consciously, could have taken place in 1962." See "New SKYFALL DB5 Videoblog," James Bond 007 Official YouTube Channel, www.youtube.com/watch?v=usnDnEq7q5A, accessed on February 9, 2022.
2. Steven Zani, "James Bond and Q: Heidegger's Technology, or 'You're Not a Sportsman, Mr Bond,'" in *James Bond and Philosophy: Questions Are Forever*, ed. Jacob M. Held and James B. South (Chicago: Open Court, 2006), 182, 175, 185.
3. Keren Omry, "Bond, Benjamin, Balls: Technologised Masculinity in *Casino Royale*," in *Revisioning 007: James Bond and Casino Royale*, ed. Christoph Lindner (London: Wallflower, 2009), 166.
4. Martin Willis, "Hard-wear: The Millennium, Technology, and Brosnan's Bond," in *The James Bond Phenomenon: A Critical Reader*, ed. Christoph Lindner (Manchester: Manchester University Press, 2003), 153.
5. Omry, "Bond, Benjamin, Balls," 160. See also Lisa Funnell, "'I know where you keep your gun': Daniel Craig and the Bond–Bond Girl Hybrid in *Casino Royale*," *Journal of Popular Culture* 44, no. 3 (2011): 455–72, 160.
6. Justin D. Edwards, ed., *Technologies of the Gothic in Literature and Culture: Technogothics* (London: Routledge, 2015), 2.
7. Alan O'Day, ed., *Cyberterrorism* (London: Ashgate, 2004), xvi.

8. O'Day, *Cyberterrorism*, xi.

9. William S. Rodner, "Humanity and Nature in the Steamboat Paintings of J. M. W. Turner," *A Quarterly Journal Concerned with British Studies* 18, no. 3 (1986): 460.

10. Nevil Gibson, "Carry On: News for Business Travellers," *National Business Review*, June 21, 2013, www.nbr.co.nz/article/carry-news-business-travellers-ng-133653, accessed August 2, 2013. The island came to be part of the setting of the film as a result of a random encounter between Daniel Craig and Swedish film director Thomas Nordanstad in Sweden, while Craig was filming *The Girl with the Dragon Tattoo* (2011). See Aaron Schachter and Clark Boyd, "Update: The History of Hashima, the Island in Bond Film 'Skyfall,'" The World, theworld.org/2012/11/the-history-of-hashima-the -island-in-bond-film-skyfall, accessed February 7, 2022.

11. Thomas Nordanstad, dir., *Hashima, Japan* (2002), vimeo.com/4557534, accessed February 8, 2022; qtd. in Schachter and Boyd, "Update: The History of Hashima."

12. Fred Botting, *Limits of Horror: Technologies, Bodies, Gothic* (Manchester: Manchester University Press, 2008), 7.

13. Umberto Eco, *The Role of the Reader: Explorations in the Semiotics of Text* (London: Hutchinson, 2007 [1979]), 148.

14. Jack Halberstam, *Skin Shows: Gothic Horror and the Technology of Monsters* (Durham, NC: Duke University Press, 1995), 8.

15. As Ian Kinane notes, "In its attempts to remain relevant in an era of increasingly visible political activism by and on behalf of women and minority communities, there is little wonder that the James Bond franchise, which has historically promulgated a violently masculinist ideology, often at the expense of women (sexism) and people of colour (racism), is politically ambivalent and ill-defined." For a comprehensive discussion of the complex race politics of the fictional and cinematic Bond, see Ian Kinane, *Ian Fleming and the Politics of Ambivalence* (London: Bloomsbury, 2021), 36.

16. Botting, *Limits of Horror*, 13.

17. See Neil Smith, "Classic Yet Modern: *Skyfall* Aims to Please Bond Fans," *BBC News*, October 26, 2012, www.bbc.co.uk/news/entertainment-arts-20069724; and Peter Bradshaw, "*Skyfall*: Review," *The Guardian*, October 25, 2012, www.theguardian.com/film /2012/oct/25/skyfall-review, both accessed on February 11, 2022.

18. O'Day, *Cyberterrorism*, xv.

19. Elizabeth Parker, *The Forest and the EcoGothic: The Deep Dark Woods in the Popular Imagination* (London: Palgrave, 2020), 2.

20. William J. McKinney, "James Bond and the Philosophy of Technology: It's More Than Just the Gadgets of Q Branch," in Held and South, *James Bond and Philosophy*, 185.

21. McKinney, "James Bond and the Philosophy of Technology," 197.

22. Duncan Petrie, "Where the Land Meets the Sea: Liminality, Identity, and Rural Landscape in Contemporary Scottish Cinema," in *British Rural Landscapes on Film*, ed. Paul Newland (Manchester: Manchester University Press, 2016), 129.

23. "There are a lot of nods to Connery's Bond—we styled Daniel in a slightly Sixties way for this film," explains *Quantum of Solace* costume supervisor Lindsay Pugh. From *Quantum of Solace* onward, Daniel Craig's suits have been designed by American designer Tom Ford. *Skyfall* and *Spectre* (2015) costume designer Jany Temime has also reinforced the 1960s inspiration for Craig's Tom Ford suits. See Jessica Fellowes, "James Bond Week: 007 and His Girls Are Back with a Crisp New Look," *The Telegraph*, October 22, 2008, fashion.telegraph.co.uk/news-features/TMG3365681/James-Bond-week -007-and-his-girls-are-back-with-a-crisp-newlook.html; "Jany Temime: Dressing James Bond," *The Journal* (blog), Benson and Clegg, bensonandclegg.com/blogs /journal/jany-temime-dressing-james-bond, both accessed April 1, 2022.

CHAPTER 24

"IT'S ALWAYS BEEN ME"

Spectrality, Hauntings, and Retcon in *Spectre* (2015)

JAMES SMITH

As might be expected for a film called *Spectre* (2015), ideas and images of spectrality and haunting proliferate throughout the twenty-fourth entry in the James Bond franchise. Across its action, Daniel Craig's Bond attempts to unravel the mystery of the SPECTRE organization and its shadowy mastermind while simultaneously dealing with ghosts from his own past, whether in fulfilling M's (Judi Dench) commands from beyond the grave or finding the truth about his supposedly dead brother by adoption, Franz Oberhauser/Ernst Stavro Blofeld (Christoph Waltz). In doing so, *Spectre* is also a film attempting to balance nostalgic and contemporary resonances, on the one hand looking back into the Craig-era arc and the longer franchise history, while on the other engaging with urgent contemporary political debates about Western intelligence agencies and digital surveillance that had escalated even since the previous entry in the franchise, 2012's *Skyfall*.

Spectre is a revisitionist series entry in many ways. It evokes the concept of haunting in its imagery, themes, and cinematography, and this is used to establish retroactive continuity (retcon) in the Craig-era Bond arc. It reimagines Blofeld and the SPECTRE organization—Bond's arch-nemeses across many of the earlier novels and films—for the rebooted era. It also engages with contemporary debates, particularly as the first Bond film to respond to the 2013 leaks by Edward Snowden about the global intelligence apparatus operated by the "Five Eyes" powers.[1] With Bond and M now fighting to overthrow the online surveillance apparatus operated by Western governments and secretly backed by Blofeld, *Spectre* therefore represents a high-profile cultural response to the

Snowden leaks, with the film taking the unusual step (for the stalwart Bond franchise, at least) of positioning itself as an explicit critique of the operations of UK intelligence agencies.

The Specters of *Spectre*

Various reviewers, fans, and academics have noted that "themes of 'haunting' certainly mark *Spectre* from its opening images."[2] As Christopher Holliday describes, this is amplified by Sam Smith's opening credit theme song, which carries the line "A million shards of glass / That haunt me from my past," accompanied by graphics containing "images from Craig's previous three Bond films, and reflected in the disintegrating glass are characters already dead but here raised."[3] Even a brief further survey shows the extent to which "spectrality" provides a recurring concern across the film's settings, characterization, and cinematography.[4] This overall aesthetic both gestures to the psychological haunting of Bond, whose status as an orphan was a recurring topic in prior films, and attempts to establish continuity across the Craig era centered on the hidden conspiracies of Blofeld—in other words, an aesthetic deployed toward convincing the audience that it was Blofeld "all along" controlling the conspiracies and suffering that had ensnared Bond since his childhood. The remarkable opening scene depicting the Day of the Dead parade not only proffers a welter of visual reminders of the undead, but also involves "the 'spectral' dimension of the camera's movements through, across, and above spaces and characters."[5] Numerous other locations visited through the action carry distinct gothic resonances and build this aesthetic of haunting. Bond lurks at the edge of funeral processions in Rome, then journeys through the mist-and-snow-shrouded wilderness of Austria in the search for Mr. White's (Jesper Christensen) apparently eerily empty lodge. Similarly, MI6's headquarters in Vauxhall Cross has become an abandoned shell after being attacked in *Skyfall*—an ironic play on the classic gothic motif of the decaying castle, further extended by Bond's eventual rescue of the "damsel in distress" tied up at the top of the building.[6] Furthermore, Johannes Riquet and Anna Zdrenyk describe Bond's train journey to Blofeld's lair as "ghostly . . . in several ways": temporally, it evokes both "a transport into a lost imperial past" and homage to "the past of the Bond series," while aesthetically it creates spectrality through cinematography such as "a long shot of the train that interrupts the scene taking place inside; [with the effect that] the train appears unnaturally slow."[7]

The motif of haunting also manifests in the actions of several characters who seemingly occupy a liminal space between life and death. The deceased M of Dench appears to Bond from beyond the grave via a recording that arrives in the mail. Not letting "death get in the way of her job" (as Bond quips), she enacts a posthumous call for bloodshed, not only demanding that Bond find Marco Sciarra (Alessandro Cremona) and kill him, but that he conduct the macabre act of attending the funeral for his murder victim, which Bond concludes in almost psychopathic style as he then seduces Sciarra's widow Lucia (Monica Bellucci). Equally spectral is the reintroduction of Mr. White, an antagonist from across the Craig-era arc, who first features in *Casino Royale* (2006), escapes MI6's custody in *Quantum of Solace* (2008), and is missing from *Skyfall* before his *Spectre* return (with a lingering posthumous presence in *No Time to Die* [2021]). Initially alluded to as the "Pale King," a play on the "White" of his name, this is also, more subtly, an image that carries with it echoes of the figure of death ("And I looked, and behold a pale horse: and his name that sat on him was Death").[8] Mr. White carries other resonances with the undead: Bond finds him hiding in a secret vault under a house (albeit a vault occupied by computer screens instead of a coffin), and his gaunt appearance gives further resonances with some vampire-like creature surviving underground. (As Bond later describes to Madeleine Swann [Léa Seydoux], "The man I just met should have been dead weeks ago.") White's dialogue runs with this theme: he calls Bond and himself "two dead men enjoying the evening" and tells the agent, "I always knew death would wear a familiar face, but not yours." Bond's mission across the film, therefore, becomes almost a supernatural quest, mediating between the worlds of the living and the dead.

And, obviously, the key spectral presence lingering over the film is the figure of Blofeld himself, another person from Bond's past who apparently reaches out from beyond the grave, as he ostensibly died twenty years before, yet has survived to plot his revenge. While many elements of Blofeld mimic earlier moments in the franchise, there are also subtle shifts. In the title credits he is alluded to as an inky, octopus-like creature. When first onscreen at Sciarra's funeral, he is only glimpsed from behind as a mostly black silhouette (half-turning his head as if to acknowledge the viewer's gaze), and is then a figure cloaked in shadows at the head of the table when SPECTRE meets (figure 24.1).

While Blofeld is equally mysterious across the earlier films of the franchise—famously glimpsed as a hand stroking a cat in an ornate chair—the emphasis on blackness and shadows is not always as prominent. For example, in *Thunderball* (1965), in the original film scene of a SPECTRE board meeting, Blofeld's face is hidden, but behind a white screen and lights, speaking with a metallic amplified voice, and with a dashboard allowing him to electrocute his minions—elements that more signal his control of a brutally modern, technically sophisticated agency rather than make him a shadowy figure emerging from the past. And in *Spectre*, Blofeld's (overly) complicated enactment of revenge attempts to turn Bond into something akin to a zombie himself, drilling holes in his brain to remove his cognitive abilities, in the belief that a

Figure 24.1 Ernst Stavro Blofeld (Christoph Waltz), the shadowy head of SPECTRE. *Spectre* (2015).

person without the ability to see is "gone" even while "still alive," leaving the person "between life and death," with "nobody inside his skull."

The overarching payoff of this stress on haunting is an attempt to retcon the Craig-era arc: it turns out that it was Blofeld haunting the background all along, that the antagonists Le Chiffre (Mads Mikkelsen, *Casino Royale*), Silva (Javier Bardem, *Skyfall*), and White were all pawns in this plot, and that the deaths of Vesper Lynd (Eva Green) and M were secretly plotted from afar, rendering "everything" that Bond values "a ruin" due to Blofeld's machinations across the four films. Of course, like any ghost story, there is a fine line between a sinister tale and something melodramatically ridiculous, and *Spectre* does not always navigate this line as successfully as it might. James Chapman has shown how the "Sonyleak" incident revealed that during the writing process there was disagreement over whether Blofeld was a convincing enough "super-villain" and some skepticism as to whether the attempts to retcon the antagonists of the Craig-era films into one organization would work.[9] Arguably, such tensions remain. Blofeld's world-spanning villainy seems to be motivated by a relatively petty sibling grudge rather than any great betrayal (as was suffered by *Skyfall*'s Silva).[10] SPECTRE's operations, involving counterfeit pharmaceuticals and human trafficking, seem to mimic patterns of actual organized crime groups rather than the next-level global conspiracies of earlier films (with "Nine Eyes" surveillance merely allowing them to counteract governments in this enterprise rather than launch any new form of world domination). Blofeld's claims of omnipotent control of the Craig arc risks introducing retroactive plot holes as much as a neat narrative cohesion: M's death in *Skyfall*, after successfully luring Silva to Scotland and aiding Bond to fight off the attack, hardly seems like an efficient hit by a criminal mastermind. The retcon is illustrated for the audience in other ham-fisted ways: Blofeld takes the trouble to decorate the ruins of MI6's headquarters with A4 printout photos of Bond's deceased friends and foes, unfortunately giving the sense more of a site-specific art project than some terrible act of revenge. His attempts to zombify Bond meanwhile prove strangely ineffective, Bond jumping to his feet little the worse for wear even after having a hole drilled through his brain. *Spectre*'s retcon, it could be said, is as notable for what is still obscured as much as for what is made visible, leaving viewers with a nagging uncertainty of whether this evidence builds to a coherent tale of haunting or is instead more indicative of a synthetic smoke-and-mirrors.

Spectre and the Bond Franchise

If, on one level, this film's theme of haunting centers on the character of Bond, this can be taken to a further plane of reading into how *Spectre* (and by implication the Craig-era arc) deals with the specter of the franchise's history and the expectations of the Bond formula. As Chapman notes, the raiding of Bond film history is now a cliché in itself, a "process [that] began in earnest with *The Spy Who Loved Me*" (1977) and that has continued unabated in the rebooted era, despite the initial sense of some critics that *Casino Royale* marked a Bond who had shrugged off many of the more problematic formulas of the past.[11] There are an obvious range of such nods in *Spectre*: Dr. Swann's alpine "Hoffler Klinik," for example, offers a direct parallel to the research clinic run by Blofeld in the Alps in *On Her Majesty's Secret Service* (1969). The train sequence to Blofeld's base has been described as "a journey into the history of Bond films," one that "self-consciously refers to a number of previous train scenes, notably *The Spy Who Loved Me* and *Live and Let Die* (1973) (in repeating the unexpected intrusion of an aggressor), *From Russia with Love* (1963) (in recalling the glamorous interior of the Orient Express), and *Casino Royale* (in suggesting a romantic alternative for Bond when Madeleine asks him whether he could imagine a different life for himself)."[12] The positioning of Swann has attracted particular scrutiny given the earlier shift of the Craig era away from the standard "Bond Girl" formula. For Lisa Funnell, Swann represents a return to the Bond Girl through being a "composite character comprised of familiar qualities from previous Bond Girls featured across the Connery, Lazenby, Moore, Dalton, and Brosnan eras." This serves to rework the gender politics of the Craig era and ultimately reasserts the earlier problematic forms of "Bond as a successful suitor and romantic hero."[13] *Spectre* therefore suggests some of the constraints of the

Bond formula, showing that, while some of its more problematic demands may be temporarily repressed, the weight of the legacy means many of the associations are difficult to exorcize completely.

Of course, *Spectre*'s most obvious engagement with the history of the franchise is the resurrection of the SPECTRE organization and its leader, Blofeld, which serves to link the Craig era to one of the most iconic villains in the franchise (and indeed, wider film history), and continued across the subsequent film, *No Time to Die*. The "Special Executive for Counterintelligence, Terrorism, Revenge, and Extortion" was first introduced to the public by Ian Fleming in the novel *Thunderball* (1961) as a private, supranational criminal enterprise run by people drawn from various national syndicates, mafias, and intelligence services.[14] Its head, Blofeld, was a genius who as a young man came to a unique realization "about the future of the world," that control of communication and "knowledge of truth before the next man . . . was the source of all great reputations," and subsequently made his wealth by monitoring telegraphic traffic and selling information to various sides during the Second World War. Physically imposing rather than the mysterious shadowy figure of the 2015 film—in the novel, it is said his gaze could almost "suck the eyes out of your head"—for the arch-criminals of SPECTRE Blofeld was "their Supreme Commander—almost their god."[15] As described by Fleming, the SPECTRE organization conducts an audacious and fantastical range of exploits—the secret recovery of Himmler's jewels, the sale of germ warfare vials, the stealing of intelligence, the blackmail of a former SS leader in hiding, the assassination of a nuclear scientist defector on behalf of the French secret service, and the plot to steal nuclear bombs and blackmail nations for their return—and Blofeld's ostentatiously ruthless credentials are quickly demonstrated as he electrocutes one of his treacherous subordinates as the SPECTRE leadership meet. After first being mentioned on screen in *Dr. No* (1962), across the film franchise SPECTRE became recurring antagonists, whether in revenge plots to assassinate Bond (*From Russia with Love*), control of the world through space lasers (*Diamonds Are Forever* [1971]), or the murder of Bond's wife (*On Her Majesty's Secret Service*), before Bond finally eliminated Blofeld in the opening sequence to *For Your Eyes Only* (1981).

After this gap of many decades, therefore, the reintroduction of SPECTRE was met with much anticipation (and some trepidation, as the "Sonyleaks" emails indicate). Further complicating this was the fact that Blofeld himself, while absent in the recent Bond franchise, had still been "sustained" in public memory "by countless parodies—most famously, the figure of Dr. Evil in the *Austin Powers* trilogy (1997–2002)."[16] The consequence of this was that a generation of Millennial and post-Millennial cinemagoers had mostly encountered a Nehru-suited arch-villain only as a figure of ridicule and parody, providing a challenge for a rebooted franchise to negotiate the resurrection of a suitably sinister vision of Blofeld without lapsing back into the campness it had sought to distinguish itself against.

It is clear that much of the SPECTRE organization in this film remains dependent on the source material first created by Fleming in the novel of *Thunderball* (and then mediated, with some changes, through the corresponding scene in the 1965 *Thunderball* film). As before, SPECTRE is a pan-national organization hidden from outside view but wielding almost mythical reach and power. In 2015, the audience first encounter SPECTRE as an organization as it conducts its secret, face-to-face board meeting in an imposing palace. This meeting is an element that also introduces the agency in Fleming's novel, albeit in a "workmanlike board room" of the front company FIRCO (which is used as a cover address in the novel) rather than the grand architecture of a palatial meeting room (a setting again in keeping with the film's distinct gothic resonances).[17] The ruthlessness of the organization is similarly established in both novel and films by the execution of one of the leaders, although in *Spectre* Blofeld watches impassively as the victim has his eyes crushed out, but does not carry out the murder himself (as he does in the *Thunderball* novel and film via his electrocution switch). Similarly, Blofeld's later desert lair in *Spectre*, based around a fallen meteorite and aptly described as resembling "a cathedral to big data processing" (figure 24.2), is every bit as megalomaniacally implausible as SPECTRE hideouts in earlier phases of the franchise, which included hidden bases in volcanoes (in *You Only Live Twice* [1967]) or a clinic on top of the Alps.[18] Even his obsession with surveillance is in keeping with the original villain of the *Thunderball* novel: while evolving from the "cables and radiograms" of the earlier era to mass-scale datamining, both Blofelds share the belief that "accurate communication lay . . . at the very heart of power" (*Thunderball*) or that "Information is all, is it not?" (*Spectre*).[19]

Figure 24.2 Bond (Daniel Craig), Blofeld (Christoph Waltz), and Madeleine Swann (Léa Seydoux) in the digital surveillance lair. *Spectre* (2015).

There are key differentiations, of course—the adopted family link between Bond and Blofeld being one, the digital-era aspirations of SPECTRE itself being another (with the launch of their global surveillance initiative), as well as the association of SPECTRE with the "spectral" that has been charted as a dominant motif in the 2015 film. But along with subtle ironic nods for the fans—in his lair, Blofeld appears in a slick jacket still featuring the mandarin collar of earlier incarnations, and has a fluffy white cat that many will recognize as alluding to the character's signature pet—it is clear that *Spectre*'s engagement with this aspect of the franchise history is more than a blank gesture and instead a detailed negotiation with the source material.

The inheritances are layered with some complexity: as has been observed, *Spectre* does not simply "reboot" Blofeld but also loops back and "serves as prequel to the 'Blofeld series' of films of the 1960s, exploring the origins of his grotesque facial disfigurement and his hatred for Bond."[20] *Spectre*, it could be noted, is both haunted by the earlier Blofeld films and in turn haunts our subsequent viewing of them. Overall, it is fair to say the reaction from reviewers concerning *Spectre*'s raiding of the franchise's history was ambivalent, and (as Chapman has noted) often divided along national lines, with British critics happy to see a return to the classic Bond material and formulas while Americans tended to view it as a "stale retread" that lacked psychological depth. Academic analysis has been similarly split, some scholars welcoming the sense of "fun" and return of scale and spectacle, others critical of the "laundry list of self-quotation" and a "self-reference count" that "swiftly spirals off the scale."[21] But whatever the critical viewpoints, the ultimate test of the formula perhaps lies in the bottom line, and with a worldwide gross of over $880,674,609, *Spectre* suggests that the raiding of the Bond franchise still has plenty of value left in it yet.[22]

The Nightmares of George Orwell:
The Specters of Global Surveillance

Beyond its revision to the Craig-era arc and the wider presence of the franchise history, *Spectre* is also haunted by certain contemporary social and political tensions, specifically what Barbara Korte identifies as the "joint spectres of terror and seemingly protective surveillance" that dominate current discourse surrounding security and intelligence.[23] As has been argued elsewhere by scholars such as Tobias Hochscherf (and in this volume by Estella Tincknell), the Craig-era arc has been notable for its shift toward a greater "grittiness" and geopolitical awareness, with the climate of post-9/11 international terrorism and competition from the *Bourne* franchise (2002–) serving as new stimuli for the films.[24] This specter of terrorism certainly continues to linger in the background of *Spectre* itself, with terrorist attacks on "Hamburg, Tunisia, Mexico City" and South Africa referenced across the course of the film, here given an ultimate controlling logic by the fact that they are "all linked" and masterminded by the "one organization," SPECTRE.

But the most obvious tension that *Spectre* evokes is that of the contemporary cyber surveillance apparatus of Western nations, specifically those brought to the forefront of public consciousness in 2013 by the leaks of a former contractor for the United States' National Security Agency (NSA), Edward Snowden. These leaks revealed top secret information about the extensive range of surveillance being conducted by the "Five Eyes" intelligence powers, showing how such intelligence agencies routinely capture vast swathes of the data that crosses the internet, and that they also have routine access to the email, videos, photos, and stored data held by major tech companies such as Facebook, Google, Apple, and Microsoft. Snowden's revelations prompted protest by citizens and media organizations across the globe. They also provided fertile source material for the next iteration of the Bond franchise, although this came with political headaches for the broader story arc: the prior film, *Skyfall*, had taken a largely conservative stance in debates over cyber activism and transparency of the secret state, with the film's main antagonist a renegade computer hacker and leaker of information who is duly eliminated by Bond and M.[25] However, with the scriptwriters no doubt attuned to the international zeitgeist in the wake of Snowden, *Spectre* conducts almost a 180-degree political turn from *Skyfall* and repositions the Bond franchise again, offering a plot that focuses on the contemporary practices of digital surveillance by Western government agencies (rather than rogue hackers) and ultimately condemns the scale of these. Indeed, *The Guardian*'s review headline claimed the film was now "sexily pro-Snowden."[26]

As Korte notes, this debate over the omnipresent specter of "seemingly protective surveillance" clearly manifests in the subplot concerning M (Ralph Fiennes) and the new "C" in charge of Britain's Joint Security Service, Max Denbigh (Andrew Scott).[27] In what proposes to be "the biggest shakeup in the history of British intelligence," Bond's MI6 faces a "merger with MI5" and the likelihood they will "scrap the double-o program forever." Max, although disparaged as a "classic Whitehall mandarin" by Tanner (Rory Kinnear), nonetheless offers the façade of a modern, efficient leader of the intelligence community. He affects a first-name basis with his staff and an always-open door (rather than the quasi-military formality and mystique of codenames that governs MI6). He is a modernizer who wants to take "intelligence out of the Dark Ages into the light," indeed, someone who seeks to exorcize intelligence from the hidden realm within which it has previously existed. This is a metaphor carried forward by the new headquarters of British intelligence, the "Centre for National Security," a transparent, helix-shaped building that seems to invite public observation and scrutiny, quite unlike the castlelike MI6 building or the other subterranean bunkers to which the intelligence services retreat in the recent Bond films.[28]

Spectre's critique suggests that this transparency is largely a pretense, masking the deeper, often sinister conspiracies at play beyond this visible surface. (As Korte argues, the paradox *Spectre* puts forward is that "transparency has become opaque"[29]). On one level, this is because much of the more controversial work has been outsourced, whether to the drones that now do "all our dirty work abroad" or the benefactors "from the private sector" who bankroll "the most sophisticated data gathering system in history," which provides "the world's digital ghost, available 24/7"—intelligence gathering now just another of the neoliberal public/private partnerships running national security for profit. Beyond this, C is also leading a "Nine Eyes" intelligence initiative that will "decide the New World Order," data-collection dissolving national barriers and allowing access to "the combined intelligence streams of nine countries." As he states in his almost evangelical speech:

> Do not let them tell you we need less surveillance. We need more. Much more. I say again, the Nine Eyes committee would have full access to the combined intelligence streams of all member states. More data, more analysis, less likelihood of terrorist attack. Ladies and gentlemen, it's time for the security services of the world to unite. Alone, we are weak. Together, we're a global power.

Such a grasp for near-total surveillance provides the plot thread that unifies the film, for the ultimate hidden watcher and controller of the Nine Eyes system, of course, is Blofeld in his desert lair of endless screens, and C one of his visionary "disciples," collaborating in order to save the world from "chaos" and supposedly "put the power where it should be."

This Blofeld-controlled "Nine Eyes" conspiracy provides a very obvious critical evocation of the "Five Eyes" operations of Snowden's leaks. A further foil to this New World Order ambition of contemporary intelligence is provided (somewhat awkwardly) by the voice of Ralph Fiennes throughout the action. Veering between spy chief and civics teacher, M periodically punctures Max's narrative with reminders that the "Nine Eyes" are "unelected," that the new security center seems like "George Orwell's worst nightmare," or that "I know surveillance is a fact of life. It's how you use the information that concerns me, and who is using it." And, in a similar vein to *Skyfall*, where interfering politicians are rendered useless when under physical attack, Max also proves wanting when forced to act in the physical world, failing to check that his gun is loaded before falling to his death in a struggle with M. In a neat metaphor, the glass structure of the public/private-funded building proves fragile, exposing all within it to hidden risks.

This chapter has, in many places, chided *Spectre* for its implausibility and its lapses into comfortable formula, but it should be acknowledged that, for many viewers, it is exactly these elements that continue to draw them to James Bond. And, overall, *Spectre* is a testament to the resilience and adaptability of the franchise. While certainly marked by the nostalgic weight of earlier moments in the franchise, the resurrected Blofeld and SPECTRE are nonetheless given new life through their reimagining in the context of the contemporary Snowden leaks. Ultimately, *Spectre* forcefully shows the capacity for Bond to still be at the forefront of evolving cultural imaginings of intelligence and spying, even as they progress into a radical new digital era far removed from Bond's Cold War origins.

Notes

1. The Five Eyes is an intelligence collaboration agreement between the United States, United Kingdom, Canada, Australia, and New Zealand.
2. Christopher Holliday, "London, the Post-7/7 Bond Films, and Mourning Work," *Journal of Popular Film and Television* 46, no. 1 (2018): 60.
3. Holliday, "London," 61. More broadly, Holliday explores *Spectre* as a work of "haunted cinema," with particular reference to its depictions of London as the "fulcrum of the narrative."
4. The briefness of this survey also precludes any broader discussion of ideas of "hauntology," although it is noted that Mark Fisher's discussion of the cinema of hauntology could provide an apt framework for analysis of the Bond franchise. See "What is Hauntology?," *Film Quarterly* 66, no. 1 (2012): 16–24.
5. Christopher Holliday, "'Old Dog, New Tricks:' James Bond's Digital Chaos," *International Journal of James Bond Studies* 4, no. 1 (2021): 17.
6. See Lisa Funnell, "Reworking the Bond Girl Concept in the Craig Era," *Journal of Popular Film and Television* 46, no. 1 (2018): 20, for discussion of the regression of *Spectre* to the "damsel in distress" motif.
7. Johannes Riquet and Anna Zdrenyk also draw attention to "the film's overall concern with spectrality," as evidenced by Swann's echoes of the "Madeleine" of Hitchcock's *Vertigo* (1958), or with Marcel Proust's *In Search of Lost Time*. See "Between Progress and Nostalgia: Technology, Geopolitics, and James Bond's Railway Journeys," *International Journal of James Bond Studies* 1, no. 2 (2018): 18, 17.
8. Revelation 6:8, KJV.
9. James Chapman, "'A Thoroughly English Movie Franchise': *Spectre*, the James Bond Films, and Genre," *International Journal of James Bond Studies* 1, no. 1 (2017): 15. "Sonyleaks" was a major hack of Sony Pictures Entertainment's network that occurred in 2014, resulting in vast amounts of data being compromised and leaked concerning its operations and films, some of which included emails between the corporate "partners involved in making the film [*Spectre*]."
10. As a point of comparison, Silva would seem to have a more successful psychological profile: a former agent betrayed by M, his justified grievance, and M's utilitarian view of surrendering someone for torture, introduces at least a shade of ambiguity into the moral universe of the film.

11. Chapman, "'Thoroughly English,'" 9.
12. Riquet and Zdrenyk, "Between Progress and Nostalgia," 16.
13. Funnell, "Reworking the Bond Girl Concept," 19, 21.
14. As Chapman points out, SPECTRE actually predates this, originating in a collaborative 1959 film project that never saw the light of day, from which Fleming took the plot and characters (see "'Thoroughly English,'" 13–14).
15. Ian Fleming, *Thunderball* (London: Penguin, 2004), 43–45.
16. Anette Pankratz and Svenja Bohm, "Play It Again, James: Seriality in the Craig Bond Films," *International Journal of James Bond Studies* 3, no. 1 (2020): 11.
17. Fleming, *Thunderball*, 43. See also Chapman, "'Thoroughly English,'" 17, for how *Spectre* developed its mix of references to Blofeld.
18. Claus-Ulrich Viol, "Things Are Not Enough: Bond, Stiegler, and Technics," *International Journal of James Bond Studies* 2, no. 1 (2019): 8.
19. Fleming, *Thunderball*, 44.
20. Pankratz and Bohm, "Play It Again, James," 10.
21. Chapman, "'Thoroughly English,'" 18, 19; Jonathan Murray, "Containing the Spectre of the Past: The Evolution of the James Bond Franchise during the Daniel Craig Era," *Visual Culture in Britain* 18, no. 2 (2017): 263.
22. Figures are taken from www.boxofficemojo.com/title/tt2379713/.
23. Barbara Korte, "The Agency of the Agent in *Spectre*: The Heroic Spy in the Age of Surveillance," *International Journal of James Bond Studies* 1, no. 1 (2017): 4.
24. Tobias Hochscherf, "Bond for the Age of Global Crises: 007 in the Daniel Craig Era," *Journal of British Cinema and Television* 10, no. 2 (2013): 298–320.
25. I have explored this at greater length in James Smith, "'How Safe Do You Feel?' James Bond, *Skyfall* and the Politics of the Secret Agent in an Age of Ubiquitous Threat," *College Literature* 43, no. 1 (2016): 145–72.
26. Peter Bradshaw, "*Spectre* Review: James Bond Is Back, Stylish, Camp and Sexily Pro-Snowden," *The Guardian*, October 21, 2015, www.theguardian.com/film/2015/oct/21/spectre-review-james-bond-is-back-stylish-camp-and-sexily-pro-snowden.
27. See Korte, "Agency of the Agent," 6–10, for a detailed reading of the interactions between M and C.
28. See Nick Jones, "New Digs, Old Digs: Vauxhall Cross, Whitehall, and the London of Craig's Bond," *Journal of Popular Film and Television* 46, no. 1 (2018): 22–33, for discussion of this building amid wider consideration of Bond's London settings. The architecture has attracted other critical readings as well—see, for example, Korte, "Agency of the Agent," 7.
29. Korte, "Agency of the Agent," 7.

CHAPTER 25

NO TIME TO DIE (2021) AND THE SPY WHO LOVED #METOO?

TERENCE MCSWEENEY AND STUART JOY

#MeToo has influenced our culture, which is a great thing, so of course it's going to influence everything we do on Bond. . . . Over the years, attitudes have changed, and so have the Bond films. The films are representative of the times they're in.

—Barbara Broccoli, producer, *No Time to Die* (2021)

You can't change Bond overnight into a different person. But you can definitely change the world around him and the way he has to function in that world. It's a story about a white man as a spy in this world, but you have to be willing to lean in and do the work to make the female characters more than just contrivances.

—Cary Joji Fukunaga, director, *No Time to Die* (2021)

While each installment in the Bond franchise is undoubtedly a significant contribution to the series, an actor's final film as the character often plays a fundamental role in how they are remembered by the public at large. For some, the last is also the first (George Lazenby); for others, their final film is an indication that the actor is considered to have aged out of the role (Roger Moore, Sean Connery) or that the series needed some sort of course correction (Pierce Brosnan, Timothy Dalton). In the case of Daniel Craig, the actor had been vocal about his desire to leave Bond behind as early as *Spectre* (2015), when he had infamously commented that he would "rather slash [his] wrists" than return to the franchise.[1] Nevertheless, six years later Craig returned to the role in *No Time to Die* (hereafter *NTTD*), directed by Cary Joji Fukunaga, a film with one of the most turbulent production histories in the series.[2]

The years in between the release of *Spectre* and *NTTD* coincided with an equally fractious period away from the screen, encompassing not just the polarizing climate that led to Brexit (2020) in the United Kingdom and the Trump presidency (2017–2021) in the United States, but also the rise of social protest movements like Black Lives Matter, #MeToo, and #TimesUp. Indeed, much of the engagement with *NTTD* in the run-up to its release seemed to be concerned with how far the films produced during the Craig era had been affected by contemporary sociocultural discourse. By the time of *NTTD* there were more vocal calls for substantive changes to the franchise than ever before, with many of those critical of the series echoing the remarks that the film's antagonist, Lyutsifer Safin (Rami Malek) makes when he finally comes face to face with Bond, calling him "redundant." Such claims had been made for decades, both within its diegetic frames and outside of them. In *GoldenEye* (1995), for example, M (Judi Dench) famously labelled Bond, at the time played by Pierce Brosnan, a "sexist, misogynist dinosaur." These diegetic criticisms of the character can be understood as a calculated attempt by the producers of the series to diffuse broader extradiegetic tensions while allowing Bond to, on the whole, behave the way he had always behaved with only minor changes.

However, the directness and frequency of similar critiques prior to the release of *NTTD* was notable, as several commentators and journalists asked whether the cultural institution of James Bond was still relevant for audiences as the twenty-first century moved into its third decade. Ben Child, writing for *The Guardian*, wondered whether 007 was too toxic for the #MeToo era.[3] Stuart Jeffries asked the rather pointed question "Is it time to revoke James Bond's licence to kill?"[4] However, at the very same time as this, there were others making the *exact opposite* claim: that, in fact, the Craig era was defined by the impact of political correctness on the series. Some of these detractors, like Charlie Higson, author of five *Young Bond* novels (2005–2008), saw this as resulting in a "woke 007," something he viewed in resoundingly negative terms.[5] Yet others, like Léa Seydoux, who played Bond's love interest Madeleine Swann in both *Spectre* and *NTTD*, argued that the Craig era had turned Bond from a "misogynist into a feminist, which is something very important."[6] These seemingly paradoxical demands of the series and the character it has been built around are those *NTTD* attempts to reconcile: seeking to please both fans who desired the traditional adventures of their James Bond, but also those members of the audience who had come to see the character as something of an anachronism.

"No More Bond Girls"?

One area that was returned to more than any other by fans, critics, and scholars with regard to how far Craig's Bond films departed from those made prior to his five-film tenure, is the portrayal of gender, in particular women, and those characters who have been traditionally referred to throughout the history of the franchise as "Bond girls." The term had grown progressively contentious through the series, as Lisa Funnell and Tyler Johnson noted, pointing out that the use of the term "girl" to describe women simultaneously infantilizes, marginalizes, and devalues, while also stressing their sexual availability to Bond.[7] It might come as no surprise, then, that in the wake of the #MeToo movement, Daniel Craig categorically stated there were "No more Bond girls. They don't exist anymore."[8]

Craig's claim is worth exploring in more detail, especially through the lens of *NTTD*, which, as we observed earlier, was the first Bond film to be produced in the #MeToo and #TimesUp era. Furthermore, it was both made and released at a very particular time in the film industry when more attention was being drawn than ever to disparities between the representations of men and women by organizations like the Media, Diversity, & Social Change Initiative at USC Annenberg (School for Communication and Journalism), the Geena Davis Institute on Gender in Media, and the Center for the Study of Women in Television & Film. A study conducted by USC Annenberg, published the year before the release of *NTTD*, observed that in 2019 only 34 percent of roles in 1,300 films studied were played by females, with those from the action and/or adventure genres that Bond would be situated in even lower, at 27.9 percent.[9] Taken as a whole, these studies reveal an industry that is not as diverse as its detractors and defenders would frame it and certainly refute vocal accusations from social conservatives of a "woke revolution" in which Hollywood is being taken over by women, ethnic minorities, and nonheteronormatives in ways that ultimately "will kill the entertainment industry."[10]

However, it should be acknowledged that several scholars have made a case similar to the one that Craig makes above. According to Lisa Funnell, an essential aspect of the Craig era is how the qualities associated with the "Bond girl" archetype and established Bond formula have been critiqued and reimagined.[11] Funnell and others find evidence of this starting with Vesper Lynd (Eva Green) in *Casino Royale*, who is intelligent, resourceful, and critical of Bond's relationships with women. Lynd's comment that Bond considers them as "disposable pleasures rather than meaningful pursuits" echoes many of those who have written critically about the series and its representations of women. Yet Lynd is traumatized, another hallmark of women in the Craig era: damaged, and undeniably a trophy for Bond. She betrays him at the end of the film and, even though audiences learn that she has committed this act of treachery for understandably tragic reasons, her death motivates him to *become* Bond in ways not too far from the process now widely referred to as "fridging." As well as Lynd, the Craig era provided us with the similarly traumatized Camille Montes (Olga Kurylenko) in *Quantum of Solace* (2008), who has many of the same qualities described above, but dismisses Bond's sexual advances, resulting in a film that ends on what some read as an "empowering and even feminist note."[12] While these two examples might be seen as deviating from the "Bond girl" stereotype, elsewhere the Craig era produced a range of female characters the likes of whom we might consider much more conventional. In *Casino Royale* (2006), for instance, Bond seduces Solange (Caterina Murino) but stops short of sleeping with her once he obtains the information he needs, only to see her killed the next day as punishment. In *Quantum of Solace*, MI6 agent Strawberry Fields (Gemma Arterton) sleeps with Bond against her better judgment and is subsequently drowned in oil. Charlie Higson might be correct when he says that Craig's Bond is "tender, cries and gets into the shower in his tuxedo to comfort a woman," but he is still the same character who in *Skyfall* goes unannounced into the shower of another, Séverine (Bérénice Marlohe), very much an archetypal "Bond girl," and has sex with her just a few hours after deducing she had been a victim of child sex trafficking.[13] Therefore, it is more productive to view the Craig era as providing female characters with a superficial veneer of agency and the illusion of complexity that became the hallmark of twenty-first-century blockbuster film production, at the same time as not deviating substantially from the essential tenets of the Bond canon, especially in terms of the frequency with which women are kidnapped, rescued by Bond, and quite often murdered. Rarely do these women occupy the privileged and dynamic spaces reserved almost exclusively for men in the genre and only Bond in this series, and remain, at best, marginalized and, at worst, objectified, sexualized, and infantilized.[14]

The portrayal of women in the Craig era, then, can be categorized both as a progressive step forward, but also as performative, calculated lip-service to notions of female empowerment increasingly associated with the #MeToo movement and #TimesUp project. Of all the films in which Craig plays James Bond, this is most clearly evident in *NTTD*'s characterizations of three of its female characters—Madeleine Swann, Paloma (Ana de Armas), and Nomi (Lashana Lynch)— and also in the participation of award-winning writer, actor, and producer Phoebe Waller-Bridge, who was brought on as a screenwriter by the producers in a highly publicized manoeuvre that was viewed skeptically by some.

Phoebe Waller-Bridge and the "Different Alternatives" of *No Time to Die*

In April 2019 it was announced that Waller-Bridge had been personally selected by Craig to cowrite the script for *NTTD*.[15] Known for being the creator of *Fleabag* (BBC, 2016–2019) and *Killing Eve* (BBC America, 2018–2022), Waller-Bridge possesses a reputation for creating rich, complex, and strong female characters. Writing in *The Guardian*, Simon Hattenstone remarked: "[She] depicts characters who say the unsayable, do the undoable and defy every stereotype of feminine behaviour."[16] As other writers in this volume have made clear, important questions have been raised over the years concerning how the Bond series has treated women and how far the films have endorsed, legitimized, and perpetuated gender stereotypes. When asked if she would bring a "female, feminist humour" to the film, she responded playfully, remarking, "Well, we'll see, we'll see what I can sneak in." However, Waller-Bridge later insisted that she was not told to change the culture of the films as, according to her, "They were already doing that themselves."[17] Craig was questioned about whether Waller-Bridge's participation might have been motivated in part by how it would be perceived by the public. Jonathan Dean of the *Sunday Times* stated, "A cynic might suggest the new recruit has been chosen to help the film look more representative." The actor seemed offended by the suggestion, stating, "Look, we're having a conversation about Phoebe's gender here, which is fucking ridiculous. I know where you're going, but I don't actually want to have that conversation. I know what you're trying to do, but it's wrong. It's absolutely wrong."[18] Yet viewing the final film and its place in the series, it appears that Dean posed a legitimate question.

Bond's pivot to embrace socially relevant discourse while at the same time being careful to not alienate more traditional fans is one adopted by many franchises in the 2010s and 2020s, from *Star Wars* (1977–) to *Star Trek* (1979–) and the Marvel Cinematic Universe (2008–). The true extent of Waller-Bridge's contribution to *NTTD*, however, remains unclear, even though she is one of the four credited writers, alongside Neal Purvis, Robert Wade, and Cary Joji Fukunaga.[19] Many of the film's creators were keen to emphasize her importance. producer Michael G. Wilson suggested, "It's unfair to think of her as a female writer . . . she contributed to the whole plot of the film" and Craig said that her "influence permeates a lot of this film."[20] Yet Waller-Bridge's own accounts are varied, ranging from "tweaks across a few of the characters and a few of the storylines" to providing "different alternatives" for various scenes.[21] This ambiguity seemed to service the demands of those members of the audience hoping to find more to the film than had been present with previous entrants to the franchise, with Craig stressing the importance of her contribution, while at the same time making it clear that fans should not expect to see too much of a deviation from the formula that had made the series so successful. He said: "Phoebe didn't come in to change Bond. She came in to spice it up for sure, but she's a Bond fan—she wasn't about to take him in a different direction."[22] It is in the portrayal of the film's three main female characters that we see the greatest evidence of the film grappling with the past, present, and future of women in the Bond series.

Swann

NTTD begins with an extended prologue shown from the perspective of a young Madeleine Swann, who had emerged not merely as a fleeting dalliance for Bond in *Spectre* but a more serious love interest. While the film gives Swann its opening moments—during which she witnesses the murder of her mother by Safin—and provides her with more character development than many other "Bond girls," her contribution to the franchise has been widely debated (figure 25.1). It is certainly possible to read her as "feminist," as Felicity Kinsella did, since, as *Spectre* established, she is a renowned psychiatrist and an emotionally complex individual, but Mary Rose Somarriba's assertion that she is "a near match, if not equal, to Bond in combat, assassination know-how, and intellect" is a willful misreading of the character.[23] In *Spectre*, even though she tells Bond, "I can look after myself," she is frequently saved by him, prompting Crystal Bell to refer to her as a "damsel in distress."[24] This process continues in *NTTD*, where she is rescued no fewer than three times. In both films, she is shown to be a largely reactive presence, with her function primarily limited to being a pawn for Blofeld (Christoph Waltz) and then Safin, the latter of whom

Figure 25.1 Nomi (Lashana Lynch) and Madeleine Swann (Léa Seydoux). *No Time to Die* (2021).

kidnaps and takes her to an island with James's biological daughter, whom she had earlier lied to him about, in order to motivate the agent's final set-piece rescue, where he will sacrifice his life for their future.

Seydoux's own understanding of Madeleine was close to that of Kinsella and Somarriba. While promoting *Spectre*, she said, "My character is a rebel. She doesn't need Bond or wait for him to save her . . . [Madeleine] is Bond's equal."[25] One might ask, given Craig's pointed declaration that there are "no more Bond girls," how far Madeleine deviates from Christoph Lindner's assertion that "Bond girls" are defined by the fact that they are "generic, interchangeable, [and] dependent."[26] Does she possess more agency than, for example, Major Anya Amasova (Barbara Bach) in *The Spy Who Loved Me* (1977) or Melina Havelock (Carole Bouquet) from *For Your Eyes Only* (1981), two characters who are shown at times to be almost Bond's equal in an era of Bond films not recognized for their progressive representations of women? Certainly, Madeleine remains an interesting character and she is intelligent, resourceful, and sensitively played by Seydoux, but her character development, as has been the case with all "Bond girls," remains constrained by the constitutive elements of the franchise itself, in which the focus is always on Bond, with every other character a peripheral entity defined very much by their relation to him. Seydoux's comment that her character is "Bond's equal" is reminiscent of what many "Bond girls" have said in the past, eager to differentiate themselves from previous characters and the limitations that Lindner described above, with rarely any substance to them.[27]

Paloma

Ana de Armas made almost exactly the same comments about her character, Paloma, a novice spy who joins Bond on a mission in Havana, Cuba. During a promotional interview for *NTTD*, she stated, "Paloma is a really complete character. She's definitely something else that I don't think we've seen in other Bond girls in previous movies."[28] Despite the fact she only has about ten minutes of screen time, it is fair to say she made a significant impression on audiences and reviewers, who lamented that she did not play a larger role in the film. Paloma is an energetic and exuberant presence, certainly a pivot away from the solemnity of many of the female characters in the Craig era. Unlike many of her predecessors, she is unburdened by past trauma and seems to delight in her role as an agent in a way that is never afforded to the likes of Lynd, Montes, Fields, or Moneypenny (Naomie Harris). However, her characterization also remains illustrative of the paradox faced by many female characters in the Craig era. De Armas commented that female Bond characters "have been sexualized before, a stereotype, a kind of woman who will always be in danger and waiting to be rescued by Bond." While Paloma isn't rescued by Bond, she is both objectified and sexualized in ways that male agents are rarely, if ever, treated in the world of 007. Both the script and the final film make it clear that Paloma is to be viewed by audiences and Bond himself in a particular way: that is, as an object of desire and a potential sexual partner. In the script, for instance, she is introduced as "a woman in an elegant BLUE DRESS" whom "Bond approaches, ready for flirtatious banter."[29] Moments later, she starts to undress Bond, helping him change into a tuxedo, prompting him to ask, "Don't you think we ought to get to know each other just a little before we . . .?" (figure 25.2)

Neither the film nor the script makes reference to the more than twenty-year age gap between de Armas and Craig, a pattern present for many of the relationships Bond has in the Craig era, which remain indicative of the industry as a whole, among them Gemma Arterton (twenty-two years' difference), Léa Seydoux (eighteen), and Eva Green (twelve). These gaps were rarely commented on in the reception of the films, a stark contrast to the press coverage surrounding the casting of Monica Bellucci, who is only four years older than Craig, as Lucia Sciarra in *Spectre*.[30] At the party Paloma and Bond subsequently visit, which is populated by many Spectre agents, Bond asks, "What is this? Spectre *bonga-bonga*? You ever been to a party like this?" She answers, "How do you think I got this job?" Moments later, Dr. Obruchev (David Dencik) assumes that she is a prostitute, asking, "You are . . . my escort?" By way of comparison, consider for a moment the introduction of CIA agent Logan Ash (Billy Magnussen), who will later be revealed to be in league with Safin. Ash is not clad in

Figure 25.2 Bond (Daniel Craig) and Paloma (Ana de Armas). *No Time to Die* (2021).

revealing attire, nor is he asked how he became an agent; he does not forget an important password, nor is it implied that he may have used his attractiveness/sexuality to get his position, all of which are the case for Paloma in the brief screen time allotted to her.

Bond and Paloma do not have a sexual relationship in the film, but their time together ends with her telling him, "Next time stay longer": on one level, the promise of a potential future relationship, and on another, an indication that, while the agent may have settled down and be in his fifties, he is still sexually attractive to women young enough to be his daughter. The combined portrayals of Madeleine and Paloma are an indication that even in the modern era, when Barbara Broccoli has suggested "#MeToo has influenced our culture . . . The films are representative of the times they're in," there are strict limitations as to what the Bond films can do with female characters, so firmly entrenched are they within the confines of a franchise built around the virility and superiority of a middle-aged heterosexual white man.[31]

Nomi

It is Nomi, played Lashana Lynch, who emerges as the film's most interesting female character, a rare entrant in the franchise who challenges many of those elements we have noted that restrict the characterizations of Madeleine and Paloma. In *NTTD*, she appears to be the individual who is most strongly influenced by Waller-Bridge's contribution to the script, something Lynch herself seemed convinced of, stating "When I read lines that were clearly from her, it all just made sense to the kind of upbringing that I imagined Nomi would have."[32] She is introduced early in the film during a sequence that finds Bond retired in Jamaica. After meeting with Felix Leiter (Jeffrey Wright) in a local nightclub, Bond discovers that his car will not start. Nomi *happens* to be passing by on a scooter and asks whether he needs a ride home. When they arrive, Bond is both surprised and intrigued by her apparent directness: "Nice house . . . Is that the bedroom?" she asks, ahead of what viewers anticipate will be a romantic liaison in the tradition of previous Bond films. Instead, Nomi removes her wig and shifts from her pronounced Jamaican patois into an R.P. English accent, revealing to him that she is in fact a double-o agent working for MI6. Yet, as the audience soon learns, she is not just any oo agent but, in fact, has been given the iconic code number 007. Bond remarks that it is "only a number," which leads her to audibly scoff, as it obviously is *more* than just a number for her, as it is for many beyond the diegetic frames of the film.

Arguably Nomi became the most widely discussed character in the run-up to *NTTD*'s release, perhaps even more than Bond himself, as many speculated that she would replace him as 007, a prospect that was not welcomed by some fans of the series: "Political correctness gone mad!" wrote one online commentator, and "007 will always be a white man" wrote another.[33] The casting of Lashana Lynch in such an important role in the franchise is significant, as Lisa Funnell argues in "Nomi/No ME? Race, Gender, and Power in *No Time to Die*," in which she states, "As a black woman, the casting of Lynch alone challenges the legacy of white masculinity and its connection to British identity in the Bond series."[34] Those who believe that Hollywood has "gone woke" saw this as further evidence of the franchise's embrace of progressive politics, belief in which requires a calculated ignorance of the sustained empirical data that refutes such claims, and a refusal to acknowledge that, in actual fact, mainstream films remain a resolutely white, male, and heteronormative space.[35]

Unlike many of the female characters the Bond series has offered in the past, and unlike assertions made about Madeleine and Paloma, Nomi is closer to something new for the series, shown to be *almost* his equal, physically and intellectually. She is clearly portrayed as a new generation of "Bond girl": efficient, professional, highly capable, and one who is not belittled, sexualized, diminished, or objectified. She tells him, "The world's moved on," something some sections of the Bond fan community, as we have seen, found hard to accept—as does Bond, who states, "In my humble opinion, the world doesn't change very much."

The extradiegetic tension concerning Nomi's position in the franchise is integrated into the film's narrative in ways that the series has often provided a commentary on the shifting perception of Bond's relationships with women. It can be seen most clearly when Bond and Nomi walk side by side through the MI6 offices, where members of staff are visibly confused by the presence of two generations of 007. At this stage in the film Nomi is clearly threatened by Bond's return and sees him as a rival, remarking on this confusion with the comment, "That must bother you." But when M (Ralph Fiennes) invites Bond into the office before her, Bond asks, "Does that bother you?" Later when she hears that Bond has been reinstated to oo, she affects an aura of nonchalance, but asks M, "oo what?" not once, but twice.

Nomi is shown to be a different type of 007 in ways not connected directly to her ethnicity or her gender. She is distanced from Bond's risk-taking and improvisational rebelliousness, and instead defined with her line to M, "By the book, sir," which comes not too long after Bond has criticized his former employer for continuing to allow Obrachev to develop such a dangerous bioweapon as Project Heracles. The rivalry between Bond and Nomi, which is shown to be mostly insecurity on her part, shifts throughout the film to mutual respect and even a productive working relationship by its finale, when she offers to give back the code number for their mission to Safin's island: "Sir, permission for Commander Bond to be redesignated as 007 . . . *It's just a number*," echoing Bond's own earlier line.

310 NO TIME TO DIE AND THE SPY WHO LOVED #METOO?

Interestingly Nomi's ethnicity is only referred to on a single occasion, on the final mission to Safin's island, when Obruchev tells her, "I have a good vial for *you people*, good for west African diaspora . . . You know I do not need laboratory to exterminate your entire race from the face of the earth." She responds with the kind of one-liner that has been a 007 trademark for decades and indeed even makes reference to the film's title in ways that have been rare in the Craig era—"Do you know what time it is? *Time to die!*"—just before she kicks him off a high platform to a painful death below. It is unclear whether this is the moment Lynch was referring to in an interview with *Harper's Bazaar* when she suggested,

> I didn't want to waste an opportunity when it came to what Nomi might represent. I searched for at least one moment in the script where Black audience members would nod their heads, tutting at the reality but glad to see their real life represented. In every project I am part of, no matter the budget or genre, the Black experience that I'm presenting needs to be 100 per cent authentic.[36]

Lynch's comments echo those of many black performers in mainstream films, or indeed those of any minorities, where, given the disparity of opportunities, a symbolic burden is placed upon them to be somehow representative of their entire gender, ethnicity, or social group, one never placed on the white men who have overwhelmingly played central roles in the industry since the birth of the medium, in front of and behind the camera. But this is evidence of the power of cinema as a representational medium, especially in a franchise like Bond and a film like *NTTD*, which was seen in multiplexes all over the world.

Conclusion: James Bond Will Return

As we have seen numerous times throughout this volume, one of the defining parameters of the Bond series has been its ability to successfully navigate the shifting social and political coordinates of the times in which each film is produced, while still retaining the core constitutive elements that have appealed to fans since 1962. James Bond has been an enduring icon of both national and masculine identity, something that was initially relatively uncomplicated for the producers of the franchise but became progressively more challenging as the twentieth century moved into the twenty-first, especially after the emergence of social progress movements such as #MeToo and Black Lives Matter and divisive debates about what constitutes contemporary Britishness in the wake of Brexit. Bond's death at the end of *NTTD*, which was as widely criticized as it was praised, presents the producers of the franchise with what might be regarded as either a challenge or an opportunity as they attempt to

Figure 25.3 Bond (Daniel Craig) awaits his fate. *No Time to Die* (2021).

reconcile paradoxical demands for the character and the world he inhabits that are becoming increasingly polarized (figure 25.3). The Craig era was able to resolve these issues between 2006 and 2021. In some ways, this is perhaps the defining element of the five films he starred in, which managed, for the most part, to satisfy both sides of the spectrum. Cognizant of this, in June 2022 Barbara Broccoli stated that the next Bond film would be "a reinvention of Bond. We're reinventing who he is and that takes time."[37] What this will result in and whether the next installment of the Bond franchise can continue to adapt with the times as it has done since 1962 will only be known in years to come.

Notes

For the source of the first epigraph, see Baz Bamigboye, "We'll Never Have Jane Bond but We Will Still Rise to the Occasion in the #MeToo Era, Says Barbara Broccoli," *Daily Mail*, April 26, 2019, www.dailymail.co.uk/tvshowbiz/article-6961695/BAZ -BAMIGBOYE-never-Jane-Bond-says-Barbara-Broccoli.html. The second epigraph is taken from Tatiana Siegel, "No Time to Lose: Hollywood Pins Its Hopes on Bond Director Cary Fukunaga," *Hollywood Reporter*, September 22, 2021, www.holly woodreporter.com/movies/movie-features/bond-director-cary-fukunaga-no-time -to-die-1235017724/

1. Peter Walker and Nancy Groves, "Daniel Craig: I'd Rather Slash My Wrists Than Play James Bond Again," *The Guardian*, October 8, 2015, www.theguardian.com/film/2015 /oct/08/daniel-craig-id-rather-slash-my-wrists-than-do-another-bond-movie.

2. Not only did it replace its original director (Danny Boyle), but it was delayed on numerous occasions due to the global impact of COVID-19, resulting in the longest gap between two Bond films played by the same actor, and not too far from the lengthiest in the franchise history, the six years between *Licence to Kill* (1989) and *GoldenEye* (1995).

3. Ben Child, "Time's Up for James Bond: Is 007 Too Toxic for the #MeToo Era?," *The Guardian,* January 30, 2018, www.theguardian.com/film/2018/jan/30/times-up-for-james-bond-is-007-too-brutish-for-the-me-too-era.

4. Stuart Jeffries, "It's No Time to Die: But Is It Time to Revoke James Bond's Licence to Kill?," *The Guardian*, September 25, 2021, www.theguardian.com/film/2021/sep/25/its-no-time-to-die-but-is-it-time-to-revoke-james-bonds-licence-to-kill.

5. Nadia Khomami, "Daniel Craig Has Given Us 'Woke' James Bond, Says Charlie Higson," *The Guardian*, September 21, 2021, www.theguardian.com/film/2021/sep/21/daniel-craig-has-given-us-woke-james-bond-says-charlie-higson

6. Rachel Lebonte, "Daniel Craig Made James Bond Feminist, Says Léa Seydoux," Screenrant, October 8, 2018, screenrant.com/james-bond-feminist-daniel-craig-lea-seydoux-response/.

7. Lisa Funnell and Tyler Johnson, "Properties of a Lady: Public Perceptions of Women in the James Bond Franchise," *Participations: Journal of Audience and Reception Studies* 17, no. 2 (2020): 95–114; 97.

8. Maureen Lee Lenker, "What Daniel Craig Has to Constantly Remind People about Bond, and His Final Word for the Franchise," *Entertainment Weekly*, October 7, 2021, ew.com/movies/daniel-craig-remind-people-bond-final-word/.

9. Annenberg Inclusion Initiative, *Inequality in 1,300 Popular Films: Examining Portrayals of Gender, Race/Ethnicity, LGBTQ & Disability from 2007 to 2019*, Annenberg Foundation and USC Annenberg Inclusion Institute, August 9, 2020, assets.uscannenberg.org/docs/aii-inequality_1300_popular_films_09-08-2020.pdf.

10. Peter Kiefer and Peter Savodnik, "Hollywood Will Barely Dare Whisper It But the Woke Revolution That Has Driven Out White Men and Ensures That Every Production Is Ideologically Sound Will Kill the Entertainment Industry," *Daily Mail*, January 11, 2021, www.dailymail.co.uk/news/article-10391261/Hollywood-barely-whisper-wokeness-kill-industry-PETER-KIEFER-PETER-SAVODNIK.html.

11. Lisa Funnell, "Reworking the Bond Girl Concept in the Craig Era," *Journal of Popular Film and Television* 46, no. 1 (2018): 17.

12. Funnell, "Reworking the Bond Girl Concept," 17.

13. Khomami, "Daniel Craig Has Given."

14. See Lisa Funnell and Klaus Dodds, *Geographies, Genders and Geopolitics of James Bond* (London: Palgrave Macmillan, 2017).

15. Jonathan Dean, "Daniel Craig Interview: The James Bond Actor on His New Comedy Knives Out, Phoebe Waller-Bridge, the Problem with Social Media, and Why He's Not Grumpy," *Times*, November 3, 2019, www.thetimes.co.uk/magazine/culture/daniel-craig-interview-the-james-bond-actor-on-his-new-comedy-knives-out-phoebe-waller-bridge-the-problem-with-social-media-and-why-hes-not-grumpy-tzh6h538m?region=global.

16. Simon Hattenstone, "Phoebe Waller-Bridge: 'I Have an Appetite for Transgressive Women,'" *The Guardian*, September 8, 2018, www.theguardian.com/tv-and-radio/2018/sep/08/phoebe-waller-bridge-fleabag-killing-eve-transgressive-women.

17. Scott Feinberg, "'Awards Chatter' Podcast—Phoebe Waller-Bridge ('Fleabag' & 'Killing Eve')," *Hollywood Reporter*, June 24, 2019, www.hollywoodreporter.com/news

/general-news/awards-chatter-podcast-phoebe-waller-bridge-fleabag-killing-eve
-1209887/; Rebecca Jones, "How Phoebe Waller-Bridge is 'spicing up' James Bond," *BBC News*, November 8, 2019, www.bbc.co.uk/news/entertainment-arts-50331077.

18. Dean, "Daniel Craig Interview."

19. For an exploration of the first female screen-writer to work on the Bond franchise and how she went largely un-credited for her work see Melanie Williams, "Her Word Was Her Bond: Johanna Harwood, Bond's First Woman Screenwriter," in *From Blofeld to Moneypenny: Gender in James Bond*, ed. Steven Gerard (Bingley, UK: Emerald, 2020), 117–128.

20. Tom Grater, "Hunt For Next James Bond Will Begin Next Year, Says Producer Barbara Broccoli," Deadline, September 27, 2021, deadline.com/2021/09/next-james-bond
-search-begin-next-year-barbara-broccoli-1234844870/; Joe Juliens, "Daniel Craig Addresses Whether New James Bond Should Be a Woman," *Radio Times*, September 21, 2021, www.radiotimes.com/movies/james-bond-daniel-craig-woman-next
-newsupdate/.

21. Will Richards, "Phoebe Waller-Bridge Talks Adding 'Little Spices' to New Bond Film," *NME,* November 8, 2019, www.nme.com/news/phoebe-waller-bridge-talks-adding
-little-spices-to-new-bond-film-2574313; Ryan Lattanzio, "Here's How Phoebe Waller-Bridge Polished the 'No Time to Die' Script," IndieWire, February 24, 2020, www
.indiewire.com/2020/02/heres-how-phoebe-waller-bridge-polished-the-no-time-to
-die-script-1202213218/.

22. Juliens, "Daniel Craig Addresses."

23. Felicity Kinsella, "Léa Seydoux And Monica Bellucci Are the Feminist Bond Girls Fighting Hollywood's Sexism," I-D, October 29, 2015, i-d.vice.com/en_uk/article
/9kb8bz/la-seydoux-and-monica-bellucci-are-the-feminist-bond-girls-fighting
-hollywoods-sexism; Mary Rose Somarriba, "This Is Why Madeleine Swann Is Not Like the Other Bond Girls," *Verily Magazine*, November 16, 2015, verilymag.com/2015
/11/james-bond-daniel-craig-lea-seydoux-spectre.

24. Crystal Bell, "'Spectre' Promised a Badass Bond Girl But Did It Deliver One?," MTV, November 6, 2016, www.mtv.com/news/2372833/spectre-bond-girls/.

25. Ian Sandwell, "Spectre's Lea Seydoux on Her Bond Girl: 'Madeleine Swann Is Bond's Equal,'" *Digital Spy*, September 28, 2015, www.digitalspy.com/movies/a670922/spectres
-lea-seydoux-on-her-bond-girl-madeleine-swann-is-bonds-equal/.

26. Christoph Lindner, "Foreword," in *For His Eyes Only: The Women of James Bond*, ed. Lisa Funnell (New York: Wallflower, 2015), xvii.

27. For example, it is what Halle Berry said about her character, Jinx, in *Die Another Day* ("this version of a Bond woman was very different than any Bond woman I had seen before") and what Bérénice Marlohe said about Séverine in *Skyfall* ("I see her like a unique character in a unique movie more than a Bond girl"). See Nicole Zamlout, "Halle Berry Reveals Why She Accepted the Role of Jinx in 'Die Another Day,'" Collider, December 2, 2021, collider.com/halle-berry-die-another-day-jinx-role-comments
/; Adam Chitwood, "Berenice Marlohe Talks SKYFALL, Playing a Femme Fatale/Bond Girl, How She Was Cast, and More," Collider, May 2, 2002, collider.com/berenice
-marlohe-skyfall-james-bond-interview/.

28. Qtd. in Rebecca Ford, "Bond Women: How Rising Stars Lashana Lynch and Ana de Armas Are Helping Modernize 007," *Hollywood Reporter*, November 6, 2019, www
.hollywoodreporter.com/movies/movie-features/how-lashana-lynch-ana-de-armas
-are-helping-modernize-james-bond-1252345/.

29. Neal Purvis, Robert Wade, Cary Joji Fukunaga, and Phoebe Waller-Bridge, *No Time to Die*, screenplay, deadline.com/wp-content/uploads/2022/01/No-Time-To-Die-Read-The-Screenplay.pdf, 20.

30. At the time, Belluci was held up as evidence of the franchise moving with the times and acknowledging historical disparities between the ages of Bond and the women he has relationships with.

31. Bamigboye, "We'll never have Jane Bond."

32. N. A. S, "Agent of Change," Net-a-Porter, October 4, 2021, www.net-a-porter.com/en-gb/porter/article-56b2b868091b41f1/cover-stories/cover-stories/lashana-lynch.

33. Caroline Graham, "The Black Woman Who Will Be the Next 007: New James Bond Film Will Feature British Actress Lashana Lynch Taking Over the Famous Codename (But That Doesn't Stop Legendary Agent Trying to Seduce Her)," *Daily Mail*, July 13, 2019, www.dailymail.co.uk/news/article-7244671/Thought-007-never-woman-black-shes-James-Bond-hand-number-over.html.

34. Lisa Funnell, "Nomi/No Me? Race, Gender, and Power in *No Time to Die*," *Flow*, September 16, 2019, www.flowjournal.org/2019/09/nomi-no-me/.

35. See Annenberg Inclusion Initiative, *Inequality in 1,300 Popular Films*.

36. Yrsa Daley-Ward, "Lashana Lynch on Making History as the First Black Female 007," *Harper's Bazar*, September 28, 2021, www.harpersbazaar.com/uk/culture/culture-news/a34517814/lashana-lynch-black-female-007-interview/.

37. Baz Bamigboye, "Barbara Broccoli Says Next James Bond Film Is Two Years away from Production: 'We're Reinventing Him,'" Deadline, June 29, 2022, deadline.com/2022/06/james-bond-daniel-craig-next-007-reinventing-barbara-broccoli-1235053969/.

SELECTED BIBLIOGRAPHY

Bennett, Tony, and Janet Woollacott. *Beyond Bond: The Political Career of a Popular Hero.* London: Macmillan, 1987.

Black, Jeremy. *The Politics of James Bond: From Fleming's Novels to the Big Screen.* Westport, CT: Praeger, 2005.

Chapman, James. *Licence to Thrill: A Cultural History of the James Bond Films.* 2nd ed. London: I. B. Tauris, 2007.

Chapman, Llewella. *Fashioning James Bond: Costume, Gender, and Identity in the World of 007.* London: Bloomsbury, 2022.

Comentale, Edward, Stephen Watt, and Skip Willman, eds. *Ian Fleming and James Bond: The Cultural Politics of 007.* Bloomington: Indiana University Press, 2005.

Field, Matthew, and Ajay Chowdhury. *Some Kind of Hero: The Remarkable Story of the James Bond Films.* Stroud, UK: The History Press, 2015.

Funnell, Lisa, ed. *For His Eyes Only: The Women of James Bond.* New York: Wallflower, 2015.

Funnell, Lisa, and Klaus Dodds. *Geographies, Genders, and Geopolitics of James Bond.* London: Palgrave Macmillan, 2017.

Germanà, Monica. *Bond Girls: Body, Fashion and Gender.* London: Bloomsbury, 2019.

Gerrard, Steven, ed. *From Blofeld to Moneypenny: Gender in James Bond.* Bingley, UK: Emerald, 2020.

Hines, Claire, ed. *Fan Phenomena: James Bond.* Bristol: Intellect, 2015.

Hines, Claire. *The Playboy and James Bond: 007, Ian Fleming, and* Playboy *Magazine.* Manchester: Manchester University Press, 2018.

Lindner, Christoph, ed. *The James Bond Phenomenon: A Critical Reader.* Manchester: Manchester University Press, 2003.

Lindner, Christoph, ed. *Revisioning 007: James Bond and* Casino Royale. London: Wallflower, 2009.

Strong, Jeremy, ed. *James Bond Uncovered.* London: Palgrave Macmillan, 2018.

Thomas, Graham. *The Definitive Story of* You Only Live Twice: *Fleming, Bond, and Connery in Japan.* London: Sagus, 2020.

Verheul, Jaap, ed. *The Cultural Life of James Bond: Specters of 007.* Amsterdam: Amsterdam University Press, 2020.

Watt, Stephen, and Skip Willman. eds. *Ian Fleming and James Bond: The Cultural Politics of 007.* Bloomington: Indiana University Press, 2005.

Weiner, Robert G., B. Lynn Whitfield, and Jack Becker, eds. *James Bond in World and Popular Culture: The Films Are Not Enough.* Newcastle upon Tyne, UK: Cambridge Scholars, 2010.

Yeffeth, Glen, ed. *James Bond in the 21st Century: Why We Still Need 007.* Dallas: BenBella, 2009.

CONTRIBUTORS

Lucy Bolton is professor of film studies at Queen Mary University of London and the author of *Contemporary Cinema and the Philosophy of Iris Murdoch* (2019) and *Film and Female Consciousness: Irigaray, Cinema, and Thinking Women* (2011). She is the coeditor of *Lasting Screen Stars: Images That Fade and Personas That Endure* (2016, winner of the BAFTSS Best Edited Collection) and, with Richard Rushton, of the book series Visionaries—The Work of Women Filmmakers, published by Edinburgh University Press. Lucy is writing a monograph, *Philosophies of Hollywood Stardom: Ethics, Aesthetics, and Phenomenologies*.

James Chapman is professor of film studies at the University of Leicester and editor of the *Historical Journal of Film, Radio and Television*. He is the author of *Licence to Thrill: A Cultural History of the James Bond Films* (1999; 2nd ed., 2007), which *SFX* magazine described as "ludicrous, intelligent, and a bit snobbish. Bit like Bond, really." A third edition is contracted to be published by Bloomsbury Academic. He has also published a stand-alone monograph, *Dr. No: The First James Bond Film* (2022). *On Her Majesty's Secret Service* is his second-favorite Bond film (after *The Spy Who Loved Me*). Outside Bond, his research focuses on the cultural and economic histories of British cinema, most recently *The Money Behind the Screen: A History of British Film Finance, 1945–1985* (2022), which was runner-up in the 2022 "Best Monograph" awards of the British Association of Film, Television, and Screen Studies.

Llewella Chapman is a visiting scholar in the School of History at the University of East Anglia. Her research interests include British cinema, film history, franchises, costume, and gender. Her monograph *Fashioning James Bond: Costume, Gender, and Identity in the World of 007* was published by Bloomsbury in 2022, and her BFI Film Classic on *From Russia with Love* was published in October 2022 in celebration of the sixty-year anniversary of cinematic James Bond.

Laura Crossley is senior lecturer in film at Bournemouth University. Her research interests include national identity, British film, nostalgia, postmodernism, and post-colonialism. Her specific areas of interest are British spy fictions, particularly in film and television. She is researching aspects of nostalgia culture in contemporary Cold War fictions as part of a wider research project. Laura is founding coeditor of the Routledge Studies in Espionage and Culture book series and is part of the BAFTSS Special Interest Group on British Film and Television.

Klaus Dodds is professor of geopolitics and executive dean of the School of Life Sciences and Environment at Royal Holloway University of London. He is coauthor of *Geographies, Genders and Geopolitics of James Bond* (with Lisa Funnell, 2017) and writings on the popular geopolitics of James Bond that have considered the elemental and embodied qualities of the Bond franchise. His work has been published in *Popular Communication*, the *Journal of Popular Film and Television*, and *Geopolitics*, as well as edited anthologies such as *Media and the Cold War in the 1980s* (2018).

Monica Germanà is reader in gothic and contemporary studies at the University of Westminster. Her publications include *The Scottish Gothic: An Edinburgh Companion* (2018), coedited with Carol Davison and shortlisted for the Allan Lloyd Prize; *Bond Girls: Body, Fashion, Gender* (2019), shortlisted for the Emily Toth Award; and a special issue of *Gothic Studies* on "Haunted Scotlands" (March 2022). She is working on a new project exploring Scottish/Arctic cultural links with particular reference to the "otherwordly" aesthetics attached to the far north. As a creative writer, she has published short stories in various anthologies and is developing a collection and working on "Dark Waters," a ghost story set in Sicily.

Steven Gerrard is reader in film at Northern Film School, Leeds Beckett University. He has written monographs about the *Carry On* films (Palgrave Macmillan) and the modern British horror film (Rutgers University Press). Steve has edited numerous collections for Emerald Publishing focusing on gender and James Bond, gender in contemporary horror, and gender and action movies. He was creator and coeditor of the world's only academic collection devoted to Jason Statham.

In his spare time, he'd love to be either Status Quo's rhythm guitarist or the new
Doctor Who. He'll have a long wait.

Claire Hines is lecturer in film studies at the University of East Anglia. Her research
focuses on gender, genre, and James Bond in the contexts of American and
British cultures. She is the author of *The Playboy and James Bond: 007, Ian Fleming
and* Playboy *Magazine* (2018) and the editor of *Fan Phenomena: James Bond*
(2015) and has published other articles and chapters on the Bond franchise.

Tobias Hochscherf is professor of audio-visual media at Kiel University of Applied
Sciences, where he also serves as Vice-President for Research and Development. He has published widely on film and television cultures. He is the author
of *The Continental Connection: German-Speaking Émigrés and British Cinema,
1927–1949* and *Beyond the Boundaries: Contemporary Danish Television Drama*
(2017). He is associate editor of the *Historical Journal of Film, Radio and
Television* and on the editorial boards of the *Journal of Scandinavian Cinema* and
the *Journal of Popular Television*.

Christopher Holliday is lecturer in liberal arts and visual cultures education at King's
College London, where he specializes in Hollywood cinema, animation history,
and contemporary digital media. He has published several book chapters and
articles on digital technology and computer animation and is the author of
The Computer-Animated Film: Industry, Style and Genre (2018) and coeditor of
the collections *Fantasy/Animation: Connections between Media, Mediums and
Genres* (2018) and *Snow White and the Seven Dwarfs: New Perspectives on
Production, Reception, Legacy* (2021). His work has appeared in *Animation
Practice, Process, and Production*; *animation: an interdisciplinary journal*;
Convergence: The International Journal of Research into New Media Technologies;
Journal of British Cinema and Television; *Journal of Cinema and Media Studies*;
Journal of Popular Film and Television; and the *London Journal*.

Keith M. Johnston is professor of film and television studies at the University of East
Anglia. His research covers the history of different film and media technologies
in American and British cinema, including color film, stereoscopic 3D, and
special effects, as well as the development of film marketing and promotion. He
is the author of *Coming Soon: Film Trailers and the Selling of Hollywood Technology* (2009) and *Science Fiction Film: A Critical Introduction* (2011) and coauthor of
Colour Films in Britain: The Eastmancolor Revolution (2022).

Stephanie Jones is lecturer in film, television, and media at Aberystwyth University
in Wales, United Kingdom. Her research focuses on popular heroes such as
James Bond and Sherlock Holmes, with an emphasis on masculinities and

reception analysis methods. She is the author of several chapters and articles on James Bond and gender. She is coeditor of the international journal *Media History*.

Stuart Joy is the course leader for film and television at Solent University. He is the author of *The Traumatic Screen: The Films of Christopher Nolan* (2020) and coeditor of *The Cinema of Christopher Nolan: Imagining the Impossible* (2015), *Through the Black Mirror: Reflections on the Digital Age* (2019), and *Contemporary American Science Fiction Film* (2022). His research interests include contemporary film theory and practice, media and cultural theory, film history, and gender representation.

Tatiana Konrad is a postdoctoral researcher in the Department of English and American Studies, University of Vienna, Austria, the principal investigator of the research project "Air and Environmental Health in the (Post-)COVID-19 World," and the editor of the "Environment, Health, and Well-Being" book series at Michigan State University Press. She holds a PhD in American Studies from the University of Marburg, Germany. She was a Visiting Fellow at the University of Chicago (2022), a Visiting Researcher at the Forest History Society (2019), an Ebeling Fellow at the American Antiquarian Society (2018), and a Visiting Scholar at the University of South Alabama (2016). She is the author of *Docu-Fictions of War: U.S. Interventionism in Film and Literature* (2019), the editor of *Plastics, Environment, Culture, and the Politics of Waste* (2023), *Imagining Air: Cultural Axiology and the Politics of Invisibility* (2023), *Cold War II: Hollywood's Renewed Obsession with Russia* (2020), and *Transportation and the Culture of Climate Change: Accelerating Ride to Global Crisis* (2020), and a coeditor of *Cultures of War in Graphic Novels: Violence, Trauma, and Memory* (2018).

Terence McSweeney is senior lecturer in film and television studies at Solent University. He has held research positions at the University of Oxford, University College London, and the London School of Economics. He is the author of a range of monographs in the field of global visual cultures, including *The "War on Terror" and American Film: 9/11 Frames per Second* (2014) and *Avengers Assemble! Critical Perspectives on the Marvel Cinematic Universe* (2018). His *Black Panther: Interrogating a Cultural Phenomenon* (2021) won the Congrès Interdisciplinaire d'Etudes Africaines (COAFRO) Award for Best Book on African Studies (2021), a Non-Fiction Authors Association Gold Award (2022), an eLit Gold Award in the category of Popular Culture (2022), a National Indie Excellence Award (2022), and a 2022 American Book Fest Award.

Christine Muller's research draws on film and television to explore responses to stark cultural change during the first decades of the twenty-first century. She is the author of *September 11, 2001 as a Cultural Trauma: A Case Study Through Popular Culture* (2017). She serves as the associate director of undergraduate studies for the Department of the History and Sociology of Science at the University of Pennsylvania.

Stacey Peebles is H. W. Stodghill Jr. and Adele Stodghill Associate Professor and chair of English and film studies at Centre College. She is author of *Welcome to the Suck: Narrating the American Soldier's Experience in Iraq* (2011) and *Cormac McCarthy and Performance: Page, Stage, Screen* (2017), as well as a new project titled *The War Comes with You: Enduring War in Life, Fiction, and Fantasy.* She is editor of the collection *Violence in Literature* (2014) and coeditor, with Benjamin West, of *Approaches to Teaching the Works of Cormac McCarthy* (2021). She has been editor of the *Cormac McCarthy Journal* since 2010.

Frances Pheasant-Kelly is a reader in film and screen studies at the University of Wolverhampton. Her research centers on abject spaces, fantasy, and the medical humanities. She has over seventy-five publications, including *Abject Spaces in American Cinema* (2013) and *Fantasy Film Post 9/11* (2013), and is the coeditor of *Spaces of the Cinematic Home: Behind the Screen Door* (2015) and *Tim Burton's Bodies* (2021). She is working on several monographs, including *A History of HIV/AIDS in Film, Television and the Media* and *The Revenant: Towards a Sensory Cinema.*

Ian Scott is professor of American film and history at the University of Manchester. He is the author of several books on American political and historical movies as well as numerous articles and reviews. His book *In Capra's Shadow*, about the screenwriter Robert Riskin, was the inspiration for the 2015 ARTE/PBS documentary *Projections of America*, which won numerous awards and on which Ian served as script editor. (The book was reissued in updated form in 2021 by the University Press of Kentucky as *Robert Riskin: The Life and Times of a Hollywood Screenwriter.*) In 2020, Ian was a collaborator and writer on the BBC Radio 4 series *The Californian Century*, narrated by Stanley Tucci, which was nominated for the Broadcasting Press Guild Radio Programme of the Year award. He contributes regularly to the longstanding American film magazine *Cineaste*, and his writing has been featured in *BBC World Histories* and the *Daily Beast* online.

Robert Shail is professor of film in the Leeds School of Arts at Leeds Beckett University, where he also leads research in film, music, performing arts, and creative technologies. He received a Leverhulme Fellowship for his study of the Children's Film Foundation (2016) and has published widely on postwar British cinema, masculinity, genre, and stardom. An essay on Roger Moore as Bond was included in the collection *Seventies British Cinema* (2008), which he also edited. His more recent research has covered aspects of children's media in Britain, including comic books and games.

James Smith is a professor in the Department of English Studies at Durham University (UK), with research interests in the relationships between modern British culture and issues such as propaganda, intelligence, and surveillance. He is the author of *British Writers and MI5 Surveillance, 1930–1960* (2013) and led the Leverhulme Trust research project "The Political Warfare Executive, Covert Propaganda, and British Culture" (2018–2022).

Randall Stevens is an independent scholar based in Texas.

Estella Tincknell is associate professor in film and culture at the University of the West of England. She was a Bristol city councillor between 2013 and 2021, during which time she was deputy mayor and the Cabinet member for culture. She was coeditor of *The Soundtrack*, a journal of film and the moving image, until 2016, and has published widely in the areas of film, media, and culture, including *Ageing Femininities, Troubling Representations* (2012) and *Jane Campion and Adaptation* (2013). Her "Double O Agencies: Femininity, Post-Feminism and the Female Spy in *Casino Royale*" appeared in Christoph Lindner's 2009 edited collection *Revisioning 007: James Bond and* Casino Royale. She is currently writing a book about masculinity, modernity and the "long 1960s" in British film and television crime narratives.

Julie Lobalzo Wright is an assistant professor in film and television studies at the University of Warwick. She is the author of *Crossover Stardom: Popular Male Music Stars in American Cinema* (2018) and coeditor of *Musicals at the Margins: Genre, Boundaries, Canons* (2021) and *Lasting Screen Stars: Images That Fade and Personas That Endure* (2016). She has published widely on film stardom, animation, and musicals.

INDEX

Printed and bound by CPI Group (UK) Ltd, Croydon, CR0 4YY

01/01/2024

08215110-0001